BLESSED ARE THE PEACEMAKERS

BLESSED ARE THE PEACEMAKERS

Martin Luther King Jr.,
Eight White Religious Leaders, and
the "Letter from Birmingham Jail"

S. JONATHAN BASS

UPDATED EDITION

With a New Foreword by **PAUL HARVEY**

and a New Afterword by **JAMES. C. COBB**

Louisiana State University Press
Baton Rouge

Published by Louisiana State University Press
www.lsupress.org

Louisiana Paperback Edition, 2002
Updated Edition, 2021

Designer: Barbara Neely Bourgoyne
Typeface: Sabon
Typesetter: Coghill Composition, Inc.

Cover photo: Martin Luther King's police mug shot from Friday, April 12, 1963.
Courtesy of the Birmingham Police Department.

Library of Congress Cataloging-in-Publication Data
Names: Bass, S. Jonathan, author. | Cobb, James C. (James Charles), 1947– writer
    of afterword. | King, Martin Luther, Jr., 1929–1968. Letter from Birmingham Jail.
Title: Blessed are the peacemakers : Martin Luther King Jr., eight white religious
    leaders, and the "Letter from Birmingham Jail" / S. Jonathan Bass.
Description: Updated edition / with a new foreword by Paul Harvey and a new after-
    word by James C. Cobb. | Baton Rouge : Louisiana State University Press, 2021. |
    Includes bibliographical references and index.
Identifiers: LCCN 2020048964 (print) | LCCN 2020048965 (ebook) | ISBN 978-0-
    8071-7478-4 (updated edition) | ISBN 978-0-8071-7591-0 (pdf) | ISBN 978-0-8071-
    7592-7 (epub)
Subjects: LCSH: King, Martin Luther, Jr., 1929–1968. Letter from Birmingham Jail. |
    Civil disobedience—Alabama—Birmingham—History—20th century. | Civil rights
    movements—Alabama—Birmingham—History—20th century. | African Americans—
    Civil rights—Alabama—Birmingham—History—20th century. | Clergy—Political
    activity—Alabama—Birmingham—History—20th century. | Clergy—Alabama—Bir-
    mingham—Biography. | Birmingham (Ala.)—Race relations.
Classification: LCC F334.B69 N415 2021 (print) | LCC F334.B69 (ebook) |
    DDC 323.092—dc23
LC record available at https://lccn.loc.gov/2020048964
LC ebook record available at https://lccn.loc.gov/2020048965

To Jennifer
for her unfailing
love, support,
and confidence

Contents

Illustrations

Foreword

PAUL HARVEY

Years before Nolan Harmon appeared as one of eight Birmingham clerics who served as targets and foils for Martin Luther King Jr.'s 1963 public letter masterpiece, "Letter from a Birmingham Jail," the lifelong Methodist stalwart ran a publishing house associated with the Methodist Episcopal Church, South. One of Harmon's projects during that time was the publication of a book that became a central influence on the thought of King and is now considered a sort of early classic of black liberation theology: Howard Thurman's *Jesus and the Disinherited,* originally published in 1949. During the days of the Montgomery bus boycott, King reportedly carried around copies of Thurman's short but powerful text in his coat pocket.

Abingdon-Cokesbury Press had first rights of refusal on the book, and Thurman assumed the "southern bias" of the press would lessen or eliminate its interest in the manuscript. But, in one of the many ironies surrounding the publication of the text, that was not the case. The editor of the press, Nolan Bailey Harmon Jr., hailed from Meridian, Mississippi. He served for years as a circuit-riding minister, then journal editor, then bishop for southern Methodists. And, as is detailed in S. Jonathan Bass's tremendous work of historical research, Harmon had a long history of racial paternalism. He immersed himself in versions of a "Lost Cause" theology extolling the virtues of Stonewall Jackson and Robert E. Lee.

Most notably, Harmon was one of the eight southern "moderate" clergymen who fell under withering condemnation in King's "Letter," which actually declared southern moderates to be a greater enemy to racial progress than the Ku Klux Klansmen. Harmon had joined in a letter to King urging that civil rights protestors "observe the principles of law and order and common sense." Harmon himself thought racial progress would come only after the "slow, slow, slow processes of time." Thus, he was the perfect exemplar of the attitude King so memorably lacerated in the letter—the idea that, somehow, time would heal the wounds. As King responded, "time" was neutral and by itself would solve nothing.

But fifteen years earlier, Harmon was closely involved in marking up the first draft of Thurman's manuscript for what became *Jesus and the Disinherited*. Thurman was not one to wait for the slow processes of time. During those years, in fact, he served as the pastor of the Church for the Fellowship of All Peoples, an interracial congregation in San Francisco that might have been the worst nightmare for any southern segregationist, and probably uncomfortable for a southern white moderate like Harmon. But Harmon served effectively as an editor for Thurman's manuscript, demanding more changes of the proud African-American minister and intellectual than he was accustomed to accepting from others. *Jesus and the Disinherited* was Thurman's most succinct, and in many ways grittiest, expression of many of the fundamental ideas he pursued throughout his career: that the meaning of Jesus could be found in his status as a poor disinherited Jew living under an oppressive Roman regime.

Harmon's backstory is one of many ironies brought to mind in reading Bass's indispensable text of southern religious history, *Blessed Are the Peacemakers*. Bass tells multiple stories here related to this central document in American religion. One involves the writing of the letter itself, a process that bears some, but only some, relationship to the mythology that quickly grew up around (and was deliberately fostered and promoted about) it. Like many of Martin Luther King's triumphs, the success of the letter (and of the Birmingham campaign) depended on a fragile but essential combination of intuitive genius, incredible personal commitment and bravery, religious faith, and carefully orchestrated media manipulation to produce the desired effect.

The other story—or rather, collection of stories—detailed here in a manner not duplicated or even approached anywhere else, is the history of the eight signatories to the white clergymen's Good Friday statement, April 12, 1963. Written and published by the Methodists Nolan Harmon and Paul Hardin Jr., the Episcopalians Charles Colcock Jones Carpenter and George Murray, the Catholic Joseph Durick, the Jewish Milton Grafman, the Presbyterian Edward Ramage, and the Baptist Earl Stallings, the letter reflected a common sentiment of the times that the problems in Birmingham could be worked out through goodwill and negotiations, without the intervention of civil rights demonstrations. "We agree rather with certain local negro leadership which has called for honest and open negotiations of racial issues in our area," they said. They feared the demonstrations were "unwise and untimely."

Martin Luther King seized the opportunity of his arrest during the Birmingham campaign to cast himself as Paul in prison, writing a letter to American Christians. It was a brilliant ploy he had contemplated for some time but was awaiting the right opportunity to strike. The local authorities in Birmingham played perfectly into his hands.

Ironically, about six years earlier, King himself had expressed hope that moderate white southern leadership, exactly of the kind represented by the eight signatories to the Good Friday statement, could lead the South to a better day. Over the next years, he came to feel differently, and later in 1963 the tragic bombing of the Sixteenth Street Baptist Church in Birmingham suggested the depths to which southern segregationism still depended on the exercise of violence and brutality. Many of the eight signatories themselves knew that; some of them had been victims of the kinds of late-night harassing telephone calls and threats of personal harm that also dogged civil rights leaders. Still, they kept to the hope that King had expressed in earlier years, unable yet to make the leap of recognition that King himself had made and subsequently explained in his letter. It didn't take long for some (although not all) of the signatories to make that leap themselves. Some expressed bitterness about how King has "used" them as foils, but others realized that mattered little compared to the advances made in the larger story of the freedom struggle.

Bass's work acutely explores the complex reactions of the eight signatories, and of other whites, to King's letter and to the course of the civil rights movement more generally. The religious leaders Bass follows were caught in an impossible position, arguing for a middle ground where none in fact existed. Their stories might best be interpreted by the analysis produced by one of King's most important intellectual influences, Reinhold Niebuhr. In *Moral Man and Immoral Society,* Niebuhr had explored the paradox that good men (humans) somehow managed to produce societies that perpetrated evil. The religious leaders followed here were good men who struggled to adjust to, deal with, and produce changes in the evil system in which they themselves were caught up.

Despite his work with Thurman, Bishop Harmon never fully understood this, but other signatories who did moved over the years to search for a new and more just common ground.

Bass relates their stories with care and sensitivity, offering explanations but not excuses and giving us deeper insight into the unforgettably dramatic transformations, both in society and in individual souls, produced by the black freedom struggle.

Preface

The purpose of this book is to tell the history of Martin Luther King Jr.'s "Letter from Birmingham Jail." Why and how was it written? How and where was it prepared and published? Who were the eight white ministers addressed in the letter? What were their backgrounds, and how did they react to King's composition? What do their careers tell us about the white religious community during the civil rights era?

Answering these questions and telling this story proved to be no simple task. What I have done is to offer the reader individual biographies of the eight white clergymen addressed in the letter. In addition, at the center of this study is a pragmatic look at King's prison epistle. The body of the book basically has three distinct yet closely related parts. Following the introduction and the stage-setting first chapter, Chapters 2 through 4 are devoted to the eight white clergymen's backgrounds; Chapters 5 through 7 examine the production and publication of the "Letter from Birmingham Jail"; and Chapters 8 through 10 explore the eight's reaction to the letter and their subsequent careers. In these pages I hope you will find a balanced and generally objective study of the histories of the letter and of the leading white church and synagogue leaders in Alabama in 1963.

In writing this book, many wise and wonderful people touched my life. The words of the Reverend Martin Luther King Jr. inspired me to make a deeper commitment to the causes of justice and racial reconciliation. Bishop Joseph A. Durick, until his death in 1994, was a constant source of inspiration and information. His overwhelming humility, strength, and grace made a unique impact upon my life. He never let me leave his Bessemer, Alabama, home without a prayer, a blessing, and a word of encouragement. The late Rabbi Milton Grafman, the late Bishop Paul Hardin, Bishop George M. Murray, the late Bishop Nolan B. Harmon Jr., and the Reverend Earl Stallings opened their homes and their hearts and spent endless hours relating stories and providing documentation. A special word of thanks must go to Earl Stallings, who, despite the passage of more than thirty-five years, has great difficulty talking about the trauma he faced in Birmingham. I am grateful for his willingness to reexamine those painful years.

Others connected with the civil rights movement or Birmingham's religious establishment contributed significantly to this manuscript; they include Norman Amaker, Katherine Ramage Love, Sister Mary Margaret Durick, the Reverend Doug Carpenter, Father Joe Allen, Dee Lucas, the Reverend Fred Shuttlesworth, the Reverend Francis X. Walter, the Reverend Wyatt T. Walker, the Reverend John Porter, John Seigenthaler, John Chandler, Paul Hardin III, William Simmons, Billy Allen, the Reverend Darold Morgan, the Reverend James Auchmuty, the Reverend Marvin Spry, and the Reverend William Ford. In particular, I acknowledge the support of Stephen Grafman and his willingness to share documents and to offer specific suggestions and forthright criticisms along the way.

The personnel at the following archival collections also provided important assistance: Birmingham Public Library Department of Archives and Manuscripts; the Archives at the Martin Luther King Center for Nonviolent Social Change, Inc., Atlanta, Georgia; Special Collections, University of Illinois at Chicago; American Friends Service Committee Archives, Philadelphia, Pennsylvania; Special Collection Department, Samford University; World Methodist Archives, Lake Junaluska, North Carolina; Pitts Theological Library, Archives and Manuscripts, Emory University; Catholic Diocese of Birmingham Archives. I also gratefully acknowledge the financial support of the Bernadotte Schmidt Fellowships and a grant from the Alabama Baptist Historical Commission in helping complete this project.

This project started with a simple suggestion from David Edwin Harrell (then of the University of Alabama at Birmingham, now of Auburn University) to "take a look" at the words and deeds of Birmingham's leading white ministers of the 1960s. With this topic in mind, I sought the wisdom of Marvin Y. Whiting, then archivist at the Birmingham Public Library, who directed me to the Bishop Charles Carpenter Papers. Dr.

Whiting provided abundant instruction and encouragement. Harriet E. Amos Doss, who has helped me in more ways than I am able to calculate, guided me through the early stages of this project. At the University of Alabama at Birmingham (UAB), Dr. Doss directed my post-master's research project that ultimately became two published articles: "Bishop C. C. J. Carpenter: From Segregation to Integration," which appeared in *The Alabama Review*, and "Not Time Yet: Alabama's Episcopal Bishop and the End of Segregation in the Deep South," which was published in *Anglican and Episcopal History*. Selections from these articles appear in Chapters 2 and 8.

My dissertation director, James C. Cobb, now at the University of Georgia, consistently provided trustworthy guidance and direction. I am also grateful to Paul H. Bergeron, editor of the now completed Andrew Johnson Presidential Papers Project, for his steady support and friendship. No words could ever express my profound respect for Professor Bergeron and the impact he made on my academic career. Civil rights scholar Cynthia Fleming contributed in countless ways as an editor, a patient adviser, and an unyielding defender. Thanks also to Ed Caudill for introducing me to the field of mass communications history.

I am greatly indebted to Culpepper Clark of the University of Alabama, who has provided over ten years' worth of great friendship, thorough criticism, farsighted counsel, and spicy Mexican food. The manuscript was read in its entirety by UAB's Tennant S. McWilliams, who has always gone the extra mile for his former students. Even in the most harried of moments, Dr. McWilliams provided rock-solid advice and that extra boost of confidence, motivation, and reassurance when it was needed most.

The editorial staff at Louisiana State University Press are true professionals. I especially thank Sylvia Frank for her unwavering commitment to this project. Much of the strength of this manuscript comes from the wise and gentle comments of Professor Dan Carter. I thank him for his kindness and clear interpretative suggestions. I would also like to thank John Easterly and Eiv Boe.

My colleagues at Samford University in Birmingham provided crucial encouragement and advice as I completed the final revisions. I am indebted to my department chair, John Mayfield, for his comments and criticisms of parts of this manuscript. Elizabeth Wells, archivist and coordinator of Samford's Special Collections, played a critical role in helping me reach the last stages of this project. I also happily thank David Chapman, J. Roderick Davis, David Bains, Paul Holloway, Gregg Morrison, and David Roberts for their encouragement and feedback.

I am particularly indebted to my closest friends, each of whom offered support, suggestions, and prayers: Clint and Lisa Clifft, Jasper Levio, Kevin McGuire, Richard and Lydia Meek, Steve Rutherford, Gorden and Sally Thomason, and Kathleen Zebley.

This project would never have been completed without the support of my family, especially my parents, Samuel and Faye Bass, my parents-in-law, Lee and Donna Synnott, and my brother, Cary Bass, and his family: Kay, Joshua, and Sarah.

With a broad smile on my face, I thank my daughter Kathleen Elizabeth for bringing so much joy into my life. Lastly, with all my heart, I offer special thanks to my wife, Jennifer L. Bass: my best friend, counselor, supporter. We traveled this journey together.

Abbreviations Used in the Notes

ACMHR	Alabama Christian Movement for Human Relations
AFSCA	American Friends Service Committee Archives
BPLDAM	Birmingham Public Library Department of Archives and Manuscripts
ESCRU	Episcopal Society for Cultural and Racial Unity
FBCB	First Baptist Church, Birmingham
MECS	Methodist Episcopal Church, South
NCC	National Council of Churches of Christ in the U.S.A.
PCUS	Presbyterian Church in the United States
SBC	Southern Baptist Convention
SCLC	Southern Christian Leadership Conference
SUSC	Samford University Special Collection
WMA	World Methodist Archives

BLESSED ARE THE PEACEMAKERS

Introduction

The old Louisville and Nashville Railroad tracks stretched south close behind the white-painted concrete-and-brick buildings of the Birmingham Jail. Late in the evening, the engineers operating the massive steam engines had to let off a long, steady whistle blast as they approached the Avenue F crossing. In 1923 those lonesome wails inspired Jimmy Tarlton, a prisoner arrested for selling bootleg whiskey, to pen the "Birmingham Jail" folk ballad. "Write me a letter," he lamented, "save it for mail; send it in care of the Birmingham Jail."[1]

This book is the story of another famous composition from the city jail, an open letter written by civil rights leader Martin Luther King Jr. Composed forty years after Tarlton's ballad, the "Letter from Birmingham Jail" emerged as the most important written document of the civil rights protest era and a widely read modern literary classic. Personally addressed to eight white Birmingham clergy, the letter captured the essence of the struggle for racial equality and provided a blistering critique of the gradualist approach to racial justice.

Much like the lyrics of "Birmingham Jail," King's letter became part of American folklore. The image of King writing the epistle from a prison cell remains among the most moving images of the era. Nonetheless, this image and the literary appeal of the "Letter from Birmingham Jail" mask a more complex tale.

Beyond the public enthusiasm for the manuscript, the letter had a deeply personal impact on the apparent audience, the eight Birmingham clergy. They were among the most prominent religious leaders in the state of Alabama: Methodist bishops Nolan Harmon and Paul Hardin; Episcopal bishops Charles Carpenter and George Murray; Catholic bishop Joseph Durick; Edward Ramage, pastor of the prestigious First Presbyterian Church of Birmingham; Rabbi Milton Grafman of the Reform Temple Emanu-El; and Earl Stallings, who filled the pulpit at the First Baptist Church of Birmingham. A ninth minister, a young Catholic priest, Joseph Allen, was a silent member of this group and served as an aide to Bishop Durick.

A clash between Martin Luther King and these white clergy seemed inescapable. Perhaps in a less emotional time, in a calm setting, these ministers would have met face-to-face and discussed their differences; but this was Birmingham, 1963: a city where segregation was rigidly enforced by custom and law.

In April of that year, this group of religious leaders joined a vast number of black and white critics from throughout the country who felt King's civil rights demonstrations in Birmingham were ill-timed. They said so in a public statement printed in the local papers. These ministers provided King and his colleagues an avenue to answer this widespread criticism. King rebuked the eight white ministers for what he felt was their timid commitment to moral issues and justice. He despaired over their failure to take more decisive leadership during the racial crisis, even while vicious white racists branded them as Communists, "nigger lovers," liberals, and integrationists.[2]

As residents of Birmingham, the eight religious leaders witnessed rising tensions. Deeply concerned, they struggled to find an appropriate response. Only three months earlier, following Governor George Wallace's inaugural declaration for segregation, they had made a stand in support of the dignity of all people. "Every human being is created in the image of God," they had proclaimed, "and is entitled to respect as a fellow human being with all basic rights, privileges, and responsibilities which belong to humanity." Harassment and death threats had quickly followed.[3]

Now, in April 1963, they asserted with equal conviction that mass civil rights protests in the streets would provoke violence, just like Wallace's bellicose rhetoric. In addition, they felt demonstrations were particularly ill-timed because of a recent change in the Birmingham city government. The racial and ideological differences between Martin Luther King and the white clergy would find a public forum in the mass media. The white ministers released their public statement to the local press in hopes of discouraging violence in the streets of Birmingham and providing compassionate support for gradual racial progress. They also hoped that the new city government, given the chance, might realize meaningful progress in healing racial divisions. King, however, had other ideas.

Martin Luther King realized that it was critical to counter the arguments of those who equated the actions of the civil rights movement with those of violent defenders of the status quo. He answered the white clergy's public declaration with the powerful "Letter from Birmingham Jail." More than thirty-five years later, most consider the composition an exemplar of American public address. King and his staff's purpose for writing the letter, like that of all open letters from jails, was to persuade a larger audience. A moral movement such as his needed a compelling document in the epistolary tradition of Christianity. The eight clergy provided the immediate occasion and served as the ostensible audience, but they were secondary to this larger national objective. As one movement activist readily admitted, the essay had clearly been written with an "eye for media consumption."[4]

King and the Southern Christian Leadership Conference proved particularly successful in attracting national press, swaying public opinion to embrace the goals of the civil rights movement, and obtaining federal intervention. King and the nonviolent demonstrations provided inspiring and challenging images for the press and the American public: drama, tragedy, and stirring rhetoric. Like earlier martyrs, the demonstrators confronted the determined and sometimes violent defenders of a repressive social order on a public stage.[5]

The letter played a key role in the SCLC's plans for securing national media attention. Widely published in a multitude of press outlets in the months following the Birmingham movement, the document's prominence soared. As King's fame and the letter's reputation grew, so too did the infamy of the document's apparent audience. Although their names appeared at the top of the first page of the letter, King and his associates never intended addressing envelopes, licking stamps, and mailing eight copies of the so-called correspondence to these ministers. None of the white religious leaders ever received a personalized, signed, or delivered copy of the composition. The document became a press release.

The letter provided a general critique of the typical southern white religious leader who had been a constant source of frustration to Martin

Luther King. In his sweeping criticism, King believed moderate white clergymen had offered precious little leadership in combating racial injustice during the civil rights era. When the letter first appeared in 1963, the eight clergymen had a passionate reaction. After reading the document, several had feelings of bitterness, others skepticism, while a few remained confused and perplexed. But because they remained silent and refused to join a public debate, their respective views on the letter were never fully considered by journalists or scholars. The ministers spent the rest of their lives quietly defending their convictions. Most of the eight believed Martin Luther King had committed an injustice with a misleading portrait of their individual racial convictions—and it wasn't surprising that the characterizations were inaccurate, since the civil rights leader knew none of these men. As Rabbi Milton Grafman remembered, King never made any attempt to understand the eight clergy's motivation for speaking out. "Were we Klans people?" Grafman asked. "Were we liberals? Were we moderates? He knew nothing about us."[6]

Neither did readers and interpreters of the letter. Over the years, characterizations of these clergy have varied; they have been described as liberals, moderates, conservatives, reactionaries, segregationists, racists, bigots, obstructionists, misguided zealots, and Pharisees. In 1963, *all* of these clergy considered themselves moderates and gradualists—although each had his own idea of what those terms meant. "There are many ways to fight injustice," one of the ministers wrote in 1963, and many types of gradualism. The fight demanded time, patience, and moderation, they believed.[7]

Throughout the region, white southern moderates exhibited a hodgepodge of convictions about segregation and discrimination. A few held no solid opinions on the race issue. Most possessed intense feelings—some for, others against segregation—but they took no public stand because of a variety of reasons. Nevertheless, others did take bold stands. As one observer noted in 1960, the distinguishing feature of all moderates was their support for "gradual accommodation of the South to new ways of thought and behavior." This was unjust procrastination in King's mind.[8]

Regardless, the vaguely defined gradual approach had mainstream support among many Americans, both black and white, who believed a slow period of desegregation was the best solution, not a fast flash of forced integration. After all, the United States Supreme Court had mandated that the country proceed with desegregation at "all deliberate speed." Political leaders, like Dwight Eisenhower and John F. Kennedy, had spoken of civil rights in equally gradualist terms. In Birmingham, the center of the civil rights conflict, many local citizens, including these white clergy, felt that the gradual approach was the only way to preserve social order. The prospects of mass demonstrations to end segregation and violent confrontations to prevent integration were the wrong answers.

This moderate, middle-of-the-road approach to the southern race question left the eight clergy vulnerable to criticism from all sides of the civil rights issue. King and other civil rights activists denounced them; arrogantly uninformed, many white northerners wrote each of them harsh letters of reproach. The most hostile condemnation, however, came not from King or northern liberals, but from southern white racists. Each clergyman experienced petty harassment and received scores of hate letters, midnight phone calls, and death threats. A few of the ministers endured bare-knuckled segregationist reprisals, such as cross burnings, vandalism, and assault. For militant white segregationists, even timid gradual reform equaled racial treason.

While confrontations with Klan elements were frightening and disturbing, they were, at the same time, vindicating. For the eight clergy, as with other like-minded whites in the region, threats, intimidation, and violence validated their moderate stands. Had they faced criticism only from King and other liberal elements, their moderation would have seemed inadequate; but when violent segregationists turned up the heat, the eight felt a little more godly. This also provided the eight with a common sense of purpose as moral and spiritual leaders of the community.

Although the eight clergymen possessed a common regional and racial identity, they were individuals from a variety of religious and denominational traditions. They included two Episcopalians (Carpenter and Murray), two Methodists (Harmon and Hardin), one Baptist (Stallings), one Presbyterian (Ramage), one Roman Catholic (Durick), and one Jew (Grafman). Each of the eight ministered within the southern context of these faiths. They were a curious blend of liberal intellectuals, conservative theologians, Social Gospel advocates, revivalists, reformers, and Calvinists. Most had deep religious roots as the sons and grandsons of circuit-riding preachers, temperance reformers, cantors, southern patriots, and the like. Generational differences, family and religious backgrounds, life experiences, and personal convictions all contributed to the mix.

The overwhelming majority of the eight clergymen, like the South itself, were Protestant. Throughout much of the twentieth century, each of the Protestant denominations represented in the group of eight clergymen practiced a regional brand of conservative Christianity that primarily focused on conversion, moralism, and institutional growth. Like most Southern Baptist ministers, Earl Stallings concentrated on "saving souls" and other basic evangelistic efforts. Ed Ramage remained true to the traditions of the Presbyterian Church in the United States (PCUS) and emphasized the "spirituality" of the church and avoided involvement in political issues. The Methodist Episcopal Church, South, had narrowed its once broad social concerns to elementary moral crusades in favor of Prohibition or against other vices. Nolan Harmon ministered in this setting. Even within the context of the nationally centralized Protestant Episcopal Church, Charles Carpenter maintained a regional temperament that often seemed to contradict that of national leadership.[9]

At times, even Roman Catholic and Jewish religious leaders in the region provided uniquely southern interpretations of their faiths. Early in his career, Catholic bishop Joseph Durick accepted regional social values as the natural order of society while he practiced the "universal" Catholic faith. Historically, southern Catholics opposed integration the same as southern Protestants did. In addition, southern Jews expressed their regional identity and often quietly accepted the social order out of fear for their own safety. Rabbi Milton Grafman did little to challenge southern social traditions in his first decade in Birmingham.[10]

Regardless, viewing these eight clergymen only in the context of their religious communities does not fully explain their actions and reactions during the civil rights era. Although they agreed on a few basic moral and ethical principles and signed joint public statements, they had conflicting and often evolving ideas about civil rights and race relations, just like the rest of the South's white moderates. Episcopal bishop George Murray possessed a far-reaching social vision that often seemed to contradict the views of Charles Carpenter, yet he loyally served as Carpenter's assistant. Likewise, Paul Hardin moved beyond the narrow confines of a "moral" Methodist ministry to embrace social and racial equality. His outlook seemed at odds with that of his colleague Nolan Harmon.

Several of these ministers' racial outlooks evolved over time. During the 1960s, Earl Stallings's traditional Southern Baptist soul-saving rhetoric also provided a message of Christian and racial unity. Ed Ramage transcended the limited "spiritual" identity of the PCUS and took a strong stand against segregation. Inspired by reforms in the Roman Catholic Church in the early 1960s, Joseph Durick rejected regional values and stood for social justice. Likewise, Milton Grafman actively confronted racial injustice throughout the civil rights era. Their racial attitudes reflected the diversity of opinions among Alabama's white religious establishment during the time period.

None of these clergy fits exactly into the usual classifications of white southern racial perspectives, namely, liberal, moderate, or conservative. Life experiences and generational differences played a key role in determining their convictions. The two oldest clergymen, Harmon and Carpenter, reared in a period of racial paternalism and social-moral reform, had stronger ties to the status quo and had the most difficulty dealing with even the most gradual social change. Four of the youngest among them, Durick, Grafman, Hardin, and Murray, emerged as the most progressive and receptive to change. The injustices of the region burdened them. Following the dramatic events of 1963, each made even bolder stands for racial justice—with one going so far as to endorse the tactics used by Martin Luther King. Caught in the middle were two city pastors, Ramage and Stallings. Shaped by personal tribulation during the Great Depression, they were sympathetic and willing to take bold stands, but they lacked the institutional support to endure as strong progressives. Hence, over time the upheaval in Birmingham would have the most direct impact on them; pressure from within their own congregations convinced both to pursue ministries outside Alabama.

This book offers the first comprehensive history of Martin Luther King's "Letter from Birmingham Jail." It is the story of how clergymen from different religious communities responded to the racial crisis in the Deep South; of how King and his associates planned, composed, edited, and distributed the letter; of a document's impact on the civil rights movement, the American public, and the eight white clergy, a story deeper than shallow headlines and popular myths. As Rabbi Milton Grafman wrote in 1963, there was a "story behind the Birmingham story" that evoked a "different reaction from unbiased people who heard it for the first time." Now, more than thirty-five years later, the eight clergy's perspective and their role in the Birmingham struggle, as a group and as individuals, can be considered in a dispassionate light.[11]

This is also their story. Understanding their viewpoints and examining the lives and careers of these white ministers reveals a great deal about the role that church and synagogue played during the civil rights era of the 1950s and 1960s. It also shows, above all, the complexity of southern race relations and how the racial dilemma trapped self-styled gradualists or moderates between integrationists and segregationists.

1   "Aristocracy of the Damn Fools"

James McBride Dabbs, a keen observer of South, once wrote that anyone in the region who expressed even the slightest concern with race
relations immediately became a member of the "aristocracy of the damn
fools." For their part, a small group of white Alabama clergymen, Nolan
Harmon, Paul Hardin, Charles Carpenter, George Murray, Joseph Durick, Joe Allen, Ed Ramage, Earl Stallings, and Milton Grafman, felt like
fools caught in the middle between radical segregationists and civil
rights activists.[1]

In the South of the 1950s and 1960s, if citizens listened, they could
hear the calm words of moderation from white leaders like these eight
clergymen. Their still small voices on racial matters appealed to those
nonvocal citizens of Alabama looking for reasonable and tempered solutions to the crisis. "Their [moderates'] self respect," one writer discovered, "requires gentility, orderliness, due process, good manners." As
long as these whites could help blacks and "keep these dimensions of
their personality, they were willing to do so." But, for Martin Luther
King, the push toward justice required a total commitment to his tactics,
and the civil rights leader expected nothing less from white church leaders. When they expressed reservations, King dismissed them. Few white
racial moderates possessed the vision, King later wrote, "to see that
injustice must be rooted out by strong, persistent and determined
action."[2]

On the other side of the issue, hard-line segregationists were equally determined in their efforts to "root out" and silence moderates. "The waves have rolled over him," one journalist wrote of these tempered whites during the crisis. "They will again. The clamor of the angry and defiant men now and then have drowned him out. It will again."[3]

In many ways, the advocates of moderation and gradualism were the forgotten voices of the civil rights era. In the rush to cover the dramatic events of the 1950s and 1960s, the media overlooked a variety of opinions concerning segregation in the South. Only those whites and blacks who yelled the loudest seemed to make the headlines. The most lasting press images of the 1950s and 1960s placed a one-minded, violent white South before the American public. Television screens and newspaper photographs revealed mostly angry faces and hateful voices. "It was the South's misfortune," said one observer, "that violence and absurdity were often the only southern symbols that reached the rest of humanity."[4]

The extremist actions of white segregationists convinced this small group of Alabama church leaders to speak out publicly in January 1963. They put aside religious and personal differences and provided a public display of tempered, Judeo-Christian unity. Their calm words brought praise from integrationists and ridicule from radical segregationists. In April 1963, they spoke out against what they viewed as black extremism. This latter pronouncement brought condemnation from Martin Luther King Jr. and other integrationists sympathetic to his tactics. Clearly in the middle, these religious leaders disagreed with the integrationist cries of "now" and the segregationist demands of "never." They hoped for a utilitarian solution to the racial crisis—placing the needs of the many over the wants of vocal minorities, both black and white. In their estimation, both the belligerence of defiant white southerners and the mass-demonstration tactics of the civil rights activists led to violence. Violence, above all, was the enemy that threatened peace, harmony, and order, undermined the moral climate of the region, and served as the opponent of progress.

This small group of prominent clergymen assembled from time to time in 1963 to discuss racial tensions in the state. As spiritual leaders, they believed that they possessed the cultural authority to publicly address moral concerns. They were an informal group with no formal name, although a few of them called themselves the "Committee of Reconciliation." Most often they communicated with each other on an individual basis, through private phone calls or clandestine luncheon engagements. They had no weekly meetings as an organization nor any particular agenda—fate and frustration just brought them together. "Sometimes, we've just been huddling together," Milton Grafman noted in early 1963. "Sometimes we've just been commiserating. Sometimes we've tried to express to each other our sense of frustration and disillusionment with the forces that seemed to prevail in our state and in our city."[5]

Much of their frustration came from seeking the precarious middle ground between hard-line segregationists and liberal integrationists. As one Alabama minister noted in 1963, this middle ground was a dangerous place for white clergymen. "The problem," he observed, "is how to lead without being appropriated by one or the other extreme which immediately destroys the effectiveness of your leadership. When thus appropriated, you are effective only with the one faction. Neither the opposite one nor the moderate group will listen to you any longer." The pastor believed that moderate religious leaders had to "pool wisdom" and act as a "fellowship rather than in isolated instances."[6]

By working collectively, ministerial groups, like these Birmingham clergymen, hoped to avoid a severe backlash. The defense of a tempered and gradualist position on race and the opposition to segregationist violence was the one great moral issue in this racial crisis on which various clergy could unite. In many southern cities, ministerial associations publicly criticized white resistance and called for peaceful compliance to integration measures. Most of the statements skirted the core issues of racism and injustice and allowed unity among broader cross sections of pastors with diverse opinions.[7]

In 1957, a group of the most prestigious ministers of Richmond, Virginia, purchased advertising space in local newspapers to attack massive resistance. "To defy the Supreme Court and to encourage others to do so, in our judgment, is not only poor strategy; it is poor citizenship," they proclaimed. A few months later, several Atlanta clergy made a public stand in favor of law and order, open communication between the races, and "first class citizenship" for all southerners. In Chattanooga, Tennessee, a group of ministers issued a statement deploring "violence, hate and bigotry in any form, against anybody." In Dallas, three hundred Protestant pastors together pronounced "enforced segregation" a moral and legal sin and encouraged citizens to cooperate with integration efforts. In 1959, ministers and rabbis in Miami advocated a moderate solution to the integration crisis and condemned all "hatred and scorn for those of another race." Throughout the racial crisis, statements from clergy appeared in other southern cities, including Houston, Texas; Columbus, Georgia; Little Rock, Arkansas; and Baton Rouge, Louisiana. In Alabama, ministerial associations in Huntsville, Montgomery, and Mobile issued statements as well, but not in Birmingham.[8]

Those vocal white ministers in other southern cities urged the Birmingham clergy to make similar public statements "concerning the race question." When the issue came up at the January 13, 1958, meeting of the executive committee of the Birmingham Ministers Association, President R. L. Dill Jr. possessed a "negative attitude" concerning the idea, and encouraged the group to remain silent.[9]

Segregationist sentiment prevailed among the 320-member white ministerial association. One of the most dignified and vocal pro-segregationist ministers was John Buchanan, pastor of Birmingham's large and powerful Southside Baptist Church since 1937. On one hand, he vigorously attacked Ku Klux Klan activities in the late 1950s; on the other, he publicly proclaimed that the good Lord had designed the "customs and practices of segregation." In his mind, Klan violence was immoral, but segregation was not. Many ministers of his age had no problem reconciling these notions.[10]

Throughout the first half of the twentieth century, southern white ministers saw Jim Crow as neither an urgent moral dilemma nor an immense social affliction. The racial and religious perspectives of many of the city's white clergy in the civil rights era remained tied to long-held notions of days gone by. Previously, Progressive Era ministers in Birmingham, both Social Gospel advocates and moral crusaders, supported the passage of Jim Crow laws. For pastors of this generation, racial separation and disfranchisement provided social uplift for blacks and served as the "moral" solution to the race problem. Many of these religious leaders saw no contradiction in advocating Jim Crow while condemning lynchings or supporting paternalistic social programs to "uplift" the "Negro" community. They embraced "separate but equal" notions and worked to make Jim Crow more humane.

As one Birmingham Methodist leader noted at the time, "God had not built the universe on a dead level. The two races will remain distinct and separate as years go by." Even the most liberal white ministers embraced these notions that placed blacks in a second-class world. Alfred J. Dickinson, pastor of First Baptist Church of Birmingham from 1901 to 1918, emerged as a Social Gospel advocate involved in a variety of progressive causes. Dickinson saw himself not as an elite man of the cloth, but as a humble servant of the "sack cloth." Yet he saw segregation and disfranchisement not as an evil or a sin, but as a necessity for progress. In his mind, disfranchisement would end black-voter manipulation by both "mischievous" northerners and "immoral" anti-prohibitionists. Alabama needed to limit suffrage, Dickinson emphasized, to "those who have the moral appreciation of its sacred nature not to debauch it, and the intelligent apprehension of its function to exercise it hereunto." The state would be prudent, he added, to eliminate the "ignorant and vicious Negro vote and stop white men from corrupting any more of them." In the minds of Dickinson and others of his generation in Birmingham, segregation and disfranchisement maintained community morality and provided a measure of social uplift for all citizens, both white and black. Anyone who tried to end separation of the races, he added, "can but be counted our enemy."[11]

While a limited version of the Social Gospel flourished in Birmingham during Dickinson's day, the 1920s through the civil rights era saw most local pastors possessing a much narrower vision. Birmingham's white religious leaders focused their cultural authority on "obvious" moral concerns like drinking, gambling, adultery, divorce, prostitution, and other vices. "With important individual exceptions," one historian later concluded, the city's white Protestants "saw personal failure clearly but were blind to underlying social sins." The Protestant Pastors Union (the forerunner of the Birmingham Ministers Association) concentrated almost exclusively on a decline in community moral standards during the 1920s. A few of the more reactionary members even supported Klan raids of gaming establishments, brothels, and speakeasies as ways to enforce community morality. Local pastors encouraged congregations to return to the straight and narrow and keep the Sabbath day holy. Preachers urged "good" Christians to honor God on Sunday by leaving automobiles in garages (except to go to church), not accepting invitations to "big dinners," and forgoing picnics, excursions, newspapers, and wedding ceremonies. "The Sabbath," an Alabama Presbyterian leadership concluded, "was not to be a day of feasting and amusement."[12]

During the 1930s, the Pastors Union continued to deemphasize social problems and highlight moral concerns. Early in the decade, its membership proclaimed its loyalty to the Democratic Party and the New Deal, but warned President Franklin Roosevelt of the "evil consequences" of repealing the Eighteenth Amendment. "We are reluctant indeed to be forced into antagonism to our party," the pastors wrote FDR in 1933, "but we deliberately and fearlessly proclaim our unwavering and determined adherence to our moral religious convictions regardless of where they may lead or what they may involve." As America inched closer to involvement in a global conflict late in the decade, the ministers called for American neutrality, but after Pearl Harbor in 1941 they united behind the "moral" war effort. Following the war, the clergy chose a more inclusive name for the organization (Birmingham Ministers Association) and invited Catholics and Jews to participate.[13]

The presence of Catholic and Jewish clergymen only reinforced the Protestant emphasis on morality. The ministers were outspoken in their criticism of Alabama governor James "Big Jim" Folsom's sinful nature. At a breakfast in Harlingen, Texas, in the late 1940s, Folsom ordered a bottle of beer and loudly proclaimed that the "only thing better than beer is whiskey." The clergy sent the governor a letter and encouraged him to live a "sober and righteous" life. The children of the state were looking to Folsom to set a good example. "What you do will have its effect on many of them," they wrote. "We are vitally concerned in their moral well being, and we feel that you owe it to them and to the office which you hold to set a good example in your own life."[14]

By the civil rights era, the emphasis on traditional morality continued. A few socially conscious pastors remained active in Birmingham, but the problems directly associated with segregation and disfranchisement were seldom, if ever, addressed. For example, a local Ministers' Discussion Group, made up of "congenial clergymen and educators of modern training and outlook," met monthly to discuss contemporary social and theological issues. From the group's founding in 1929 until 1959, these white religious leaders, among the city's most liberal, discussed race problems a scant five times—twice in 1933, twice in 1943, and once in 1947.[15]

Throughout the first half of the twentieth century, however, social separation from blacks did not mean total isolation. More than a few white pastors crossed racial lines and developed warm friendships with their black counterparts. In the 1920s, the Reverend James E. Dillard, pastor of the Southside Baptist Church, and the Reverend Henry Edmonds of the Independent Presbyterian Church were just two of the city's white pastors who built close personal and working relationships with prominent black pastors such as the Reverend John W. Goodgame at Sixth Avenue Baptist. Yet despite their close bonds, these pastors knew their designated roles and their appropriate places in the social and moral structure.[16]

Broad cooperation between black and white ministers, however, was nonexistent. In 1947, white pastors invited the Birmingham Baptist Ministers' Conference, the city's largest and most prestigious organization of black ministers, to participate in an interracial "Festival of Faith Rally" at Legion Field. When the black pastors learned that the rally would be segregated, they refused the invitation.[17]

At almost the same time a few local white religious leaders perhaps sensed the changing racial climate. In 1946 a special committee of the Southern Baptist Convention drafted a "Statement of Principles" on race. Adopted by the full convention the following year, delegates pledged, among other things, to "strive as individuals to conquer all prejudice," to "protest against injustice and indignities against Negroes, and to become active in cooperating with black Baptists in "building up of their churches, the education of their ministers, and the promotion of their missions and evangelistic programs." Perhaps inspired by this spirit of good will, the all-white Birmingham Baptist Association appointed a special task force to reach out to black Baptists. Taking the lead was James Edward Rouse, pastor of South Avondale Baptist Church, and Henlee Barnette, a professor of sociology at Howard College. Barnette and Rouse attended a meeting of the all-black Birmingham Baptist Ministers' Conference and asked to address the meeting. A few ministers moaned and stamped their feet in an objection to the white interlopers' presence. "Brethren," one black minister proclaimed, "this is the first time any white people have ever come to our meeting and I think we ought to hear what they have to say."[18]

Putting aside the usual paternalistic rhetoric, Barnette told the gathering that he was coming as a Christian brother seeking mutual understanding. Apparently, although not well documented, Rouse and Barnette's efforts resulted in an interracial conference of Birmingham's Baptist pastors at the Sixteenth Street Baptist Church in the spring of 1947. Little progress resulted from such efforts, and Rouse and Barnette had both left the city for other opportunities that same year.[19]

Following these failed attempts, opinions on the race question hardened. During these years, formal communication between black and white pastors became increasingly strained. For many of Birmingham's older white clergymen, the U.S. Supreme Court's 1954 *Brown v. Board of Education* decision had, in the words of John Buchanan, complicated and damaged race relations in the South. "The present court from its cloistered chambers has overlooked the reality of the situation," he added. "Our people must exercise sober and sound judgement in facing this crisis." Soon after the *Brown* decision, a poll by *Pulpit Digest* revealed that a majority of white southern ministers favored the Supreme Court decision, including 53 percent in Alabama. The gap between pulpit and pew, however, was disquieting. Vocal segregationists were determined to prevent these pastors from acting upon these "liberal" notions. "The worst obstacle we face in the fight to preserve segregated schools in the South," one hard-liner emphasized in 1955, "is the white preacher. The patriots of Reconstruction had the preachers praying for them instead of working against them."[20]

In spite of the intimidation, informal interracial contact between the city's religious leaders continued, but most white pastors failed to comprehend the new sense of urgency in the black community; nor did they acknowledge the immoral nature of segregation. Attitudes had changed little, and social customs were too deep and opinion too rigid for a rapid great awakening among the religious leaders of the region. Old traditions were slow to die. "Moral leadership seemed woefully inadequate," one writer concluded in the 1960s, "where opinion was so rigidly fixed, where expression of divergent viewpoints was so little tolerated, and where forces of repression were so organized and aroused."[21]

In 1960, an outside consulting firm compiled the "Birmingham Metropolitan Audit," a detailed analysis of the city's "personality" and "leadership." Using data gathered by a small group of local businessmen, the final report concluded that while most citizens maintained high moral standards, Birmingham's white populace had yet to determine whether or not segregation was immoral. Until that issue was agreed upon, the consultants added, "we cannot subtract segregation from the mores and morals of the community." In other words, the white citizens of Birmingham were moral as long as segregation was not deemed immoral.[22]

The "Audit" also concluded that the race question remained "much on Birmingham's mind," with a growing number of residents "gravely" preoccupied with the issue. Many of these citizens were searching for new answers to the racial crisis. By the early 1960s, a few younger white moderates in Birmingham, including several religious leaders, recognized the moral disparity between Jim Crow and Judeo-Christian brotherhood. As tensions in the state reached a boiling point in January 1963, a small group of Birmingham clergymen issued a joint statement against hard-line segregationists and for human rights. Nearly a decade after the integration crisis began, this was the first public rebuke of segregationists and the first acknowledgment of black civil rights by any group of white clergy in Birmingham.[23]

On January 9, 1963, Episcopal bishop George Murray invited several ministers for a "dutch lunch" the following week at the old Tutwiler Hotel on Twentieth Street North in downtown Birmingham. For many citizens, the old Tutwiler Hotel was a local landmark and the embodiment of the Birmingham establishment. Early in the century, local business executives had financed and built the twelve-story hotel because Birmingham lacked suitable accommodations for visiting U.S. Steel executives from the Northeast. Named after one of the investors, industrialist Edward Magruder Tutwiler, the hotel opened its doors on June 15, 1914. For years, the proprietors bragged that the facility was the dispenser of "true southern hospitality" in Birmingham.[24]

The Tutwiler's grand style accommodated occasional famous guests and several infamous incidents. In 1927, only a few months after his famed transatlantic flight to Paris, aviator Charles Lindbergh stayed in the Louis XIV suite. His boyish charm and lanky good looks so impressed Una Franklin, a reporter for the Birmingham *Age-Herald*, that she described Lindbergh as the "one boy with whom I could fall in love." A decade later, actress Tallulah Bankhead caused quite a scandal in the city when she held an outrageous wedding reception in a suite on the thirteenth floor. "Isn't this all so ridiculous?" she boasted.[25]

When the southern Democrats bolted from the 1948 National Democratic Convention, they used rooms 922, 923, and 924 of the Tutwiler as a temporary "Dixiecrat" headquarters. One evening during the boisterous political gathering, a group of delegates hanged Harry Truman in effigy from a hotel balcony with a sign draped across his chest proclaiming "Truman killed by civil rights." Three years later, on September 21, 1951, one former Dixiecrat delegate, Eugene "Bull" Connor, was involved in Birmingham's scandal of the decade. A city police detective discovered Connor and a woman other than his wife in room 760. [26]

The rooms of the Tutwiler contained a rich history. In 1963, though almost fifty years old, the hotel still maintained some measure of its earlier splendor and glory. When George Murray invited the clergymen to gather at the Tutwiler, he urged each of them, for their own safety, to keep the meeting a secret. "You must keep this off the record," he advised. Murray summoned the white ministers who would later compose the Good Friday statement and also the Reverend Soterios D. Gouvellis of the Holy Trinity–Holy Cross Greek Orthodox Church in Birmingham, Rabbi Eugene Blackschleger of Temple Beth-Or in Montgomery, and J. T. Beale, the secretary-director of the Christian Churches of Alabama.[27]

Before the group could meet, the intensity of the racial rhetoric in the state reached a fever pitch. In the gubernatorial election of 1962, Alabamians elected George Wallace to his first term as governor of the state. On Monday, January 14, Wallace stood on the steps of the state capital in Montgomery and took the oath of office near the spot where Jefferson Davis, a hundred years before, had taken the oath of office as the president of the Confederate States of America. In his inaugural address, Wallace sent a message to all those who dared tread upon the sovereign state of Alabama. The new governor drew his "line in the dust" and tossed the "gauntlet before the feet of tyranny" and proclaimed "segregation now . . . segregation tomorrow . . . segregation forever."[28]

As the state and national media widely publicized Wallace's bellicose rhetoric, the small group of clergymen gathered on January 16, 1963, at the Tutwiler. Hoping to persuade white Alabamians against any further massive resistance, George Murray decided that his colleagues should follow the lead of other ministerial groups around the South and issue a public statement appealing for "law and order and common sense" and a peaceful compliance to desegregation orders.[29]

The clergy simply revised a statement composed by the Huntsville Ministers Association in October 1962. Episcopal minister Emile Joffrion, a member of the Huntsville group, had mailed a copy of the statement to Bishop Murray. Previously Joffrion sent the resolution to Alabama governor John Patterson, who emerged as an outspoken advocate of massive resistance. "We find ourselves in disagreement with the position you have taken in the past," the minister wrote, "and especially with your most recent statements, concerning the racial situation in Alabama." Most Alabamians, Joffrion believed, were tired of this type of leadership that had led other states into a "tragic and hopeless trap."[30]

The Birmingham clergy believed that the defiance of radical segregationists, like that of Patterson's successor, George Wallace, would further increase tensions and lead the state into a pit of racial turmoil. In times of trouble and change in the "cherished patterns of life in our beloved Southland," the eleven ministers emphasized, it was essential for clergymen in positions of responsibility and leadership to express their honest convictions. They were not self-appointed leaders, but had been chosen by Alabamians of several religious faiths (Protestant, Catholic, and Jewish) to carry the heavy responsibility of serving as shepherds to their flocks. Speaking in a spirit of humility, the ministers recognized that they had never possessed all the answers to solve the complex racial problems in the South. Nevertheless, the religious people of Alabama expected and deserved active and vocal leadership with a "firm conviction."[31]

Many forthright residents of Alabama opposed desegregation of the education system in the state. "As southerners," the clergy emphasized, "we understand this." Nevertheless, the ministers believed defiance was neither the "right answer nor the solution" to the race question. Inflammatory and rebellious rhetoric by hard-line segregationists led only to discord, violence, disgrace, and confusion for the "beloved state" of Alabama.[32]

The group directed seven points to the opponents of desegregation (Wallace was never named in the statement), and the same notions they would direct toward integrationists in April: (1) hatred and violence had no sanction in American religious and political traditions; (2) disagreement over laws and social change should never lead to defiance, anarchy, and subversion; (3) courts and legislatures had the power to review and change laws, but laws could "not be ignored by whims of individuals"; (4) citizens had the right to amend the Constitution or impeach a judge through proper action, but in the meantime, America's way of life depended on obedience to court decisions; (5) no person's freedom was safe unless everyone's freedom was equally protected; (6) the First Amendment right of free speech must be "preserved and exercised" without fear of recrimination or harassment; (7) by being created in God's image, every human deserved respect and all "basic rights, privileges, and responsibilities."[33]

The situation confronting the South called for earnest prayer, clear thought, understanding love, and courageous action, the ministers concluded. "Thus we call on all people of goodwill to join us in seeking divine guidance as we make our appeal for law and order and common sense." Calling the statement an "interesting illustration of ecumenicity moving rapidly," Episcopal bishop Charles Carpenter personally delivered a copy of the statement to the editors of the *Birmingham Post-Herald* and the *Birmingham News* to ensure no slip-up in publication. "I believe we may have done a little good," Carpenter wrote a few days later, "and at least we have shown that this group of eleven assorted ministers feel at one in this matter."[34]

The statement appeared in Birmingham's two daily newspapers on January 17, 1963, and in other newspapers across the country via the wire services over the next week. Most journalists assumed that the clergymen had issued their statement in direct response to Wallace, but the meeting had been planned before the governor's address. "So happens that it was very well timed," Milton Grafman said later that week, especially in the wake of Wallace "breathing defiance" and defacing the image of Alabama.[35]

Alabama's *Methodist Christian Advocate* enthusiastically embraced the ministers' statement as pointing the way to a peaceful and harmonious Alabama. "Be it ours to follow in the conviction that right shall at last prevail." With their courage, convictions, and honesty, these eleven white clergy had earned the right through long and effective leadership to serve Alabama as "spiritual guides." Several letters to the editor in local newspapers also praised the efforts of the white ministers. One writer believed church leaders and other men of good will had remained silent too long—racists had seized the day and were leading citizens down the "back alley of hate and violence." The writer called on all ministers to follow the clergymen's example and cast off timidity and fear and lead citizens along the paths of good will.[36]

An editorialist for the moderate *Post-Herald* described the statement as a "creed of the good citizen" and a guide for thinking and action. In a lengthy piece, an editorial writer for the conservative *Birmingham News* viewed the ministers' rhetoric with uncertainty. The state needed vocal opposition, the writer concluded, and other leaders needed to step forward and speak out. In this light, the *News* encouraged the continued exercise of free speech. Cryptically, however, the editorial writer believed the ministers had erred in expecting freedom of speech without the retaliation and harassment from those on the other side of the issue. Anyone who spoke publicly on racial matters, the *News* assumed, should anticipate such responses. E. L. Holland Jr., the paper's editorial page editor, wrote Earl Stallings a few days later and thanked the Baptist minister for his efforts but again warned of the coming counterattack. "I now await, glumly," Holland wrote, "the other groups who, surely, will be coming forward."[37]

The segregationist backlash indeed came quickly. Each of the men received an outpouring of vicious letters, harassing midnight phone calls, and, as Carpenter later wrote, "other expressions of hatred" from radical segregationists. "I like a negro on his side of the fence," one writer explained, "but when he crawls over on my side, I don't like it." Many segregationists believed that this small group of white ministers had discarded God's Word for a testament of integration. "Are those gentlemen of the Cloth so ignorant of the teachings of Holy Writ that they want us to peacefully submit to integration contrary to God's instructions?" one segregationist wrote. "Do they ask that we obey man rather than God? Do they think there is law and order in the most integrated city in the United States? To accept integration is no guarantee of law and order. Quite the contrary is true. From the considered instructions laid down by God, it would seem some violence to prevent integration is better for a country than integration, with its widespread lawlessness."[38]

One letter writer believed the eleven "frocked politicians" had overstepped their bounds, violated the spiritual nature of the church, and endorsed the sin of integration. A fundamentalist minister encouraged Alabamians to ignore the statement and remain unyielding to the whims of these Reds, pinks, or so-called liberals. Birmingham lawyer Maurice Rogers wrote to each of the clergy and branded their statement disgusting, cowardly, ill-timed, ill-advised, and inappropriate. The eleven "hypocrites and conformists" needed to keep their mouths shut and stop meddling in race relations. After all, he concluded, George Wallace was America's last hope to maintain freedom. "If you have any convictions, which apparently you have not, then you should stand in your own pulpit and preach it and not hunt up others whose religious views you despise to sign edicts with you. The truth is your socialist statements have no part in your religion and no basis in your various doctrines hence you cannot preach the sort of thing now proclaimed."[39]

These impassioned segregationists vocally and sometimes violently demanded no deviation from the status quo. "Not all of them [white southerners] feel as strongly as I do," said one Alabama segregationist. "I'm rabid on the subject." In their minds, there was no middle ground on the issue of race—white folks had to either support Jim Crow or embrace integration. "You are either for segregation, or you are for integration, without prefix, suffix, or affix . . . ," one proclaimed. "As long as we live, so long shall we be segregationists, and after death, God willing, thus it will still be!"[40]

In spite of attempts to maintain freedom in the pulpit, pastors that refused to preach the gospel-truth of Jim Crow had to endure steady criticism from hard-line segregationist laymen. "If your preacher doesn't preach segregation from his pulpit," a Methodist parishioner recommended, "you cut his salary to a dollar a year and sell his parsonage." One Alabama Methodist churchgoer gruffly advised sympathetic ministers to hit the "well paved roads" heading north, and radicals repeatedly urged whipping "weak-kneed preachers" into line by withholding tithes and sabotaging the pastor's program with steady persecution. If a minister crossed the line, churchgoing segregationists used harsh, "Spanish Inquisition–like" reprisals to purge a pastor from a local church. These activist segregationists were adamant. "We believe in segregation," one said during the civil rights crisis, "and I mean *believe* it, like we believe in God." Many southern white Christians shared this opinion and apparently placed more faith in Jim Crow than in Jesus Christ. "The day I have to go in church and have to smell stinking niggers," one Alabama segregationist wrote, "that's the day I'll stay away and take a chance on my hopes of Heaven."[41]

The explosive nature of the segregationist rhetoric had a direct impact on a southern white clergyman's ministry. No matter the depth or shallowness of a pastor's racial convictions, the majority remained silent on the issue and preserved their ministry and their economic livelihood. As one author suggested, "silence was golden, or at least there was some relationship between silence and gold." Even more important for these white clergy were their roles as shepherds. Their job was to tend to the spiritual needs of their congregation, not to lead a social revolution. At the time, critics demanded that white religious leaders do more to aid the civil rights cause. "There are places in the South," one pastor observed, "where a clergyman's forthright advocacy of even gradual integration might mean not only his own dismissal but the wholesale withdrawal of members from his church." Certainly, in hindsight, they could have done more, but they would have moved too far out in front of their congregations and ended their principal role as spiritual stewards.[42]

Of those clergymen that addressed the racial issue, most avoided direct mention of it and instead focused on generic allusions to Christian brotherhood. "There are an awful lot of sermons these days about brotherly love," one white pastor noted in 1963, "but darned few of them are specific about who the brothers are." In order to preserve his pastorate, a white clergyman had to carefully chose the words he uttered before a congregation. As one historian later argued, a minister's simple calls for justice and brotherhood were "far from irrelevant in tense southern communities and, in some situations, required a measure of courage."[43]

Hard-line segregationists clearly understood the meaning of these sermons and launched efforts to "straighten out" those clergymen who "preached the brotherhood of man." These radicals branded the pastor's message as "Marxian" Christianity or "revolutionary social" Christianity. "This is the dream of the socialist planner," one radical wrote. "Many unsuspecting ministers and congregations, influenced by the hierarchy of the various denominations, are being led astray. These so call [sic] Christians are, as a matter of fact, Socialists." Others questioned the kind of love being professed from the pulpit. Was it love for the poor, the sick, the hungry? Or was it the kind of love that sustained the racial crisis? "I think ministers should preach the gospel of Jesus Christ," a segregationist proclaimed in 1957, "instead of sending out feelers to ascertain how the congregation and the public react to the brotherly love sermons."[44]

Other ministers lost pulpits simply by stating publicly that Christian duty demanded a response to the race problem or by pleading for moderation, which was for some synonymous with integration. In Alabama and throughout the South, individual white ministers who made statements on the race question found themselves targeted for persecution by extremists. One observer of the southern scene noted that in 1963 white ministers in Birmingham "who expressed themselves on integration were leaving their pulpits at the rate of one a day." This perhaps was an overstatement, but at the very least, a tremendous amount of turnover was occurring in Birmingham church leadership during the civil rights era. As one church official noted at the time, as many as one hundred pastors throughout the South had left their pulpits over the race question during 1963 alone. Radical intimidation was taking its toll.[45]

While segregationists believed moderates were proceeding too fast, integrationists believed they were moving too slow. For years, Martin Luther King scolded white church leaders for not doing more. For King and the Southern Christian Leadership Conference, crisis-packed demonstrations provided the empowerment and the publicity the movement needed for fund-raising and bargaining. Most white ministers believed such activities prevented slow and peaceful change in the region. They urged blacks to remain patient and wait for a more convenient season for racial equality. Sudden changes in the status quo would cause an upheaval in southern society that they feared would hurt both blacks and whites; the region needed slow, gradual change. The dilemma demanded time, they concluded; time for more education, time for more debate, time for better laws, time to establish racial harmony, and most of all, a time when peace and order would be maintained. They failed to understand the new sense of urgency among many southern blacks.

On the surface, the small group of white clergymen who gathered in January and again on Good Friday, April 12, 1963, seemed the complete opposite of Martin Luther King and his confidants. These white ministers wanted to maintain harmony and peace. On the other hand, King looked to create a crisis and bring tensions to the surface. SCLC preachers wanted extensive press coverage of the crisis to reveal southern injustice, to raise money, and to create national pressure to force local change. The white ministers hoped the national media would ignore the city. As King fasted that Good Friday before his march to jail, the white religious leaders ate lunch. The black ministers stayed at the only lodging available to them, the Gaston Motel; the white clergy met at the finest hotel in Birmingham. The Birmingham clergy desired to end the demonstrations; King wanted them to continue. King believed the quest for civil rights should be contested in the streets. The white religious leaders hoped to see the cause pursued gradually, in the court system.[46]

In the minds of the eight clergy, and many thoughtful citizens both black and white, the moderate judicial approach was transforming Birmingham. Only a few days prior to their Good Friday gathering, citizens voted against hard-line segregationist Bull Connor's bid to become mayor in favor of the more tempered Albert Boutwell. While the eight saw this event as a sign of hope, Martin Luther King and civil rights activists had a different perspective: Boutwell was a segregationist who needed to be pressured through direct confrontation. "King was never one to wait upon problematical differences in official attitudes," one observer later reflected. Street demonstrations, however, in the eyes of the eight white clergymen, were not the peaceful, ethical, or moral solu tion to the racial problem. As the city's leading moral and spiritual authorities, they once again felt a duty to speak out.[47]

They gathered anew at the Tutwiler Hotel, and following a lunch, the clergy retired to Bishop Nolan Harmon's hotel suite to compose a formal statement for the local press. Harmon was a relative newcomer to the Birmingham situation; only a few months before, Methodist leaders had chosen him to serve as the leader of the North Alabama Conference. Harmon divided his time between Alabama and his home conference in western North Carolina. When in Birmingham, he made his home in the Tutwiler.[48]

During the days proceeding the Good Friday meeting, Harmon had preached a series of Holy Week messages in Winston-Salem, North Carolina; unwittingly, the titles of his sermons seemed to reflect the tensions in Birmingham: "Who Is This?" "The Impossible Task," "Things That Cannot Be Shaken," "The Paradox of God," and "Bearing the Marks." Each of the clergy gathered that Friday in the hotel could identify with Harmon's religious and civil reflections. In a lively debate, the men discussed their solutions to the race problem, and Rabbi Milton Grafman typed drafts of the statement on Bishop Harmon's portable typewriter.[49]

Grafman sat down at the old manual typewriter and the other clergy gathered around him offering suggestions for the statement. Catholic bishop Joseph Durick told Grafman to begin the statement with the blessing: in the name of the Father, the Son, and the Holy Spirit. "Wait a minute," Grafman said as he glanced over his shoulder at the Catholic leader; "I won't be able to sign that." Embarrassed, Durick realized his mistake and let someone else suggest the format of the statement.[50]

Optimistically, the religious leaders believed all Birmingham residents had an opportunity for a "new constructive and realistic approach" to the racial dilemma with the apparent end to Bull Connor's regime. The city, however, was confronting a series of demonstrations by some black citizens and the white clergy believed these protests were directed and led in part by "outsiders" (the statement never mentioned King by name). The white ministers recognized the natural impatience of black citizens, who felt their hopes had been unfulfilled. Regardless, the clergymen considered the use of demonstrations in realizing these hopes "unwise and untimely." Instead, they agreed with certain (unidentified) local black leaders who had called for honest and open negotiation of racial issues. The ministers believed that local residents, both black and white, had the knowledge and experience to deal with the Birmingham situation and could best handle negotiations.[51]

Conversely, the use of nonviolent direct action was an incitement to hatred and violence, because, although technically peaceful, those tactics had contributed nothing to solving local problems. The ministers viewed civil disobedience through nonviolent action as an unjustified and extreme measure during days of "new hope" in Birmingham. The religious leaders commended the community, the local news media, and the law enforcement officials in their efforts to remain calm during the first week of demonstrations. They also urged the citizens of Birmingham to show restraint and asked law enforcement officials to continue to "protect our city from violence." Proceeding in this paternalistic tone, they advised "our own negro" community to withdraw support from the demonstrations and unite in a local effort to work peacefully for a better Birmingham. When rights had been denied, the cause must be pressed in the courts and through local negotiation and "not in the streets." The ministers concluded by appealing, simply and vaguely, to blacks and whites to observe the principles of "law and order and common sense."[52]

The Good Friday statement and the names of the white ministers appeared in the two Birmingham papers on Saturday, April 13, 1963. Although the ministers made several references to their January "law and order" statement and much of the language was similar, the April pronouncement seemed hasty and lacked the thoughtfulness of their earlier issuance. The white clergy were naive, misguided, and obtuse in their choice of words and phrases in their statement, especially the terms "law and order" and "outsider." They were rhetorically smart to use the "law and order" phrase in January against segregationists, but it was an unwise choice to admonish integrationists. Civil rights activists recognized these expressions as racist code words with connotations of harshness and intolerance. In the years following the publication of the "Letter from Birmingham Jail," some scholars believed the clergy's appeal revealed a "segregationist intent."[53]

For many white southerners, invoking the principles of law and order was a stalling technique, a "civilized" way to maintain the status quo. A few of the older white clergy shared this perspective. Radical segregationists, however, enforced the principles of law and order to maintain white supremacy at any cost, whether through intimidation, violence, vigilantism, or murder. When the Supreme Court outlawed segregation in public schools or in transportation terminals, segregationists simply ignored these decisions. Maintaining local customs and ignoring federal laws would help preserve order in the region, they surmised, and order clearly meant keeping blacks in their "proper" place in society.

Others, like several of the younger clergymen, had a broader interpretation of the law-and-order concept. They expected that all southerners, both black and white, should obey *all* the laws of the land to maintain civil order. "For some time," remembered Bishop George Murray, "most of us [eight clergy] had pleaded with people to obey the laws of the land. Obey the law; obey the law; obey the law: we said it over and over again." In 1954, the U.S. Supreme Court had handed down the *Brown v. Board of Education* decision, declaring "separate but equal" educational facilities unconstitutional. *Brown* was "now the law of the land and we urged whites to obey this," Murray continued. "Circumventing the law undermined law and order in the region." When Martin Luther King and the SCLC began demonstrations in Birmingham, the eight clergy felt bound to speak out. "It was the same principle," the bishop continued. "I saw no inconsistency as we asked Dr. King to stop parading in the streets and obey the laws against demonstrations. This would help maintain civil order and not provoke violence. He should have pursued change in the courts, not in front of television cameras." This emphasis on law, order, and court action suggested that each of these ministers viewed the racial crisis as a legal problem and not a moral issue.[54]

In addition, the eight clergy had a narrow definition of the term "outsider." King, they believed, was not an outsider to the region or even the state, but simply an outsider to the city—a noncitizen. "I don't ever recall my looking upon him as being an extremist or an outsider," Bishop Joseph Durick wrote in 1971. "He was often called that, but he was only an outsider to Birmingham—but not to Alabama." The ministers had hoped for a solution based on "commonsense" negotiations among local leaders. Rabbi Milton Grafman, however, later admitted the ministers' statement should have been better phrased. "We certainly didn't come out smelling like a rose," he said. Durick was more graphic, calling the statement little more than "verbal diarrhea." Each of the ministers felt a sense of frustration with the ultimate reaction to their statement.[55]

No matter where they stood on specific racial issues, the eight white clergy were all trapped in the middle. Gradualists or moderates, of any persuasion, had little ground to stand on as activists and segregationists kept up the pressure. They were all "damned fools."

2   In the South By and By

Charles Carpenter and Nolan Harmon had grown up in an era much different than their younger colleagues. Their age and their family background gave them a closer bond to the mores and traditions of the South. Both born in the 1890s, they heard stories told of the great southern struggle through war and Reconstruction, but during their untroubled formative years they remained sheltered from the storms of the past and the storms of the future. "It was as if," wrote one southern observer, "from this quiet midstream vantage point, the long and devious ways in the past, now in the way of being forgotten, were to be matched by the long and difficult ways of the future."[1]

The two genteel bishops shared similar regional perspectives with a small but vibrant group of white southern progressives between the two World Wars. Many of these southerners possessed a commitment to Christian brotherhood and an elitist compassion for blacks. They embraced a Christian paternalism that compelled many religious leaders to ministries of spiritual and moral uplift or social support. Many Christian leaders and laypeople crossed the racial divide to share the Gospel message or provide educational opportunities, medical facilities, or some concrete need for the "other" race. "Anyone who thought about black people at all in these years," concluded one writer, "was able to find some person to patronize—the cook, the laundress, the janitor in the office."[2]

Idealists like Charles Colcock Jones Carpenter actively pursued opportunities to aid southern blacks in social progress, but *only* within the framework of segregation. A moralist like Nolan Harmon, a third-generation temperance reformer, looked foremost to save souls, while encouraging whites to simply provide Godly and virtuous examples for childlike blacks. Despite their activities and rhetoric, these white southerners were unable to see Jim Crow as a great moral evil hanging over the region. Seeking only to make separate but equal more humane and preserve southern traditions, leaders like Carpenter and Harmon offered progressive but custodial guidance. "As long as Jim Crow was not threatened," added one observer, "it had been relatively easy for white southerners to demonstrate their racial liberalism."[3]

By the post–World War II era, however, blacks and a few sympathetic whites confronted the injustices of southern segregation and disfranchisement. This new sense of urgency and militancy stunned the white South. "This awakening of a once docile race," novelist Erskine Caldwell once wrote, "is disturbing to traditional attitudes of southern whites. . . . Century-old traditions are threatened with extinction." Old-style white progressives had no less of a problem in finding an appropriate response to the race question: some embraced the change, others remained sweaty-palmed gradualists, while a few became outspoken defenders of the southern way.[4]

In confronting the root of southern racial injustices, Harmon and Carpenter were at best ultra-gradualists and at worst morally blind defenders of the status quo. On an almost daily basis, depending on the specific issue, their actions and rhetoric moved up and down this scale as they struggled to comprehend the massive changes in the South during the 1950s and 1960s. Their lack of bold action left them vulnerable to criticism from all sides of the racial confrontation.

The most ridiculed of this group was Carpenter. Carpenter, whom the uncompromising civil rights activist Fred Shuttlesworth characterized as the "great articulate segregationist," epitomized the typical genteel and charming southern religious leader—bound much closer to the status quo than most of his younger colleagues. Conversely, many white segregationists condemned the Episcopal leader and his old-style racial liberalism as treasonous. "I think you would be amazed to know," George Murray wrote a friend in 1965, "that in Alabama, Bishop Carpenter is criticized as an integrationist by a very great many people."[5]

Carpenter was an enigma. A complex individual with contradictory rhetoric and deeds, he often appeared to sympathize with both sides of the segregation issue. In examining the words and deeds of the white clergy addressed in King's letter, it is Carpenter's commitment to desegregation that appears the most questionable. Often ambivalent, hypocritical, and misunderstood, he struggled to find the right answer to the race question. His consistent advocacy of slow reformation clearly displayed his fear of rapid change and inability to adapt to new circumstances. A speedy end to segregation, he believed, would lead to social chaos and violence. Many colleagues and friends challenged the bishop to lead the drive for change; however, Carpenter was unable to envision a future without segregation, the racial system familiar to his generation and in fellowship with his paternalism.

An intimidating, burly, and husky figure, Carpenter stood six-foot-four and weighed 275 pounds. As an undergraduate at Princeton University, "Chuck" reigned as the Ivy League heavyweight wrestling champ. In an exhibition bout at the Hotel Commodore in New York City in 1921, Carpenter went the distance with world heavyweight wrestling champion Ed "Strangler" Lewis. A *New York Times* reporter noted that the young collegian made an impressive display of defensive maneuvers that "thwarted Lewis's every attempt" to pin Carpenter to the mat. Noted for his vice-grip headlock, Lewis tried "every trick at his command and all the strength of which he possessed" to defeat his young college rival. When the match ended in a draw, the crowd of 2,500 jumped to their feet and let out a thunderous cheer for Carpenter that "reverberated through the corridors" of the hotel. Lewis advised his young opponent to become a professional wrestler. Carpenter, however, said he preferred to wrestle with theological matters.[6]

After graduating Princeton, Carpenter attended Virginia Theological Seminary and furthered his Herculean reputation. When Carpenter and a group of seminarians heard that a professor's house was burning to ashes, they rushed from their classrooms to help save his possessions. Swarming into the house, the students salvaged "everything from beds to kitchen utensils." Carpenter went to the cellar and emerged with a burlap sack of green onions under one arm and the furnace under the other. The young seminarian also gained campus fame as a skillful Jew's harp player, a class clown, and a fearless prankster. In order to "demonstrate" the theory of evolution, Carpenter climbed the seminary water tower dressed in a leopard-skin (Tarzan) outfit. Hanging by one hand and beating his chest with the other, he was reported by a classmate to have let out a roar that would frighten even a jungle gorilla. "If there was any doubt about man descending from the apes," he continued, "it would be on the apes' side, their descending from man."[7]

Carpenter completed theological training in 1926, and behind the wheel of his Model T Ford named Prudence, he traveled to Waycross, Georgia, to launch his ministry. In this small southeast Georgia hamlet near the Okefenokee Swamp, he won the heart of Alexandra Morrison and married her on November 21, 1928. He soon moved on from Waycross and made subsequent stops as rector of St. John's Church in Savannah and the prestigious Church of the Advent in Birmingham, Alabama. On April 27, 1938, Alabama clergymen and parish representatives elected Carpenter to succeed William George McDowell as bishop of Alabama. "Gentlemen," Carpenter told the delegates, "I take this as an order." The young religious leader ordered his first bishop's vestments from a company that found his measurements so improbable that they asked the diocesan secretary to verify his size-nineteen neck. At the same time he ordered a pair of custom-made dress shoes, and the manufacturer sent Carpenter's order in two large boxes—one for each shoe.[8]

Over the next few decades, Carpenter became a much-loved figure throughout the diocese. By the civil rights era, this giant man was struggling with the prospect of rapid change in the social order, wishing the South had simply gone along under the old system of segregation for at least a while longer. The bishop believed Christianity offered no "detailed answer" to the problems created by segregation. "If we make enough Christians," he naively declared, "integration will take care of itself."[9]

During his formative years, Carpenter had developed a peculiar attachment to the Old South. Born in 1899, he grew up in the home of his maternal grandfather and namesake Charles Colcock Jones Jr. in Augusta, Georgia. The young Carpenter spent hours reading the mounds of family letters and books. During the heyday of the New South era in the 1880s and 1890s, Carpenter's grandfather had demanded a return to the agrarian ideal of an earlier era. A "bellicose southern patriot," Jones contended the South's industrialization insulted "the graves of the Confederate dead" and marked an end to "true civilization in favor of barbarism."[10]

A generation earlier, Jones's father, the Reverend Charles Colcock Jones Sr., founded several Presbyterian missions to the slaves, including the Dorchester Mission near Savannah (ironically, where King planned the Birmingham civil rights campaign). Jones's efforts failed because of his inability to cope with the dilemma of ministering to what he viewed as a morally inferior race. From the beginning of time, he wrote, the black race occupied the "position designed for it in nature and Providence, and no changes and no efforts can ever, on the whole alter it for the better."[11]

One hundred years later, the Presbyterian minister's great-grandson wrestled with his own American dilemma. Like his ancestors, Bishop Carpenter grappled with the rapid changes forced upon his beloved South. Carpenter deplored racial discrimination, his assistant, Bishop Coadjutor George Murray maintained, but at the same time he believed segregation had worked well. Carpenter's stand on civil rights issues reflected this contradictory view, an attitude common among southerners of his generation.[12]

Like the majority of whites in the region during the post–World War II era, Carpenter proclaimed his loyalty to the Democratic Party and the "southern states-rights tradition." Following the party line, he denounced the 1954 *Brown* decision as a violation of that time-honored tradition. Blacks and whites, he believed, had been working "along pretty satisfactorily" and "making progress" in race relations before the court decision. Carpenter had grown bitter in the years following *Brown* as he watched an interracial commission in Birmingham dissolve following pressure from radical segregationists. In 1951, Carpenter had joined, and chaired for a time, a biracial group of prominent citizens, seeking to improve communication and understanding between the races. The Interracial Committee of the Jefferson County Coordinating Council held monthly meetings at diocesan headquarters in the Episcopal Church of the Advent. The group, despite lofty aspirations, steered clear of controversial issues—especially integration. As one of the sponsors noted, "segregation is strictly observed." The committee, however, had six goals for improving the lives of blacks in Birmingham: better hospital care, employment of black police, day care for children of working parents, improved housing, improved transportation, and improved recreation facilities. As always, Carpenter's approach was to provide social uplift within the context of Jim Crow.[13]

With massive resistance on the rise in Alabama in the mid-1950s, the group called upon all Alabamians to remain peaceful, avoid violence, and not allow all of the racial "progress" of the last century to be "swept away in the resentment and fury of real or imagined wrong." It seemed that Carpenter and the committee believed the muted dialogue of inter-racial meetings constituted tremendous progress in the segregated South. It was time, he pleaded, for "all men and women of good will, whatever their color, to stand up unmistakably in word and example, against the use of force in the settlement of our differences."[14]

In response, angry whites harassed and threatened Carpenter follow-ing the publicized statement. To belligerent whites, Carpenter had com-mitted racial treason. Staunch segregationists phoned Carpenter's house in the wee hours of the morning and offered to ride the bishop out of Alabama on a rail. "Why don't you come on over and try one on for size?" he would tell them. Members of the Ku Klux Klan also phoned with death threats. Callers always had an open invitation to visit the bishop's office to "talk about it." No one ever showed up in answer to his invitation.[15]

One citizen believed the bishop belonged to the gilded "scum" of society and condemned him for compromising southern "Anglo-Saxon supremacy" by serving on a committee with blacks and Jews. "May God of heaven take note," he proclaimed, of the moral decay of civilization in the wake of racial progress. "You are certainly a fine specimen to be playing out front as a do-gooder," he scolded Carpenter. "No doubt, however, to hear you talk and write so piously, our innocent and unin-formed will swallow your dope—hook, line, and sinker."[16]

Members of the anti-integration White Citizens Council in Bir-mingham circulated published material violently attacking the interra-cial committee. Rather than standing their ground against such pressure, the committee simply disbanded. Ironically, the group made a final pub-lic statement on April 13, 1956, calling for continued open discussion of "mutual problems" between white and black moderates. The committee offered no suggestions or displayed any willingness to continue to pro-vide an open forum. Building racial tensions made meaningful dialogue "more necessary than ever," they demanded. Yet fear and intimidation ended such public efforts in Birmingham for the rest of the decade.[17]

In the bishop's eyes, the Supreme Court decision had, in Carpenter's words, "seriously retarded" race relations and led to new militancy on both sides of the issue. The bishop feared violent clashes and civil disor-der throughout the region. "We have received a severe set-back," he added, "and at present those of us who are deeply concerned over the situation are trying to feel our way through the maze of difficulties which beset us."[18]

As racial tensions mounted in the South, the Episcopal leader advocated only leisurely avenues of change. Carpenter consistently spoke of "tremendous progress" in race relations in Alabama, but he conversely opposed any measure that would make rapid improvements. The bishop imagined gradual solutions for what he called opportunities rather than problems.[19]

For years, Carpenter's office was high in the catacombs of the Episcopal Church of the Advent in downtown Birmingham. Until new offices were constructed in the 1950s, a cramped attic space above the church's large assembly hall served as diocesan headquarters. The long, steep, narrow stair case to the top prompted the quick-witted Carpenter to dub his office "Mount Ararat," a reference to the biblical lofty resting place of Noah's Ark; a fitting abode for the high-minded Charles Carpenter, a religious leader seeking to stay above the upheavals of the 1950s and 1960s.[20]

Early in the modern civil rights era, Carpenter emerged as one of the most widely publicized outspoken critics of civil disobedience in Alabama. During the 1950s, as blacks throughout the South organized to combat segregation, many southern whites defied compliance to desegregation mandates. Carpenter believed that the boycott, as well as the resistance of radical segregationists, damaged what he blindly viewed as the South's long tradition of "amiable and harmonious" race relations. "We must do all that we can to preserve this harmony and concord which are seriously threatened today," he wrote in the diocesan journal in 1956, "and I am calling upon you all as Christian people of both races who have advanced together through the years to resist the efforts" of sowers of discord and to "hold fast the friendships and confidences that have meant much to most of us and have been the basis for the building of pleasant relationships and mutual progress."[21]

The civil rights activists, those "incident makers" and "rabble rousers," only wanted trouble, Carpenter believed, and created undue tension and dangerous situations. Carpenter loathed the actions and civil disobedience of both the nonviolent civil rights activists and the often violent white resisters. Southerners, the bishop once wrote, must not allow themselves to be dragged into the "depths of foolish pride, prejudice and unreasoned . . . animosities by shallow minded opportunists who thrive on aroused animosities."[22]

During the spring of 1960, as the sit-in movement spread across the South, Carpenter again publicly condemned direct action and civil disobedience, noting that such tactics provided nothing productive for race relations in the region. The sit-in movement was "holding up, instead of aiding" black progress. "Personally, I'm sorry," he added, "for I don't think the demonstrations will be productive or good."[23]

National Episcopal church leaders felt differently. A statement declaring support for the sit-in movement and civil disobedience by units of the National Council of the Protestant Episcopal Church appeared in newspapers around the country in late March and further inflamed Carpenter. These Episcopal leaders believed Christian doctrine supported civil disobedience when laws had degraded individuals. Carpenter, however, rejected these claims. He complained that the document had little value and had only received public attention because of "artificially inflated press propaganda." Carpenter called on all Episcopalians in the Diocese of Alabama to ignore the statement because of the "inadequate presentation" of the region's racial situation. He further asked the national council to repudiate the document, which would "condone lawlessness if carried to its ultimate conclusions."[24]

In a strongly worded letter to the National Council, Bishop Carpenter declared civil disobedience "just another name for lawlessness." To allow individuals to choose which laws to obey or disobey was like "playing with dynamite," contended Carpenter, and led to confusion, and there was too much of that already. "We already have entirely too much 'civil disobedience' in our country as it is," he added, "and there are many who will be delighted to have an excuse for disobeying the laws further." The sit-ins were causing the South "great difficulty," Carpenter concluded, and the press release gave a general impression that the Episcopal Church supported such tactics. "You may imagine we had a pretty difficult time trying to explain this situation."[25]

One of the authors of the statement, the Reverend John B. Morris, contended that the statement was of "value to all Christians of all churches in the present crisis." Morris harshly characterized Carpenter as the "chaplain to the dying order of the Confederacy." Consequently, the National Council rejected Carpenter's pleas, affirmed the "appropriateness" of the document, and encouraged church members to give the statement "serious consideration and study."[26]

Carpenter's old friend and colleague Bishop Will Scarlett of Maine disagreed adamantly with Carpenter's opinion of the sit-ins. In a letter to Carpenter, Scarlett believed that the bishop was not on God's side when he denounced civil disobedience and that his position hurt the church and the country both at home and abroad. He exhorted Carpenter to shed his moderate-gradualist approach and become an active leader in the fight for civil rights in Alabama. Scarlett saw the "opportunity of a hundred years" for his friend. "This was in line with my suggestion years ago," Scarlett counseled, "that the sight of the great Bishop of Alabama ridden out of his State on a rail because of a courageous and enlightened speech would be one of the greatest events of many years."[27]

Responding to Scarlett, Carpenter noted that his goal was to simply stop "irresponsible publicity" rather than to hinder the quest for equal rights. Carpenter sent Scarlett a copy of the memorandum for inspection, adding that the group had attempted to resolve "tension as best we could." Carpenter was certain that Scarlett could appreciate how "we might get a little irritated when irresponsible publicity was suddenly flooded upon us." Nevertheless, Scarlett still disagreed with Carpenter's opinion of the sit-in movement. Those who had "quietly and nonviolently" occupied segregated lunch counters were not to blame for the violence, Scarlett maintained. The blame rested upon the mindset which denied them the right to sit at lunch counters and receive service.[28]

Later that year Carpenter attended a House of Bishops meeting where he found most Episcopal bishops expressing skepticism over Alabama's desire to solve its racial problems. While Carpenter attempted to assure his colleagues of the state's move toward progress, most of the Episcopal leaders scoffed and dismissed the bishop's claims. Whenever he rose to speak, he found his audience expecting him to "give the rebel yell, wave the Confederate flag and sing Dixie," Carpenter believed.[29]

By 1961, the entire nation witnessed the brutality of Birmingham's radical segregationists and the hand-wringing frustration of the city's moderates. Carpenter and several other Birmingham leaders and citizens, both black and white, agreed to discuss the city's race relations on a nationally televised CBS news program entitled "Who Speaks for Birmingham?" On March 6 the CBS crew filmed an interview with Bishop Carpenter in Birmingham for a program to be aired two months later. By that time the situation in Birmingham had taken a violent turn.[30]

On Mother's Day, May 14, while Carpenter addressed a meeting of Episcopal churchmen, a group of Freedom Riders arrived at the Trailways bus terminal in downtown Birmingham. City Commissioner of Public Safety Bull Connor ordered policemen out of the vicinity as Klansmen attacked the riders. CBS newsman Howard K. Smith, host of "Who Speaks for Birmingham?" watched as Klansmen dragged passengers out of the bus and beat them with lead pipes, key rings, and bloody fists. "They knocked one man, a white man, down at my feet," recalled Smith, "and they beat him and kicked him until his face was bloody, red pulp." Almost simultaneously, "as if on signal," the attackers dispersed as the police arrived. Smith watched several Klansmen "discussing their achievement of the day" right under Connor's office window.[31]

CBS had scheduled "Who Speaks for Birmingham?" for the following Thursday, May 18. The incident at the terminal became an epilogue to the program. That Thursday night on national television the entire country saw the tremendous problems of a racially divided city. In the interview, CBS producer David Lowe asked Carpenter if communication existed between "thinking members" of both races. "That's our biggest weakness," he responded. Blacks pushed for complete integration and whites would not consider such terms. Leaders had shelved the "gradual approach," he added, and much-needed communication remained difficult. Local leaders endeavored to resolve the racial crisis; however, Birmingham was "in a situation," Carpenter insisted, and "we know it."[32]

Later that spring, Carpenter addressed the Freedom Ride incident in his monthly column for Alabama's Episcopal journal. A small group of cowardly men, he wrote, had brought disgrace and shame to Birmingham by beating visitors in an unfair fight. Sounding more like a wrestling commentator than a minister, Carpenter skirted the issue of racial justice and commented: "The right to [a] fair fight is not to be denied, but the bullies beating a man HELD by other men is dastardly." Southern chivalry, Carpenter continued, was at a low ebb.[33]

These misguided and disgraceful white combatants had fallen into the trap laid by the Freedom Riders, the bishop believed. The civil rights protestors wanted to create a scene, make trouble, and a few witless citizens were more than obliging. These were the "devastating results," Carpenter wrote, that always follow an uncontrollable mob action and when a "few stupid men consider themselves above the law and take matters brutally into their own hands to force their will on others with whom they disagree and whose lives they threaten."[34]

Once again, Bishop Carpenter's ambiguous words on television and in his column brought a storm of criticism from both segregationists and integrationists. The true patriots of the South, wrote one segregationist, praised the mobs of attacking Klansmen for their courage to defend white women from enforced integration. "Thank God," he continued, "there are still men of honor living in the South, not mealy-mouthed bishops whose sermons are written and published by the jew-owned publishing houses." The writer hoped the white mobs soon would give Carpenter and other Alabama traitors the same treatment the Freedom Riders received.[35]

On the other hand, northern integrationists urged Carpenter to make a stronger stand on behalf of racial justice. "To practice empathy," one suggested, "black your self some night and go around as a Negro." This exercise would propel Carpenter to write a bold new Sunday sermon. "But then you'd no doubt be afraid to preach the . . . [sermon]," she continued, "and tell your people how wrong they are in holding the colored people down." Everyone had the right to learn together, play together, and pray together. Another letter writer pleaded with Carpenter to look beyond the safe confines of his own environment to gain an understanding of what was right and just. "I hope that the present riots stimulate you and your community to take a firm stand and follow through on your Christian responsibility to protect and promote the rights of mankind."[36]

The racial climate in the city continued to deteriorate over the succeeding months. Perhaps more than any of the eight white clergy, Carpenter struggled with the change forced on the city. Martin Luther King's demonstrations during the spring of 1963 made Carpenter especially angry. He saw King and other civil rights activists as outsiders and pleaded with them to move to Birmingham on a permanent basis. "It would be much more effective than coming and marching and then leaving because then we have got to pick up the pieces," he insisted. The bishop's solutions to racial injustices, however, as with many older gradualists, offered few immediate changes. "We are having difficult times," he wrote in 1963, "but somehow I'm sure we will find the answers if we work alone [without outside interference] patiently and try to keep our heads."[37]

An equally passionate advocate of gradualism and calm mediation was the oldest of the white ministers, Methodist bishop Nolan Harmon Jr. Scholarly and urbane, he always dressed in impeccably well tailored suits and skillfully polished shoes. The Methodist leader had a slight build and a long, gaunt, weathered face, dark deep-set eyes, and thick white hair. In 1956, the Methodist Church elected Harmon bishop of the Western North Carolina Conference. Five years later, the death of Bishop Bachman Hodge of Alabama forced Harmon into assuming the leadership of part of Hodge's jurisdiction, then covering the entire state of Alabama. After redrawing the conference lines, the church selected Harmon to supervise the North Alabama Conference in addition to his duties in North Carolina.[38]

As Harmon soon discovered, Alabama's Methodists were a contentious lot and were hotly divided over the race issue. A few years before in 1954, the conference's bishop at the time, Clare Purcell, and seven other southern bishops opposed the national church's support of the *Brown* decision. Delegates to the annual conference meeting that year passed a resolution favoring segregation in public schools, noting that "it is our honest conviction that for the good of whites and Negroes that separate schools be maintained." Ministers joined local lay leaders in forming the Association of Methodist Ministers and Laymen to fight merger with the all-black Central Jurisdiction and to inform church members of pro-integration efforts by Methodist leaders. By the early 1960s, racial tensions were again on the increase in Alabama, and the circuit-flying Harmon hoped to mediate a law-and-order solution to the crisis.[39]

Harmon's formative years led him to cherish the peacemaker's role and to deplore social strife from activists of any kind. Born in Meridian, Mississippi, on July 14, 1892, Nolan Bailey Harmon Jr. was the son, grandson, and great-grandson of ministers. His father and paternal grandfather were passionate and controversial Methodist ministers and temperance reformers in the South. During Reconstruction, grandfather John Wesley Harmon had left a Methodist pastorate to become the founding editor of a temperance paper, the *Southern Organ,* in New Orleans. For his views, he survived several mob attacks and two arson attempts at the newspaper building. In later years, the elder Harmon was a stern, somber man with a flowing white beard, who struck fear into the heart of young Nolan and his three brothers. They dreaded his occasional visits. In turn, the old man thought no better of his grandchildren, believing the bothersome brood had "reached the milepost of nuisance."[40]

Bishop Harmon's father, Nolan Bailey Harmon Sr., had grown up in a cultured home in New Orleans and was among the first southern Methodist ministers to study at Vanderbilt University. He too was a moral crusader. As his son later remembered, Nolan Sr. was "never happier than when pitching into some contest for what he felt was right." During the Progressive Era, he preached against the evils of liquor as the president of the anti-saloon league in San Antonio, Texas. He received numerous threats from the beer-drinking German immigrants and mescal-drinking Mexicans in the frontier town. Always prepared, young Nolan Jr. slept with a shotgun near his bed just in case the roughnecks attacked the Harmon home.[41]

During his high school years, Nolan Jr. received the call to preach. Much to his father's delight, the youngster walked the aisle during a revival meeting and shook the hand of a visiting evangelist, pledging to become a full-time minister. Harmon received his education at Millsaps College in Mississippi and began seminary training at the Candler School of Theology at Emory University in Atlanta in 1916. America's entry into Europe's Great War in 1917 compelled the young man to volunteer for service as a chaplain. He never saw the front lines of Europe, but survived a stateside bout with influenza during the great epidemic of 1918. After serving his tour of duty, Harmon never returned to finish his education at Emory; instead he began preaching in 1919. The next year, the young minister attended graduate school at Princeton University and studied history and the classics. On campus at the same time, he and Chuck Carpenter apparently never crossed paths. Harmon took a few classes at the seminary, just prior to the Fundamentalist-Modernist controversy at the Presbyterian seminary. And despite having a New Testament class under the Fundamentalist sage J. Gresham Machen, Harmon developed a moderate theological underpinning and often joked that modernists considered him a fundamentalist and fundamentalists considered him a modernist.[42]

With a master's degree in hand, Harmon served as an itinerant minister and traveled wherever the bishop sent him. His first assignment was circuit riding in the small towns of Goshen and Emory in Maryland. By then, automobiles had replaced the horse as the primary mode of transportation for itinerant preachers, and Harmon's reliable 1914 Ford stirred up a storm of dust as he raced along the red clay roads. "It would GO!" Harmon later remembered, "I mean move, transport itself, get on with it, and with all on board. . . . It was no jet driven speedster, but just kick the clutch down low—plenty low—slip it in gear, release the clutch and pull the right trigger under the steering wheel, and nothing could stop it."[43]

Traveling down the backroads of Virginia and Maryland, Harmon frequently stopped to visit Civil War battlefields and once retraced the Valley campaign of Confederate general Stonewall Jackson. His romanticized notions of the Old South even compelled the Methodist parson to preach frequently on the virtuous life of Robert E. Lee, much to the irritation of a few Yankees in his congregation. In turn, they asked him to preach a message about Abraham Lincoln, which he gladly did. Harmon's passion for history and a natural flair for writing brought him to the forefront of Methodist thinkers as an editor of a conference paper and then as the book editor of the reunified (both northern and southern branches) Methodist Church from 1940 to 1956.[44]

Unlike his father and grandfather, Harmon shied away from ministerial activism and vocal protest. Witnessing the threats and intimidation from people with aroused passions had convinced the Methodist bishop to avoid social and political conflicts during his ministry. He would provide the calm voice of reason and order. During the depths of Great Depression, as many Americans grew restless, Harmon urged all citizens to preserve their liberties by obeying laws. "There is no freedom where there is no law," he announced from the pulpit in 1936. "Therefore when you break the law, you destroy freedom."[45]

Regardless, the fiery prohibitionist rhetoric of his father and grandfather had a profound impact on Harmon's ministry. Following World War I, he praised the ratification of the anti-liquor Eighteenth Amendment, and condemned bootleg activities as a "best bet of the devil." In 1928 he denounced Democratic presidential candidate Al Smith for urging a repeal of the amendment. "Out of all things happening in the present campaign," Harmon wrote in his conference paper in 1928, "there is one thing that stands out like chain lightening on a midnight sky, and that is that the election of Al Smith to the presidency will be a tremendous blow to prohibition." Throughout the rest of his career, Harmon frequently condemned the use of alcohol by all races of people.[46]

Like many southerners of his generation, Harmon had developed a paternalistic, caretaker view of blacks. In the 1920s, he asked his congregation to provide a good example, because blacks were like children and often imitated the "dominant" race. We must teach them, Harmon once said; "how will they learn otherwise?" Yet in direct contradiction, Harmon called segregation a great social chasm and advocated equal rights for blacks in law, business, civic affairs, and religion. As with many white southerners of his era, Harmon never confronted this inherent contradiction between paternalism and equality.[47]

As a preacher, Harmon's sermons focused on the basics of salvation rather than the "fruit" of the Gospel. For the enlightened Christian, the lessons of citizenship, sobriety, and a social conscience were self-evident and simply followed a "lively faith." As a straight-and-narrow evange-list, Harmon rejected liberal theological notions, especially the Social Gospel. Through the years, the church had fought against social evils and for social engineering programs, but this had created a "*this-worldly* mind" among church people. "A this-worldly mind is a poor mind," Harmon wrote, "with which to face the winds of eternity, or even present enemies."[48]

In the early 1960s, Harmon bristled at the suggestion by the young professor of religion Samuel S. Hill Jr. that the church had to come to terms with vast cultural changes and not simply continue preaching conversion of the individual, "as though that were enough." The bishop, however, believed redemption was the beginning of relevancy for the church in society and culture. He pointed to Methodist patriarch John Wesley as an example of someone who paid little attention to culture and simply "started out to get people right with God." In time, British culture had to come to terms with a converted people, not vice versa.[49]

The church, Harmon emphasized, was on a divine mission and would never become a "sociological pressure machine." When confronted with sending a delegate to a conference on safe driving, Harmon believed the church had a more important mission: to get folks ready for eternity, "with or without seat belts." The bishop, however, underscored that he had never called for silence from the pulpits on the important social issues of day—especially the race question. Nevertheless, Harmon believed the church's stand on justice, righteousness, and the "eradication of old evils" remained self-evident. This was similar to the argument that colleague Charles Carpenter had used: make enough Christians and the race question will take care of itself.[50]

To many, the nagging racial problem in the Methodist Church was the Central Jurisdiction, which mandated segregated black conferences and leaders. The 1939 reunification of the northern and southern Methodist Churches had created six jurisdictional conferences—five geographical and one racial for the nineteen black conferences. At the time, the *Christian Century* noted that the Methodists had "written segregation into the very constitution of their church." Harmon later argued that the plan was not based on Jim Crow traditions. The whole jurisdictional system, he added, "had been worked out long before there was racial tension" in the region.[51]

Regardless, the unification plan and jurisdictionalism created tension within the church and, with each successive general conference, non-southern Methodists attacked the separation with increasing emotion. By the 1950s, the church was under intense pressure to eliminate the racially distinctive jurisdiction. In 1956, at the General Conference in Minneapolis, Harmon had seconded a motion to allow the segregated black conferences to transfer into white conferences or jurisdictions. The Methodist leader argued that "defense of a minority" had led to the jurisdictional division, and that "racial involvement was simply incidental." The shift into a geographical jurisdiction, however, required a formidable two-thirds majority approval by black and white Methodists at conference and church levels; a nearly impossible task. As one author later noted, Methodist leaders achieved only limited success by treating the issue as a structural problem rather than a moral dilemma.[52]

Clearly, Harmon supported the jurisdictional divisions. Just as the New Testament church had done centuries before, "so now in our day, the same church may and should work through its separate divisions," the bishop emphasized in 1962. "I also feel that the great Church of Christ is the richer if we all are not pressed into a spiritual sameness." Above all the separation would allow southern church leaders to meet the "peculiar needs and opportunities" in their own districts. Southerners were just naturally more regionally conscious, Harmon added. "Call this regional consciousness *provincialism*, if you want to, but it is the way it is, and we know it."[53]

Although years later Harmon, in a more hyperbolic moment, claimed to have relieved the "brooding tension" and fostered an immediate sense of relief over the church's segregation issue with his 1956 speech, the Central Jurisdiction remained a point of conflict until the Methodist's merger with the Evangelical United Brethren in 1968. The terms of this unification brought about an end to a separate jurisdiction for blacks.[54]

As the civil rights movement gained strength in the South, Harmon recognized the inequity of the southern racial system. Southern whites had dealt unfairly with blacks, he emphasized in the early 1960s, and God knew the church had failed to end injustice in society. Harmon hoped for peace and justice between persons of all races, but he heartily disapproved of the sudden assault by civil rights demonstrators on southern customs and the "great people" of the region.[55]

The Methodist sage considered Martin Luther King's nonviolent demonstrations militant and antagonistic no matter how orderly they appeared on the surface. Harmon's opinion of nonviolent direct action never changed. In later years, he still complained that King had simply put on the nonviolent movement for show and heightened racial tensions in the South. Little more than "inflammatory grandstanding," the demonstrations damaged southern race relations through a deliberate and organized effort to inflame an explosive situation. Without these highly visible confrontations, Harmon believed, the demonstrations roused little media interest and public support.[56]

Mass demonstrations violated Harmon's sacred view of law and order. He consistently deplored the violation of the principle by civil rights activists and radical segregationists. Squarely in the middle of the issue, he rejected any disregard for federal laws by segregationists; as well as defiance of local segregation ordinances by black activists. Regardless, he saw no moral inconsistency in this position. No majority had the right to deny any minority the fundamental rights of citizenship, he presumed, and any law that denied these rights was an injustice. Nevertheless, when King advocated breaking a "bad law," this went against the long history of Western jurisprudence. Continued agitation and an "excited confrontation" between black activists and white belligerents, Harmon believed, might win needed legal rights, but at the expense of community civility. The Methodist leader believed a measure of good will was needed to secure good laws and provide a "sure scaffolding" for future racial harmony.[57]

Neither a "vast outside power" (the federal government) nor the "well meaning but misdirected forays of outsiders" (the civil rights movement) would bring about justice and peace between the two races. Justice and peace, Harmon believed, would come only by the "slow, slow, slow process of time." Only the good, upright, and forward-looking people of the region and the nation would bring about a gradualist solution to the racial tensions in the South. These people would be impelled by their "own spirit," not forced by others to do away with inequity and establish what was good. Alluding to the length of time needed, Harmon prayed for God to "give us and our children, or our children's children, the will to see that day."[58]

In short, Harmon and Carpenter, as the eldest of this group of Birmingham clergy, had the most difficult time dealing with change in the social order. They remained inconsistent and bewildered figures—paternalistic, yet calling for basic rights for blacks; often defenders of the status quo, other times critics of segregation. Harmon and Carpenter were torn between tradition and social progress. Despite a social conscience in certain areas, as elitists they sought to remain above the fray.

Like many southern pastors of the pre–World War II era, they were charming, "even courtly in manner," as one noted observer of southern religion once wrote. "They practiced tolerance and eschewed crudeness or bombast." Most southerners admired them for their chivalrous style, dignity, and refinement. A commitment to the status quo or cryptic gradualism would be this generation of ministers' response to the civil rights era and the race question. As Erskine Caldwell explained, these whites continued to postpone and delay, promising to make good on the promises of equality "in the sweet by-and-by of tomorrow and tomorrow and tomorrow." A younger generation of southern religious leaders would have to come to grips with the massive changes in society. "Each generation," wrote one observer in the 1960s, "seems a little less inclined toward bigotry than the one before."[59]

3   Turning the Corner

Even the younger generation of whites in the Deep South, Bishop George Murray explained to a northern colleague in the 1960s, had instruction while on their "Mother's knee," that blacks were "inferior, dishonest, diseased, degenerate," happy with segregation, and perhaps not quite human. "I have to remember that had my own mind not been presented with an alternate point of view while I was still in my twenties," the bishop underscored, "I might have found it much more difficult to make a complete about face." This younger generation, Murray believed, had a "tragically difficult task" of adjusting to a "whole new set of relationships" between blacks and whites. "Ours is an inherited problem," he wrote, "and this generation is suddenly called upon to solve it. In a sense, we are required to begin a race from a starting point which is way ahead of us."[1]

When his boss, Charles Carpenter, came under fire for refusing to directly confront segregation, Murray explained to critics that they "must first of all remember that he is one generation removed from us." Older and more set in their ways, Carpenter and Nolan Harmon were unable to turn the corner and see segregation as a moral problem. Most of the other clergy addressed in Martin Luther King's "Letter from Birmingham Jail" were younger and were more accepting of change than their older colleagues. As events unfolded around them, the younger group came to see southern racial problems as a great moral dilemma. Like their older associates they too were paternalistic, but as one observer noted, these 1950s and 1960s southern white progressives moved beyond this fatherly elitism to "recognize the full humanity of blacks." At the very least, this paternalism had brought these whites into contact with blacks and provided the spark of a racial awakening. In turn, most of these younger clergymen actively confronted racial issues in their churches and in the community.[2]

In 1963, much like Harmon and Carpenter, they spoke only of gradual change. Regardless, these clergy maintained a broader perspective and seemed less inclined to traditionalism and narrow regional biases. As members of religious minorities in the South, Catholic bishop Joseph Durick and Rabbi Milton Grafman had encountered religious intolerance and retained a greater compassion in dealing with racial issues. As a local preacher and later a bishop, Paul Hardin emerged as a critic of the South's traditional racial mores. And unlike Charles Carpenter, George Murray spoke in clear and certain terms of his distaste for segregation.[3]

At times, Murray felt frustrated by Carpenter's brand of gradualism. "Time and again I have felt that perhaps he should have moved a bit faster," Murray wrote in 1965. In hindsight, however, the "little bishop" believed there was some wisdom in Carpenter's lack of action. "Had matters been in my hands and the moves been faster, we might have run into disaster," Murray added. Despite their differences, Alabama's two Episcopal leaders maintained a close relationship. The pair made a "good team," the senior bishop used to say, because Carpenter was conservative enough to keep the laymen content, and Murray was liberal enough to keep the young clergy happy. "Maybe we'll muddle through this [racial] crisis on that basis," Carpenter told Murray.[4]

Although mindful of Carpenter's unwillingness to confront segregation, Murray saw his own job as bishop as twofold: to take a leadership role in social issues and to serve as a pastor to the clergy and their families. During the 1950s and 1960s, a few of the younger Alabama Episcopal clergy were making bold stands on racial issues. "I tried to back them up," Murray once said. When a priest came under fire from conservative laypeople, the young bishop would travel to the parish and preach on the evils of segregation and discrimination. "I wanted them to see that this was a broad moral issue that had the support of the church hierarchy," he later recalled. In turn, Bishop Carpenter often had to return to the same parishes to smooth tensions with the laity. "His comparative conservatism," Murray wrote in 1965, "has kept him in contact with people with whom I fear I have long ago lost contact. Perhaps this makes us a good team."[5]

Murray maintained a liberal commitment to a socially active Christianity, not unlike the one Martin Luther King advocated. The church had to become applicable to all of life or it simply existed as a meaningless institution, Murray told a group of Episcopal laymen in 1961. He believed the church had a duty to win souls for Christ and alleviate social ills, including segregation. "I am convinced on Christian and patriotic grounds that I must oppose racial discrimination and injustice," he once wrote.[6]

Murray, however, never advocated immediate integration. He was neither an integrationist nor a segregationist, he claimed, but a desegregationist. Accordingly, Murray was also firmly committed to the gradualist approach. "I do not agree with Martin Luther King on his methods and his approach to the civil rights program," Murray wrote in 1964. King's use of civil disobedience was the wrong answer in confronting the social injustice of segregation, he believed. "I am convinced that civil disobedience is justified only as a last resort," he added, "when the whole force of government is clearly being applied against the law of God." The federal judiciary, Murray believed, championed civil rights, providing King an alternative to resorting to "extreme" measures. "Therefore, I do not believe it [civil disobedience] to be justified in these times in this country."[7]

Born on April 12, 1919, in Baltimore, Maryland, George Mosley Murray was the youngest of the white ministers addressed in Martin Luther King's "Letter from Birmingham Jail." A dignified and distinguished man, Murray possessed an eloquent, proper speaking voice that one acquaintance described as refined as the sound of "crystal when it's tapped," an aristocratic accent he apparently picked up from his father and British grandfather. When only an infant, George and his family moved to the Birmingham area so his father, Gerard, could take a job as an engineer with U.S. Steel. His mother, Emma Eareckson, a registered nurse, worked as head of pediatric nursing in U.S. Steel's company villages.[8]

The Murray family settled on a four-acre spread in what was then a small countryside community of Hueytown, just west of Birmingham. Mother Emma isolated George and his brother from the neighborhood boys, believing the country rabble were not good enough to play with her children. "I must say," Murray once remembered, "we were kind of snobbishly brought up." While the neighborhood kids were riding bikes and shooting squirrels with pea-shooting air rifles, the Murray children learned tennis on their own private clay court.[9]

With two working parents, the family employed a black woman to cook, clean, and look after the boys, and she was provided a place to stay in a small servant's house in the backyard. George's parents treated the domestic help with respect, but they also believed blacks had their "place" in society and they were expected to stay in it. "I grew up thinking that segregation was natural," George said. His parents told him to never say Mr., Mrs., or Miss to a black person. "That wasn't proper," his mother told him. "That wasn't done. Call them by their first name."[10]

Following graduation from Hueytown High School, Murray attended the University of Alabama and studied banking and finance. During his senior year, he decided to become an Episcopal minister, but Bishop Carpenter encouraged the lad to get a taste of the real world before going to seminary. Carpenter had stayed at Princeton University for a while after graduation and coached wrestling. "What's good enough for you is good enough for me," Murray told the bishop. After receiving his degree in 1940, Murray took a job as an auditor for General Electric in Charlotte, North Carolina, but when the United States entered World War II the next year, he volunteered for the navy.[11]

He went through a whirlwind training at the midshipman school in Chicago, a regular "ninety-day wonder," and received his commission as an ensign. After serving as an instructor in the gunnery school for a year, Murray grew restless, a stateside navy officer anxious for South Pacific action, so he volunteered for submarine duty. He joined the crew of the USS *Pintado* in 1943, and as the submarine steamed toward the naval base at Pearl Harbor, Murray realized he had a major problem— severe seasickness, so bad he fell asleep one night on deck leaning against the periscope. His captain transferred him ashore for a time, but Murray rejoined the crew. "I had to either get better or die," he later recalled. "I got better."[12]

Following discharge from the navy after the war, and with perhaps more "experience" than Carpenter had in mind, Murray enrolled in Virginia Theological Seminary and embraced a liberal theology and social commitment. The ideas he learned in seminary also had a tremendous impact on his racial attitudes. "I think my attitude was completely turned around from moderate segregationist while I was there," he later recalled. Several of the seminary's faculty were actively involved in working for integration and civil rights. "I was totally convinced that they were right," Murray added. There was no grand epiphany for the young seminarian, just a slow realization that the love of God was for everyone, regardless of color. This totally persuaded Murray that segregation and racism were sins, and he needed to work personally towards changes in the status quo.[13]

Murray earned his divinity degree in 1948, and Bishop Carpenter sent the young minister back to the University of Alabama, this time as an Episcopal chaplain. He gained a reputation as an able fund-raiser for the diocese and led the expansion of campus ministries. In 1953, a special convention of the diocese of Alabama elected Murray, only thirty-four, as Carpenter's right-hand bishop.

With racial tensions on the rise in Alabama, Murray took an increasingly active role in the affairs of the diocese. In the fall of 1961, leaders in the newly formed Episcopal Society of Cultural and Racial Unity planned a Prayer Pilgrimage in the spirit of the Freedom Rides that would proceed through the Deep South to "show concern" for segregated educational institutions operated by the Episcopal Church. The group, led by an Episcopal minister, John B. Morris, planned to stop in Birmingham to promote "greater understanding" between Episcopal clergy.[14]

Bishops Murray and Carpenter warned Morris that if he was coming to Alabama to break laws, he could expect no cooperation. "We believe the best approach to today's situation is through lawful and orderly processes," they concluded. As Alabama's bishops continued to balk at the proposed bus ride, Morris accused the church leaders of blocking open communications. Murray, however, believed Morris, a staunch civil rights activist, had chosen the one method (direct action) which made real communication impossible. The best approach to the racial situation was through a "lawful and orderly" process, not through a campaign to cause embarrassment and "confusing publicity." The bishop believed Morris and his group were attempting to drive a "wedge of mistrust" between the bishops and their clergy. Murray asked Morris if he wanted to strengthen the church for people to find their way or wanted to create dissension. The activists were undermining the work of those who had a heavy responsibility and had worked "creatively and not destructively" to further racial progress. While Murray hoped for southern racial equality, he strongly opposed the activists' methods and deplored their efforts as harmful to the church's ministry. The only clear goal Morris had in making the pilgrimage was to obtain publicity; he was confused about any other purposes, Murray wrote. The bishop urged Morris to submit to church leadership and work with people of "various convictions on the subject within a framework of responsibility, rather than taking pot shots from outside."[15]

Much to Murray's disdain, Birmingham's local newspapers printed several articles on the planned bus trip. This created a false image in the minds of many white southerners, Murray believed, that the Episcopal church was participating in demonstrations. "It has made us less effective in accomplishing what we were already working on," he added. In spite of what many northerners believed, some white southerners were "already fighting a battle on this score, and it is we who must fight it." New York and Chicago had their own social evils, and Murray believed that the local clergy in those cities knew best how to handle the problems. "I trust them to act reliably," he added, "and to call on me if they do need help. It seems to me that we might be accorded the same trust here in the South."[16]

When the Prayer Pilgrimage rolled through the South in the early fall, Morris decided to bypass Birmingham on the journey. A few weeks later, when Morris requested another conference with local clergy to "bring persons together to face the issues," Murray and Carpenter responded with an emphatic no. There were plenty of clergy in the diocese who knew a great deal more about racial issues than Morris, Carpenter wrote. "If the time comes when we need you to help us," he continued, "you may be sure that we shall get in touch with you, but confine your work to places outside Alabama." Morris later said he would be "unable to do this."[17]

While pressure continued to intensify in Birmingham, U.S. district judge Hobart H. Grooms Sr. quickened the pace of desegregation on October 24, 1961, by ordering all of the city's recreational facilities integrated by January 15, 1962. Rather than integrating, the hard-line city commissioners—Eugene "Bull" Connor, Art Hanes, and James "Jabo" Waggoner—ordered all facilities closed. The city's action outraged and united white moderates in Birmingham and gave Bishop Murray a new sense of resolve in confronting racial injustice.[18]

The Southern Regional Council, a group dedicated to open communication between races, dispatched representative Benjamin Muse to observe the situation and the "sudden awakening" of moderate leadership in Birmingham. In no other southern community had Muse seen "such a general mobilization of community leadership on the moderate side of a segregation issue as had occurred during the past two months in Birmingham." The SRC representative also commended Bishop Murray's liberal attitude in combating racial prejudice. Muse, however, believed the bishop coadjutor remained critical of those who wished to "go too fast." In a conversation with Muse, Murray said that he had to move gradually to avert an "aggressive counter-movement" by Episcopal segregationists.[19]

During Holy Week 1962, Murray addressed the problems facing Birmingham in a series of services at the Church of the Advent in downtown. The bishop wondered what Jesus would see in Birmingham if he looked across the valley from atop Red Mountain. Murray believed his Savior would observe "little children offended and puzzled" in Birmingham. The bishop had a difficult time explaining to his own children why city officials had closed the public parks and the Kiddieland amusement center rather than letting the black children share equally in the enjoyment. "They [Murray's children] just do not understand," Murray said. Foreshadowing King's rhetoric in the "Letter from Birmingham Jail," Murray believed he had gained a new understanding of the struggle black families faced in a segregated society. How does a black family explain to their little child why they "couldn't stop and let him go on some rides" at Kiddieland. "Jesus truly offended in a little child!" Murray emphasized. "Can we not see where this path of retaliation and meanness leads us?"[20]

The time has come, Murray wrote a colleague a few weeks after the service, to "say these things and still continue my ministry here. I believe I am right." Several parishioners at the Church of the Advent expressed shock and outrage over Murray's comments. The bishop called their reaction "a sad commentary on our situation" in Birmingham, Christian brothers and sisters unable to discuss the "most burning and troublesome issue of our time." Many moderates in the city had become "so suppressed" that they were unable to seek a solution. Murray confessed he had found "little grace" in helping racial progress occur in Birmingham. Nevertheless, he pleaded for Alabama Episcopalians to "come out of our shells" in order to understand one another "openly and honestly and in Christian love."[21]

Murray called for a new atmosphere of open and direct communication between blacks and whites; an environment where all Birmingham citizens had the opportunity to express honest convictions without being branded a Communist and without being harassed by anonymous letters and telephone calls. People of different opinions and different races needed a place to sit down calmly and seek real solutions based on a "searching after the will of God," Murray said. Some believed these discussions had no place in the church. The bishop disagreed. Jesus spent time in the temple in "creative controversy," discussing the important social issues of the time. "I believe we would not accuse him of any wrong-doing," Murray added. An exemplary life was much better than exemplary talk, the bishop believed. "Those things which we learn from God by honest seeking will be most effectively shown forth by the way we as a church actually practice them," Murray wrote.[22]

This open communication, however, needed to exist among local residents, and the church offered the perfect setting for such negotiations. Murray often wondered if groups in opposition really attempted to understand one another. He believed the church needed to encourage reconciliation and provide a place for people to come together and talk. During 1962 and 1963, Bishop Murray hosted and moderated several interracial meetings between local business, religious, and civic leaders at the diocese headquarters in downtown Birmingham. Miles College president Dr. Lucius H. Pitts praised the meetings for showing that white men of good will in Birmingham were willing to "approach our problems with saneness." Regardless, as with earlier interracial efforts, they provided a bold forum for discussion, but a weak platform for launching any meaningful change.[23]

During the demonstrations in the spring of 1963, Murray invited Martin Luther King to come to these gatherings to discuss the Birmingham crisis. King, however, never participated. Instead, Andrew Young, Fred Shuttlesworth, and others represented King and the SCLC. Negotiating was a job no one in the movement wanted, Young later recalled. "They thought it was a waste of time," he added, "and perceived it as sucking up to white folks." Murray remembered what he saw as a presumptuous Fred Shuttlesworth telling them that he welcomed the support of the interracial gathering, but "any other ideas" regarding compromise were out of the question. Shuttlesworth had grown weary of the failed promises of the white power structure. "White folks have always been crooked," he later reflected. "Even when they're straight, there is a crook in some of what they do, where the system is concerned. The system wants to put down protest."[24]

Joseph Durick's racial attitude during his formative years and through the 1950s was typical of that of many Americans of the time period. Like most whites in the South, the Catholic leader passively accepted segregation as the natural order of society. With an aura of timelessness to the institution, Durick also saw segregation as merely "the way of life we had." The bishop admitted that he and most white southerners had an almost instinctive, take-for-granted attitude and never recognized the injustice of segregation. Whites held a widespread belief that blacks were treated honorably as long as they remained in their place.[25]

As the injustices of racial separation became more apparent to Durick, he publicly proclaimed segregation a great "social and moral evil." Regardless, the bishop believed the quest for racial equality demanded time. Many of the more enlightened religious leaders in the region were attempting to break down a long-standing way of life and never expected to transform the mind of the South overnight. Throughout the racial crisis in Birmingham, Durick encouraged Alabamians to gradually cross over to a new social order and transcend "emotion-packed demonstrations" and violent confrontations. Using a racial crisis to provide an immediate and reckless transformation of an "immoral social order" was illogical and harmed the gradualist cause that had worked "ever so many years," Durick wrote. The church had not failed with the gradual approach, and the leaders were not "going to abandon that way in order to seize upon something more dramatic," the bishop emphasized.[26]

Born in Dayton, Tennessee, on October 13, 1914, Joseph Aloysius Durick was the seventh of twelve children born to immigrant parents: a Slovak father, Stephen, and an Irish mother, Bridget Gallagher. The Duricks ran a mom-and-pop grocery business in the small industrial town of Bessemer, Alabama, only a few miles west of Birmingham. Bridget had traveled to Dayton shortly before Joseph's birth to stay with some relatives and escape Bessemer's dirt and grime. Dayton would gain international fame a decade later with the sensational Scopes Monkey Trial, but in 1914 the sleepy East Tennessee town provided a quiet resting place for a weary mother. The town, however, lacked an essential institution: a Catholic church. So as soon as her young child was old enough to travel, Bridget Durick brought him back to Alabama, stopping at St. James Church in Gadsden for a quick baptism.[27]

Joseph Durick grew up in Bessemer during the height of anti-Catholic violence in Alabama, including the murder of a Birmingham priest by a disgruntled, fly-by-night Protestant minister. Following World War I, with an influx of new immigrants to the Birmingham area, mostly Catholics, many native whites looked to a reincarnated Ku Klux Klan to safeguard traditional southern culture and mores. The new immigrants practiced a strange religion, some thought, that would undermine established customs, especially Prohibition laws. As the power of Klan groups in Jefferson County reached unprecedented heights, a national magazine declared Birmingham the "American hotbed of Anti-Catholic fanaticism."[28]

Tensions reached a climax in 1928, when the Democratic Party nominated a "wet" candidate in Catholic Al Smith for president; state and local politicians proudly and loudly waved the anti-papist banner. One of Alabama's U.S. senators, the bombastic "Cotton" Tom Heflin, predicted that immediately following a Smith victory, the pope would hop on a submarine and sneak into Alabama's Mobile Bay and forcibly convert all Alabamians to Catholicism. Although Smith carried Alabama by a slim margin, Jefferson County voters gave Republican Herbert Hoover the nod. For Joseph Durick, these images of bigotry toward Catholics helped the young man develop a sympathetic perspective in confronting religious and racial intolerance.[29]

Influenced by the priests at St. Aloysius parish in Bessemer, Durick had lifelong desire to become a Catholic clergyman. Regardless, he almost chose a less orthodox vocation. An accomplished saxophone player by his early teens, Durick had a passion for jazz music and flirted with a career as a professional musician. Jazz was all the rage in the 1920s and the young sax performer joined the Rhythm Kings band at the tender age of thirteen. Durick later insisted that one tongue-in-cheek incident convinced him to choose Jesus over jazz and become a priest. The Rhythm Kings often performed on a weekly jazz broadcast aired on WBRC radio in Birmingham. In an effort to aid a budding romance, Durick promised an on-air dedication to a special young woman from Bessemer High School. Nonetheless, as he focused on the music during the show, the dedication slipped his mind. With only one number remaining on the playlist, Durick rushed forward and insisted the announcer dedicate the final song to his sweetheart. The youngster had failed to check his sheet music and an amused announcer dedicated King

Oliver's jazz standard, "Mule Face Blues" to Durick's soon-to-be-lost love.[30]

After graduating Bessemer High School, Durick entered St. Bernard College in Cullman, Alabama, as a seminarian and quickly discovered all of those jazz gigs had left him weak in his Latin studies. Durick graduated in 1933, however, and traveled to St. Mary's Seminary in Baltimore, Maryland, to complete course work in philosophy.[31]

In 1936, the bishop of the Diocese of Mobile, Thomas Joseph Toolen, sent Durick to study in Rome at the Urban College for the Propagation of the Faith—the church's missionary school. Arriving with his saxophone in hand, Durick studied with students of thirty-six different nationalities, broadening his perspective on race and Christian unity. "I came to respect all men," Durick later recalled. "The missionary college in Rome encouraged me to get to know and understand all nations and all people groups." At the same time, he recognized the need for strong church leadership in times of crisis. Benito Mussolini had reached the height of his fascist dictatorship in Italy, and Durick witnessed Pope Pius XI's struggle to find an appropriate response to this ruthless totalitarianism. By 1940, war was spreading across Europe, and Durick asked Vatican officials for an early ordination. Granting his request, Durick was ordained a priest for the Diocese of Mobile on March 23, 1940.[32]

That same year, Bishop Toolen assigned Durick to aid a fledgling group of priests and nuns in evangelistic efforts in central Alabama. "Come on home," Toolen told Durick, "and learn to change a tire!" Somewhat apprehensive, the young priest returned to Alabama and began his career as a roadside preacher. With a strange blend of Fulton Sheen evangelism and Billy Sunday zeal, Durick and a handful of missionaries traveled from town to town in an old station wagon with trailer in tow, having to stop often to add water to an ailing radiator or to patch a flat tire.[33]

With little experience, Durick struggled to deliver his first street-corner sermons, leading his supervisor, Father Frank Giri, to joke that the young priest never "let the English language get in his way when he preached." Regardless, Durick learned quickly. He adopted the informal language of Protestantism and developed an imaginative, down-home style of preaching—not unlike that of many a Baptist and Pentecostal evangelist in the region.[34]

By 1943, Durick had replaced Father Giri as the leader of this missionary group, which then came to be known as the "North Alabama

Mission Band." It seemed an ideal assignment for Durick, once the saxo-phone-playing youngster with dreams of becoming a traveling musician but now wandering about entertaining wayward souls. He preached from a makeshift pulpit, and with the aid of a rudimentary, battery-operated organ he played "nonheretical" Protestant revival standards, "Blessed Assurance," "In the Sweet By and By," "Oh, What a Friend We Have in Jesus," and "Old Rugged Cross."[35]

As the "band's" director, Durick expanded the group's missionary efforts to include rural areas throughout central Alabama, including Warrior, Calera, Sylacauga, Mulga, Jasper, Montevallo, Trussville, and other small towns. Arriving in a community, the priests canvassed each neighborhood door-to-door to promote interest in the revivals. These evangelistic efforts, although uncommon among Catholics, matched Durick's personality and religious convictions. "I was always anxious," Durick once said. "I believe very firmly in what I believe. I would be willing to die for it. That's how much I believe in it."[36]

After a day of knocking on doors, the band held a service in the back of their trailer, or in an open field, or on the front steps of a local home. "I am a Catholic priest," Durick said as he began each service with a personal introduction, although he told the gathering that Catholic priests "don't go in much for personal advertisement." The doctrine he was about to preach was universal, he explained, and embraced by mil-lions of Catholics throughout the world. Regardless, Durick promised that the religious convictions of each person would be respected at "all times." Following a sermon on various Christian truths and a few hymns, Durick and the other priests took questions from the audience.[37]

Most Protestant Alabamians looked upon the strange visitors with contempt. "I have no use for Catholics" and "I don't like your kind" were frequent responses. One woman, with a slightly devilish view of priests, asked Durick why he had no "horns" on his head. "I'm kind of young," Durick explained. "I haven't grown mine yet." One young man asked why Catholics "trip when they go into their Church?" A rather odd view of kneeling, Durick thought. Others in the crowd asked more serious questions: "You call your priest Father, the Bible said, 'call no man your father upon the earth.'" Quite true, Durick responded. A priest, however was simply a "father to his spiritual flock just like my father or yours." The young priest explained how his father had brought him into the world and a priest, by baptism, gave spiritual life to his soul. "Our fathers brought us up and cared for us," he added. "A priest nourishes the spiritual life of his flock by administering the sacraments."[38]

Klan activists tried to intimidate the priests with anti-Catholic banners posted near revival meetings. Threats of violence, however, never materialized. Durick emphasized that "breaking down bigotry" was always one of the central aims of street preaching. "If I had been taught the things you had been led to believe about the Catholic Church," Durick often told Protestants, "I would hate it too."[39]

With Durick in charge, the missionary efforts helped "disabuse" many Protestants of their "evil notions of the church" and led to the addition of almost a thousand converts, some twenty missions, and six churches in central Alabama.[40] The success of the revivals led Durick to organize and chair the Outdoor Apostolate of the South as a training ground for priests interested in missionary work. "I don't know how much good we did," Durick later remembered, "but it helped my preaching. I preached so much, after a while I thought I was Bishop [Fulton] Sheen."[41]

The Catholic Church in the Birmingham area flourished in the 1940s and 1950s, with a sizable number of converts, additional missions, and a new central high school. In 1954, the Vatican redesignated the Diocese of Mobile as Mobile-Birmingham, a reflection of the growing power and prestige of Catholics in the northern part of the state. The diocese covered a sprawling 58,821 square miles, including ten counties in northwest Florida—a large area for the seventy-year-old Thomas Toolen to shepherd. Catholic leaders also acknowledged this problem, and late that year, Durick received the title of auxiliary bishop.[42]

On Christmas Eve 1954, ten minutes before offering a Midnight Mass at St. Margaret's Church in Birmingham, Durick received a dispatch announcing his appointment. Stunned by the news and sworn to "Apostolic secrecy," Durick meandered through the liturgy. "Ah, brother," Durick's sister said after the service, "I don't know what's wrong but whatever it is, everything is going to be alright." Flush with excitement, he called Archbishop Toolen early Christmas morning and thanked him for the "wonderful present."[43]

A few days later, an editorial writer in the diocesan newspaper hailed the new auxiliary bishop as "an outstanding missionary in a vast missionary diocese." Durick had traveled down every highway and into every hamlet and village throughout the territory, preaching Catholicism and providing religious instruction. As a regional native, Durick understood the temper of the South. "He knows it for what it was, is, and, more important, what it can be," the writer concluded. The Catholic Church would find a friendly welcome from the "religious-minded, God-fearing people of the Southland" once they understood the true church and "not the caricature left by the distorted fables told about Her."[44]

In March 1955, Bishop Fulton Sheen preached at Durick's consecration at St. Paul's Cathedral in downtown Birmingham. "It is a beautiful thing," said Sheen, "when the church will choose a bishop from a trailer and put him on a throne." He reminded Durick never to forget the "trailer and the crossroads and the common people." The young bishop never would, especially in his dealings with those suffering from racial and economic injustices.[45]

Publicly, Toolen expressed delight in having Durick as an assistant. "He has done many outstanding and important works, and whatever he has been asked to do he has done well," Toolen said in early 1955. Privately, the two Catholic leaders would disagree over the race question. The elderly Toolen needed his new assistant's help in leading the growing Catholic population in the Birmingham area—placing Durick, the nation's youngest bishop, in the midst of the rising racial upheaval in the city. As Durick took a more active role in community affairs, he always consulted Toolen before signing any resolutions or making any public statements. "Can I sign your name next to mine?" Durick often asked respectfully. "Nah, you sign it, Joe," Toolen answered. "Leave my name off."[46]

Many whites simply wanted no direct challenge to the status quo, and Toolen was a strong advocate of working within the framework of segregation. The leader of the state's Catholics for over forty years, Toolen gained a reputation as America's "number one missionary bishop." When he first came to Alabama in 1927 as a young, forty-one-year-old bishop, the state only had 45,000 Catholics; when he retired in 1969, that number had increased to 140,000. During his years as Catholic leader of the Mobile-Birmingham Diocese, he directed the building of 189 churches, 23 hospitals, and over 100 schools. Toolen reached across the racial divide in Alabama and provided quality medical care and educational opportunities for blacks. Regardless, he remained a conservative supporter of the status quo. By the 1950s and 1960s his lack of interest in the race question put him at increasing odds with his assistant in Birmingham, Joseph A. Durick.[47]

As one keen observer of black-white relations in the region noted, the elderly Toolen was apparently unwilling to "come to grips" with the race problem, while Durick appeared more open and liberal. Durick recognized that this was no simple disagreement. "It goes much deeper," he told Toolen. "I and my generation will have to face up to the question and you and your generation will not. You're past that age." The times, Durick later remembered, had simply passed by the elderly archbishop.[48]

Only a few months before Durick's appointment, the U.S. Supreme Court had handed down the *Brown* decision. As tensions in the state continued to rise, Alabamians began devising ways to avoid compliance. State Senator Albert Boutwell helped draft the Alabama School Placement Act in 1955, allowing local superintendents to make the final decision as to where students could attend school. The measure was so effective that ten years later only 4 of the state's 114 school districts once designated all-white contained any black students.[49]

As the movements for and against civil rights spread throughout the state, Durick invited Toolen to move to the forefront and integrate Alabama's Catholic schools. Durick was less than enthusiastic about leading the effort, but he sensed the church needed to take the lead. Traveling by automobile on a quiet backroad in northwest Alabama, the young bishop meekly confronted the elderly prelate. "Bishop," Durick asked in a trembling tone, "do you want me to start in the first grade desegregating our schools?" After a long, painful silence, Toolen responded with a firm, "No!" The elderly archbishop delayed integrating the diocesan school system until 1964; he believed that integration would lead to violent reprisals against the church. He too feared a change in the social order, the only way of life Toolen had ever known. In the same way that Pope Pius XI struggled in his response to fascism, Toolen grappled to find an appropriate answer to the race question. The events in Birmingham during 1963 would help Joseph Durick to emerge from the shadow of Toolen and embrace a new social order.[50]

As tensions continued to rise, Birmingham's Jewish community also became increasingly uneasy. It was impossible for anyone to judge the temper of the South without living in the region, Rabbi Milton Grafman wrote in 1956. No one could truly understand the anxiety and heightened emotions from the outside. "There is a tension," Grafman added, "and an atmosphere that I honestly never expected to feel." It had become quite evident to the rabbi that an unfortunate by-product of the segregation issue was an ugly surfacing of radical anti-Semitism—with an intensity foreign to most of Birmingham's Jewish community.[51]

While Alabama had a fairly strong history of blatant anti-Semitism, Birmingham's white Protestants usually limited their discrimination against Jews to more subtle forms of social ostracism. The city's Jewish community faced relatively little harassment from Ku Klux Klan elements prior to the civil rights years—even in the 1920s. A few Jewish businessmen in the area were well acquainted with the KKK's leadership and actively courted Klan patronage. Perhaps most popular was Cousin Joe's Pawn Shop, owned by Joe Denaburg, where Klansmen bought and sold pistols. Denaburg apparently used to joke about being the KKK's principal sheet provider in the area.[52]

Regardless, the intense reaction of many white southerners following the *Brown* decision renewed fear, violence, and terrorism in Birmingham and elsewhere in the South. The Cold War only added to the intensity of the rhetoric. Fear of Communist infiltrators creeping into social, political, and economic institutions blurred the distinction between legitimate discourse and sedition. During this myopia, a more virulent form of the Ku Klux Klan flowered, as did several new racist organizations, including the somewhat "civilized" White Citizens Councils and the odious National States Rights Party. These white southern radicals seized the anti-Communist banner and intimidated anyone willing to discuss racial matters. If white supremacy alone failed to keep blacks down and whites united, one journalist observed, then the anti-Communist torch "would surely do the trick."[53]

Birmingham had had a long history of political red-baiting and other anti-Communist activities. When Communist Party organizers used the city as a staging area in the 1930s, local police introduced a "Red Squad" to intimidate them. Several years later the Birmingham City Commission enacted the Communist Control Act, giving Commissioner of Public Safety Bull Connor freedom to harass suspected revolutionaries, usually those that questioned the racial status quo. The state of Alabama adopted a similar law, which required Communists to register with the Department of Public Safety or face a hefty fine.[54]

Throughout his political career, Bull Connor consistently used the paranoid political style in whipping up fears of Communist infiltrators spreading strife, dissension, and mistrust in the city's churches. "It may be unfair to fleas, but fleas and Communists are a lot alike," Connor once said. "It doesn't take a whole hide-full to make you mighty uncomfortable." These agents of strife, Connor warned, had infiltrated every phase of American life and were undermining the Christian way of life. "If you think the Communists confine their activities to stirring up poor negroes and whites, you'd never be mistaken." Agents, he added, had gained a strong influence in the Protestant, Catholic, and Jewish churches in the South. Joining these red-baiting antics was onetime Birmingham mayor Art Hanes, who accused the city's religious leaders of distributing Communist literature and advancing the integrationist cause in local churches. Like many radical segregationists, Hanes saw no distinction between Communists, blacks, liberals, gradualists, integrationists, and Jews.[55]

Civil rights for black Americans had long been a tenet of the American Communist Party. Accordingly, southern segregationists ascribed all civil rights activities to a Communist scheme led by the nation's Jewish population. Integration, they believed, was a "Communist-Jewish conspiracy plotting to overthrow white-Christian mankind." Terrorists bombed Jewish temples and centers in Miami, Nashville, Jacksonville, Atlanta, and Gadsden—then described these efforts as a Jewish plot to gain sympathy. Adolf Hitler, some segregationists suggested publicly, had the best solution for the Jews.[56]

In 1958, two men from the National States Rights Party drove by Rabbi Milton Grafman's Temple Emanu-El and yelled at the janitor, "You'd better get out of here—this will probably be the next temple to be bombed." Synagogue leaders quickly sought volunteer watchmen to stand guard and installed floodlights around the building. A few months earlier, fifty-four sticks of dynamite and a load of nitroglycerine had failed to detonate outside a basement window of the conservative Temple Beth El, only two blocks or so from Temple Emanu-El.[57]

Even loose identification with those favoring integration might bring reprisals from radicals. In February 1956, Rabbi Milton Grafman was one of several prominent clergymen invited to speak at the University of Mississippi's Religious Emphasis Week. Among the ministers scheduled to appear at the Ole Miss gathering was the mild-mannered Alvin Kershaw, an Episcopal rector in Oxford, Ohio. A minor celebrity in the early years of television, Kershaw had won $32,000 on the TV game show *The $64,000 Question*. He had correctly answered a jazz question on Louis Armstrong's early band and the musical improvisational technique known as scat. When the Episcopal minister later announced that he would contribute a slice of his winnings to the NAACP, Mississippi officials withdrew the invitation to speak on campus. Ole Miss chancellor J. D. Williams explained that Kershaw's willingness to "speak his mind fully on integration" would provide the spark to "ignite an explosive situation" on campus. "I felt it would be unwise for his purposes and for ours for him to come to the campus this year," Williams, an old friend from Grafman's days in Lexington, Kentucky, wrote the rabbi. In response, Grafman and the other ministers quickly canceled plans to attend the event. "I regret exceedingly," Grafman wrote Williams, "that I find it impossible to participate."[58]

In a joint statement, Grafman and the other clergy expressed outrage that an institution of higher learning would screen potential speakers and exclude those with "controversial" opinions. "The action of the university," they continued, "is an affront to the maturity and intelligence of its student body, faculty, staff; and it is a disservice to education, democracy, and religion." The ministers emphasized that the love of God and fellow man was "fundamental to our faith," and this compelled them to cancel their participation in the forum. "Under the circumstances," they added, "to do anything else would make a mockery of the religious, democratic, and educational principles we hold dear."[59]

The actions of these religious leaders received widespread coverage by the regional and national media. Many northern colleagues praised Grafman for his honesty and courage. "Up here it is comparatively easy to take a forthright stand on the segregation issue," one rabbi wrote, "but I know how much real courage that requires in your part of the country." Another rabbi recognized that northerners were far from the battleground for racial justice in the South. "It's easy for us to talk," he wrote; "it's easy for us to act." For Grafman, he added, each word and each step was a major dilemma.[60]

When the story on Grafman's stand appeared in the Birmingham newspapers, however, harassment and threats quickly followed. The constant phone calls became so obnoxious that the rabbi purchased a shrill police whistle and blew his warning signal in the ear of many a would-be harasser. Birmingham and the South in general had been quite hospitable to Grafman and "his race," one anonymous "neighbor" wrote the rabbi. "However if you don't approve of our way of life and the way of life in Mississippi, we would like to suggest that you live somewhere else." The writer suggested Grafman move his family to New York, where "teaming hordes" of Jews, foreigners, and blacks lived and worked without segregation. Another anonymous person wrote

Grafman that if the Mississippi air was too unholy for him to breathe or speak in, then so was the air in Birmingham. "For your information we have the same kind of air and the same kind of people here, only we have been too tolerant of you."[61]

Born in Washington, D.C., on April 21, 1907 and raised in Pennsylvania, Milton Louis Grafman had developed a strong commitment to justice as a young high school student. In his 1924 yearbook he emphasized his desire to see justice prevail and looked to a future career either as a lawyer or a rabbi to attain this goal. The Holocaust of the 1930s and 1940s emerged as a source of "tremendous personal anguish" for Grafman and reinforced his resolve to seek justice. During a trip to Europe in the fall of 1938, he wrote to his family in America that Nazi cruelty was "beyond description" and he feared that no one would believe his stories once he returned home. "Nothing they would do," he wrote at the time, "would now come as a surprise."[62]

In addition to this unwavering commitment to justice, Grafman had a deep love of Judaism that helped refine his response to race relations. During Grafman's childhood, his father, Reuben, served as a chazzan, or cantor: the leader of the musical part of a Jewish religious service. Reuben Grafman began teaching Hebrew to Milton at the age of three and spent every Saturday afternoon with his son discussing the Bible, the Talmud, and Jewish philosophy. As he grew older, Milton had a "natural" desire to become a rabbi. "I chose to dedicate myself to my God and to my people," he once recalled, and to serve them in a "fine, decent, ethical, moral, and upright manner."[63]

Grafman began his college career at the University of Pittsburgh and finished his degree at the University of Cincinnati. He completed his rabbinical training at Hebrew Union College (also in Cincinnati) and was ordained in 1933. That same year he accepted his first full-time position at Temple Adath Israel in Lexington, Kentucky. The rabbi would spend the next sixty-two years working and living in the South.[64]

During the fall of 1941, Grafman accepted an invitation from the Reform congregation at Temple Emanu-El in Birmingham to interview for a position there and to preach a trial sermon. He sensed that many Jews around the country were questioning God's mercy and justice as word slowly spread of the Nazi concentration camps in Europe. The forces of anti-Semitism controlled much of European continent, but Grafman tried to reassure his audience in Birmingham's Temple Emanu-El. "The horrible events of today are the results of man's stupidity and cupidity," he said. The world that God had created was essentially good. "It's the people in it who make it a painful place," the rabbi added; in the end, God's will would predominate.[65]

The congregation quickly hired the thirty-four-year-old Grafman and he assumed his duties at the temple during one of the darkest times in World War II, December 8, 1941, the day after the Japanese bombing of the American base at Pearl Harbor, Hawaii. The new rabbi spent much of his early years at Temple Emanu-El deeply concerned with the plight of Jews during the Holocaust and later an outspoken Zionist supporter of the creation of the nation of Israel.[66]

Consistently seeking to improve Christian and Jewish relations, Rabbi Grafman founded and promoted an annual Institute on Judaism for Christian Clergy to "wipe away prejudice, intolerance, and hatred with knowledge." Each year, a renowned Jewish scholar lectured to as many as 150 Christian ministers. "The idea motivating this Institute is simple enough," said Grafman in 1949. "I feel it is important that we of the clergy, know and understand each other better and have a finer mutual appreciation of our respective faiths."[67]

The Jews of Temple Emanu-El maintained a close bond with many white Christian civic and religious leaders. The temple had a long history of social activism and interfaith cooperation under the leadership of Grafman's predecessor, Rabbi Morris Newfield (who served the temple from 1895 to 1940).[68] Over the years, splinter congregations from Presbyterian, Southern Baptist, Congregational, and Unitarian churches held services in the temple. Rabbi Grafman's efforts helped to convince the Protestant Pastors Union to change their name to the Birmingham Ministers Association and the group in turn invited Grafman to join. In 1974, he became the first rabbi to head the association.[69]

During the civil rights era, Grafman believed that working together with other religious leaders would advance racial justice and protect his synagogue and himself from violence. The congregation at Temple Emanu-El supported his role as a peacemaker, and the rabbi never feared addressing controversial subjects, including race, in a public forum or from his own pulpit. Grafman's appearance, however, was physically unimpressive: he was small in stature, had a rim of closely cropped dark hair half-ringing a bald head, wore bland, and at times rumpled, conservative clothes, and looked bookish with his black horn-rimmed glasses. Yet when Grafman believed God had revealed a word of truth, he spoke with the fire of a biblical prophet. When the rabbi prefaced his remarks with "You're not going to like what I'm going to say," the congregation at Temple Emanu-El braced themselves for a candid message.[70]

Across town at First Methodist Church, Paul Hardin's sermons likewise often provided a swift kick in the seat of the pants for many of his four-thousand-member congregation. During his eleven years in the pulpit, Hardin never avoided preaching on contentious topics, including racial tensions. He believed if a congregation prevented a pastor from preaching on such matters, the members had deprived themselves of information and knowledge they painfully needed. "Now my primary interest is not debating," he once said. "I'm much more interested in the fact that scriptures never show Jesus in an apologetic defensive mood. He's always out to attack!"[71]

The church, Hardin believed, needed to regain the offensive and "wage successful combat" against the nation's social ills: crime, delinquency, immorality, discrimination, drugs, alcohol, and "other evils" that plagued society. "All of this, and more," Hardin proclaimed, "is the legitimate concern of a church that is relevant to the world around." Methodists mature in their faith needed to embrace a "militant church" that placed strong emphasis on both personal redemption and social concern. "We might as well make up our minds," he continued, "whether we're going to drift passively with a treacherous current or fight for the right of all men to live what Jesus called the abundant life."[72]

This battle for human dignity must include the black community, the minister believed. Hardin asked his flock to search their own hearts for racial bigotry, and he petitioned the congregation, as Christians, to treat blacks as Jesus would in every circumstance. "We might try to imagine," he added, ". . . what I would think and do if I were of the other color." Hardin noted that he always tried to keep these two reasonable considerations in mind in his interracial dealings. He rejected the idea of racial supremacy—a concept rooted in fear. "We might as well face it," Hardin told his congregation in 1951, "there are many white people who are inferior to many colored people in mentality and ability, and also, sometimes, in character."[73]

Those who hated the black race were either "morally ignorant or spiritually ill," Hardin believed. He never understood how mature adults harbored hatred of anything or anyone. Hatred deep in the heart was a deadly sin and had no place in the church or at the altar. He explained to this mostly middle- and upper-class congregation that economic fear of blacks had resulted in hatred among less-educated and ignorant whites. He believed that most southerners had been "grossly misrepresented" in their racial attitudes toward blacks. During this time he instructed the ushers in the church to welcome all visitors, regardless of race. "I'm counting on you," Hardin told them, "to see that no one will be turned away because of their skin color."[74]

While Hardin encouraged his congregation to treat blacks with dignity, other whites in Birmingham committed terrorist acts. In the late 1950s, members of a small radical Klan group abducted a young Birmingham black man, Judge Aaron, castrated him, and poured turpentine on the wound to intensify the pain. Hardin condemned the senseless violence from his pulpit (he later said he had been the only white minister in the city to do so) and called the "so-called defenders" of the southern way of life Birmingham's worst enemies. Phone threats began that afternoon and persisted for almost a month, with callers telling the "nigger-loving" preacher to get out of town or he was dead. The harassment culminated in a cross-burning on Hardin's front yard during the wee hours of the morning.[75]

Despite several bold statements from his pulpit, however, Hardin remained firmly committed to a gradual approach to race relations. The South would never see the goal of racial equality achieved overnight. The black-activist push for immediate integration and the white-segregationist cries of never were both unrealistic in the region. "Only by calm, persistent, and consistent efforts under level-headed, intelligent, and dedicated leadership can true brotherhood become a reality," Hardin believed.[76]

Southern communities desperately needed breathing space for the people of good will to work together for a solution to problems. The presence of "deeply dedicated visitors" attracted extensive national media attention, but Hardin questioned whether their presence made "any contribution to the permanent solution of local problems and the feeling of good-will between local Negroes and whites."[77]

Born on November 7, 1903, in Chester, South Carolina, Paul Hardin Jr., like his colleague Nolan Harmon, had deep ancestral ties in the Methodist church. Hardin's father and namesake, however, was a successful businessman during the early years of the twentieth century, but he speculated in the fledgling automobile industry and went bust following World War I. Regardless, he sent young Paul on to Wofford College in South Carolina in 1920, where he studied for a career in law. He had never considered becoming a minister until he received the calling during his senior year. Though Hardin was at first reluctant to heed the summons to God's service, he nevertheless borrowed money from family and friends and enrolled at Candler School of Theology at Emory University in 1924. Resentful and uncertain, he arrived on campus full of self-doubt and possessing a negative view of Methodist ministers. "Frankly," he once remarked, "I just thought they were sort of an odd sex . . . inclined to be, shall I say, effeminate." Although diminutive, Hardin loved competitive athletics, and when he discovered the "theologs" had a football team at Emory, he changed his brash opinion. "I had no idea," Hardin later said, "that boys who were going to be ministers played football." It was an eye-opening and a bone-jarring revelation for Hardin, especially when a teammate knocked the young seminarian out cold in his first scrimmage.[78]

He earned his divinity degree in 1927 and began his career in western North Carolina filling the pulpit at seven different churches during his twenty-two years in the conference. In 1949, Hardin moved to Birmingham as pastor of the thriving downtown congregation at First Methodist. A powerful church with a solid history of prestigious ministers and prominent families, Hardin realized he had to live up to big expectations. At the beginning of his first Sunday service at the church he sat down in a massive pulpit chair and realized that his shoes didn't even reach the floor. A bit rattled, Hardin deviated from his planned sermon and made an impassioned plea to the multitude of worshipers: "You all have got to help me; this whole thing is too big for me; my feet don't even touch the floor." Moved by the pastor's honesty and humility, the congregation rallied around their new leader.[79]

After eleven years, the promotion to the episcopacy in 1960 led Hardin from the prestigious pulpit in Birmingham back to his home state of South Carolina. A few months later he returned to Alabama to oversee the new conference covering south Alabama and the Florida panhandle. Racial tensions had intensified in Birmingham during 1961, and both Hardin and Nolan Harmon had to spend increasing amounts of time in their troubled conferences in the Deep South as well as maintain leadership of their conferences in the Carolinas. An outspoken, progressive voice in Birmingham's white religious community, Hardin presented an interesting contrast to the straight-and-narrow Harmon. In spite of their differences, the pair maintained a close relationship and hoped to act as peacemakers during the racial crisis in Alabama.

Older white southerners, like Harmon and Charles Carpenter, could not envision a future without segregation. A younger generation had learned to accept the inevitability of integration, but they still hoped to control the process according to their own timetable. "I told myself some time ago that we might as well get ready for changes in the South," one Birmingham resident said in the 1960s. "Just the same I don't understand these Negroes. Why do they want to lose the good will of the white man? Why do they insist on pushing so hard?"[80]

In 1963, all of the white clergy addressed in Martin Luther King's "Letter from Birmingham Jail" rejected this push for immediate integration. In their eyes, gradual change remained the peacemakers' way of encouraging a calm transformation of the social order. Regardless, Harmon, Carpenter, Murray, Durick, Grafman, and Hardin remained somewhat isolated from the direct confrontation of energetic integrationists and militant segregationists. On the other hand, Ed Ramage and Earl Stallings became direct targets for both sides. Their personal and professional agony during the racial crisis was "acute and real," a Birmingham native recognized at the time. "How far can a minister go in proclaiming a Christian principle at the risk of alienating his people and breaking the unity of the church?" he wondered. Ramage and Stallings would find out during the spring of 1963.[81]

4 "Grand Fraternity of the Harassed"

Unlike their colleagues of other denominations and faiths, Ed Ramage and Earl Stallings had no shelter from violent reprisals. As leaders in an episcopal form of church government, Harmon, Hardin, Durick, Carpenter, and Murray took little institutional risk in speaking out; neither did Rabbi Grafman, who had solid support from his congregation at Temple Emanu-El. Despite constant harassment, threats, and criticism, the bishops and the rabbi never feared losing their jobs or their livelihood. Southern Baptist and Presbyterian ministers, however, lacked the protection and support of a church hierarchy.

Hence in 1963, Ramage remained in a vulnerable position as the senior pastor at First Presbyterian. Most Presbyterian churches had a representative form of church administration—led and governed by a group of elders elected by the congregation. While this eliminated direct retribution from the congregation, Ramage was, nonetheless, at the mercy of several outspoken segregationist elders. Likewise at First Baptist, Pastor Earl Stallings was unprotected from hostile segregationists. As a Southern Baptist in a congregational form of church government—ruled directly by the congregation—Stallings had little sanctuary or recourse. In 1963 and 1964, the Southern Baptist minister would face what he described as one of the "greatest dilemmas" of his life in Birmingham.[1]

The drama of the civil rights demonstrations in Birmingham touched the life and ministry of Earl Stallings more directly than any of the other white clergymen addressed in Martin Luther King's letter. As part of an overall plan to highlight the hypocrisy of segregation, the SCLC targeted Stallings's First Baptist for black visitors on Easter Sunday morning, April 14, 1963, and for several weeks thereafter. The prospect of blacks violating the social customs of a local church had the reaction King and the SCLC had hoped for: bringing tensions to the surface in a white church and attracting the attention of the national press. These unique visitors inflamed radical segregationists not only in Stallings's church but in Ramage's too and brought tremendous pressure and threats upon the two pastors.

That bright, cool Easter morning at First Baptist Church, Earl Stallings was preparing to preach "A Message for This Day," the opening sermon in a week-long soul-saving revival. Born March 20, 1916, in Durham, North Carolina, James Earl Stallings was the youngest of four children in a single-parent home, his father having skipped town when Earl was just a boy. The family lived at 110 Trinity Avenue, right across the street from Grace Baptist Church, where, as a young lad, Earl felt the tugging of the Holy Spirit and accepted Jesus as his savior and was baptized.[2]

The lean years of the Great Depression forced Earl and his mother, Mattie Bagwell Stallings, to move in with his sister, Margaret, and brother-in-law, W. F. Beam. In search of a better job in the soft-drink business, Beam relocated the entire family to the scrub-pine metropolis of Pine Bluff, Arkansas. The move couldn't have been worse for young Stallings. "Times were so bad," he later reflected, "and money was so short, I got discouraged." Seeking freedom from Arkansas, he wrote to his grandfather back in North Carolina, and the elderly gentleman sent Stallings a bus ticket to their home in Winston-Salem. With only one dollar and one Indian nickel in his pocket, the youngster began the lengthy journey back to his home state.[3]

In Winston-Salem, Stallings had the option of attending school or finding a job. With his family and much of the rest of the country struggling to make ends meet, he found work as a clerk at an A&P grocery store and postponed his final two years of high school. In these days, before self-service stores, clerks ran to and fro behind long counters gathering products for shoppers and ciphering their bill on a paper bag. Soon after he started work, his mother moved to Winston-Salem, where the pair found a small apartment. His mother's weak heart prevented her doing any work outside the home, so at age fourteen, Stallings had the heavy burden of serving as the head of the household. Nonetheless, Stallings soon had another opportunity to complete his education over in Knoxville, Tennessee, but once they relocated, hard times again forced Earl to forgo school and obtain employment as a clerk at a local A&P.[4]

Soon after Stallings began work, he commenced a lengthy courtship with a young woman he met at the store, Ruth Langston McMahan. Three years later they wed, and Stallings established an open-air fruit stand on the street near their apartment in the Knoxville community of Fountain City. As the couple settled into married life, Stallings felt God's calling to enter the ministry. With little formal education and even less money, the task seemed impossible. Ruth, however, had the answer. "I'll go to work and you can go back to school," she told Earl. "I'm not going to be married to an uneducated preacher." In the fall of 1937, Stallings began his "reeducation" as a twenty-one-year-old high school junior at Harrison-Chilhowie Academy, a Southern Baptist boarding school near Knoxville. He shared a room with his young nephew and visited Ruth, who had found a job as a receptionist at the Reeves-Leach Infirmary, on the weekends.[5]

He graduated in the spring of 1939 and enrolled the following fall at Carson-Newman College, a Southern Baptist school just up the road in Jefferson City, Tennessee. He lived for a time in a shabby old dormitory nicknamed the Barn by students, before his wife joined him and they moved into a small apartment over the gymnasium. Stallings soon had his first preaching jobs at two historic Baptist churches near campus: Buffalo Grove on the fourth Sunday of each month and Dumplin Creek on the second and third Sundays.[6]

Dumplin Creek Baptist, founded in 1797, was the onetime church home of backwoods hero Davy Crockett. When Earl Stallings assumed the Dumplin pulpit in 1940, the congregation had lost little of its coon-skin-cap flavor. During services, the women sat on one side of the sanctuary, chewed snuff, and spat into tin cans, while the men sat on the other side, chewed tobacco plugs, and spat out the window. Ruth Stallings found the practice a bit unsightly, but her stomach literally soured at the thought of passing only one tobacco-stained cup during the Lord's Supper. The Communion queasiness, however, soon passed, as the churchwomen sold hand-made quilts to purchase sanitary cups.[7]

These lean years taught Stallings many important lessons for his later ministry. "The Great Depression taught me the true values of life," he later recalled. "It ultimately came down to the fact that I had to make a stand in Birmingham, because of the values that I learned in my early life." Those ideals included honesty, personal integrity, a willingness to assume responsibility, and respect for the dignity of all humankind, regardless of race, Stallings added.[8]

Stallings graduated with his bachelor's degree in 1943, and went on to earn his master's in theology from Southwestern Baptist Theological Seminary in Fort Worth, Texas, four years later. His first job after seminary was at the Ridgedale Baptist Church in Chattanooga, Tennessee. After leading the congregation through a period of remarkable growth, he accepted the pastorate at the First Baptist Church of Ocala, Florida, in 1951. Under his leadership, church attendance more than doubled, and Stallings became a leader in the Florida Baptist Convention, serving as president in 1956 and 1957.[9]

In 1961, a delegation from First Baptist Church in Birmingham traveled to Ocala to pay a visit. Pastor Grady C. Cothen had recently vacated the prestigious Birmingham pulpit to become executive director of the Southern Baptist Convention in California. Upon leaving, he recommended his friend Earl Stallings as a possible successor. In November 1961, the pulpit committee submitted a "general report" on Stallings to the deacons at the Birmingham church, and concluded that the Ocala pastor was "well-groomed" and made a "good appearance" while preaching. He was doctrinally sound and possessed an "evangelistic and missionary fervor" in his ministry. Stallings was outgoing, warm, friendly; had a pleasant speaking voice and used few, but "pleasing," gestures. His administrative abilities were unmatched, because he had worked as a "business man" before being called to save souls and preach.[10]

Before he accepted the position, Stallings was partially aware of the difficulties in pastoring the First Baptist Church of Birmingham. Over the previous decade, the church had gained a reputation as a "meat grinder" for pastors and staff—chewing them up and spitting them out after only a few years. When the pulpit committee visited Stallings in 1961, the church was searching for its fourth pastor since 1952 in a period of increasing uncertainty and instability. Previously, from 1901 to 1952, only three pastors occupied the pulpit in a time of great stability and growth. By 1952, the congregation was flourishing, with almost 3,500 members.[11]

Located at Sixth Avenue North and Twenty-second Street in Birmingham, the First Baptist Church building resembled a grim medieval fortress—with roughly chiseled Bedford stone and stark Moorish spirals—rather than a house of worship. During the civil rights era, as demographic changes in the community surrounding the church heightened fears of integration, an increasing number of members retreated behind these thick walls in a faithful effort to maintain southern traditions and provincial values.[12]

A former staff member later recalled that First Baptist's membership possessed a tangled web of highly complex alliances, blood ties, family feuds, and cliques. This left a new minister in a "precarious position," surrounded by a political minefield that he knew little about and over which he had no influence or control. The tug-of-war between factions within the church placed each new pastor in a no-win situation. This made building a loyal churchwide following a near impossible task for an independent-minded pastor and created a revolving door in the church's pulpit.[13]

As racial tensions increased, segregationist pressure on the church leadership increased as well. For a pastor to succeed with his ministry, he had to submit to the whims of reactionaries in the congregation. A submissive leader would maintain the social structure within the church, avoid controversial subjects from the pulpit, and support the status quo in the community by remaining silent on matters of race. If a pastor violated this unwritten code, the segregationist response would be persistent and cruel. As journalist Ralph McGill observed during the racial crisis, southern white ministers, much like losing football coaches and baseball managers, became expendable when support failed, or hardcore members plotted to repudiate the so-called liberal or Communist pastor. While others at First Baptist maintained a more tolerant viewpoint, the segregationist factions seemed to control the power structure in the church through unrelenting intimidation.[14]

Even prior to the racial crisis, Pastor John L. Slaughter, who had occupied the pulpit from 1938 to 1952, was the first minister to run into serious trouble with the divided minds at First Baptist. When he criticized one powerful clique at the church, the subsequent feuding between rival factions nearly split the congregation. The controversy ended only with Slaughter's resignation in 1952. When the church hired James Thomas Ford in November of that year, the pulpit committee assured the young pastor that "our church had no cliques." Confident of a successful ministry, the determined Ford introduced a progressive plan of church expansion. "The only way to grow a great church," he said at the time, "is to grow a harmonious team, with each person and activity complementing the other." Tangible support for the program, however, never materialized. By the summer of 1953, the preacher complained to the deacons that the congregation was unsupportive and uncooperative and had "failed to carry-out the promises and commitments . . . of his ministry." He begged the deacons, as "partners of the pastor," to help create a "spirit of harmony and unity among the membership."[15]

With the "unsettled conditions" lingering into early 1954, First Baptist adopted a new church covenant that outlined basic beliefs and doctrines. "We engage, therefore, by the aid of the Holy Spirit to walk together in Christian love," the covenant proclaimed. Members would endeavor to uplift the body of the church and "contribute cheerfully and regularly to support the ministry, the expenses of the church, the relief of the poor, and the spread of the gospel through all nations." Churchgoers must also avoid intoxicating liquor, and watch over the sick. They had to remain just in dealings, faithful in commitments, exemplary in all behavior, and avoid "all tattling, backbiting, and excessive anger."[16]

For some members, this was just hollow rhetoric. In early 1955 Ford jump-started his earlier reform efforts and outlined a "preaching program" to strengthen the pulpit ministry. Although he received an "enthusiastic" endorsement from the deacons, his ideas again received little support from factions in the congregation. By the summer months he had grown weary of reconstructing his "pastoral relationship with the church" and resigned. "Let us all thank God for whatever worthwhile ministries we have been permitted to perform together," he told the congregation in July 1955, "and sincerely ask his forgiveness for our failures."[17]

As First Baptist began searching for a new pastor, a special committee solicited advice from church members as to the type of pastor, church staff, and ministry they wanted. "We need a strong forward program," one member wrote, ". . . and [we] can't afford to be petty or little about any of these points." Another churchgoer admonished the congregation to pray, work, and love more. "Let our criticism be open and above the board," the individual wrote.[18]

While many in the congregation hoped for stable and flexible leadership from the pulpit, turnover in the pastoral leadership continued to plague First Baptist. In April 1956, the church called the well-liked T. Sloan Guy Jr. as minister, but by early 1959 he had moved on to lead the Southern Baptist Hospital Commission in New Orleans. During a widespread search for the next pastor, one member of the pulpit committee discovered that the problems at First Baptist were "well known in many places other than in Birmingham." After considering some fifty-five candidates for the position, the church turned to the leadership of Grady C. Cothen in the fall of 1959. "He is a fine-looking man," noted committee participant Mrs. W. R. Russum, "impeccably dressed; dignified, but not coldly formal." Despite his good looks, warm personality, and general popularity among the congregation, Cothen resigned after only two years.[19]

Determined to avoid the problems of his predecessors, Earl Stallings came to Birmingham in January 1962 full of optimistic enthusiasm. Throughout his first three months, he visited every member and regular visitor in the large congregation, whose numbers had declined by this time to two thousand people. This personal contact, he hoped, would lay the foundation for unity among the divergent elements at First Baptist. By the spring of 1962, he launched an aggressive plan to expand ministries. Stallings targeted evangelism efforts in two key areas of the city: in the low-income housing project across from the church and in the affluent homes over the mountain. "We needed them to come downtown," recalled Bill Simmons, First Baptist's minister of education at the time, "because we needed their leadership and . . . their stewardship to pull off what we needed to do." The over-the-mountain folks would provide a moderating influence in the congregation and help provide financial support for the costly inner-city ministry.[20]

Throughout 1962 and into early 1963, the growth plan showed glimpses of success. Attendance was picking up after several years of steady decline. A youthful, dynamic, and hardworking church staff was in place: Stallings, Simmons, Billy Allen in youth and college ministries, and John Chandler, a holdover from the Cothen era, leading the music program. Everything seemed to be going well until Easter Sunday, April 14, 1963.

Stallings had little time to react to the prospect of black visitors that resurrection Sunday. Less than an hour prior to the start of 10:55 A.M. church services, a reporter gave the pastor the news. Soon afterwards, civil rights activist Andrew Young and two college-age black women entered the crowded sanctuary. Ushers handed the trio cards and seated them four or five rows from the back of the church. Almost immediately, nearly seventy white worshipers left in protest. Stallings later commented that these segregationists "did not characterize the way most of us felt about welcoming them to our worship."[21]

Two more black women arrived a few minutes after the start of the service and sat with the other activists. During the offertory, the head warden at the Birmingham Jail, Bob Austin, handed Young the offering plate. Young placed an offering envelope in the plate (one church leader claimed the envelope was empty and had "thank you for an almost Christian reception" scrawled on the outside). Young insisted later that church officials refused to accept his offering—an accusation denied by the church staff.[22]

Following the service, church members gathered in the streets alongside several reporters and photographers to observe the church's visitors. SCLC leaders and the news media anticipated a direct confrontation with segregationist elements at First Baptist, but as the visitors exited the sanctuary, Stallings greeted Young and his group on the steps of the church with a heartfelt smile and a warm handshake. Young handed Stallings a form letter explaining the demonstrators' motives. They had come to First Baptist on the day of resurrection to seek a new life together with "our separated brothers and sisters." Some called this act a "kneel-in," but the civil rights activists simply hoped to worship in a house of prayer "for all people."[23]

Despite segregationist pressure, Earl Stallings never considered turning black visitors away from First Baptist. "If the people came to worship," Stallings wrote a few days after the incident, "we had no Christian justification for closing our doors, and if they came to provoke an incident, we were determined to have no part in this action." The church had intended to welcome blacks for years. Since 1954, the church maintained an open-door policy for any black visitors. Pastor Ford had initiated the action following the *Brown* decision, and each succeeding pastor (Sloan Guy, Grady Cothen, and Earl Stallings) had reaffirmed the policy. Only the week before Easter Sunday 1963, the board of deacons had done the same. Of course the issue remained a moot point as long as blacks never appeared at church services.[24]

The gracious reception by Stallings and a few sympathetic church members had surprised the black visitors and disappointed journalists on the scene. "Well, we didn't get a story," one reporter told Bill Simmons, "but you did the right thing." The next morning, papers all over the country, including the *New York Times,* printed a large photograph of a cheerful Stallings shaking hands with one of the black visitors. Some would find encouragement and inspiration in this image of Christian unity, while others deplored this "integrationist" stand in the church house door.[25]

Members of Stallings's former churches in Florida and Tennessee wrote words of encouragement, as did each of the pastor's surviving predecessors at First Baptist Church. John Slaughter, J. T. Ford, Sloan Guy, and Grady Cothen knew firsthand the simmering tensions under the surface at the church. "When I read in the paper that you had not turned away those who came to worship with you," Slaughter wrote, "I gave thanks unto God that you had met a crisis in the spirit of Christ." Slaughter encouraged Stallings to allow the experience to draw the congregation closer in love and fellowship. "Anything less than that," he added, "would be a tragedy indeed." The remark was an ominous foreshadowing of the days to come.[26]

Stallings had hoped and prayed that his stand would serve as "a witness" to further the kingdom of God. From all over the country, people offered words of encouragement. "People like you restore my faith in the church," one woman wrote. A seminary student attending Yale Divinity School thanked Stallings for "pointing the way for all of us" to stand for God. Ministers around the South also found inspiration in Stallings's stand. "Your demonstration . . . of real Christian ethics helps me to stand back up and a little taller, as an otherwise embarrassed Alabamian," one pastor in Texas wrote. The symbolism contained in the picture, one Florida pastor noted, was of "inestimable worth in its ability to convey to the public, and the world, that Southern Baptists regard themselves as a part of the answer to the problem of race, and not as a part of the problem."[27]

Around the world, missionaries found great merit in Stallings's display of Christian unity. During the racial crisis, foreign missionaries had a difficult time explaining the brutal images of white defiance in the American South. "How can this be in a Christian country?" new converts asked. William and Martha Gilliland, missionaries in Nigeria, thanked Stallings for the "dignity and spirit" in accepting blacks at First Baptist. "You have given an unmistakable witness in your local situation," they wrote. "By your action yesterday you have strengthened our own hands for witnessing to Nigeria."[28]

In Birmingham, Southern Baptist women active in the Woman's Missionary Union offered strong words of encouragement. "In my judgment," one WMU official wrote Stallings, "you stand tall as a minister of the gospel of Christ." She remembered Stallings often in her daily prayers and petitioned God to provide the pastor "courage and strength adequate for the days ahead." She also hoped that other Christians might follow Stallings's stand, which was "restrained enough to be helpful, yet positive enough to be understood." A few of the WMU workers were members of First Baptist and praised Stallings for his leadership. "I shall be praying," one member wrote, "that we, as a church, may be spiritually mature enough to see this matter through in the way that Christ would have us to."[29]

Other individuals in the congregation wrote brief notes of support or offered quiet words of encouragement. "We are for you 100%," the "Blue Print" Sunday School Class wrote the minister, "as our Pastor and as a man's man. . . . "We pray for God's guidance and God's leadership for you as you minister unto these people."[30]

On the other side of the issue, segregationists were more explicit in their responses. Members of the Visitation Sunday School Class at First Baptist scolded Stallings for permitting the "ill-advised and unwarranted" misuse of the church. "We are of the Christian persuasion," these church members wrote, "and seek to imitate the example of Christ in those areas of our lives that bring us into contact with other people, other groups, other beliefs." The most "Christ-like" way to deal with the situation, they suggested, was to drive out these groups just as Christ had forced the "money changers from the temple." These black visitors had not come to worship, this group believed, but to advance the aims of their organization.[31]

"I think what happened in our church Easter Sunday was the most awful thing that could have happened," seventy-two-year-old Willie Mae Bartlett wrote Stallings. She believed the worst part of the day was Stallings's stand in the church door and his handshakes with "those negroes." Bartlett had attended First Baptist for sixty-five years and had "enjoyed every bit of it, but never did we have to mix." She now asked the deacons to "send my letter" of membership so she could go to another church.[32]

Southern Baptists from outside Alabama also blasted Stallings for his stand. "I hope Martin L. King will be real proud of you," one Georgian wrote the pastor. "Any one that can back up that bunch of low down Negro [sic] that are sent down here to the South to cause the trouble . . . and call themselves a Baptist Minister is beyond me. . . . Men like you make me sick." A segregationist in Louisiana encouraged Stallings to

become a "real Baptist" and not remain a "confused Kennedy Baptist."
By welcoming blacks to First Baptist, Stallings had aided the integrationist cause and helped the "Kennedy Clan" in Washington. "I'm ashamed
of you as a Baptist Minister," the writer continued. "Communists work
through such individuals as you in getting their movement going." A
Florida Baptist announced that he resented Stallings's actions to such an
extent that he was "going over" to another denomination. "And if they
integrate," he continued, "I'm going over to still another church or
none. Those niggers didn't go to your church to worship, they went to
integrate. Why be the suckers?"[33]

The events of Easter Sunday 1963 had overwhelmed those in the middle, infuriated hard-core segregationists, and dissatisfied civil rights
activists. Still hoping for a public showdown, three black men and two
black women returned the Sunday following Easter for another visit. A
receptionist pinned on each protester a red and white ribbon with a
small badge that had the words "A Welcome Guest." For many, however, the blacks were anything but welcome. Visiting once had been a
fluke, but coming back again was a habit.[34]

As soon as blacks attended, reactionary segregationists in the congregation began pressuring Stallings and the deacons to change the church
policy. A quarterly church meeting in late April 1963 digressed into an
aggressive and mean-spirited confrontation with vocal segregationists.
One church member presumed he had the right to choose the type of
people he worshiped with and he "didn't choose to worship with
Negroes." Jail warden Bob Austin claimed to have recognized some of
the visitors as "having been in jail for violation of the law" and he
"didn't like to worship with them." Segregationists argued that the
black visitors had insincere motives in attending the church and were
only interested in publicity. Blacks, therefore, should "not be admitted
to future services," they maintained.[35]

The decade-long divisiveness among rival cliques in the church had
hardened just as brooding tensions over the race question came to the
surface. The controversy over the black visitors in the spring of 1963
was just the opening engagement in a drawn-out conflict for the heart
and soul of the First Baptist Church of Birmingham.

A couple of blocks away at First Presbyterian, the Reverend Edward
Vandiver Ramage also received pressure from outspoken segregationist
factions in his church. Born on October 2, 1908, in the small hamlet of

Weaverville in the mountains of western North Carolina, Ramage was the son of well-educated parents. His father, Samuel Johnson Ramage, had studied voice at the University of Pennsylvania before embarking on a career in the lumber business in North Carolina. His mother, Elizabeth Jane Vandiver, taught English and the classics at Columbia College in South Carolina. A spinstery thirty-three when she married in 1902, she bore three children and raised them by herself after Samuel's premature death in 1917. The strong-willed Elizabeth taught her children classical literature and the holy scriptures in a strictly pious home. This convinced young Ed at an early age to become a preacher—as did spending each summer at the nearby Presbyterian camp at Montreat.[36]

A wandering sort, Ed Ramage bounced from college to college, first Davidson in North Carolina, next Emory near Atlanta, then back to Davidson, and returning again to Emory before he attended the conservative Columbia Theological Seminary in Decatur, Georgia, from 1929 to 1932. Ramage completed his formal education during the depths of the Great Depression, and he quickly discovered that no one needed the services of a "full-fledged Presbyterian parson." The young minister had nowhere to go. His immediate family had fallen on hard times and had scattered around North Carolina, living with aunts, uncles, and cousins. Seminary administrators allowed Ramage to stay in the dormitory, but the dining hall had closed, and with no money, he lived for time on stale bread discarded by a bakery near campus and tap water. "There is nothing quite as desolate as a school just after all the students have gone," he later recalled. "I sat there alone and listened to the quietness" with an empty stomach. One evening, when a friend invited him to dinner of roast beef, rice, hot rolls, and lemon ice-box pie, Ramage ate himself sick.[37]

Each morning, Ramage would go to the mailbox hoping for a job offer, but none came. He spent the rest of the day wandering about the Georgia countryside with bands of unemployed men looking for work. "I walked and walked," he later recalled, "but no job. There just weren't any to be had." One day he packed his meager belongings in an old knapsack and began hitchhiking his way to the mountains of North Carolina. "Things may be better there," he hoped. Ramage made it to Greenville, South Carolina, and begged a bowl of hominy grits and fried bacon from the manager of the local bus station. "You don't look like no preacher," she said with a smirk. "Besides, I ain't never seen a preacher begging for food." He spent the night in the depot on a hard knotty-pine bench, and by first light he was once again on the highway thumbing a ride along busy Highway 25.[38]

A pickup truck soon stopped, and Ramage tossed his meager belongings in ahead of him and climbed in the back for the winding ride up into the Blue Ridge Mountains. The crisp morning air blew hard against his face as he soaked in the beauty of the countryside. "I had no money," he later wrote. "I had no food. I had no home. But the world was bright and beautiful." Returning to North Carolina, Ramage found work as a "grease monkey" in a small garage near his hometown, earning twelve dollars a week. After months of struggling to make ends meet, he received a job offer during September of 1932 to pastor three churches, Main Street, Lindale, and Barker's, scattered over thirty miles of countryside in and around the northwest Georgia town of Rome. He earned seventy-five dollars a month and preached in an oversized hand-me-down shirt and a threadbare suit, worn so often that the seat of the trousers had been replaced three times.[39]

As he grew older, Ramage never forgot those lean years and his bouts with hunger, poverty, and unemployment. "I understand life and its issues a little more fully," he later wrote, "and am better equipped to face its rough places. I have an abiding fellow feeling for those who live with hunger and poverty as their companions, and am a little more willing to share what I have with them." The Presbyterian minister maintained a compassion for the less fortunate in society and those alienated by poverty or race. Regardless, during his days in seminary, Columbia was a bastion of biblical conservatism, where students learned that the Presbyterian Church in the United States (PCUS) had a "special mission" to minister to the "spirituality" of the church. Ramage accepted these notions and upheld this spiritual sacredness by abstaining from preaching on "social issues" like racial discrimination.[40]

From his pastorate in Georgia, Ramage moved on to lead congregations in Decatur, Alabama, and Oklahoma City, Oklahoma, before he received the call from First Presbyterian of Birmingham in 1946. Located on the corner of Fourth Avenue North and Twenty-first Street, "Old First" was the first church to erect a building in the fledgling city of Birmingham in 1872. The church had a long history of excellent ministers, including Welshman Trevor Mordecai, who filled the pulpit during the 1920s and had a large following, including future U.S. Senate chaplain Peter Marshall.[41]

As a thirty-seven-year-old "seasoned" bachelor, Ramage enjoyed playing the field in the dating scene. To help him with the social duties usually reserved for the pastor's wife, he brought to Birmingham his widowed Aunt Grace "Geekie" Vandiver Cann to serve as his hostess (Ramage's mother having functioned in this capacity in Oklahoma City until her death in 1942). But soon after coming to "Old First," a young church member, Katherine Morrow Watters, caught his eye. Fourteen years younger than Ramage, the vivacious Watters had earned degrees from the University of North Carolina in art and sociology (under the tutorage of Howard Odum). Graduating during the early 1940s, she found a job as a production illustrator with Bell Aircraft in Marietta, Georgia, assisting experimental engineers as they attempted to fit prop-driven B-29 aircraft with jet engines. An accomplished artist, she returned to Birmingham following the war and went to work as a medical illustrator. Their courtship was rather clandestine, to prevent any whispered conversations among nosy church members. He soon proposed, and they were married at First Presbyterian on April 20, 1948. Performing the ceremony was Ramage's old friend and fellow clergymen Henry Edward "Jeb" Russell, the brother of the outspoken segregationist senator from Georgia, Richard Russell.[42]

Six years later, when segregation became a burning issue following the *Brown* decision, the General Assembly of the PCUS adopted a resolution urging "all of our people to lend their assistance to those charged with the duty of implementing the decision, and to remember that appeals to racial prejudice will not help but hinder the accomplishment of this aim." Back in Alabama at the 1954 meeting of the state synod in Birmingham, the Permanent Committee on Christian Relations urged laypeople and ministers to make a public stand against racial discrimination. The synod rejected the idea.[43]

The General Assembly, however, continued to issue sympathetic statements, compelling lay leaders and a few pastors in the Birmingham Presbytery to ask the national church to stop. These "inflammatory" pronouncements that pointed the "finger of scorn and shame at our area" were "ill-advised," the presbytery believed, and would only increase tensions. Nonetheless, the General Assembly emphasized that the "racial problems of our time" were so far-reaching and so urgent to "require our attention and action."[44]

As race relations in the region continued to worsen, the General Assembly invited the "Christian people of the South . . . to demonstrate the effectiveness of the Gospel in solving a difficult problem in human relations whose far-reaching effects are incalculable." In 1961, the Synod of Alabama called upon all church members to "examine their hearts and conscience in this matter, and to seek creative and constructive means under the guidance of the Holy Spirit by which men of different races may learn to live together in peace, understanding, mutual respect and love." The synod urged a public statement be read in every PCUS church in the state. The synod confessed partial responsibility and guilt "in action and attitude" for the rising racial tensions and lawlessness in Alabama. There was no easy solution to the problem, they continued, but Presbyterians could not be at odds with the Gospel. "Though there are differing opinions concerning the application of the Gospel to individual and corporate life, we affirm that the Christian Faith can never support or encourage racial prejudice or violence stemming from and based on such prejudice." The session at First Presbyterian unanimously voted to insert the statement in the church bulletin, but "only as a resolution from the synod of Alabama and not as action taken by the session of First Presbyterian Church."[45]

Like many white Christians, members of Old First hoped to simply avoid this volatile issue, but on Easter Sunday, the church would be forced to confront the dilemma. That morning, Ed Ramage sat in his pastor's study and nervously awaited the beginning of the service and the entrance of the rumored visitors. Sunday school teachers prepared children and adults alike for the appearance of the black worshipers. A few church members stayed away, convinced that police would be stationed at the doors to prevent rioting. One family chose to spend the morning at a local Jewish delicatessen "drinking iced tea, eating matzos, and meditating on the ironies of southern Christianity."[46]

Following the processional and call to worship that Easter Sunday, the congregation stood to sing "Jesus Christ Is Risen Today." During the hymn, two black women, including Dorothy Vails, an instructor at Miles College, entered the sanctuary. Apologizing for the large Easter crowd, an usher greeted the pair at the door and escorted them down the center aisle. With each successive row of pews, the congregation noticed the visitors and dropped their hymn books in disbelief. The singing slowly tapered off like a sing around of "Row, row, row your boat" gone astray, until only a few churchgoers continued to vocalize the hymn. Ramage's wife Katherine later described the experience as a rolling wave of static electricity standing everyone's hair on end. In the thick tension, Mrs. Ramage thought the air in the sanctuary would "crackle."

A handful of churchgoers immediately left in protest and apparent disgust.[47]

The only seats available for the duo were near the front of the church—a young boy and his parents moved into the aisle to let the women enter the pew. An elderly man smiled and handed one of the protestors his hymn book and pointed to page number 204.[48]

Ramage's Easter sermon was simply entitled, "Jesus." A remarkable extemporaneous speaker, Ramage never typed a prepared sermon text or used extensive notes. After much prayer and contemplation, he often jotted three words on the back of an envelope and preached for forty-five minutes. This Easter morning in 1963, however, Ramage was painfully aware of the events transpiring in his church and throughout the city. He preached a brief, rambling sermon that bounced from point to point. While discussing the serious problems facing humanity, Ramage seemed to point to the inner feelings of many in his congregation, noting that the "real warfare" was not between opposing groups but deep in the "invisible realm" inside individual people, "where sinister forces, flaming and frantic," contended.[49]

Hoping to avoid a media incident following the service, Ramage ended his sermon prematurely, and the congregation stood and sang the benediction hymn, "The Day of Resurrection." Following the service, the two women were welcomed "most cordially" by church members, Vails later told a newspaper reporter. Ramage greeted the activists at the door and invited them to "come again" and worship at First Presbyterian. "They had a lovely service," Vails added, "which we enjoyed very much."[50]

Almost immediately, Ramage began receiving death threats. Late-night phone calls started, and he had all four of his tires slashed on the automobile the church had purchased for him. Ramage's wife feared for the safety of their children and their home at 2500 Aberdeen Road. One Presbyterian colleague wrote that Ramage had been inducted into the "grand fraternity of the harassed" in the South. Belligerents in the church formed a committee of laypersons to investigate and expose the Communist treachery at First Presbyterian. A few weeks following the Easter Sunday incident, one unyielding segregationist member explained that the only salvation for the church was to "get rid of the Communists," and she pointed a quivering finger toward Ramage and identified him as "one of the biggest."[51]

On the surface, Ramage endured the events with his generous nature.

Inwardly, the minister agonized over the raging firestorm within his congregation over racial issues. Old friends stopped speaking to one another, others found new church homes with a less "liberal" pastor, and even families divided over the dilemma. When the racial ideals of one young woman from First Presbyterian took a more liberal turn, her parents reacted with deep resentment toward the church. "Much of their bitterness toward the church," she wrote Ramage, ". . . springs, I feel sure from their disappointment in me." Strains from the economic downturn in Birmingham, family worries, and her mother's "time of life" had only made the couple "less able to cope with changing ideas and more ready to blame their disappointments on 'communist infiltration' and subversion." Regardless, the young woman had found great joy in seeing the church "facing the moral issues involved in social change." She hoped "fervently that it may guide men's minds into acceptance, Christian acceptance, of change instead of bitterness."[52]

In that spirit, Ramage told the church elders in a regular meeting of First Presbyterian's Session, "we are committed to open the doors of worship to all who come." A few days later, the church elders gathered for the first of series of special meetings to discuss the issue of black visitors, and Ramage emphasized that he coveted church unity but not at the sacrifice of Christian principles. One of the elders, Birmingham insurance magnate "Colonel" William J. Rushton, reportedly replied, "To hell with Christian principles—we've got to save the church!"[53]

For many segregationists, the only way to save white southern churches was to purge "integrationist" pastors from their pulpits. For Ramage and Stallings, the purging process began on Easter Sunday 1963. Many in their congregations clung to the traditions of Jim Crow over religious and moral considerations. Unlike so many white southern ministers, Ramage and Stallings had chosen to act as spiritual leaders rather than social followers, but once they defied the whims of extremists, the two city pastors faced un-Christian persecution.

5   Eyes on the Press

Birmingham and the SCLC

In Birmingham, the reminders seemed everywhere. "White Only" and "Colored Only" signs dangled above water fountains and lunch counters; they remained fastened to the doors of restrooms, dressing rooms, and waiting rooms. Proprietors displayed the signs prominently over the entrances to hotels, restaurants, and laundry-mats. Laundry trucks inscribed with WE WASH FOR WHITE PEOPLE ONLY zipped down the city's streets. Many white southerners never gave much thought to these symbols of segregation or to the injustices of Jim Crow customs, laws, and etiquette. For whites, this was the southern way of life. Black southerners, on the other hand, had to face these constant reminders of second-class citizenship. "I tell you, it's a funny place this South," a black resident of Birmingham concluded in the early 1940s. "This place is all right in a way, but a man has to be less than a man to get along most of the time."[1]

Jim Crow was originally the name of a shuffling dance popular among slaves in the early nineteenth century. Prohibited from using certain forms of musical expression and dance, slaves performed the Jim Crow like a walking-jig that required fancy footwork and the ability to conceal and deny its appearance to whites. After observing an old slave doing the Jim Crow in the 1830s, a white stage performer, T. D. "Daddy" Rice, borrowed the dance and its name for a wildly popular black-faced minstrel show. In front of large crowds of cheering whites, Rice would sing: "O, Jim Crow's come to town, as you all must know. /

An' he wheel about, he turn about, he do jis so, / An' every time he wheel about he jump Jim Crow."[2]

The term seemed an appropriate description for the odd system of southern segregation that emerged in the years following the Civil War. On the stage of southern life, the races performed their designated roles, in which strange codes of conduct, long enforced by whites, became ritualistic habits for both races. Most of these rituals were a way of implying black inferiority and white superiority. The two races never greeted one another with friendly handshakes; never walked to a common destination side-by-side; never shared tables at local restaurants and ordered glasses of sweetened tea and slices of lemon pie; black and white couples never jitterbugged together in crowded southern dance clubs; and the races never broke bread or shared Communion in the same church. Social interaction, let alone any social equality, was forbidden.

Whites rarely called black men "Mr." or "Sir"; rather, they referred to them by their first names or last names. If the name of a young man was unknown, whites called him "boy," "Jack," "John," or "George." Older men were often referred to as "uncle." Whites addressed young black women by their first name or a sullen "hey you" or "you there," and older women were greeted with "auntie." Most often, police officers and other authorities just barked out "nigger" to all blacks regardless of age or sex. Even business letters had to conform to the decorum. Letters from white companies addressed to blacks rarely began with the standard salutation "Dear Sir" or "Dear Madam," but simply the person's first name. One black mother was so disgusted by all of these degrading rules, she decided to name her child Mister. When asked by a white insurance agent about the reasoning behind the unusual name, the mother replied, "Well, I know he'll grow up to be a man some day and since you are going to call him by his first name anyway, I thought I'd name him mister."[3]

Many black men removed their hats in the company of white people—not necessarily as a sign of respect but as a precautionary measure. "White people expect it," one black man said during the 1940s. "I do it just to keep out of trouble." Failure to obey the etiquette might, and frequently did, lead to violence. In order to sidestep any violation of Jim Crow customs, some blacks avoided all possible contact with whites. One fellow even crossed the street every time he saw a white person coming toward him. "I let them have they side of the street," he said, "and I goes on."[4]

By 1963, Birmingham, Alabama, had become synonymous with this odd and oppressive system of segregation. Considered the industrial center of the South, Birmingham was a tough, dirty town, with a lingering black smog so thick that streetlights often burned during the daylight hours. The United States Steel Corporation controlled most of the city's industry from faraway Pittsburgh. As absentee owners, the corporation exploited the area's natural resources, utilized a pool of cheap labor, hindered diversification of the local economy, and turned a blind eye to violence and terror—all in the name of higher profits, tax breaks, and favorable perks. If the city had a golden era prior to 1963, it existed only in the minds and dreams of local officials and residents. For most citizens, the area's economy had stagnated as the city shifted from blue-collar to white-collar jobs during the 1950s and 1960s. Unemployment and competition for jobs grew fierce, adding to the racial tensions and climate of unrest.

Founded in 1871 during the heyday of the New South era, early promoters boasted that Birmingham would soon rival Pittsburgh as the nation's steel and iron center. Entrepreneurs had built the new city on some farmland in a sparsely populated valley running through Jefferson County in north-central Alabama. The hills surrounding the city offered rich deposits of iron ore, coal, and limestone—key ingredients for iron and steel making. Nicknamed the "Magic City" because of its rapid growth, Birmingham was a peculiar blend of northern capital, Old West frontier brutality, and New South hype. As one overzealous city father noted, Birmingham was the "Magic City of the World, the marvel of the South, the miracle of the Continent, the dream of the Hemisphere, the vision of all Mankind."[5]

Reality, however, never matched the hopeful rhetoric. Years later, in 1937, George R. Leighton reported for *Harper's Magazine* that Birmingham was still a city of "perpetual promise," never quite living up to optimistic, flamboyant civic boosterism. On top of Red Mountain, a large cast-iron statue of Vulcan, the Roman god of fire and metal, served as the great symbol of the city. Holding a hammer in one hand and a spear in the other, Vulcan emerged as a strangely pagan symbol for a place that boasted of being a "city of churches." Nevertheless, wildly exaggerated hype continued throughout the racial turmoil. Even in 1963, Mayor Art Hanes bragged that Birmingham was the nation's "last outpost of gracious living [and] warm hospitality."[6]

From at least the mid-1880s, segregation by custom was commonplace in Birmingham. Private utility rules and old habits separated blacks and whites on the city's early streetcars, and a pattern of residential segregation persisted without government ordinance. For forty years, the promise of jobs persuaded thousands of blacks to leave the rural South for low-skilled employment in this north-central Alabama city. By 1920, of the cities with one hundred thousand or more population, Birmingham had the highest percentage of blacks, at 39 percent. In turn, many whites felt the need for a strong measure of social control. During the twenties, city officials enacted a series of laws separating blacks and whites in virtually all situations, including education, public facilities, and even innocent matches of dominoes, cards, and checkers.[7]

The enactment of segregation laws in Birmingham and other areas of the South gave those whites with the closest contact with blacks the voice of government authority. Railroad and streetcar conductors, bus drivers, ticket agents, bartenders, restaurant owners, sales clerks, cab drivers, ushers at public events, church deacons, and even ignorant bullies had the right to demand and enforce racial separation.[8]

This voice of authority was particularly forceful and often brutal in Birmingham. Some of the city's streetcar conductors carried loaded pistols or shotguns as a not-too-subtle reminder of Jim Crow laws and customs. One hateful conductor incited the resentment of many black passengers in Birmingham. "He tries to treat you in a pretty rough way sometimes," one patron noted in the 1940s. The passenger resented having no other recourse but to take the abuse and ride the streetcars with a burning anger. When blacks could afford to, they purchased automobiles to escape the humiliation of the mass transit system. Yet some whites made certain blacks knew their proper place as well on the South's roads and highways. These white people paid little attention to traffic laws and evoked a "racial right of way" when blacks were involved. As one observer noted, when whites saw black drivers, they usually kept "going like it was a disgrace to stop at a stop sign to let a nigger pass." Some blacks took these strange occurrences with biting humor, like the black motorist who ran a red light and explained to a white officer that he was simply obeying separate-but-equal traffic signals. The driver had seen whites traveling through green lights and told the officer that he "thought the red light was for colored folks" to go through.[9]

In addition to a variety of statewide segregation ordinances, local ordinances relegated blacks to separate railroad cars, waiting rooms, washrooms, drinking fountains, hospitals, schools, restaurants, cemeteries, and, although there was only one judicial system, separate Bibles for taking oaths. Black citizens in Birmingham had to purchase apparel by sight, because local department stores prohibited blacks from trying on clothing in the stores' white-only dressing rooms. During the ten or eleven days of the Alabama State Fair in Birmingham each year, African Americans had just one "black day" that they could attend.[10]

With rigid segregation the defining feature of the city, Birmingham had a difficult time presenting a positive image to the rest of the nation. The city was just over ninety years old in 1963, so Birmingham had developed no natural aristocracy to help refine the city's wild, frontier edges. In addition, the more affluent sections of the surrounding county were on the other side of Red Mountain and sealed off from the rest of Birmingham. Safe in their isolated communities, these elitist whites looked over the mountain and down their noses at the working-class folks in the valley. They were quick to criticize the city's problems, but slow to help find solutions.

Adding to the image woes was Birmingham's shortage of quality leadership and unfailing promoters. The city lacked a persevering New South booster (in the mold of Atlanta's champion, Henry Grady) to help define and give the young city direction and purpose in its infancy. By the middle of the twentieth century, Birmingham still needed aggressive, pro-growth leadership similar to Atlanta's mayor William Hartsfield. During the racial crises in the South, Hartsfield had trumpeted consistently the public relations image of Atlanta as the city "too busy to hate." In Birmingham, no progressive pacesetter or image-conscious group emerged to cultivate and sell a positive impression of the city to national business executives or the country at large. In the public's eye, racial segregation and violent acts of terrorism had defined Birmingham as a city too busy hating.[11]

Even prior to the nationally publicized racial problems, image-conscious Birmingham had battled wave after wave of negative portraits. Before the city's founding, Black Belt politicians in the state's capital at Montgomery joked that Jefferson County was so poor, even buzzards had to pack a lunch before flying over it. By the end of the nineteenth century, the city had already gained a reputation as "Bad Birmingham"—a frontier town filled with steamy saloons, houses of ill-repute, and daily gunfights. The homicide rate was so high at the turn of the century that writers in the national press referred to Birmingham as the "Murder Capital of the World." By the 1920s, Progressive reforms had helped close the saloons and whorehouses, but had done nothing to really improve the city's image or curb its appetite for violence. "Hold-ups and other crimes in Birmingham," a local writer concluded at the time, "have become so prevalent that people may well ask themselves if it is safe to leave their homes after dark."[12]

Tied so closely to the nation's lifeblood of heavy industry, economic downturns shook the very foundations of Birmingham's fragile existence. Poor civic self-esteem and consistent financial problems led one hand-wringing pessimist to the conclusion that "hard times came first to Bir-mingham and stayed the longest." The onslaught of the Great Depression in the 1930s confirmed this notion in the minds of many. The Bir-mingham area had the nation's highest unemployment rate, leading Pres-ident Franklin D. Roosevelt's administration to consider the city the "worst hit town in the country." World War II helped revive the steel industry and led a few locals to boast that Birmingham was the "Great Arsenal of the South"; yet local leaders still had no vision for the future or even the will to repair the city's horrible reputation. With no catchy slogan or image to sell Birmingham to the public, the national media con-tinued to focus on the city's harsher features. About the only nice state-ment the national media made about Birmingham was a 1945 *Saturday Evening Post* story which described the city's downtown area as "slightly more attractive" than Atlanta's. During the early civil rights era, the national press's focus on the city and South in general only intensified.[13]

By the 1960s the city's image had become an obsession for many citi-zens. Before Martin Luther King's arrival there, the national media had already examined the peculiar nature of race relations in the Magic City. Poor civic images and constant press scrutiny had given the city's resi-dents a heightened sense of inferiority and paranoia. Constant criticism made most whites defensive and willing to lash out at any negative por-trait of their hometown. Responding to the public mood, politicians like Eugene "Bull" Connor often railed against "junkateering journalists" and preached that Birmingham had been held back because of "Com-munism, socialism, and journalism."[14]

High-strung white residents and community leaders reacted hysteri-cally following the visit of a "carpetbagger" journalist from New York City during the spring of 1960. *New York Times* reporter Harrison Salisbury traveled to Alabama during the first week of April to write an in-depth story on race relations in Birmingham. After spending five days interviewing a narrow variety of residents and walking the city's streets observing the local scene, Salisbury composed two blistering articles on the "fear and hatred" gripping the Magic City.[15]

He admitted in the first article that "no New Yorker can readily measure the climate of Birmingham today." Yet the Pulitzer Prize–winning journalist, accustomed to covering the paranoia and veiled secrecy of the Soviet Union, provided a clear picture of the racial and political polarization in the city. Focusing almost exclusively on the vicious activities of radical segregationists and the work of political and social activists, Salisbury concluded that whites and blacks in Birmingham shared a "community of fear": "Every channel of communication, every medium of mutual interest, every reasoned approach, every inch of middle ground has been fragmented by the emotional dynamite of racism, reinforced by the whip, the razor, the gun, the bomb, the torch, the club, the knife, the mob, the police and many branches of the state's apparatus."[16]

All channels of cross-racial communication were closed and moderate voices cowered in safe places to avoid violent reprisals. Salisbury noted that Birmingham's whites and blacks never talked freely and lived in a virtual police state ruled by Connor. City officials tapped telephone lines and intercepted mail. "The eavesdropper, the informer, the spy" were a fact of life, Salisbury wrote. Even a nameless Birmingham pastor closed his door before speaking openly about race.[17]

Later identified as the "pastor," Rabbi Milton Grafman insisted the *Times'* reporter had traveled to Birmingham with a preconceived idea, and twisted the facts to fit that conception. When he approached the rabbi about an interview, Salisbury claimed that he was "gathering information" and not writing an exposé on Birmingham. Grafman also pointed to that supposedly fearful closed-door meeting. Because of the location of his office along a lengthy hallway, the rabbi always closed the door to discuss personal matters, just to make sure his visitors were comfortable and at ease to talk freely. Some years later, following Salisbury's death, the *New York Times* wrote that some of the paper's journalists had whispered that the famed newsman had "sometimes exaggerated" his reporting. "He had a nearly boundless confidence in his reporting," the *Times* concluded, "and intuitions that would lead him to conclusions . . . few editors at the time dared challenge." Apparently, as Grafman maintained, Salisbury saw what he wanted to see in the rabbi's closing of the door.[18]

Grafman displayed the defensiveness that the majority of white Birmingham had in reaction to the national media and the city's poor public image. Like most whites in town, Grafman resented the way the *Times* had singled out Birmingham from all the other cities in the Deep South with racial tensions. Salisbury indicted, tried, and convicted every citizen of bigotry and hatred, the rabbi believed. The reporter had focused only on the negative and failed to search for those citizens trying to turn the city around. Regardless, Grafman later insisted all the negative publicity helped Birmingham turn a "moral microscope" on the city's racial problems. The publicity also helped the nation consider the question of the black race's place in American society.[19]

Nevertheless, Salisbury deeply angered many of the city's elites. Soon after the stories appeared, the *Birmingham News* reprinted the article under the headline: "N.Y. Times slanders our city—Can this be Birmingham?" and branded the journalist's work "a shoddy, vicious type of reporting."[20] Mortimer Jordan of the Chamber of Commerce and William P. Engel of a local citizens' group composed a lengthy reply printed in the May 4, 1960, edition of the *Times* refuting the image presented by the paper. The citizens of the Magic City only wanted objectivity and an "open door policy" between the national media, such as the *New York Times,* and the South. Yet the tenor of the reply showed that the articles had struck home and had highlighted the side of Birmingham that most whites refused to acknowledge even existed.[21]

In response, the *Times'* editors made no secret of their "general editorial policy" in favor of integration and equal rights for blacks. Even so, managing editor Turner Catledge acknowledged that Salisbury's article had not stressed the "obvious fact that an overwhelming percentage of the citizens in Birmingham lead happy and peaceful lives in a growing and prosperous community."[22]

Yet Salisbury's portrait seemed all the more accurate when Bull Connor and the other city commissioners dragged the reporter and everyone he interviewed before a grand jury in a libel suit for "false and malicious reporting of racial tensions" by the *New York Times.* Connor believed it was "high time someone put a stop to irresponsible Yankee journalism." Radio, television, and newspaper journalists from the North had forsaken, either through "ignorance or evil intent," the principles of "responsible journalism to cry havoc over victims and situations that don't exist." Salisbury's articles, Connor thought, were a "cheap attempt" to smear the "good name" of Birmingham.[23]

The thin-skinned Birmingham residents, like most white southerners no matter what their racial outlook, had grown weary of the constant criticism from other regions of the country. As one observer of the southern scene noted at the time, "it wasn't so much the race issue as just being constantly criticized in the nation's press, which put so many on the defensive."[24] This was certainly true in Birmingham during the early 1960s.

In Birmingham and other areas of the South, national reporters used a simple formula to cover the racial crises. "We wrote our stories like western movie scenarios," remembered one veteran reporter, and Birmingham emerged as the 1960s version of the O.K. Corral. Birmingham commissioner of public safety Bull Connor was cast as the "big, fat, sloppy sheriff with his cigar, dogs, and cow prods" (the bad guy) and Martin Luther King was the good guy. This type of reporting trapped journalists into presenting every story as a "cops-and-robbers shoot-em-up." Just like those old, worn-out Western plots, press coverage of the South followed the same formula. "There's the good guys, there's the courthouse, there's the bad sheriff," observed another journalist. "Just change the names and the name of the town and the story was already written because this had become a ritual kind of reporting."[25]

Many white southerners, like the eight white clergy addressed in King's letter, complained at the time that, seizing upon the poor behavior of belligerent segregationists, the national press had failed to communicate a fair and complete portrait of the social structure of the region and depicted all white southerners as worse than they really were. Journalist Claude Sitton of the *New York Times* later recognized that national reporters focused almost exclusively on the scene of racial strife in the South and failed to tell readers, for good or bad, that life continued at a normal pace for a majority of citizens.[26]

In reality, there was little doubt Birmingham had tremendous racial problems. By 1963, the city had an ugly past and a bleak future. In his quest for racial justice in Birmingham, Martin Luther King Jr. and other SCLC activists worked to keep the image of the city as the definitive symbol of segregation in the public's eye. "If we can crack Birmingham," King said, "I'm convinced we can crack the South."[27]

By promoting Birmingham as the nation's ultimate example of evil, the civil rights leader was encouraging outside pressure to end segregation. Alabama's largest city was the chief obstacle to racial justice and a problem that must be solved, hence King encouraged his followers, and sympathizers from around the country, to help charge the ramparts of the wicked. He was heightening the sense of crisis in the city by describing Birmingham as the most segregated in America; the "tragic city" (rather than the Magic City); "Old Burninghell" or "Bombingham"; the "Johannesburg of the South"; the "dark city"; "America's most racially bigoted city"; the "worst city on earth (besides Johannesburg, South Africa)"; or a "poor excuse for a city." As events unfolded in April and May 1963, Birmingham had become once again the worst elements of its own image.[28]

While attacking Birmingham's image in general, the movement also focused on the city's individual symbol of segregation, Bull Connor. As one national news magazine reported in 1963, Connor was as much a monument to segregation in Birmingham as Vulcan was a shrine to the city's steel economy. Better dressed than the loin-clothed statue, Connor was notable for stylish hats, horn-rimmed spectacles, dark suits, stiff white shirts, and fashionable ties. A stubby, sweaty man with a roaring voice, Connor had gained notoriety as the radio announcer for the Birmingham Barons baseball team during the 1920s and early 1930s. He used his popularity to launch a political career and soon dominated city politics. During the civil rights era, Connor ruled much of city government with an iron fist and often bragged that he needed just "two policemen and a dog" to solve the city's racial problems.[29]

Connor's image as the typical southern racist politician and his volatile temperament suited the SCLC's purposes well. King's chief lieutenant, Wyatt Walker, knew that if the movement pushed Connor to the edge, he would strike back and benefit their cause. "My theory was that if we mounted a strong nonviolent movement, the opposition would surely do something to attract the media, and in turn induce national sympathy and attention to the everyday segregated circumstance of a black person living in the Deep South," Walker said.[30]

The Reverend Wyatt Tee Walker was the executive director of the Southern Christian Leadership Conference. With a knack for organization and a natural media savvy, Walker directed most of the SCLC's publicity and fund-raising efforts. He considered himself King's chief representative, key administrator, and the behind the scenes "son of a bitch." With the SCLC struggling to find direction in the late 1950s, Martin Luther King asked Walker to bring order and discipline to the organization. While seeking new venues of direct action, King believed he had found an administrator with a broad vision of racial justice and a micro-management style to take care of small details. "I'm strong," an immodest Walker insisted. "I'm proud. And I'm transparent. Anything I tell you I can do, I can do it. And I probably have done it."[31]

Distinguished, somber, and all business, Walker wore fashionable thin-lapeled suits and stiff white shirts with giant spherical cufflinks. His receding hairline came to a V-shape that pointed to a furrowed brow and black horn-rimmed glasses and gave him a sinister appearance. Walker's chronic smoking added to the effect. His cold, calculating eyes and authoritative yet noble voice struck fear into the hearts of SCLC subordinates. A tireless individual with high standards for himself and his staff, Walker worked from early in the morning to late at night during movement activities. He also demanded his staff work the same hours. Oftentimes, his young secretary, Willie Pearl Mackey, would fall asleep at her desk, unable to keep up the pace. "Everything was rush with him," Mackey remembered. "He worked the 'H' out of everybody. I would feel guilty not working right along with him."[32]

Walker's self-confidence, arrogance, forthrightness, and heavy-handed administrative style rubbed many in the SCLC the wrong way. "They thought I was the Ayatollah," Walker later recalled. A poor work ethic or chronic tardiness among SCLC staffers irritated Walker, and he took many of them to task. "We live off the public money," he told one worker, "and you can't come strolling in here at ten minutes after nine with a split sandwich and coffee in your hand. At nine o'clock I want to hear the typewriters singing."[33]

Walker, however, was much more than an able administrator. His natural charisma and a well-developed public relations ability helped keep King and the SCLC in the national spotlight. Although many of Walker's skills were intuitive, he was influenced by George Lawrence, a former newspaper reporter for the influential black newspaper the *Pittsburgh Courier*. After several years in journalism, Lawrence entered the ministry and became the pastor of the prestigious Antioch Baptist Church in Brooklyn, New York. Antioch Baptist was SCLC's leading New York affiliate and Lawrence gladly gave Walker a crash course in basic public relations skills, revealing the knack for finding a journalistic hook and getting a reporter interested in a story.[34]

To keep Martin Luther King in the media spotlight, Walker studied the civil rights leader's style and made mental notes of King's favorite phrases, stories, metaphors, and emotional pleas. "His language was much more florid than mine," Walker later recalled. "I'm a kind of meat and potatoes preacher." Yet Walker had the ability to almost completely assume King's voice in various ghostwritten newspaper articles and speeches.[35]

Regardless, King and Walker's first effort to attract press attention and federal intervention failed. In Albany, Georgia, demonstrations received virtually no positive publicity and no symbols of injustice to be exploited in the media. The SCLC discovered their chief villain, Albany's crafty police chief Laurie Pritchett, was a smooth operator who also recognized the importance of the media. Turning the tables on King and Walker, Pritchett obtained positive press coverage for the segregated South and became, as SCLC officials complained at the time, the "darling of the press." Conversely, the Albany failure damaged King's national image and called into question the use of nonviolent direct action in confronting racial segregation. Martin Luther King needed a victory and Birmingham's Fred Shuttlesworth had the perfect place.[36]

"Birmingham is where it's at, gentlemen," Shuttlesworth told King and other SCLC officials. "I assure you, if you come to Birmingham, we will not only gain prestige but really shake the country. If you win in Birmingham, as Birmingham goes, so goes the nation." King and others in the SCLC agreed, believing that a direct-action campaign in Alabama's largest city would provide a new image for King, restore the power of nonviolence, and bring in some much-needed cash. Eventually, the "Letter from Birmingham Jail" emerged as a key element in realizing each of these goals.

In early January 1963, King and his associates began planning for a mass campaign in Birmingham with Shuttlesworth and his SCLC-affiliated organization, the Alabama Christian Movement for Human Rights. Shuttlesworth saw segregation as the ultimate evil and continued to battle for equality while being beaten, bombed, and arrested. King believed Shuttlesworth was a courageous figure, whose "audacious public defiance" of segregation in Birmingham was an inspiration and a source of encouragement for blacks throughout the region. Yet as one observer noted in 1958, Shuttlesworth was also "head strong and wild for publicity." He remained a marginal figure among Birmingham's black religious leaders—even among those activists confronting segregation. Regardless, his radical and uncompromising attitude remained the perfect foil for Bull Connor.[37]

The key for success in Birmingham, as Martin Luther King instructed Wyatt Walker, was to find a way to make Connor "tip his hand." As journalist Pat Watters observed, the SCLC implemented a cunning strategy in Birmingham by triggering Connor's "stupidity and natural viciousness" as an archfiend and villain for full exploitation in the media. To help create the appearance of a crisis, the movement would "string out" the marches until large crowds of onlookers had assembled. "They'll gather to see what's going to happen," Walker explained to King, "and we can depend on Bull Connor to do something foolish." In turn, more people on the scene meant more drama, intensified a sense of crisis, and resulted in better news coverage. Extensive press reports inspired many Americans to send donations to King and to pressure the federal government to take action. "That's the story of the Birmingham movement," Walker later recalled, "and the key to how we made the maximum use of the media."[38]

Had Bull Connor ignored the protesters, Walker insisted, there would have been no publicity and, in turn, no movement. "I often mused to myself," Walker remembered, " 'Suppose Bull Connor had let us go to city hall and pray?' He was such a stupid man. After four or five days of going to City Hall and praying, there was no story. He didn't have enough sense to understand that. He just kept stopping us and putting people in jail."[39]

Even prior to King's movement in the city, many of Birmingham's citizens hoped to end Connor's political domination. Civic and business leaders had led an effort to replace the old Progressive Era, Connor-controlled, three-man city commission with a mayor–city council form of government.

The move to change the form of government had been a frequent topic of debate in Birmingham politics for more than a dozen years. In 1949, when several adjacent municipalities had voted to stay out of Birmingham, some said it was because of the city commission form of government. By the middle of the 1950s, Jefferson County legislators had passed several laws paving the way for a voter referendum, provided that 10 percent of the eligible voters had signed a petition. In 1957, the first petition drive fell short. Two years later, civic and business groups were grumbling that "Birmingham's present form of government had outlived its usefulness." It took three more years to gather enough voter signatures to call the special election. Those citizens frustrated with the outdated mode of government hailed the election as a revolutionary milestone in Birmingham's short history.[40]

In November 1962, Birmingham citizens, both black and white, voted overwhelmingly in favor of the new government. Another election would be held the following March to elect a new mayor and council. Connor wanted the job of mayor, as did several others, including the moderate segregationist and former Alabama lieutenant governor Albert Boutwell—the favored candidate of the business community.

In contrast to the unpredictable and explosive Connor, Boutwell was a quiet and mild-mannered individual who always chose his words carefully when speaking in public. He avoided sensationalism and self-promotion. Regardless, he was still a segregationist, although a "polite" one, and had sponsored the Alabama Pupil Placement Act, which had allowed the state to avoid compliance with the *Brown* decision. "It is the sheerest folly to resort to panic and pure defiance," Boutwell had once said. "Our resources lie not in disorder but in firm legal resistance."[41]

In his campaign, Boutwell promised a new civic image for Birmingham, much different than the dirty, violent portraits of the past. In turn, Connor scoffed and labeled his rival "The Image"—a public relations puppet of the city's business elites. No candidate received a majority of the votes in the March 5, 1963, election, and the city scheduled a run-off election between Connor and Boutwell on April 2. The race had become a "showdown," Connor proclaimed, "of whether two foreign owned newspapers," the *Birmingham News* and the *Birmingham Post-Herald,* and a bloc vote were "going to rule Birmingham" or whether the people of Birmingham were "going to rule themselves."[42]

On Tuesday, April 2, nearly 75 percent of Birmingham's registered voters participated in the election, giving Boutwell an impressive eight-thousand-vote victory over Connor. Ironically, the press reported that only 50 percent of the city's whites voted for Boutwell. The margin of victory had been decided by a solid block of the eight thousand registered black voters. "The newspapers didn't beat me," Connor claimed after the election, "the Negro vote did."[43]

The next morning Boutwell proclaimed the dawn of a new era in Birmingham and pointed to the optimistic spirit of citizens. A *Birmingham News* editorial cartoonist captured the spirit (and the feelings of many local residents) in a front-page drawing of a bright sun rising over the city. For many in Birmingham, this was a watershed event—one whose significance was more than just symbolic. A majority of the citizens of Birmingham had tossed aside the belligerent segregationists in city hall in favor of less confrontational regime; one that on the surface, at least, appeared much more accommodating. Yet as the new mayor celebrated his victory, two dozen nervous protesters invaded lunch counters at four downtown stores.[44]

At the beginning of the movement, King restated his commitment to nonviolence and emphasized the special mission blacks had to end segregation. "You must always refuse to use violence on your opponent," he said. "I know sometimes this is hard to do, but our cause is great and noble, no physical violence and no violence of spirit. Remember our white brothers are just misguided. We are not going to give up and we must let them know that, but we must not lower our love for our white brother."[45]

King and other movement leaders had apparently postponed the beginning of the demonstrations on two different occasions to avoid disrupting the election and the campaigning. Although they later denied this point, the movement needed Bull Connor in office to provide the violence and the national publicity needed to reveal the injustices of segregation to the American public.[46]

Fortunately for King and the movement, hopes for a smooth transition of city governments were dashed when Connor and lame-duck city commissioners James "Jabo" Waggoner and Art Hanes contested the election, contending that their terms of office did not expire until November 1965. The commissioners refused to relinquish government control until the Alabama Supreme Court ruled on the case. Boutwell and the new city council, however, were determined to take the oath of office on April 15. The prospect of two governments operating simultaneously led *Birmingham News* managing editor John Bloomer to quip that Birmingham was the "only city in the world with two mayors and a King."[47]

Unpredictable politics seemed a natural expression of the city's frontier mentality. This was not the first time Birmingham had two competing municipal governments. A fight over licensing fees among local breweries in 1907 had prompted an anti-prohibition faction to change the form of city government in an effort to oust prohibition-minded mayor George Ward. Ward, who was in Europe at the time of the coup, returned to find John L. Parker the new mayor. As uncompromising on the issue of prohibition as Bull Connor would be on segregation, Ward brought a pistol and a company of armed supporters to a city council meeting in September 1907 in an effort to maintain control. An astonished minister ran from the meeting into the streets of Birmingham predicting a "terrible slaughter in city hall." No violence occurred, however. Ward's display of grit and determination led to Birmingham's becoming a dry city on January 1, 1908.[48]

Over fifty years after the Ward controversy, Connor was equally determined to hold on to his power. He remained in firm control of the police and fire departments. "I don't know how long I will be here," Connor declared, "but King can rest assured that as long as I am here, he better tell his crowd not to violate any laws." He predicted that he would "fill that jail full if Negroes violate segregation laws." Of course this was what the movement hoped for.[49]

As Connor maintained control, King announced four goals to help blacks realize racial justice in Birmingham: desegregation of lunch counters and other public facilities, fair hiring practices, charges dropped against demonstrators, and the establishment of a biracial commission with the power to institute peaceful school desegregation plans. The plan built on earlier student protest efforts. A year before, during the spring of 1962, local black college students had organized and implemented a boycott of Birmingham businesses. The student movement had almost identical objectives to King's demands, including desegregation and fair hiring practices. The boycott proved highly successful, with Easter sales dropping some 12 percent below 1961 levels, until it faded during the early summer. The students had provided many of Birmingham's black citizenry a new spark of energy in confronting segregation. In turn, local merchants were also willing to negotiate. During the fall, the student efforts and the prospect of mass demonstrations led by King during the SCLC convention of September had prompted local stores to remove the "colored only" signs. Connor, however, saw to it that the signs quickly returned. When the demonstrations began in April 1963, Fred Shuttlesworth insisted to the press that demonstrations had occurred because the business community had reneged on the September desegregation pledge.[50]

After the first day of protests, the arrest of demonstrators at Britt's lunch counter inside the J. J. Newberry's department store on Nineteenth Street North proceeded with little attention from average citizens. Birmingham's whites and the two major newspapers focused on the change in city government, the beginning of spring practice for Paul "Bear" Bryant's University of Alabama football team, and the hometown movie premiere of Harper Lee's *To Kill a Mockingbird* at the Melba Theater. Huge crowds jammed the street in front of the theater to catch a glimpse of the movie's two child stars: Birmingham natives Mary Badham and Phillip Alford. Ironically, the story line depicted white bigotry and black injustice in Alabama during the 1930s and illustrated the meaningful role a paternalistic, decent, and moderate white southerner could play during a racial crisis. Regardless, the movie apparently had little impact on the racial outlook of Birmingham's white community during the spring of 1963.[51]

Albert Boutwell believed the people of Birmingham had given him a mandate to solve the city's problems. "I pledge to you, all our citizens," Boutwell proclaimed, "that I will work for a solution." The vast majority of Birmingham residents had a "deep and abiding respect for law and order and for their fellow man." The new mayor urged local blacks to consider carefully before they followed the leadership of strangers. The protestors were people who only wanted to "stir strife and discord here and then who will leave our citizens to pay the penalty of this discord, once they have worked their mischief and have put upon us, whites and Negroes, an atmosphere of tension and violence." Demonstrations and sit-ins would accomplish nothing, Boutwell believed. "I do not need to tell the people of Birmingham that this is an attempt to stage a big show . . . to make headlines throughout the country," he said. King and the demonstrators were more interested in sensational headlines to raise money than in the welfare of the black community. "Birmingham must not give these outside agitators an opportunity to be glorified," he added. "I urge everyone, white and Negro, calmly to ignore what is now being attempted in Birmingham."[52]

With this in mind, editors of the two local daily newspapers, the *Birmingham News* and the *Birmingham Post-Herald,* decided to downplay coverage of the demonstrations. On April 4, a *Birmingham News* editorial called on citizens to ignore the demonstrators. These outsiders created "strife and discord" in the city's streets and only desired headlines and publicity. Prophetically, the *News* predicted that they would receive media coverage in full measure if the demonstrators provoked the city. But at the time, their "sideshow" was "playing to an empty house." A *Post-Herald* editorialist believed local black leaders needed to "send the trouble-makers away" and end the lawlessness they promoted. The demonstrations had accomplished nothing beneficial for Birmingham's black community. "On the other hand, they created racial friction, risked the possibility of serious trouble and made it impossible to continue" efforts to solve local problems.[53]

During the preceding months, the two papers featured page-one stories on civil rights demonstrations in other areas of the South. During early April 1963, editors buried small stories on the Birmingham protests in the interior pages. This editorial decision made few people happy. Alabama governor George Wallace complained of a complete blackout of news coming out of the state's largest city. "News is news," he stressed. In his quest for more extensive press reports, Wallace had an "unwilling ally" in civil rights activist Fred Shuttlesworth. Shuttlesworth hoped Birmingham's newspaper publishers would get the message that the demonstrations had become "front page business" in Alabama. The black leader recognized the irony and humor in agreeing with George Wallace. "I think Mr. George wants to come in to see what we're doing," Shuttlesworth told a group of supporters. "Well, let's do a great big job so when he comes around to see what we're doing, we'll ask him to help us. Come on in, Mr. George, we're all here."[54]

While Shuttlesworth, Martin Luther King, and other SCLC officials hoped for positive news coverage, the press and the public showed little interest during the first few days of the movement. The demonstrations to win the "heart and conscience" of Birmingham's population met stiff resistance not only from local segregationists, but from gradualists and liberals of both races too, as well as a flood of national criticism. The first extensive news coverage occurred after a violent confrontation with Birmingham police on Sunday, April 7. Bull Connor provided the brutal images of segregation that Walker and the SCLC had looked for when he released a squad of growling police dogs. Walker jumped for joy and proclaimed over and over: "We've got a movement. We've got a movement. We had some police brutality. They brought out the dogs. We've got a movement."[55] Nevertheless, Connor quickly withdrew the symbols of brutality and the media once again lost interest.

To help ease rising tensions in Birmingham, the new mayor and members of the new council, not yet in office, promised to openly discuss black grievances in return for King's withdrawal. The Justice Department and Attorney General Robert Kennedy urged a postponement of demonstrations until Boutwell and the new council were in firm control. America's foremost white evangelist, the Reverend Billy Graham, believed King had complicated the racial situation in Birmingham. The timing of mass protests was questionable, and Graham urged civil rights leaders to "put the brakes on a little bit." The minister hoped to see a "period of quietness in which moderation prevailed."[56]

The *Washington Post* editorialized that a "few weeks more without direct action in Birmingham was a short time to wait to see if political action were successful." A few days later, the *Post* called marches on

Palm Sunday of "doubtful utility." Birmingham has already achieved a victory, or a near victory, through the best possible way, the democratic election process. "This administration deserves a fair trial." *Time* magazine also criticized the SCLC campaign as a "poorly timed protest" and noted that for many blacks in Birmingham, King's efforts had "inflamed tensions at a time when the city seemed to be making some progress, however small, in race relations." Within a few days, a group of Birmingham's most progressive clergy would join this chorus of mainstream critics and denounce the poor timing of King's protest.[57]

In the Magic City, black responses to King and the demonstrations varied. "To whites who have always thought of the Negro segment of this community as representing a phalanx of single-minded people," one northern journalist observed, "it often comes as quite a shock to learn that the average Negro community is as splintered and divided as the average white community."[58]

Emory O. Jackson, the editor of the black newspaper the *Birmingham World* was among the most outspoken critics during the early days of the campaign. Jackson questioned the wisdom of King's tactics to end segregation. The editor saw "room for discussion over the timing, the tactics, but not the big target—enforced racial segregation and its by-products." Jackson branded direct-action campaigns "wasteful and worthless" and pleaded with all responsible citizens to show a degree of restraint in the community's best interest. To confront the complex issues of segregation and racial discrimination, the editor concluded, the black community needed a diversified plan of attack. As with many traditional black leaders, Jackson believed the court system was the proper battle ground for civil rights.[59]

Immediate integration and equality through a "one-blow, knockout punch" (via direct action) was too much to expect, the editor wrote. As a "quickie, shortcut" method, King's primary tactic was easily abused or misused. This was clear, Jackson believed, when direct action degenerated into a "deliberate disrespect of the law" and the court system. Jim Crow laws were bad laws and needed to be destroyed wherever they existed, he emphasized. "But it can be knocked-out by due process." Following the due process of law allowed the implementation of direct action to enforce court decisions, not vice versa.[60]

Other black leaders also remained skeptical of King. Millionaire and conservative civil leader A. G. Gaston opposed the demonstrations and called on black citizens to rally around "local colored" leaders, and for both races to work together in a harmonious spirit of brotherly love to solve the racial conflict. Overall the city's black pastors provided only lukewarm support for King's campaign. Wyatt Walker later estimated that fewer than 10 percent of Birmingham's black clergy participated in the movement. The Reverend J. L. Ware, one of Birmingham's most prominent and influential black ministers and a longtime outspoken critic of segregation, trumpeted the bad timing of King's campaign. Other black pastors uncomfortable with the prominent leadership role of Fred Shuttlesworth in the demonstrations were also critical. King countered the ministers with a powerful theological sermon, stressing the addition of the social gospel to enrich the gospel of individual salvation (a point later emphasized in the "Letter from Birmingham Jail"). King surmised that a "dry as dust" Christianity prompted a "minister to extol the glories of heaven while ignoring the social conditions that caused man an earthly hell." The true witness of a Christian, he avowed, was a commitment to social concerns and the greatest example of an "inner, spiritual church." "If you can't stand up with your people," King told Birmingham's black ministers, "you are not fit to be a preacher."[61]

His persuasive argument before the ministers on Monday, April 8, earned King vocal support from the black clergy, including a unanimous statement of support by Ware's Baptist Ministers' Conference. King believed that any mass demonstration had to face the outcries from those who said it was poorly timed. "Our cup of endurance runneth over," he said. The demonstrations had been planned for the day after the election, no matter the victor, and would test the good faith of Birmingham's new image. He had no plans to stop. Protestors would use some form of nonviolent direct action in Birmingham every day, King predicted, until "peaceful equality" had been assured. The civil rights leader added that he believed the new mayor would never desegregate the city voluntarily. In a few weeks, King and the SCLC used the "Letter from Birmingham Jail" (and the eight clergymen) as a way to provide a detailed answer to these widespread criticisms. King, however, needed more than a verbal argument to sway skeptical blacks to accept his tactics and physically champion his crusade. He must present himself as a living sacrifice for the movement and demonstrate the power of nonviolence in breaking down the barriers of segregation. This was certainly of symbolic importance for many African Americans in Birmingham.[62]

Since the campaign's commencement, many blacks wondered if King was indeed willing to go to jail and present his body as a personal witness in this crusade for racial justice. As the movement's primary spokes-man and fund-raiser, King needed to stay out of jail to rally the faithful and to recruit more disciples. The suspense and speculation increased as the civil rights leader waited for the most strategic time to brave an arrest. During the early days of the movement, King told supporters that he would face imprisonment, because it was better to "go to jail in dig-nity than to accept segregation." The anticipation grew at a mass rally in the First Baptist Church of Ensley on Monday, April 8, when King's closest friend and associate, the Reverend Ralph Abernathy, announced that he and King were leading a crowd of protestors to jail during the middle of that week. "Are you going to jail with me?" Abernathy asked the crowd. The eyes of the media and the nation would be upon every-one involved. "If you go with me President Kennedy will be looking in, Lyndon Johnson will be looking in and Old Bull will be shaking in his boots," he assured them. King, however, postponed leading a demon-stration several times before announcing the decision to lead a march on Good Friday. "Ralph Abernathy and I will make our move. I can't think of a better day than Good Friday for a move for freedom," he told an enthusiastic crowd at the Wednesday, April 10, rally. On Good Friday, Jesus had made the ultimate sacrifice at Calvary, and now King symboli-cally followed in his footsteps to free a captive people.[63]

The same evening King announced the Good Friday march, Bir-mingham city attorneys received an ex parte injunction from Circuit Judge William A. Jenkins, forbidding King and over a hundred other movement participants from sponsoring, encouraging, or participating in mass demonstrations without a permit. King had received word early in the day on Wednesday that the injunction would be served. When Jef-ferson County deputy sheriff Raymond E. Belcher entered the restaurant at the Gaston Motel a few minutes after 1 A.M., King and Walker had assembled a group of reporters to witness and record the event. Belcher served the papers and quickly exited as cameramen snapped pictures of King, Abernathy, and Shuttlesworth reading the injunction. Shuttles-worth called the injunction a "flagrant denial of our constitutional rights" that would "in no way . . . retard the thrust of this movement." Following the brief show for the media, King instructed Walker to pre-pare a formal press statement in response to the injunction and schedule another news conference for the next morning. The decision to disobey the injunction had been made several weeks before, at a March meeting in entertainer Harry Belafonte's New York apartment. There, King and movement leaders decided that if the courts issued an injunction to discourage demonstrations, "it would be our duty to violate it."[64]

At a Thursday morning press conference, King, Abernathy, and Shuttlesworth appeared before the assembled press dressed in denim work clothes, the movement's "sacrificial uniform," as they called it. King read from Walker's prepared statement and announced that in good conscience he could not obey an injunction that was an "unjust, undemocratic, and unconstitutional misuse of the legal process." The civil rights leader told the media he would lead the Good Friday march, go to jail, and stay as long as necessary. Previously, King and the SCLC had obeyed federal injunctions "out of respect for the forthright and consistent leadership" of the higher courts in integration matters. "However," he continued, "we are now confronted with recalcitrant forces in the Deep South that will use the courts to perpetuate the unjust and illegal systems of racial separation."[65]

Abernathy told reporters at the gathering that Christ had died on the cross nearly two thousand years ago and "tomorrow we will take it up for our people and die if necessary." Fred Shuttlesworth later agreed that the decision to send King to jail was symbolic. "It came at a time when the whole Jesus on the Cross significance was before the whole world for Easter," Shuttlesworth said. As King wanted, the movement "transformed the jails into church houses."[66]

Not leaving anything to chance, Wyatt Walker telephoned Birmingham Police chief inspector W. J. Haley and announced the decision to "make a march" to City Hall on Good Friday at 12:15 P.M. "In my opinion," Haley told Walker, "that would be a violation of the city ordinance." The inspector told Walker to obtain a permit or face certain arrest. "Convey that information to Martin Luther," he added.[67] Walker was providing police with the exact time and approximate location to ensure an arrest and, he hoped, plenty of press coverage.

That Thursday night at a mass meeting in the Sixth Avenue Baptist Church, Abernathy reiterated the pledge to march to City Hall on Good Friday. "We are going to turn this town upside down and inside out tomorrow," he told the crowd. "I'm not going to fail tomorrow and M. L. King's not going to fail tomorrow and lots more of us are not going to fail tomorrow. . . . We are going to a higher judge than Judge Jenkins."[68]

Later that evening, the bondsman who worked for the movement notified SCLC officials that funds were insufficient to continue providing bail. That "decision" was so distressing, King later recalled, "that it threatened to ruin the movement." Privately King began rethinking his decision to participate in the march. The movement had a moral responsibility to the people in jail. The easiest way to raise the much-needed funds for bail was for King to leave Birmingham and crisscross the country speaking to large crowds and passing the offering plate—after all, he was the movement's principal fund-raiser. Yet King had given a promise to march. For hours he agonized over the decision. Perhaps, his incarceration would give the movement a crucial boost and would perhaps provide extensive national press coverage. But what of the bail money?[69]

On Good Friday morning, King had awakened with the rising sun and immediately began praying, still searching for an answer. King and Ralph Abernathy refused to eat breakfast that morning, beginning a day of fasting—their customary ritual before "making a witness" by going to jail. As the morning wore on, King's closest friends and aides slowly gathered behind the pastel-painted door of his hotel suite, room 30 on the upper tier of the Gaston Motel. A. G. Gaston had opened the motel in 1954 because blacks had no place to stay in Birmingham. "Negroes needed a good high class motel," Gaston once said, "so I built one." Ever the pragmatist and opportunist, the black business leader had a simple philosophy: "Find a need and fill it. Successful businesses are founded on the needs of people."[70]

The needs of the people of Birmingham were at the forefront of King's mind that Good Friday. "I have never seen Martin so troubled," one associate later said. "He knew it was vital to keep up the morale of those already jailed, and he knew how it might flag if bond couldn't be posted for them at the time they expected to be released." The civil rights leader listened attentively to the advice of his counselors. Wyatt Walker frequently darted out of the discussion to apprise news reporters and order subordinates in rapid-fire "ten second encounters." In King's room, some urged postponing the march until the following week, when more money might be in the SCLC's coffers. The civil rights leader, however, thought the "movement was mushrooming" and waiting might ease passions and press interest. Sitting in a small, low-resting chair, King stood up and retreated into his bedroom for a few moments of solitude and prayer. He soon emerged from the room and announced his intent to march. "The path is clear to me," he said. "I've got to march. I've got so many people depending on me. I've got to march." He hugged his father and shook hands with his friends. Following a final prayer, King and his associates hurried to the Zion Hill Church.[71]

6   The Prison Epistle

Martin Luther King Jr. was late. A cheerful gathering of churchgoers had waited over two hours anticipating the civil rights leader's appearance. Lengthy prayers, old spirituals, and assorted warm-up speakers maintained the audience's enthusiasm in the small sanctuary of the Sixth Avenue Zion Hill Baptist Church. The church seemed to overflow this day, Good Friday, April 12, 1963: those inside packed every inch of seating space, while others stood in the aisles, and a few curious souls peeked through the back doors hoping to catch a glimpse of King. Other members of Birmingham's black community lined the front stairs of the church and the sidewalks of Sixth Avenue North. A few whites were on hand as well, mostly an assortment of journalists and a collection of police officers, both plainclothes detectives and uniformed patrolmen. They all waited. King's civil rights activities almost never ran on time, because, as one participant explained, the movement was "on eternity's time."[1]

Wearing matching gray fatigue shirts and denim work pants, King, Abernathy, and Shuttlesworth finally arrived at the Zion Hill Baptist Church at nearly 2 P.M. Zion Hill was a little over a block from the Gaston Motel, near the corner of Fourteenth Street and Sixth Avenue North. The church building was unremarkable, with four square brick columns supporting a small portico and four narrow steps leading from the sidewalk to the front doors. Founded in the late 1930s, the congregation dwelt in the shadow of the large, powerful, and patriarchal Sixteenth

Street Baptist Church. On Good Friday 1963, however, the small church emerged as the focus of attention.

Only fifty official protestors had volunteered to join King in his march to jail. They were mostly well-dressed young black men and women from Birmingham (King and Abernathy were the only two out-of-towners). Many were of college age; others were as young as fifteen. One white man participated, Robert Brank Fulton, a professor at the black Miles College. The two senior citizens of the group were Henry Haynes, at age eighty-one, and Lila Baylor, sixty-one. Throughout the Birmingham campaign, a handful of elderly blacks served as a source of inspiration to many of the younger protesters. "We didn't have no opportunities when we was coming up," one said at a movement rally, "so we don't mind risking our lives for our grandchildren. What else we got to live for?"[2] From the Zion Hill pulpit, King told the crowd that only a "redemptive influence of suffering" would change Birmingham. The civil rights leader hoped to provide a true model of suffering by marching to jail as "a good servant of my Lord and Master, who was crucified on Good Friday." As the civil rights trio moved toward the doorway, someone in the crowd looked at King and said: "There he goes, just like Jesus."[3]

Christians had always celebrated Good Friday as a day of marching and suffering. Jesus had dragged a wooden cross through the streets of Jerusalem on his journey to crucifixion and certain death. Now King had stepped forward from his Gethsemane in the Gaston Motel to pick up that cross and march for racial justice. Singing the movement anthem "We Shall Overcome," the official protesters stepped through Zion Hill's double doors, with King, Abernathy, and Shuttlesworth leading the way. They quickly descended the stairs and marched along the north side of Sixth Avenue's broad sidewalks; with Shuttlesworth closest to the street, King in the middle, and Abernathy on his left. They passed a few shotgun houses (so named because of their long, slender shape and the notion that a shotgun blast through the front entry would pass straight out the back door), Mary's Sandwich Shop, the Sixth Avenue Meat Market, and Mrs. Gussie Smith's house. Despite the forecast for rain, this was a pleasant spring day: some clouds billowed about and the temperature was a mild seventy-three degrees. Spring had arrived early in Birmingham this year; the dogwood trees had already reached their peak, and the bright white blooms had changed to their summer green.[4]

Parked automobiles lined the streets as the marchers advanced. After only a short distance, Shuttlesworth quietly slipped behind and left the march. He had briefly joined the march because, as he later said, "the symbols of the movement should be seen together." He had hoped to stay out of jail to make further plans, but Birmingham police would later arrest him as well.[5]

Leading the marchers side by side in columns of two, King and Abernathy proceeded in the afternoon sun, both carrying coats draped over one arm for warmth in the cold Birmingham Jail. They crossed Fifteenth Street and passed St. Paul's Methodist, Mrs. Lucille Parker's furnished rooms, some apartments, and the imposing Sixteenth Street Baptist Church.[6]

Spectators lined the marchers' path—sometimes three and four people deep—most standing on the lawns of houses. Out of respect, many wore Sunday clothes: women in crisp white dresses and little girls in frilly Easter apparel; men and boys in ties and dress slacks. Another large group of blacks shadowed the demonstrators from across the street: some jumped, clapped, and shouted words of encouragement; others sang freedom songs; some knelt on the sidewalk in silence. Elderly men pulled their hats from their heads and left them dangling between their fingers or placed them over their hearts. A plump, older woman in a fashionable dress and bleached white gloves knelt with a little boy. She wept as the civil rights leader passed by.[7]

Before the march began, King had given Wyatt Walker specific instructions: "Wyatt, whatever you do, don't you get arrested." Looking more like a member of the press, Walker brought along his camera and snapped photographs that would help him begin obtaining extensive press coverage and dramatic symbols of brutal segregation. As the demonstrators moved along, Walker chatted in a friendly manner with members of the Birmingham police force and other law enforcement officials. "I did not know you took pictures," he told a bemused Willie B. Painter, who was documenting the march for Alabama Department of Public Safety.[8]

Birmingham police had placed barricades along the marchers' route and prevented automobile traffic from entering the area. Over eighty police officers were on the scene, including forty-eight patrolmen on three- and two-wheel motorcycles; at least a dozen plain-clothes detectives and special-detail men; and scores of other officers, who trooped around on foot. Three patrol wagons and five or six squad cars swarmed around the vicinity. Police moved all white spectators out of the district, as one officer later said, to "keep any breach of the peace from happening" and to protect the people "inciting trouble" (the marchers). The only whites allowed to observe were the police and members of the press. Newspaper photographers, TV cameramen, and reporters swarmed around the marchers like scores of bumblebees attacking an early-spring yellow bell bush.[9]

Moving at a moderate pace, the protesters crossed Sixteenth Street and encountered a barricade in the next block at the intersection of Sixth Avenue and Seventeenth Street. Catching the Birmingham police off guard, King, Abernathy, and the marchers suddenly crossed the street and moved south on Seventeenth Street (alongside Kelly Ingram Park) away from City Hall and toward the central business district. After another block, the marchers turned left on Fifth Avenue and walked alongside the Parkview Barbecue and the Run-a-Ford Auto Rental. Police caught up with them near a Hill's supermarket. Eugene "Bull" Connor stood in the middle of the street and bellowed, "Stop them. . . . Don't let them go any farther." King's group had marched a little over three blocks.[10]

A lanky patrolman wearing a shiny white helmet and aviator sunglasses pulled his motorcycle on to the sidewalk and into the marchers' path. He snapped down the kickstand and whirled off his vehicle and stomped toward King and Abernathy. A three-wheel motorcart also pulled onto the sidewalk, as paddy wagons and police cruisers screeched to a halt in the street. King, Abernathy, and many of the other marchers immediately dropped to their knees on the sidewalk and bowed their heads in prayer. Another officer gave the motorcycle patrolmen orders, and he brought King to his feet. Abernathy also stood up, and the patrolmen hurried the pair into the street. Pudgy, middle-aged Jack Warren, head of the patrol division, stepped over and gingerly squeezed the back of King's black leather belt and led him away. King waited calmly as Warren unlocked the side door to the police vehicle. The other patrolman grabbed Abernathy by the back of his shirt and propelled him toward a waiting van. Other officers arrested the balance of the protesters and headed toward the Birmingham Jail, located at 501 Sixth Avenue on the city's south side.[11]

Some years earlier Bull Connor had planted the first of four hundred rose bushes in an effort to transform the jail, often called the "Southside Hilton," into a botanical showcase for the city. Assistant wardens dressed in blue wash trousers, regulation blue police shirts, and black bow ties led King through the heavy iron doors up to the second floor of the "new" building, erected in 1912, and placed the civil rights leader in an isolation cell—supposedly for his own protection.[12]

The fifty-four-square-foot third isolation cell had only a few scant furnishings for King: a six-foot cot with metal slats and no mattress, a sink, a toilet, a metallic mirror on the back wall, and no overhead light. The burden of absolute solitude greatly distressed King and sent him descending into a period of deep depression. The civil rights leader recalled those hours as the "most frustrating and bewildering" he had ever lived. He pondered the effect his jail term had on the movement, fund-raising, and community morale.[13]

While King had time to contemplate his predicament, Wyatt Walker remained at the scene of the arrest and worked to keep the restless crowd of onlookers calm. Several of the black spectators had grown agitated as Birmingham police officers attempted to scatter the mass of people. As the crowd moved down the street back toward Kelly Ingram Park, Walker waved his arms around like a windmill on a breezy day, instructing the crowd to make "one circle around the block." As the onlookers milled about, police moved in and dispersed the group. Many gathered with Walker on the steps of the Sixteenth Street Baptist Church for an impromptu prayer and song service.[14]

Walker quickly returned to his office in the A. L. Smith Building at Fifth Avenue and Fifteenth Street, across Kelly Ingram Park from the Gaston Motel. He immediately began calling press contacts and relaying the story of the Good Friday march. Walker also phoned a long list of King's most ardent supporters and requested that they begin contacting the White House. "I was hoping to get the nation all upset about Dr. King in jail," Walker remembered.[15]

Around seven-thirty that evening, NAACP Legal Defense and Education Fund attorney Norman Amaker attempted to visit King at the jail. For over three hours Amaker tried to persuade jail officials to permit a confidential meeting with the civil rights leader. They refused a private meeting, but Amaker could meet with his client with guards present. Amaker balked. He immediately relayed the news to Walker and returned to the Gaston Motel. In turn, Walker phoned a civil rights official in the U.S. Attorney General's Office and later sent a telegram to President John F. Kennedy, requesting the president use the influence of his office "to persuade the city officials of Birmingham to afford at least a modicum of human treatment" for the imprisoned movement leaders.[16]

According to most historical accounts, police held King incommunicado for at least twenty-four hours. At the time, however, Birmingham police chief Jamie Moore called those claims ridiculous. "Apparently some people think our jail is to be used as office with frequent long distance calls and press conference," Moore barked at a reporter. "We have rules and regulations." Perhaps the police chief was correct. Ralph Abernathy later said that it had "never occurred to us that we might be entitled to call a lawyer ourselves." Apparently the leaders chose to quietly submit to the tactics of the Birmingham Police Department for the publicity. Jail administrators wanted King bailed out as soon as possible, but movement officials insisted that King remain in jail. "My instructions were not to bail him out," Amaker later recalled. "I could have done that anytime. They knew that. Everybody knew that." King had to remain behind bars, Amaker recognized, "to focus the attention of the media and national public opinion on the Birmingham situation."[17]

The next morning, Amaker and local attorneys Orzell Billingsley and Arthur Shores went to see Bull Connor in City Hall and gained permission to go see King. Amaker returned to the jail for a brief visit. On Sunday afternoon, Billingsley and Shores met with King, and on Monday attorney Clarence Jones made a lengthy visit. At some point during these visits by the movement legal trust, King apparently read or received news of a published statement by a group of eight white clergy from Birmingham. Unlike King's other confrontations in Birmingham, this campaign would not take place on the streets or at a lunch counter, but in the pages of America's newspapers, journals, and magazines.[18]

If King read the statement in the newspaper then someone presented him a copy of the Saturday Birmingham papers (the morning *Post-Herald* or the afternoon *News*) or perhaps the Sunday *New York Times*. Exactly when and how he read the statement remains unclear and confusing.[19]

Wyatt Walker later indicated that he had "relayed the news" of the statement to the jailed civil rights leader. Most likely, Walker had sent King the newspaper and urged a written response. The "Letter from Birmingham Jail" could have been addressed to any one of the chorus of critics from throughout the country. Yet for the accomplished public relations strategists in the SCLC, this seemed a golden opportunity for publicity: an entire media crusade centered on the biblical image of a lone apostolic leader, confined to a jail cell, writing a letter of admonishment and love to his accusers and fellow churchmen.[20]

This scenario seems likely, since someone other than King had the initial idea of publishing a response to the eight white ministers in Birmingham. In the Sunday, April 14, *New York Times,* journalist Foster Hailey reported that unidentified individuals in Birmingham were "drawing up an answer" to the eight clerics. They planned to tell the white clergy that the time for compromise had passed and blacks in Birmingham wanted an immediate move toward integration. Waiting was no longer an option. Since the *Times'* Sunday edition deadline was Saturday at approximately 3:30 P.M. (Central Time), it seemed unlikely that King had received and read a copy of the statement and relayed the information via a brief attorney's visit to movement headquarters and then to Hailey. Most likely Wyatt Walker had leaked word of an already planned prison letter to the *Times* correspondent.[21]

On the surface, the production of the "Letter from Birmingham Jail" appeared to be a spontaneous event, with little or no planning involved. From the beginning to the end, King and Walker had planned the Birmingham campaign to secure maximum press coverage. Like the letter itself, the Birmingham movement was a culmination of all of King's ideas, theology, experiences, and civil rights tactics. Remarkably, the idea of producing a document like the letter had been in place for some time. What King and the movement needed was the perfect moment, the appropriate place, the right immediate audience in the eight Birmingham clergy, and an impassioned press corps.

The idea of publicly rebuking southern white religious leaders had long appealed to the civil rights leader. King had even considered writing a piece in the form of an open letter on several occasions prior to the Birmingham campaign. At the close of the 1950s, King joined the editorial staff of the *Christian Century* with hopes of writing "occasional articles and letters" to influence Protestant leadership and express his deep disappointment in the white church. Previously, in his book on the Montgomery Bus Boycott, King had foreshadowed his future Birmingham composition by noting that "with individual exceptions the white ministers, from whom I had naively expected so much, gave little." Yet several months after joining the *Christian Century,* editors planned a special Christmas issue with a series of open letters "in such a form that they can actually be sent to the people to whom they are addressed as well as appearing in the columns of the magazine." King, however, did not write a public letter at this time, but perhaps deemed this a worthwhile avenue to reach the public at large.[22]

During the Albany movement of 1962, the idea of a prison epistle penned by King foreshadowed the Birmingham document and its media campaign. Harvey Shapiro of the *New York Times* had contacted SCLC officials and solicited King to write a letter during his incarceration in the small south Georgia town. For some reason, perhaps due to the extensive problems in Albany and the poor press coverage, the idea was dismissed. A Chicago lawyer and King adviser, Chauncey Eskridge, following a consultation with Billy Graham's public relations specialist, had advised King to not write anything for the mass media while in jail. The notion of a prison epistle was simply postponed for a year, until all the factors seemed perfect for King and the SCLC to compose and release the letter.[23]

If King read the statement in the Saturday, April 13, edition of the *Birmingham News,* he saw a rather nondescript story on page two under the headline "White clergymen urge local Negroes to withdraw from demonstrations." Editors had placed the statement directly under a photograph of King, Abernathy, and a line of demonstrators—the caption read "chanting marchers end in jail." The clergymen's names, Carpenter, Durick, Grafman, Hardin, Harmon, Murray, Ramage, and Stallings, appeared in alphabetical order before a complete text of the statement.[24]

Martin Luther King began writing his response under "somewhat constricting" conditions—writing around the margins of the newspaper in which the white ministers' statement appeared. During a brief, guard-supervised exercise period, Ralph Abernathy had a whispered conversation with King about writing the response. "Did they give you anything to write on?" Abernathy asked. "No," King replied, "I'm using toilet paper." Apparently a generous black jail attendant provided King with additional scraps of paper for the essay, and later in the week, SCLC attorneys provided a notepad.[25]

As he began the rough outlines of the letter, King's only light in his jail cell was scant daylight deflected from a small opening high atop the back wall. "You will never know the meaning of utter darkness," King later wrote, "until you have lain in such a dungeon, knowing that sunlight is streaming overhead and still seeing only darkness below." As late as Friday, April 19, New York attorney Stanley Levison complained that King still had no light in his jail cell.[26]

Back at movement headquarters, Wyatt Walker informed his personal secretary, Willie Pearl Mackey, that Dr. King was writing an answer to the white ministers' statement. The response was coming soon, Walker warned Mackey, and she should be prepared to "do her best at typing the letter." The twenty-one-year-old secretary had a passion for racial justice. Born in a rural Georgia farming community in 1941, Mackey had moved to Atlanta following her high school graduation in the late 1950s. She confronted racial injustice at one of her first jobs as a "counter girl" at a popular Emory University student eatery called "The Den." During the 1960 sit-in movement, a group of white students donned blackface and used the lunch counter for a "prank photograph." Deeply offended, Mackey walked off the job and never returned. She quickly found employment in food service at Atlanta's Piedmont Hospital and began studying business at Georgia State University. One afternoon, she watched in horror as an elderly coworker was denied treatment for a heart attack because the hospital refused to treat blacks. Mackey and several other employees quit in protest.[27]

Once again looking for work, Mackey found a kindred soul in her neighbor, Dorothy Cotton, the director of the Citizenship Education Program for the Southern Christian Leadership Conference. With Cotton's encouragement, the young woman applied for a job opening as a secretary with the SCLC. Hired in February 1962, Mackey's passion and dedication impressed Wyatt Walker, and within a few months, the SCLC executive asked her to work as his private secretary. "I was very insecure in the beginning," Mackey remembered, but the other secretaries helped her satisfy Walker's demands. "He was a no nonsense person," she added. "He had an arrogant streak about him. He's a perfectionist, but I'm glad our paths crossed. He was caring; a teacher." She quickly learned how to handle many of Walker's public relations responsibilities, including typing and distributing press releases, directing media contacts, and receiving fund-raising contributions. Since she typed most of the media releases, Mackey would understandably type the "Letter from Birmingham Jail."[28]

King apparently used his attorneys to shuttle notes and drafts of the letter to and from Walker. Arthur Shores, Orzell Billingsley, Norman Amaker, and Clarence Jones all claimed that they served as couriers. Jones remembered one visit in particular, where King pulled the newspaper containing the white ministers' statement from under his shirt and explained the strange scrawl of handwriting around the margins of the paper. "I'm writing this letter," he told Jones. "I want you to try to get it out, if you can."[29]

At movement headquarters, Walker began receiving the scraps of paper filled with King's "chicken scratched" handwriting. During the week the civil rights leader was in jail, Walker slowly began piecing together the literary jigsaw puzzle, matching sentences, words, and phrases and placing them into logical order. Throughout the day and into the night, Walker buzzed through the office and deposited scraps of paper onto Willie Mackey's desk, and she began typing the first drafts of the letter on her IBM electric typewriter. Sometimes the transcriptions were difficult to comprehend, as she followed King's musings and Walker's deciphering around the edges of newspaper pages. Mackey frequently stopped and asked Walker to provide his interpretation of what he thought King was trying to say in the reply to the ministers. "This is the only thing that makes sense," Walker told Mackey as he examined the piece of paper. "I'm sure this is what he is saying." He handed the scrap back to Mackey and the whirlwind typing proceeded.[30]

When Mackey rubbed her eyes and huffed out a deep sigh during the frustrating task, Walker reminded her how important the document was to King. "Miss Willie, this has to be right," he demanded. Walker let his young secretary know in "no uncertain terms" that she would have to work nonstop to get the letter completed.[31]

Working late into the evening, Mackey often found herself alone in the office typing King's composition. One night as she attempted to leave, she discovered that all of the exits to the building had been locked from the outside and there was no way to get out. "Apparently everyone had forgotten about me," she remembered. Undaunted, Mackey managed to coax open a push-bar-handle door, and she exited into a dark, empty street in Birmingham. Frightened and alone, she said a prayer for the Lord's protection and briskly walked across the park to the Gaston Motel. During another marathon typing session, she placed her head down and fell asleep on the typewriter. Rather than waking her, Walker lifted his young secretary from the chair and helped her to the couch. He sat down and continued the typing.[32]

When Mackey finished the rough drafts, Walker apparently gave the typed pages to one of the movement lawyers to smuggle back to King in the Birmingham Jail. King made corrections and returned them to Walker. Mackey never recalled seeing any of the corrections in King's handwriting, only in Walker's. "I think he was more or less trying to make sure that I was able to read it," she later recalled.[33]

With the issuance of the eight white clergymen's statement, Walker believed, King's cup had overflowed, and the letter was going to be a historic document. "This is going to be one of the most important pieces of this era," Walker said as he transcribed, compiled, composed, and edited.[34]

The text focused upon a central theme of justification. King defended the civil rights movement in Birmingham (and elsewhere), its timing, and the use of nonviolent direct action. He addressed six major issues: negotiation, timing, breaking laws, triggering violence, the myth of time, and extremism. He also focused on two significant sub-issues: rebuking white moderates and disillusionment with the white church in general.[35]

To prove his points King used biblical references, quoting classical and modern philosophers, theologians, church and Western historical figures. Furthermore, to lift the rhetoric to a higher level, King symbolically assumed the voice of the apostle Paul. As one author discovered, King stylistically exploited parallels between Paul's life and his own. Like Paul's writings, the letter seemed more like a sermon than a correspondence and was meant for a larger audience than those addressed. Similar to Paul, King remained separated from his audience, spoke with apostolic authority, and used prison as an "ironic pulpit" for encouragement and admonishment.[36]

The text of the "Letter from Birmingham Jail" opened with King's salutation to the eight white clergy, his symbolic audience. The civil rights leader explained that he rarely took time out of his schedule to respond to individuals critical of his work and ideas. King received volumes of dissenting mail every day, ranging from mild criticism to hate-filled condemnation. Yet he believed these eight white Birmingham ministers were men of "genuine goodwill" and sincere in their criticisms, so he hoped to answer them with patience and reason. What emerged from King's pen was an eloquent letter of justification and admonishment.[37]

First, the civil rights leader answered the white ministers' charge that outsiders were leading the demonstrations. He explained that he was in Birmingham because of organizational ties to Fred Shuttlesworth's Alabama Christian Movement for Human Rights (an SCLC affiliate). Moreover, King was in Birmingham because of the injustice in the city. Just as Old Testament prophets and New Testament apostles had carried their messages to other nations, King was compelled to take the "gospel of freedom" beyond Atlanta. Like Paul, King claimed the authority of an apostle (deriving from the Greek word *apostolos,* meaning an ambassador, a messenger, or "he that was sent"). Just as Paul had, the civil rights leader professed he had faithfully answered the "Macedonian call for aid." This was a biblical reference to Acts 16:9–10, where Paul had a vision of a man from Macedonia begging him to "come over . . . and help us." Paul immediately got ready and left for Macedonia, concluding that "God had called us to preach the gospel to them."[38]

Furthermore, King rebuked the religious leaders for using the shallow, provincial outside-agitator argument. The civil rights leader emphasized a common destiny for all communities and states in America and stressed his unwillingness to "sit idly by" in Atlanta and remain unconcerned about injustices in Birmingham. "Injustice anywhere was a threat to justice everywhere," he insisted.[39]

Continuing, the minister chided his fellow clergy for deploring the demonstrations and apparently disregarding the condition of the black community and race relations in the city. He alluded to a superficiality among the white ministers and believed the eight men would reject a social analysis that only dealt with effects and not underlying causes. He agreed that the demonstrations were unfortunate but found it even more unfortunate that Birmingham's white power structure had left no alternative (2–3).

King pointed out that the movement had gone through the four basic steps in a nonviolent campaign: fact collection, negotiation, self-purification, and direct action. The civil rights leader emphasized the "hard, brutal, and unbelievable" facts of the racial injustice that engulfed Birmingham. He called the city the "most thoroughly segregated" in the country and stressed the widespread image and sinister reality of police brutality, unsolved bombings, and unjust treatment of blacks in the judicial system (3).

Local blacks attempted to negotiate a change in these conditions, King noted, but Birmingham officials refused to bargain in "good faith." In September 1962, local blacks turned to the city's business leaders and received several commitments, including the promise to remove the humiliating "colored only" signs in department stores. The Reverend Fred Shuttlesworth called a moratorium on demonstrations, but the business leaders (under pressure from Connor) had broken the promise and the signs remained (3).

Confronted with "blasted hopes," King insisted that "we had no alternative" (although he was not personally involved) other than to continue along the road to direct action and begin the process of self-purification. He explained to the ministers the Paul-inspired concept of demonstrators using their "very bodies" as living sacrifices in an appeal before the conscience of the city and the nation. The SCLC's direct-action campaign targeted the business community during the busy Easter shopping season (3–4).

King emphasized, however, that they postponed the movement twice until after the mayoral election and again until after the runoff so the demonstrations would not "cloud the issues" of the campaign. This postponement aided the community and demonstrated that the SCLC had moved carefully and responsibly into direct action, the civil rights leader believed (4).

He then moved on to a justification of the use of direct action—the most important part of the letter in light of the failures in Albany. The purpose of nonviolent direct action was to create a crisis and establish "creative tension" to force a community to negotiate. While King had preached and worked against violent tension, he saw nonviolent tension as necessary for growth. He compared these methods to Socrates' creation of intellectual tension for individuals to rise above myths and experience the "unfettered realm of creative analysis and objective appraisal." Nonviolent tension in a society helped citizens to rise above racism to the "majestic heights of understanding and brotherhood." King concurred with the white ministers' call for negotiation, but he believed he had the best way to facilitate such an open discussion. For too long the South had tragically attempted to exist in "monologue rather than dialogue," he explained (4–5).

King then turned to the white ministers' contention that the demonstrations had been "unwise and untimely" in light of the change in city government. He believed the new administration needed prompting to act as much as did the old. No millennium had dawned in Birmingham with the election of Albert Boutwell, and although King found him more "articulate and gentle" than Bull Connor, he also believed the new mayor was equally dedicated to preserving segregation. The black minister surmised that only pressure from civil rights activists would enable Boutwell to see the hopelessness of massive resistance. Addressing his friends, King noted that he had achieved nothing in the civil rights arena without resolute pressure on whites, who seldom gave up privileges voluntarily. He pointed to Reinhold Niebuhr, who stressed that groups were more immoral than individuals (5).

Continuing, King eloquently wrote what *New York Times* journalist Foster Hailey had reported the day after the civil rights leader had been arrested: the time for gradual change had passed and blacks now insisted on immediate desegregation. For years, the civil rights leader had heard the word "wait" from those people who had never experienced the "stinging darts" of segregation. Nearly 340 years had passed, and blacks still waited for their constitutional and "God-given" rights. To further illustrate his point, King used his most emotional and persuasive plea: an over-three-hundred-word sentence—a series of dependent clauses exploring the troubled souls of segregated southern blacks in the long night of waiting:

> when you have seen vicious mobs lynch your mothers and fathers at will and drown your sisters and brothers at whim; when you have seen hate filled policemen curse, kick, brutalize and even kill your black brothers and sisters with impunity; when you see the vast majority of your twenty million Negro brothers smothering in an air tight cage of poverty in the midst of an affluent society; when you suddenly find your tongue twisted and your speech stammering as you seek to explain to your six-year old daughter why she can't go to the public amusement park that has just been advertised on television, and see tears welling up in her little eyes when she is told that Funtown is closed to colored children, and see the depressing clouds of inferiority begin to form in her little mental sky, and see her begin to distort her little personality by unconsciously developing a bitterness toward white people; when you have to concoct an answer for a five-year old son asking in agonizing pathos: "Daddy, why do white people treat colored people so mean?"; when you take a cross country drive and find it necessary to sleep night after night in the uncomfortable corners of your automobile because no motel will accept you; when you are humiliated day in and day out by nagging signs reading "white" and "colored;" when your first name becomes "nigger" and your middle name becomes "boy" (however old you are) and your last name becomes "John," and when your wife and mother are never given the respected title "Mrs.;" when you are harried by day and haunted by night by the fact that you are a Negro, living constantly at tip-toe stance never quite knowing what to expect next, and plagued with inner fears and outer resentments; when you are forever fighting a degenerating sense of "nobodiness;" then you will understand why we find it difficult to wait. (5–7)

A time had come, King noted, when the "cup of endurance" overflowed and a people were no longer willing to tolerate such injustice and despair. The civil rights leader hoped the white ministers could understand the "legitimate and unavoidable impatience" of most blacks (7).

Subsequently he appraised the law-and-order theme emphasized in the white ministers' statement. King explained why he had been willing to obey some laws and break others. He pointed to two types of laws, just and unjust. He cited St. Augustine's admonition that an unjust law was "no law at all" and St. Thomas Aquinas's belief that an unjust law was a human decree not rooted in eternal and natural laws. In distinguishing between just and unjust laws, he described the just law as a code in line with moral or Godly edicts; while the unjust law was in discord with these laws. All segregation ordinances, King resolutely presumed, were unjust because they distorted souls and damaged the personalities. Paraphrasing the Jewish philosopher Martin Buber, segregation substituted an "I-it" for an "I-thou" relationship and relegated people to the "status of things." Accordingly, theologian Paul Tillich had maintained that sin was separation: hence, King saw segregation as an "existential expression" of human separation, estrangement, and sinfulness (7).

King continued to make several more distinctions between just and unjust laws. The civil rights leader considered an unjust law a code inflicted by a majority on a minority, that the majority was unwilling to apply to itself. He pointed to the "devious methods" used to prevent blacks from registering to vote and questioned whether the Alabama legislature that enacted the segregation laws had been democratically elected. Sometimes on the surface a law appeared just but was unjust in its application. For example, King stated that it was just to have an ordinance to require a parade permit. The ordinance, however, became unjust when used to maintain segregation and deny the right to peaceful protest (8).

He hoped the white ministers would understand the distinction he presented. He never advocated defying a law as belligerent segregationists had defied the *Brown* decision and other integration measures. Disobeying an unjust law must be done with love, not hate; with an obedient attitude and a willingness to accept the consequences. Reflecting the words and actions of Henry David Thoreau, King firmly believed a person expressed the "highest respect for the law" by breaking a code they deemed unjust and willingly accepting a jail term to "arouse the conscience of the community." For example, had King lived in Nazi Germany under the iron rule of Adolf Hitler, he would have illegally eased the suffering of his "Jewish brothers," or had he resided in a Communist country where the government suppressed the Christian faith, he would have advocated disobeying the anti-religious codes. His ideas rooted in the Judeo-Christian heritage, the civil rights leader also pointed to Old Testament figures Shadrach, Meshach, and Abednego as early practitioners of this manner of civil disobedience (8–9).

King next turned his attention to the white moderates. He had almost reached the unfortunate conclusion that the greatest stumbling block in the black stride toward freedom was neither the belligerent members of the White Citizens Councils nor the Ku Klux Klan, but the white moderate. King believed white moderates were more devoted to "order" than to justice; they preferred a negative peace (the absence of tension) to a positive peace (the presence of justice). They had consistently told blacks that they agreed with the quest for racial equality, but rejected the use of direct action. While urging blacks to wait for a "more convenient season," white moderates lived with a mythical concept of time by paternalistically determining the hour of another race's freedom. This "shallow understanding" from men of good will, King believed, was "more frustrating than absolute misunderstanding from people of ill will." Drawing a parallel with Christ's renunciation of lukewarm Christianity in the book of Revelation, King rejected a lukewarm acceptance from white moderates as "more bewildering than outright rejection" (10).

Turning to the white ministers' central theme, King rejected the clergy's concept of law and order as a dangerous roadblock to social progress. The civil rights leader believed law and order existed to establish justice for all citizens. The tension in the South was a necessary transition from an "obnoxious negative peace" (wherein passive blacks accepted a life of injustice) to a "substantive-filled" positive peace (wherein all people had respect, dignity, and worth). The nonviolent civil rights movement had not created the tension in the South, it had simply brought to the surface the hidden tension for everyone to see. "Like a boil that can never be cured so long as it is covered up but must be opened with all its pus-flowing ugliness to the natural medicines of air and light," King wrote, "injustice must likewise be exposed with all of the tension its exposing creates, to the light of human conscience and the air of national opinion before it can be cured" (10).

The white ministers erred, King believed, in denouncing the civil rights demonstrations as a precipitant to violence. This was similar to condemning a robbery victim because the money in his possession precipitated the crime, or condemning Socrates because his philosophy and commitment to truth precipitated the "misguided popular mind to make him drink hemlock." Was not this criticism, King asked the white ministers, like condemning Jesus because His devotion to God's will precipitated crucifixion? "We must come to see, as federal courts have consistently affirmed, that it is immoral to urge an individual to withdraw his efforts to gain his basic constitutional rights because the quest precipitates violence. Society must protect the robbed and punish the robber" (10–11A).

The civil rights leader again criticized the white moderates' concepts of time. King referred to the letter he had received from a white Christian in Texas urging slow, gradual change and accusing black activists of seeking equal rights in a great "religious hurry." This tragic misconception of time was irrational, King argued, and rested upon the naive idea that time inevitably cured society's problems. Belligerent segregationists made more constructive use of time than the white moderates. This generation, the civil rights leader concluded, would repent, not only for the belligerence of segregationists, but for the "appalling silence of the good people." Progress never rolled in "on wheels of inevitability," King emphasized, but through the untiring endeavors of God's "co-workers." Without these diligent efforts, time became an ally of social stagnation. The time was "always ripe to do right," he demanded. Now was the time to provide blacks with democratic guarantees and "transform our pending national elegy into a creative psalm of brotherhood." Now was the time to raise the public agenda from the "quicksand of racial injustice to the solid rock of human dignity" (11A–11B).

Nevertheless, the white ministers had considered King's efforts to achieve these immediate goals as extremist. Countering this charge, the civil rights leader argued that he stood as a moderating force between two opposing forces in the black community: the complacent black (those drained of self-respect by years of oppression or those profiting from segregation) and the militant black nationalist ("those nourished" by frustration over continuing discrimination and concluding all whites were the devil—especially Elijah Muhammad's Nation of Islam). Through the influence of the black church, King advocated a "more excellent way of love" through nonviolent protest. If blacks had never cultivated this ideology, he was certain that "floods of blood" would engulf southern streets. Accordingly, if whites refused to support nonviolence and dismissed protesters as extremists and outsiders, millions of blacks would turn to the black nationalists, leading to a "frightening racial nightmare" (11B–12).

Oppressed people never remained oppressed forever, King contended. Consciously or unconsciously, the freedom movements in Africa, Asia, South America, and the Caribbean had engulfed America's black community with a sense of urgency to push toward the "promised land of racial justice." This explained and justified the public demonstrations. Blacks had few outlets for their frustrations, so let them march, King exhorted; let them stage sit-ins and Freedom Rides. "If his repressed emotions do not come out in these nonviolent ways, they will come out in ominous expressions of violence." This was not a threat, King emphasized, but a "fact of history." He had urged blacks to channel discontent through nonviolent direct action which the white ministers had condemned in their statement as an act of extremism (12).

The civil rights leader, however, gained a "measure of satisfaction" from the extremist label. To illustrate his point, King pointed to Jesus, the prophet Amos, the apostle Paul, Martin Luther, John Bunyan, Abraham Lincoln, and Thomas Jefferson as examples of historical extremists. The South, the nation, and the world desperately needed more creative extremists for love and justice. He had hoped white moderates would recognize this need. Nevertheless, members of an oppressor race had little understanding of the "deep groans and passionate yearnings" of the oppressed. Even fewer whites had the vision to see justice prevail through "strong, persistent and determined action." Some of the South's whites, however, understood and embraced the goals of the civil rights movement. King pointed to Ralph McGill, Lillian Smith, Harry Golden, and James McBride Dabbs as sympathetic and articulate voices from the southern white community. Other whites had marched and suffered with King in many southern cities. Unlike the moderates, these whites had acknowledged the movement's importance and discerned a need for action to "combat the disease of segregation" (12–14).

King next turned specifically to his disappointment with the white church and its leadership. Recognizing the "significant stands" the white ministers had taken in fighting segregation, the civil rights leader commended Earl Stallings for making a "Christian stand" and welcoming the black visitors to First Baptist Church on Easter Sunday.[40] These actions, King believed, were simply notable exceptions. During the Montgomery Bus Boycott in the mid-1950s, King had hoped for the support of the white church and its leaders. Nonetheless some church leaders opposed the movement, while others "remained silent behind the anesthetizing security of stained-glass windows" (14).

King had optimistically expected Birmingham's white religious leaders to recognize the justice of the civil rights movement and, with a "deep moral concern," serve as a door to the power structure. "I had hoped that each of you would understand," he wrote. "But again I have been disappointed." He longed to hear southern religious leaders exhort their congregations to obey a desegregation ruling, not because it was simply the law, but because it was a moral imperative. As blacks suffered injustice, white churches had remained aloof and simply mouthed "pious irrelevances and sanctimonious trivialities." King also criticized church leaders for failing to emphasize social issues. Most churches emphasized an other-world religion with a bizarre "distinction between body and soul," and sacred and secular. Religion in the South had accommodated the social order and emerged as a "taillight behind other community agencies rather than a headlight leading men to higher levels of justice" (14–15).

King often observed the stately churches in Mississippi and Alabama and wondered "What kind of people worshiped here?" "Who was their God?" "Where were their voices when the lips of Governor Barnett dripped with words of interposition and nullification?" "Where were they when Governor Wallace gave a clarion call for defiance and hatred?" (The white clergy found this statement particularly offensive in light of the stand they made against Wallace in January 1963). "Where were their voices of support when bruised and weary Negro men and women decided to rise from the dark dungeons of complacency to the bright hills of creative protest?" (15–16)[41]

King wept "tears of love" over the church's indifferent attitude. There was no deep disappointment without deep love. The church was the body of Christ, but it had been "blemished and scarred" by social negligence and the fear of nonconformity. The church was once a powerful social force. The early church was not "merely a thermometer that recorded the ideas and principles of popular opinion; it was a thermostat that transformed the mores of society." Early Christians pressed on in the face of intimidation and adversity. Though small in numbers, they maintained a giant commitment to God and brought an end to the ancient evils of infanticide and gladiator contests (16).

King believed, however, the modern church had a weak and ineffectual voice with an "uncertain sound." The southern church was a defender of the social order through silence or vocal support. If the church was unable to recapture the spirit of the apostolic age, society would dismiss it as "an irrelevant social club with no meaning for the twentieth century." Perhaps organized religion was too closely tied to the status quo to save the world. King believed he must turn his faith to the "inner spiritual church" as the world's last hope (16–17).

Nevertheless, some in the church had thrown off the "paralyzing chains of conformity" and stood for King's concepts of racial justice. These "noble souls" had marched in Albany, Georgia, or participated in Freedom Rides. Some had gone to jail. Others had lost their pulpits. Their witness was the "spiritual salt" that had preserved the "true meaning of the Gospel in these troubled times" (18).

Even if the church failed to confront the status quo, King never despaired or feared the outcome of the Birmingham struggle. Although scorned and abused, the black destiny was bound with America's destiny. Before the Pilgrims came to the New World or Jefferson wrote the Declaration of Independence, blacks lived in America. They had suffered through slavery. "If the inexpressible cruelties of slavery could not stop us," King wrote, "the opposition we now face will surely fail" (18).

Before closing, King turned to the white ministers' praise for the Birmingham police force. Had the ministers seen police dogs bite six blacks or observed the harsh treatment in the Birmingham Jail, he argued, their viewpoints would be different. King admitted the police department (in these early weeks of the movement) had been rather restrained and even "nonviolent" in handling the demonstrators. "But for what purpose?" he asked. They were using a moral system (nonviolence) to maintain an immoral status quo (segregation). Paraphrasing T. S. Eliot, King saw "no greater treason" than carrying out the "right deed for the wrong reason" (18–19).

The civil rights leader wished the white ministers had praised the demonstrators for their courage and capacity to suffer. "One day the South will recognize its real heroes," he wrote, pointing to such examples as the University of Mississippi's first black student, James Meredith, and the old black woman in the Montgomery Bus Boycott, who proclaimed with "ungrammatical profundity" that her feet were tired, but her soul was rested. One day the South would recognize that these "disinherited children of God" had stood for the American dream and Judeo-Christian values. They had moved an entire nation back to the true spirit of democracy as advocated by the founding fathers (19–20).

In his conclusion and with a note of irony, King surmised that he had never written such a lengthy letter ("or should I say a book?" he added). He believed he had taken too much of the white ministers' "precious time." Had the civil rights leader composed the letter from a comfortable desk, it would be much shorter, he presumed. But what activities were there in the confines of a jail cell, other than writing lengthy letters, thinking odd thoughts, and praying long prayers. If King had overstated the truth or was unreasonably impatient, he begged the ministers' forgiveness. If he had said anything in the letter that understated the truth, or indicated a patience for anything less than brotherhood, he begged God's forgiveness (20).

Once again assuming the reassuring voice of the apostle Paul, King hoped the letter would find the ministers "strong in the faith." He also looked forward to meeting each of the religious leaders, "not as an integrationist or a civil rights leader but as a fellow clergyman and a Christian brother." Lyrically, he hoped the "dark clouds of racial prejudice" would pass away and the "deep fog of misunderstanding" would lift from fearful communities, and "in some not too distant tomorrow the radiant stars of love and brotherhood" would "shine over our great nation with all their scintillating beauty." He closed the letter with the salutation, "Yours for the cause of Peace and Brotherhood," Martin Luther King Jr. The initials of Wyatt Walker's secretary, Willie Pearl Mackey, appeared at the bottom of the text: MLK:wm (20).

The document had all the appearance of a personal letter, but the early mass-produced versions of it bore no signature. Clearly, movement leaders had a broader audience in mind for the prison epistle.

7 Gospel of Publicity

The bright Saturday sunshine was almost blinding. After eight long days in the Birmingham Jail, Martin Luther King and Ralph Abernathy emerged into the glare, which seemed even more intense as it reflected against the white walls of the jail buildings and the shiny black asphalt. Squinty-eyed and wearing week-old beards, the civil rights duo looked haggard as they slowly made their way toward a small group of support-ers and a handful of journalists gathered outside the fence. King told reporters that he had been persuaded, contrary to the commitments of his conscience, to allow the $300 bail to be paid so that he could leave jail and continue planning the campaign. The civil rights leader said he had no regrets about violating the injunction. "Morally, we had no other alternative," he added. A week later, Judge William Jenkins held King, Walker, Abernathy, Shuttlesworth, and seven other ministers in con-tempt for a deliberate and blatant disregard of his court order and fixed punishment at five days in jail and a $50 fine. The SCLC immediately began a lengthy appeal process.[1]

During King's imprisonment, and despite Wyatt Walker's best efforts, national news coverage had dwindled. As King settled back into the Gaston Motel, he told his staff that the movement needed a jump start because the press and the American public were losing interest. "You know, we've got to get something going," King told his aides. "The press is leaving, we've got to get going." This practical side to King shocked John Porter. "I want God with us," he told King, "not the press." Porter yearned for a civil rights victory via righteousness and God's might, not through the power of the press. Nevertheless, he soon realized that in the twentieth century, "the Lord and righteousness . . . also worked through the modern media."[2]

SCLC associate James Bevel had an intriguing and controversial idea: recruit thousands of students to overwhelm Eugene "Bull" Connor's police force. This children's crusade provided fresh volunteers for the most striking public demonstrations of the campaign. The plan worked to perfection, as a journalist on the scene emphasized, with marches "planned down to the finest detail."[3]

On Friday, May 3, youthful demonstrators pushed Connor over the brink, and he ordered widespread use of police dogs and fire hoses. The confrontation generated Saturday headlines across the country and was the beginning of an unprecedented week of worldwide media coverage focusing on Birmingham—transforming the city into a "global symbol of America's racial malaise." During these dark days of the Cold War, the Soviet press gleefully exploited the images in Birmingham and an apparent inconsistency in U.S. foreign policy. "We have the impression," reported Radio Moscow, "that American authorities both cannot and do not wish to stop outrages by racists."[4]

The U.S. media obtained possibly the most important visual image of the entire campaign that Friday with a dramatic still photo by Associated Press photographer William Hudson. The public was appalled at the sight of a Birmingham police dog named Leo, held tight on a leash by officer R. E. "Dick" Middleton, attacking a fifteen-year-old black boy named Walter Gadsden.[5] Almost overnight, scores of newspaper, magazine, radio, and television journalists descended upon the city (joining veteran reporters of the Birmingham crisis), searching for every possible angle on the racial situation.[6] Apparently many of the Birmingham grassroots protestors understood the importance of national news exposure in breaking down racial barriers. During lulls in the demonstrations, blacks yelled at police to "bring on the dogs; bring on the water."[7]

The drama in Birmingham ingrained the images of the defiant white South in a desperate shootout with the noble forces of the civil rights establishment. Most Americans believed at the time (and perhaps still believe) that the violent clashes in Birmingham took place all over the city. The demonstrations, however, rarely left the two or three blocks around the Sixteenth Street Baptist Church. "It was a masterpiece of the use of the media," remembered one progressive white Birmingham official. Prior to the marches, the television networks only devoted fifteen minutes to the national news and fifteen minutes of local news. Suddenly, as King's troops marched a short distance, the SCLC had solicited "enough news film to fill all of the newscasts of all the television stations in the United States."[8]

Television news shows such as NBC's *Huntley-Brinkley Report* and others reported all of the dramatic scenes. "There was no way Dr. King could have bought that kind of coverage," one Birmingham observer noted. Wyatt Walker agreed. "That was really some coup for us," he said, "with very limited resources and a very unpopular cause in the most violent city in the South. It went all over the nation and then all over the world."[9]

Behind the scenes, as the racial tensions in the city remained high and bail money ran low, the SCLC began a major national fund-raising effort just prior to the completion of the "Letter from Birmingham Jail." A half-page advertisement donated by northern supporters to "reach like minded friends" appeared in the May 7, 1963, *New York Times* as an appeal from Birmingham to the "conscience of America." Blacks in Birmingham had endured decades of discrimination in one of the largest segregated cities in the Western Hemisphere, but they had now marched forward. Despite the nearly fourteen hundred blacks in jail at the time, the community's "will to freedom" had remained vibrant. "We urgently need your help. Please extend your support and extend the Frontier of Democracy—TODAY in the Deep South." The names of King and Shuttlesworth appeared under the text, as did a request for checks payable to the SCLC.[10]

The SCLC also circulated form letters in May signed by King to various contributors throughout the nation. Printed on King's personal stationery, the form letters explained to supporters that King had only been temporarily released from jail to coordinate movement activities. He emphasized that nothing remained of the SCLC's thin resources and pleaded for contributions made with "maximum generosity" from those dear friends who shared hopes and aspirations for racial justice. "Please let the embattled Negroes of the South know that they are not alone," he pleaded. King pointed out, however, that if his solicitation reached the addressee following a partial victory in Birmingham, their money was still needed to provide a solid foundation for the movement and to take the battle for human rights farther into the Deep South.[11]

Seeking a solid compromise in Birmingham, President John F. Kennedy and the Justice Department pressured King and city officials to end the confrontations. Through the mediation efforts of Assistant Attorney General Burke Marshall, King and white business leaders reached an accord on the evening of Thursday, May 9. At a joint press conference the next day, King announced the city of Birmingham had "reached an accord with its conscience." Shuttlesworth read the points of the settlement to media: a desegregation of public facilities (including lunch counters, drinking fountains, rest rooms, and fitting rooms) at downtown stores within ninety days; better employment opportunities for blacks at these stores within sixty days; the release of jailed demonstrators on bond or personal recognizance; and the appointment of a biracial committee within two weeks. The settlement was far short of the movement's original objectives.[12]

With the fund-raising campaign under way, Wyatt Walker released the "Letter from Birmingham Jail" to the media during the first two weeks of May. "We went through the press release process," secretary Willie Mackey later recalled. "We had a list and sent the letter out just like we did any other SCLC release."[13]

With the tension in Birmingham still high, the press paid little attention to the document initially. When the dramatic confrontations ended, the media slowly turned to the letter as a "famous pronouncement of moral triumph" by the victorious King. For Walker and the SCLC, the document began serving its intended purpose as a public relations tool to maintain press interest and to spread the story of the movement in Birmingham. The document also functioned as a symbolic finale to the Birmingham campaign.[14]

The media and the American public quickly became captivated by the prison cell epistle. The supposed story of how the letter was written, was of course, quite striking: the leader of a great moral struggle between the forces of good and evil, confined to a jail cell (like the apostle Paul), writing a letter of love to eight white pharisees. It quickly became part of the civil rights folklore. This image will long be remembered with other important memories of the black struggle for equality, like that of the students at lunch counters and King on the steps of the Lincoln Memorial. And just like these other images, the story *behind* Martin Luther King's "Letter from Birmingham Jail" was also created for the media and the American public.

The idea that King had written this great, refined work of polished prose in a period of less than seventy-two hours, on or before April 16,

1963, was a key part of the letter's appeal for the press and the public. This story capitalized on the symbolism of the time King spent in jail. Just like other movement efforts to secure publicity, the SCLC staff planned to the finest detail the production and publication of the "Letter from Birmingham Jail." The real story of the production of the letter was less symbolic and more practical. "We had a movement to try to win," Norman Amaker later reflected. "We had to do what was necessary."[15]

In reality, Martin Luther King wrote parts of the letter in jail and continued writing, editing, and revising drafts (with the assistance of Walker and other SCLC officials) several days after the date on the manuscript. April 16 marked not the end of the composition, but the beginning. Norman Amaker, King's principal courier, agreed. "As many people will do when they are writing something," Amaker argued, "they will put down the date when it began, but that does not mean the end. I've gotten letters mailed weeks after the date on the letter."[16]

For scholars, journalists, and other curious sorts, written verification of how the letter was written just does not exist. The only proof that King penned this entire text under these exact circumstances and in the short time frame conveyed was based exclusively on the testimonies of those involved in the document's production. These people still closely guard King's image and remain unwilling to challenge any of the legends surrounding the civil rights leader. Regardless, evidence suggests a different scenario.

King and his staff continued to work on the document after he left jail. In the text of the document, King selectively quoted from a letter to him by an anonymous writer (which was signed simply "yours, In Christ's Service"). Setting forth the arguments of many white moderates, the letter writer believed all Christians knew that blacks would eventually receive equal rights. Nevertheless, the writer asked King if he and his followers were in "too great of a religious hurry?" It had taken Christianity almost two thousand years to accomplish what it had, because biblical teachings of Jesus Christ took time to come to earth. King wrote in the letter that he had received this correspondence the morning of April 16 from a "white brother in Texas" (although the letter made no mention of gender). Unquestionably, King received this dispatch at some later date. The letter had an afternoon, April 15, postmark from Dallas, Texas, and movement officials later stamped an April

25, 1963, date across the top of the page (presumably the date received).[17]

Other evidence also points to King's continued work on the "Letter from Birmingham Jail" after April 16. King complained to Stanley Levison on May 20, 1963, that while he was writing the document, the text had grown so long that he had slashed several additional sections—perhaps as many as fifteen thousand words. That many additional words would have more than tripled the size of the letter, from twenty pages of typed double-spaced text to almost seventy-five. If all of this had occurred while King was in jail, he would have written, by hand, well over a hundred pages of text in a relatively short period of time. He would have accomplished this with no desk and writing only during daylight hours, and even then in poor lighting. As one observer suggested, this many pages of handwritten text would have been an extraordinary feat for any author even under the best of circumstances. Furthermore, in the transcription of the phone-tapped conversation between the civil rights leader and Levison, King never remarked that he had written *any* of these sections while in the Birmingham Jail.[18]

King explained that he had written and later removed a forceful section from the letter on the concept of how the struggle to "save the soul of America" had freed both blacks and whites. In addition, he had omitted a long section on the gap between American foreign and domestic policy. While fighting the Cold War abroad, America had condemned the Communist block for human rights violations. This appeared inconsistent in light of the racial problems on the U.S. domestic front. "I was appealing to them on the basis of understanding this," King said. "There's more I could put in on this." King apparently viewed the letter as a document that had not been set in stone while he was in jail and might be expanded or contracted at his whim. "In adding to it," Levison told King, he was making the document "even stronger."[19]

Editor Hermine I. Popper further strengthened the text of the letter for King's book on the Birmingham campaign, *Why We Can't Wait,* released in 1964. Popper discovered several details in the text "which had not actually occurred at the time" King was in jail. To sustain the biblical aura of the letter, it remained essential to maintain the appearance that King had written the entire composition while incarcerated. In a conversation with Popper, Levison again acknowledged that King had revised the letter at a later date and inserted "additional material."[20] Levison advised Popper to include the material, but in a "very general way," presumably to indicate that King had written these sections while in jail. As an example, Levison told Popper to change the passage about police dogs attacking six unarmed blacks. "Just leave out the six and put the remainder in," he said. Popper subsequently changed the original text from: "I don't believe you would have so warmly commended the police force if you had seen its angry violent dogs literally biting six unarmed, nonviolent Negroes" to the text printed in *Why We Can't Wait:* "I doubt that you would have so warmly commended the police force if you had seen its dogs sinking their teeth into unarmed, nonviolent Negroes."[21]

These questions of timing and authenticity suggest that the production of the "Letter from Birmingham Jail" was part of a highly organized overall campaign for publicity. Other evidence also hinted that King and the SCLC had written and distributed the document for media consumption. Before the movement began, Fred Shuttlesworth, King, and Ralph Abernathy had agreed to issue only joint statements to the press. As Shuttlesworth later emphasized, if this agreement had been followed, the letter would have been signed by "all of us . . . simply because we had agreed to do things together."[22] At the very least, the letter did not accord with Shuttlesworth's expectations. He apparently saw the manuscript as a publicity document and a cooperative effort by King and others within the movement.

The eight white clergy addressed in the document provided the best evidence of the broad purpose of the "Letter from Birmingham Jail." One author has suggested that the letter was a "private communication" between King and the eight white ministers. Regardless, the white clergymen never received a personalized, delivered, or signed copy of the letter from King.[23] The media, not the white ministers, were the real focus of the document.

Surprisingly, the SCLC staff apparently discarded King's handwritten notes and early drafts of the document that had been secretly smuggled in and out of the Birmingham Jail. As one observer noted, SCLC staffers working on the letter, and especially Wyatt Walker, should have recognized the historical significance of King's scribblings and preserved them. After all, Walker had noted on several occasions that he "always sensed" that King was making history. Years later, Walker maintained that throwing King's notes away was a simple accident. With the truce signed, many of the SCLC staffers began moving out of Birmingham and back to Atlanta. "Wyatt, everybody is leaving," King told his associate.

"Somebody has got to stay around here and break this operation down." Walker realized this was more than a suggestion. "Well, I guess it is me."[24]

Along with his secretary, Willie Pearl Mackey, Walker began sorting through files and separating items to keep and those to discard. Mackey had saved the note and drafts of the letter just long enough to make sure she had typed the document accurately. After the campaign was over, in her mind, the scraps of paper were just trash. "You could tell I'm green as grass and from the country," she later recalled. "Had I been one of those slicksters, I would have kept all of these things. They were in my possession. . . . I threw them in the trash can. I didn't have sense enough back then to keep stuff like that." When Walker later realized what had happened, he said it made him sick. "What happened to the original? I had it in my hands. I always had a sense of history, of things to save. That got away from me."[25]

Adding to the confusion surrounding the letter's production were the slightly different versions of the document produced by the SCLC publicity corps. A mimeographed version in the Mayor Albert Boutwell Papers in the Birmingham Public Library Department of Archives and Manuscripts omitted the name of Bishop Paul Hardin in the list of those addressed. A hand-typed carbon copy, obtained by Bishop Joseph Durick at a later date, included Hardin but had editorial corrections in handwriting different from that of the Boutwell version. In addition, the two versions had been typed on different typewriters. This may explain the assertion by Addine Drew, one of King's friends in Birmingham, that she too had obtained the civil rights leader's notes from jail (apart from Walker) and asked Rose White at Miles College to type up the letter.[26] Moreover, by the following year, an extensively edited version of the document appeared in King's book on the Birmingham campaign, *Why We Can't Wait.*

This evidence, however, does not imply that members of the SCLC staff had written the entire letter. King did make extensive use of ghostwriters for most of his public writings and speeches. Yet in closely examining the text of these early press release versions of the document, the composer, presumably King, was writing random thoughts from memory. Many of the direct quotations in the document were inexact or paraphrased, suggesting someone writing from recollection. For example, in one of these typed versions of the letter the author paraphrases a passage from T. S. Eliot's *Murder in the Cathedral,* saying that "there is no greater treason than to do the right deed for the wrong reason." The letter was later changed for King's book to a direct quotation: "The last temptation is the greatest treason: To do the right deed for the wrong reason."[27]

Despite the impersonal uses of the document, it had a strikingly personal appearance. In virtually every reproduction of the letter, the names of the eight white ministers appeared at the beginning of the text. Adding to the personal guise of the document, King directly addressed the white ministers as "you" some 40 times. He also used the personal pronoun "I" 139 times. The typed manuscript had 20 pages, 48 paragraphs, 325 sentences, and roughly 7,110 words.[28] This was a rebuttal to the white ministers' 1 page, 7 paragraphs, 18 sentences, and 428 words of typed text.

The SCLC presented the document to the public as an open letter—a letter addressed to specific people, but intended for a larger audience. This remains part of the letter's appeal, as it moves on two fronts: first as an apparent private correspondence among American Judeo-Christian religious leaders and second to the country's citizens en masse.[29]

Despite the moving rhetoric of the letter, King and the SCLC staff provided little new material for the text of the document. The endeavor was simply a synthesis of ideas, themes, sermons, and writings King had produced over the years. As one King observer discovered, the civil rights leader frequently borrowed from himself—readily interchanging material from speeches, sermons, and writings. King's "Challenge to the Churches and Synagogues" was one of clearest precursors to the "Letter from Birmingham Jail." Delivered three months earlier at a National Conference on Religion and Race in Chicago, the speech addressed many of the same themes as the Birmingham document: justification for the movement, admonishment of and disappointment with the white church, and the "urgency of now" in the black struggle for equality.[30]

Throughout the text of the letter, King directly quoted from the Chicago oration. For example, in both the speech and the letter, King blasted the white church for demonstrating more caution than courage and remaining "silent behind the anesthetizing security of stained-glass windows." In both instances, the civil rights leader used phrases such as "jet like pace," "horse and buggy speed," "pious irrelevances and sanctimonious trivialities," and other examples.[31]

King and others involved in the composition also used other sermons as the basis for the "Letter from Birmingham Jail." From King's sermon

"Transformed Nonconformist," they drew similar quotes and examples from the historical and biblical figures like Jefferson, Lincoln, Bunyan, and Shadrach, Meshach, and Abednego. In both this sermon and the letter he noted that the church had become a "weak and ineffectual trumpet making uncertain sounds." Additionally, in numerous sermons and writings, King referred to the "ungrammatical profundity," of the elderly black woman in Montgomery, who had tired feet, but a rested soul.[32]

As author Keith Miller discovered in his study of King's rhetorical sources, the civil rights leader also skillfully "borrowed" arguments and ideas from others and blended them with his own identity and language. In the text of the letter, King's primary sources included Harry Emerson Fosdick, Harris Wofford, George Kelsey, H. H. Crane, the *Christian Century*, and black folk preachers. Several passages from these sources sound remarkably similar to sections of the letter. From Fosdick, King had borrowed such words and phrases as: "leaven in the lump of the race," "ecclesia," and the story of how early Christians had ended the horrors of "infanticide and bloody gladiatorial contests." Crane had written: "Instead of being *conformed* to this world, [man] can *transform* it. . . . For when he is what his Maker obviously intended him to be, he is not a thermometer; he is a thermostat." King wrote: "In those days the church was not merely a thermometer that recorded the ideas and principles of popular opinion; it was a thermostat that transformed the mores of society." Regardless of the sources of the letter, such a system of borrowing material would have made the editorial assistance of those involved in the document's production much easier.[33]

By the middle of May 1963, the *New York Times* was among the first media outlets to consider publishing the letter. Editor of the *New York Times Sunday Magazine* Harvey Shapiro told Stanley Levison that three or four of King's people had phoned from Birmingham about the document. The *Times* had decided to publish an edited version of the document with a "little introduction setting forth the circumstances of the piece" in the Sunday, May 26 edition. Just a few days before, Shapiro had asked King to write a feature article based on the letter, but after events took a violent turn in Birmingham, the civil rights leader had his "hands full" and had no time to write another piece.[34]

The cross-town rival *New York Post Sunday Magazine,* however, obtained a copy of the letter and published extensive excerpts on May

19, without King's authority. The civil rights leader surmised that Walker had "let a copy get out of the reach of the people that were supposed to see it." The *Times* subsequently pulled the press release from the publishing schedule and refused to "touch it." A week later, the liberal Christian journal *Christianity and Crisis* published extensively edited excerpts in the May 27 edition.[35]

The American Friends Service Committee (Quakers) also obtained a copy of the letter during early May. Executives circulated the document among the AFSC staff and explained that King's composition was an articulate rationalization of nonviolent protests and a practical answer to perplexing questions that people had as they attempted to understand the broader impact of the Birmingham movement. By May 13 the AFSC had received permission from the SCLC to print the letter for wide dissemination and had corrected the numerous typographical errors in the press release.[36]

The Quakers published fifty thousand copies of the document in pamphlet form for national distribution (at ten cents a copy) among religious groups, labor unions, human relations organizations, and government agencies. Released to the public on May 28 under the title "Tears of Love," the pamphlet included the white ministers' statement and an introductory letter from AFSC executive secretary Colin W. Bell.[37]

For over three hundred years, the Religious Society of Friends (Quakers) had been deeply sympathetic to the concerns of human freedom. Bell noted that sixteenth-century Quakers had demonstrated for the right of peaceful association, for freedom of worship, and against the injustices of tyranny. This had often brought the religious order into conflict with established society. Bell pointed to George Fox as a Quaker who had practiced civil disobedience as a "witness to the supremacy of God's commands over the dictates of men." Like King and other civil rights activists, members of the Society of Friends were often imprisoned for their supposedly disruptive actions and unreasonable demands. Many of the freedoms for which they fought had become the "bulwarks of our society." Quoting the white ministers, Bell wrote that reform movements had often been "unwise and untimely" because they were the birth pains of change. People of good will often resisted reform until their consciences had overwhelmed their interests, he wrote. America needed honest and mature communication and a willingness to pursue friendships among all people who reflected a common faith in God.

King's letter furthered such efforts and was an eloquent expression of his nonviolent, direct-action approach to transform the society."[38]

On June 12, the liberal Protestant weekly magazine *Christian Century* offered the first complete reproduction of the manuscript in a media outlet. The "Letter from Birmingham Jail" had come to the attention of the editor, Harold E. Fey, in mimeographed form, and he arranged to publish the document in full. On May 22, Fey had written King and mentioned using a revised version of the letter for reproduction in the magazine. Fey preferred to omit the names of the eight white ministers to broaden the impact of King's remarks because they applied to "all of us to a considerable degree." The editor clearly hoped to make the letter's "impact as effective as possible" by appealing for contributions to the SCLC. Fey considered his editorial tasks an honor and privilege to help sustain King's "message and ministry to the churches of America."[39]

In the June 12 issue of the magazine, Fey wrote that the letter was much more than a reply to eight clergymen who claimed Dr. King was disturbing the peace. The document spoke to everyone "concerning a crisis that involves us all." Fey and the *Christian Century* published the epistle to contribute to racial justice and to help heal "a most grievous wound which this nation is inflicting upon herself." The editor suggested that readers wishing to offer tangible help send checks to the SCLC. Several years later, Fey wrote King that the letter had been the most memorable article to appear in the magazine during his editorship.[40]

On June 15, the *Saturday Evening Post* published a few excerpts from the letter in a lengthy and rather unflattering story on King, entitled "Apostle of Crisis," written by Reese Cleghorn. Cleghorn noted that King had addressed the letter to seven leading religious leaders (suggesting he had obtained the mimeographed Boutwell version) who had openly criticized the civil rights leader and "staked their prestige and positions upon a moderate solution in Birmingham." King had answered with a public letter later dubbed by his staff the "Birmingham Jail Treatise of Martin Luther King Jr." The *Post* reporter believed the King composition further separated the civil rights leader from the southern white moderates and suggested blacks now charted their own destiny. Much more than a treatise, Cleghorn noted, the document sounded like a "declaration of black independence in the civil-rights crises of the future."[41]

Through the efforts of an unnamed friend closely associated with the

SCLC, the editors of the left-of-center publication the *New Leader* discovered King's prison epistle during the summer. Intrigued by the arguments involved, executive editor Myron Kolatch phoned King and secured permission to run the full text. The letter appeared in the June 24 issue. More so than anyone else, the editors clearly stated the arguments of the eight Birmingham clergymen. These ministers, the editors believed, had reflected a nationwide anxiety over violence and a desire for blacks to achieve equality more peacefully. During King's "enforced respite," the civil rights leader authored a response to the white ministers which Kolatch believed was "one of the most important documents to come from the pen of a Negro leader, especially in a time pervaded by ambivalence." In 1988, Kolatch estimated that the *New Leader* had sold close to three thousand reprints of the letter per year.[42]

In Birmingham, SCLC staffers circulated a copy of the letter throughout the black churches during May. On July 30, the *Birmingham News* printed the first mention of the letter in the city's white press. Although unnamed, the eight clergymen were described as sympathetic with King's aims, but deploring the methods used.[43]

During August and September 1963, media outlets published the letter extensively as pre- and post-publicity for the March on Washington held on August 28. The *Atlantic Monthly* published the document under the headline "The Negro Is Your Brother." *Ebony* editors enthusiastically described King's message to the white Alabama clergy as a modern classic. The letter was highly popular among print editors because King's oral rhetoric had swayed so many people through personal appearances, television, and radio. The letter simply served as an eloquent written sermon.[44]

As the prison epistle gained notice among various media outlets, Stanley Levison worried that King might lose control of the copyright. The civil rights leader told Levison he had circulated the document and allowed publication because he believed it would not hurt sales of a proposed book on the Birmingham movement. During early May, noted radical attorney William Kunstler had proposed seizing on the events in Birmingham by quickly publishing a book centered around the letter. Kunstler originally wanted to author the book with the proceeds sent to a nonprofit organization, but Levison, always seeking ways to promote King's image, vetoed these ideas in favor of a King-authored book and the civil rights leader's control of all royalties. Levison stated that King had a difficult time living on his salary from the SCLC and he hoped the book would provide financial security. Levison considered Kunstler an opportunist who simply wanted a piece of the action and to take advantage of King with a shady book deal. The New York attorney had to scrap Kunstler's deal and secure a book contract for King with a major New York publishing house.[45]

Levison used the "Letter from Birmingham Jail" as the best way to sell the book idea. The attorney told associates that King might expand the letter by ten pages and then "expound" the document further in the book.[46] Since Levison was using the document as a way to obtain a book contract, he told King on May 23 that publishers considering the book might be influenced negatively if they discovered the document was showing up in newspapers and magazines all over the country. King admitted he had sent copies of the document to the *Christian Century* and to *Ebony*. The civil rights leader presumed he could stop publication. Levison emphasized that by incorporating the letter in a book he hoped to secure the copyright.[47]

The next day, Levison received news that King's book agent Joan Daves had received a commitment from the New York publishing house New American Library for the book on Birmingham. The director of the publishing house, Victor Weybright, read the letter and told Levison the main theme behind King's document had been the explanation of why blacks could no longer wait for moderate change. The publisher suggested "Why We Can't Wait" as the title for the expanded book version of the letter. Levison believed this phrase expressed the "issue of the hour" and the public would buy the book to find out the answer to the question. In addition, Weybright gave King permission to resume circulating the letter among the various media outlets.[48]

The most widely circulated and reprinted version of the letter appeared in *Why We Can't Wait* published in 1964. King admitted that he had indulged in the "author's prerogative" and polished the document for this publication. In fact, the civil rights leader had scarcely written any of the text for the book, relying instead on a series of ghostwriters and editors. In the editing process, King and ghostwriters Al Duckett and Hermine Popper added the name of Bishop Paul Hardin (who was probably inadvertently omitted as an original addressee) to the list of white ministers. Unfortunately, two of the white ministers' names were misspelled in the edited version (and all subsequent publications): the book version lists them as Rabbi Hilton Grafman instead of Milton Grafman, and Holan Harmon instead of Nolan Harmon.[49]

The editors combined several sentences and tightened King's prose, but did not change the substance of his argument. For example, at the end of paragraph five of the original version, King had written: "I would not hesitate to say that it is unfortunate that so-called demonstrations are taking place in Birmingham at this time, but I would say in more emphatic terms that it is even more unfortunate that the white power structure of this city left the Negro community with no other alternative." The edited version was substantially altered: "It is unfortunate that demonstrations are taking place in Birmingham, but it is even more unfortunate that the city's white power structure left the Negro community with no alternative." Subsequently, most reproductions of the letter used the edited version and presented it as the original. This further added to the view that King had written not only a great prison epistle, but a flawless literary masterpiece.[50]

Clearly, the "Letter from Birmingham Jail" was the most important written document of the civil rights era. For a people and a movement that relied almost exclusively on oral traditions and testimonies rather than written chronicles, the letter served as a tangible account of the long road to freedom. For Birmingham activist John Porter, this made the document extremely important. "This gave us a sense of the spirit of the time," Porter said, "and reminded us as of where we came from and where we still must go."[51]

As the walls of segregation slowly tumbled, the prominence of both Martin Luther King Jr. and the "Letter from Birmingham Jail" reached new heights. The eight white clergy's reputations, on the other hand, continued to descend. While the public saw the clergymen as religious rogues, King emerged as a national hero. The letter evolved into a grand statement of protest literature. Likewise, many Americans considered the white ministers' statement the last desperate cry from supporters of a racist social order. With King's murder in 1968, the civil rights leader rightfully took his place alongside other martyred icons. His death convinced many that King's letter was more than a work of literature, that it was a sacred, cherished, and divinely inspired text.

King's top staff members in the SCLC enthusiastically praised the "Letter from Birmingham Jail." Wyatt Walker believed the document was the "20th Century Magna Carta for human rights" and the "quintessential digest of Martin Luther King's theological thought at that moment in Birmingham." Although the composition did not appear in the media until after the end of the Birmingham demonstrations,

Andrew Young believed the document served as the turning point for the movement in the city. The letter clearly articulated the problems blacks faced in Birmingham, Young emphasized, and was an important rallying point for the movement. It was not enough to complain about justice. "You've got to define it," Young said, "one, two, three; state your moral case and offer your solution." King's composition set forth the philosophical justification for the civil rights movement. "More than any other written document or statement," Young later wrote, Martin's letter helped lay a strong moral and intellectual basis not only for our struggle in Birmingham, but for all subsequent movement campaigns in the South."[52]

For Fred Shuttlesworth, the arguments in the letter were nothing new. King's document spoke with the "voice of the oppressed" to people around the world. People seeking respect and recognition often made pleas for consideration and the lifting of oppression. The document, however, fell short of summing up all of what made the civil rights movement a success. "I don't think any letter ever sums up all of our human nature," he added. "It spoke a philosophy; a beginning that led to many other things. . . . I don't think anything but the Bible covers everything. . . . No one man can write all that because no one man is God."[53]

The letter had an important and constructive impact on the nation, Martin Luther King Jr. later reflected. "By now," he said in 1965, "nearly a million copies of the letter have been widely circulated in churches of most of the major denominations." This served as a catalyst for focusing international attention on the city of Birmingham. He suggested that without the document and events in Alabama, the March on Washington in August 1963 would not have been possible. "The March on Washington spurred and galvanized the consciences of millions," he added. "It gave the American Negro a new national and international stature. The press of the world recorded the story as nearly a quarter of a million Americans, white and black, assembled in grandeur as a testimonial to the Negro's determination to achieve freedom in this generation." The March on Washington, subsequently duplicated countless times by a variety of interest groups, was the ultimate made-for-television news event. Perhaps it alone surpassed the letter as the SCLC's greatest media triumph.[54]

After reading the letter, Ralph Abernathy said he doubled efforts to witness in Birmingham. "I was determined that I would no longer be afraid of jail," he reflected. The civil rights leader likened the letter to other great writings in American history and noted that Americans would read the document as long as the nation existed and remained free.[55]

Scholars and members of the media also compared the manuscript to significant historical writings and great public letters. Some considered the letter as important as Lincoln's Gettysburg Address and Kennedy's inaugural address. Others likened the document to Emile Zola's 1898 public letter to the president of the French Republic defending Dreyfus, or Thomas Mann's 1937 public letter to the dean of the Philosophical Faculty of the University of Bonn.[56]

Teachers of literature and the philosophy of civil disobedience soon made extensive use of the letter in high school and college classrooms throughout the country. The document also quickly appeared in numerous literary anthologies alongside the civil disobedience writings of Plato, Thomas Jefferson, and Henry David Thoreau; the religious compositions of C. S. Lewis, Paul Tillich, and St. Augustine; and the works of Ralph Ellison, James Baldwin, and Alice Walker. Editors praised King's composition as "one of the strongest pieces" of persuasive writing to come out of twentieth-century America. Other anthologists considered the letter a "virtuoso performance" by a master composer of rhetorical style and tone. The document had broad appeal to all U.S. citizens who were "indifferent or hostile to the Negroes' ways of seeking freedom, or unwilling to take positive steps toward getting civil rights for Negroes."[57]

In the years following the Birmingham campaign, the "Letter from Birmingham Jail" became part of American folklore. Entrepreneurs and enthusiasts began seeking new ways of capitalizing on King's fame and the mass appeal of the letter. Record producers pressured King and the SCLC into recording a phonographic version of the letter for the listening pleasure of both blacks and whites. A long-play rendition of King's composition would find its way into homes across the country and end up on the turntables of middle-class American families. In selling the idea to the civil rights leader, producers insisted that a recorded version of the prison epistle would help sympathetic listeners to understand the logic of King's arguments and provide a permanent platform for the civil rights leader's message. Television executives also tried to lure King to a broadcast studio to produce a televised version of the prison epistle. The document was "inherently pictorial" and provided a "unique message on the integration blot," one television producer commented.[58]

In 1963, composer Paul Reif set King's words to music in a lengthy choral arrangement. The chorus began with a slow chanting of "Birmingham Jail . . . April sixteen . . . nineteen hundred sixty-three." The arrangement focused on the slow road to racial equality and the rebuke of gradualism. "Wait! Wait! Wait!" shouted the singers. "Wait for a more convenient season, wait!" And ended with a booming bass voice singing "I hope this letter finds you strong in the faith, Mar-tin Lu-ther King." More recently, another composer, John Scully, presented an operatic version.[59]

With King's murder in 1968, the letter made the final transformation from an eloquent and inspiring example of protest literature into an apparent God-breathed epistle. Members of the Black Theology Project, a group of activists developing the theological implications of the Black Power movement, began a campaign in the 1970s to include the letter as the sixty-seventh book of the Bible. Led by the Reverend Muhammed Kenyatta, the activists hoped a grassroots effort would provide a biblical version of King's epistle by the year 2000. Their efforts apparently fell short.[60]

As one civil rights activist noted, King's "Letter from Birmingham Jail" "condemned you like the Bible condemns you" and compelled people to change their ways and "do the right thing." The eight white clergy addressed in letter suddenly found themselves condemned as American pharisees—a portrait they had a difficult time overcoming. King and the SCLC had simply used the ministers as convenient rhetorical targets to answer the many critics of nonviolence and the Birmingham movement. "I understood that in this document," remembered Andrew Young, "Martin was providing a comprehensive, far-ranging answer to all the objections to our campaign." Yet, because their names appeared at the top of the document, history remembered only the eight white clergy, not everyone else who had been critical—not the Kennedys or Billy Graham; not the majority of black ministers in Birmingham; not the mainstream press. Martin Luther King's rhetoric overtly and sometimes subtly condemned the eight religious leaders for many of Birmingham's sins and suggested that the white clergy, and other moderates, were black Americans' greatest stumbling block to freedom. This viewpoint emerged as the basis of most subsequent assessments of the eight ministers.[61]

The timing of the letter's appearance in the public realm was also unfortunate for the ministers. The eight had issued their public statement early in the movement, on April 12, three weeks prior to massive police retaliation and before widespread public sympathy had developed for the protesters. Conversely, the letter first appeared in the public realm less than two weeks following the most violent confrontations in the city. These images of Birmingham brutality remained fresh in the public's mind. Since few media outlets offered any explanation of the white ministers' statement or provided an appropriate context, the clergy appeared to be condemning the nonviolent protests of children, while commending the use of police dogs and fire hoses by a so-called restrained Birmingham police force.

Despite hopeful rhetoric in the letter, King never had a face-to-face meeting with any of these eight ministers. He had stated in the document that he looked to a time when he would meet each of the clergy, "not as an integrationist or a civil rights leader but as a fellow clergyman and a Christian brother." King, however, never sought a meeting with the white clergy, reflecting his complete dismissal of these men as effective agents of change. They were, however, worthy rhetorical targets.[62]

In King's overall quest to "crack" Birmingham, the white ministers were of little consequence. Other issues had King's attention: money problems, image woes, tactical shortcomings, and a personal responsibility for the lives of scores of Birmingham's children. Why bother with a group of white ministers who had told him to get out of town? Drawing on past experiences with white southern clergymen, King had neither the time nor the patience for open dialogue. Others in the movement felt the same way. Compromise was never an option—even negotiations were seen as a waste of time. "It was a job no one coveted," Andrew Young remembered. Several SCLC officials teased Young for "sucking up to white folks and playing the 'Uncle Tom.' " Even prior to the campaign, Wyatt Walker had instructed aides to simply "write them [white] churches off."[63]

Regardless, most of the eight white clergymen believed King's rhetoric was cruel and unfair. Perhaps most offensive to the eight ministers was the civil rights leader's inquiry as to where their voices were when "Governor Wallace gave a clarion call for defiance and hatred." They had indeed spoken out against "inflammatory and rebellious statements" and had faced a steady stream of harassment and intimidation from belligerent segregationists. Several paid the high price of losing the effectiveness of their ministry and eventually their pulpits.[64]

Relatively few civil rights leaders or members of the national press recognized the precarious situation in which these eight white ministers found themselves; between two powerful opposing forces, the black activist and the belligerent segregationist. Moreover, while King and his colleagues were composing the "Letter from Birmingham Jail," they either ignored or never knew that the clergy had spoken out against Wallace just a few months before.

Opinions regarding the eight white ministers and their public statement varied among Birmingham's civil rights activists. Oblivious to many of the problems the white clergy faced, the ironclad Fred Shuttlesworth believed the clergy's stand was nothing more than a simple "pebble in the ocean" of racial justice. "They ought to have started [speaking out] a long time before," Shuttlesworth contended. "Way on back, when they were beating, and castrating, and bombing, there should have been voices then." In contrast, the white ministers believed they had boldly spoken out for several years. "Let's not get hung up on the fact that they did a little bit," Shuttlesworth responded. "Yeah, yeah, yeah, they should have been speaking out. They should have done this and that." During the defiant days of the 1950s and 1960s, the civil rights leader believed Alabama's white ministers had no interest in racial justice. "Don't think that I am wicked in my statement," he added. "I am factual, O.K. You should know the truth and the truth shall make you free. You can't cover it up. Jesus died not because they thought he was wrong but because they knew he was right."[65]

While the white clergy openly sought concessions from King and the SCLC, they had never truly experienced the vast injustices of segregation and never fully understood why waiting for gradual change insulted King. "Where were their voices when a black race took upon itself the cross of protest against man's injustice to man?" King asked. Resorting to demonstrations upset the white clergy's concept of law and order. For King, sacrificing order to challenge an unjust law was a small price for freedom. Neither side was willing to compromise these sacred principles.[66]

Many within the movement saw no shades of gray in the quest for racial justice. With scores of unenforced laws on the books and years of broken promises, many civil rights activists developed the conviction that a white person was either for them or against them. As Fred Shuttlesworth believed, if the eight white clergy had been on the "right side" of the integration issue, they would have boldly "marched with the people" in the streets of Birmingham. Although he knew none of these men personally, the civil rights leader compared the eight clergy and their public statements to New Testament Pharisees who were grandstanding before the public and judging from "high ecclesiastical and pontifical positions." It was a situation where "hell-bound, pious folks were still hell-bound," he added. He considered their public statement an unjustified, futile attempt to slow the quest for equality. "Jesus would classify" all of the eight white ministers as bigots and the religious mouthpieces of belligerent segregationists, Shuttlesworth argued. The white clergy never abided with their flock and never prayed for the people involved in the movement, he continued. Had they prayed or revealed any concern and love, they would have actively participated in the movement. "They never spoke to us," the civil rights leader added. "They never encouraged me. They never prayed for me as a minister or brother. They never even spoke to me about what I was doing. They left me to the Klan."[67]

By disagreeing with the SCLC's timing and methods, Birmingham civil rights activist Abraham Woods also questioned whether the eight white clergy really hoped to improve race relations. "If they wanted justice and equality," Woods said, "they wanted it without plowing up the field. They wanted it without the thunder and lightning."[68] Few gradualists wanted such loud flashes of change in society.

Bombastic and sensationalistic, the attitudes of Shuttlesworth and Woods, however, were uncharacteristic of most local activists in Birmingham. More representative was the attitude of campaign leader John Porter, who refused to condemn the white ministers for not taking a more active role. "You have to be careful when you boast about what I did and what you did not do," Porter emphasized. Even getting involved as much as they did placed the eight white clergy on shaky ground. Porter said he saw "tremendous suffering" in the white pulpits of Birmingham. "Any attempt," he believed, "to address the [racial] issue from a moderate point of view and you were penalized gravely. It was a cut-and-dried issue." Belligerent segregationists carefully scrutinized the actions and rhetoric of the white clergy. "The intensity was just unbelievable," Porter said. In addition, economic considerations guided the white ministers. Porter's participation in the demonstrations did not jeopardize his job and financial situation. The white ministers chose not to risk their livelihood by stepping forward to support the movement in words or actions, Porter believed. "I'm convinced that all that matters is each man has to decide where he will stand," said Porter. "You cannot require everybody to stand where you stand."[69]

Others in the movement were less sympathetic and understanding. After reading the white clergy's statement, Ralph Abernathy recalled, King and other movement leaders were "totally surprised" that these men had such a narrow vision of racial equality. In turn, Abernathy later pondered what they had felt after reading the "Letter from Birmingham Jail." Had King's arguments convinced the white clergy, or were his points dismissed as more extremism and foolishness? Were the ministers "ashamed of themselves," Abernathy wondered, or had they continued to support Birmingham's violent stand against outsiders and trouble-makers? "I . . . never read any subsequent statements by these gentle-men," the civil rights leader wrote, "and perhaps that said something about their ultimate thoughts on the subject."[70]

Privately, however, each of the white clergy had a personal reaction to King's letter. The responses were a mixed bag of anger, bitterness, and bewilderment; some agreed with King's arguments, others rejected them, a few just ignored them. Regardless of the reaction, the "Letter from Birmingham Jail" would haunt the eight religious leaders the rest of their careers. Combined with the unrelenting pressure from radical segrega-tionists, none of Birmingham's peacemakers would find any personal peace.

The "symbols of the movement" *(left to right)*: A defiant Fred Shuttlesworth, a jovial Ralph Abernathy, and a pensive Martin Luther King Jr. defy a court injunction and march through the streets of Birmingham on Good Friday, April 12, 1963. *Department of Archives and Manuscripts, Birmingham Public Library*

Ralph Abernathy *(left)* and Martin Luther King Jr. *(right)* lead the small group of singing protestors walking two by two in the bright afternoon sun amidst a swarm of reporters and a crowd of onlookers. Fred Shuttlesworth had quietly left the march to help coordinate other activities. A few short blocks farther along, Birmingham police arrested the tiny parade and transported them to the Birmingham Jail. *AP World Wide Photos*

Jail wardens placed King in this fifty-four-square-foot isolation cell. The burden of absolute solitude distressed him and sent him descending into a period of deep depression. The civil rights leader recalled those hours as the "most frustrating and bewildering" he had ever lived. During his first few days of imprisonment, he began composing the "Letter from Birmingham Jail."
Department of Archives and Manuscripts, Birmingham Public Library

SCLC Executive Director Wyatt Tee Walker *(left)* assisted King in composing, compiling, editing, and circulating the "Letter from Birmingham Jail." During the week the civil rights leader was in jail, Walker slowly pieced together the literary jigsaw puzzle—taking King's words, phrases, and sentences and placing them into a kind of logical order. Walker's secretary, Willie Pearl Mackey *(right)*, typed drafts of the document.
Courtesy Willie Pearl Mackey

Dignified and urbane, Methodist Bishop Nolan Bailey Harmon Jr. made an outstanding contribution to Methodism as a preacher, writer, editor, bishop, and teacher. The oldest of the eight white clergymen, Harmon believed racial justice and peace in the South would come only with the "slow, slow, slow process of time."
Nolan B. Harmon Papers, MSS 134, Pitts Theology Library, Emory University, Atlanta, Georgia

A husky, intimidating figure, Episcopal Bishop Charles Colcock Jones Carpenter stood six feet four inches tall and weighed 275 pounds. A complex individual with contradictory rhetoric and deeds, Carpenter often appeared to sympathize with both sides of the segregation issue. A speedy end to segregation, he believed, would lead to social chaos and violence.
Department of Archives and Manuscripts, Birmingham Public Library

Dignified, distinguished, and aristocratic, Episcopal Bishop George Murray possessed an eloquent speaking voice that one acquaintance described as refined as the sound of "crystal when it's tapped." Murray maintained a far-reaching social vision that was not out of step with Martin Luther King's. Regardless, the two ministers disagreed on the right tactics to bring about equality. Murray refused to "go all out" and participate in the public demonstrations, which he thought would "automatically end my ministry here."
Department of Archives and Manuscripts, Birmingham Public Library

Prior to his selection as a bishop, Paul Hardin Jr. served as a pastor of First Methodist Church of Birmingham. Hardin later insisted that his entire ministry in Birmingham and in South Carolina contradicted the impression the "Letter from Birmingham Jail" gave. "I don't think that he meant to take advantage of a situation," Hardin reflected, "but he saw . . . the names of men who were prominent in the religious life of Birmingham and the state of Alabama, and he wanted to address that letter to that type of person, people who were well known. In a measure, I never really felt badly toward him for it."
Department of Archives and Manuscripts, Birmingham Public Library

In spite of his bookish and unassuming appearance, Rabbi Milton Grafman was often described by colleagues as an Old Testament prophet with tireless energy, keen insight, and courage to stand for justice and righteousness. "The question is," he asked his congregation during the racial crisis, "are you ready to pay the price? If you are not, God help this city. This city isn't dead yet, not by a long shot. It's almost dead. You and decent Christians can revive this city."
Courtesy Stephen Grafman

Roman Catholic Bishop Joseph A. Durick experienced an intellectual awakening rare among white southerners. As his role in the Catholic Church grew in prominence, he realized the injustice of segregation and began to advocate gradual change. The brutality of segregation in Birmingham in the early 1960s shook the foundation of the bishop's culture-based beliefs. The blinders fell off his eyes, and he could no longer wait passively with other southern gradualists.
Courtesy Nashville Tennessean

During the height of the civil rights tensions in Birmingham, one friend believed First Presbyterian pastor Edward V. Ramage had been inducted into the "grand fraternity of the harassed" in the South. Pressure from segregationists within his own congregation convinced Ramage to leave his longtime pastorate and pursue a ministry elsewhere.

First Presbyterian Church, Birmingham, Alabama, Files. Special Collection, Samford University Library, Birmingham, Alabama

The drama of the civil rights demonstrations in Birmingham touched the life and ministry of Earl Stallings more directly than that of any of the other white clergymen addressed in the "Letter from Birmingham Jail." In the face of unrelenting pressure and criticism, Stallings stood for racial justice. "We hear the call of truth, of righteousness, of justice," he proclaimed from his pulpit at First Baptist Church in the spring of 1963, "but we are not men enough to heed its challenge." Segregationists in the congregation, through petty harassment and threats, effectively ended Stallings's ministry in Birmingham.

First Baptist Church, Birmingham, Alabama, Files. Special Collection, Samford University Library, Birmingham, Alabama

Left to right: Joseph Allen, Earl Stallings, Milton Grafman, George Murray, Nolan Harmon, and Joseph Durick share a moment in front of the White House before their meeting with President John F. Kennedy on September 23, 1963. Kennedy had invited Alabama's leading white religious leaders to Washington following the bombing of the Sixteenth Street Baptist Church.
AP World Wide Photos

The moving words of King's "Letter from Birmingham Jail" deeply affected the life and career of Roman Catholic Bishop Joseph A. Durick. "I had seen segregation as wrong," he later reflected, "but not as he had portrayed it." A year after King's death, Durick (*right*) participated in a Good Friday memorial march (he is pictured here with Father William Greenspan) and spoke at a rally in Memphis honoring the slain civil rights leader.
Courtesy Nashville Tennessean

Although Nolan Harmon retired from the Methodist episcopacy in 1964, he continued to play an active role in church affairs, preaching and teaching until near his one-
hundredth birthday. A black southerner once asked Harmon if he had ever met
Martin Luther King Jr. "No," the bishop replied, "all he ever did was just write me a
letter."

*Nolan B. Harmon Papers, MSS 134, Pitts Theology Library, Emory University,
Atlanta, Georgia*

8   "Let It Alone"

Although they rarely expressed their feelings in a public forum, each of the clergymen had a personal reaction to Martin Luther King's composition, but few journalists or scholars ever examined these responses. In 1963, many Americans read King's letter and joined with a symphony of voices condemning the injustices of segregation in the South and demanding immediate integration. Few Americans understood the reasons why eight white ministers spoke out against King and his Birmingham campaign. In general, the public saw only King's perspective and held the eight clergymen in low regard.

After reading the "Letter from Birmingham Jail" for the first time in 1963, Bishop Nolan Harmon telephoned colleague Paul Hardin and expressed feelings of deep hurt. The document was unfair and unjust, he told Hardin, and had betrayed the eight white clergy. They had promoted racial justice, Harmon believed, but that apparently wasn't good enough for King. Hardin advised Harmon to ignore the document. "Bishop, I don't think I would touch it," Hardin said, "there was no way in the world that you could get a hearing now; let it alone." And for the rest of their careers, the eight ministers did mostly "let it alone."[1]

For the rest of their ministries, Nolan Harmon and Charles Carpenter, the eldest of the eight, continued to condemn the "lawless" tactics of integrationists and segregationists alike. They both remained static figures, trapped in the social system most favored by their generation of white southerners.

On April Fools' Day 1972, the last patron at the Tutwiler Hotel, Vaisilios Melonas, checked out of room 528, and the grand old building closed its doors permanently. The hotel where the eight white clergy held their gatherings was razed to make way for parking in early 1974. Bishop Nolan Harmon, who used the Tutwiler as his Birmingham home, checked out of the hotel for the final time in 1964 and returned to full-time duties as the leader of the Western North Carolina Conference. A black southerner once asked Bishop Harmon if he had ever met Martin Luther King Jr. "No," the bishop replied. "All he ever did was just write me a letter."[2]

The "Letter from Birmingham Jail," Nolan Harmon later wrote in his autobiography *Ninety Years and Counting*, was a "good one from its own standpoint," but he questioned the motives behind the document. Martin Luther King, he believed, should have sent the white ministers the letter first, instead of just releasing the document to the media. The SCLC had simply "given out" the letter to various media outlets as a "propaganda move" and used the names of prominent Alabama religious leaders to "give great emphasis to what he wrote—as indeed it did." The white ministers, the bishop later recalled, were "incidentally tagged" by King and the media as defiant bigots, unwilling to accept guidance or counsel.[3]

Had the civil rights leader listened to the white ministers, Harmon believed, Birmingham's racial climate would have been more peaceful. The demonstrations, he said at the time, had "blown away for a long time" a sense of "brotherliness and good feeling, on which proper race relations must be based rather than on legal enactments." In the same spirit, the "Letter from Birmingham Jail" aided King's quest for national prominence, Harmon believed, but helped few people in Birmingham. King won his battles in the northern newspapers, but he lost his war in the South, where it needed to be won, he added.[4]

King had called into question the motives of the eight clergy, something Harmon resented. "We who uttered our warning admit and bewail the lack of the rights that Dr. King properly calls for," the bishop said in 1963. Harmon believed that civil rights would only come through peace, patience, and order. King had brushed aside the gradual approach to the racial crisis in Birmingham and had demanded an immediate solution to all the problems of what Harmon described as the "downtrodden black people." Integration, Harmon added, was going to take more time than the letter demanded, as it "surely did." The eight white clergy recognized this, as did "other sensible people."[5]

Although he was a staunch moralist and frequently preached against societal sins, Harmon's position on segregation never evolved. He never gained a temperance fervor for civil rights issues. Even after decades of acknowledging the injustice of segregation in the South, Harmon still urged more time for change. Human nature and the "entrenched manners and customs of millions of people cannot be quickly reversed," he concluded. "Gradualism will work, and I do not mean endless procrastination." Although many thought "now is the time" for racial justice, Harmon insisted more time and the absence of tension served the situation best. He was convinced that law breaking was not the beginning of freedom but the end. Harmon held fast to his "law-and-order" philosophy and his chivalrous southern paternalism. Martin Luther King had broken the law, and no good citizen or preacher would resort to such a wrongheaded notion. Laws, no matter how just or unjust, had to be obeyed, the bishop believed.[6]

King, however, was not the only "lawbreaker" that Harmon confronted. When Alabama governor George Wallace made a symbolic stand in the schoolhouse door against integration at the University of Alabama in June 1963, Harmon stood before the Annual Conference in Birmingham and read a public protest. Neither segregationist governors nor civil rights activists had the right to defy the law, the bishop underscored. Harmon regretted that Wallace had attempted to "defy the sovereignty of the United States" and deny fundamental human rights. Such an attempt was a "moral mistake" and a "political blunder" (although it never would harm Wallace's career). The church had no business directing the affairs of state, but the church had to speak out when state leaders injured the "God given rights of any man." Harmon received several hateful letters, and a few Methodist churchgoers quit the denomination over his stand, including a Birmingham firefighter injured during the civil rights demonstrations. Nevertheless, most of the Methodist clergy in the conference supported the bishop.[7]

Harmon, however, had little support when he confronted the circulating of the "Letter from Birmingham Jail" at the Chicago meeting of the United Methodist General Board of Christian Social Concerns in August 1963. When delegates received a copy of the letter in an official information packet, Harmon believed the group had allowed two Methodist bishops (Hardin and himself) to be characterized as "obstacles to

all justice and freedom." Within hours, Harmon sent a forceful statement to the conference expressing anger that an official agency of the
church had distributed the document without notifying Harmon and
Hardin or truly understanding the situation in Birmingham. The Board
of Social Concerns had long called for justice and fairness to all, but,
Harmon asked, "What of the fairness of placarding publicly the names
of two of its own Bishops, to say nothing of the other religious leaders,
without making any attempt to reach them or to find out from other
than newspaper reports the exact situation in Alabama—what had happened before our statement was issued and what happened afterward as
the result of not heeding our warning? The fact is, the complete story of
Birmingham has not yet been told."[8] King's letter was unfair to all eight
of the white clergy, and the Methodist board had moved toward
"deplorable irresponsibility" by distributing the document. "Keep your
balance, brethren," Harmon warned, "be careful what you do, and be
as fair to your own as you want them to be fair to others."[9]

In response, the Chicago conference leaders defended their distributing the letter, because the document had so admirably "shed light upon
the complexities of contemporary human relations." The conference
also affirmed the "well known" sincerity, integrity, and Christian leadership Harmon and Hardin had shown in the cause of racial justice. Harmon scoffed, considering this only a poor excuse for an apology.[10]

A few months after leaving Birmingham, Harmon retired from the
episcopacy but not from a life of active endeavor. "One can sit down
and listen to his arteries harden," Harmon once said, "or you can keep
going at whatever you can find to do." He spent the next ten years compiling and editing the *Encyclopedia of World Methodism*, a massive
two-volume work that remains the most comprehensive guide to the
church. Harmon also found time to join the faculty at the Candler
School of Theology at Emory University in Atlanta as a visiting professor. He and his wife Rebecca purchased a home near campus, and Harmon taught two classes a semester, usually on Methodist polity and the
constitutional history of the church. Even well into his nineties, after his
wife had passed away and he lived alone, Harmon went to campus each
day for classes. Nearly all of his students received an A in his courses.
When someone asked about the improbability of teaching so many A
students, Harmon replied, "But they all do equally well because they
have an A professor."[11]

In 1983, at age ninety, he wrote his autobiography, *Ninety Years and*

Counting, reflecting upon his long service to the church. Harmon retired from his second career as a college teacher in his 96th year and died just short of his 101st birthday on June 8, 1993. Methodist bishops are elected for life, and Harmon died the oldest bishop in church history. He made an outstanding contribution to Methodism, remembered one colleague, as a preacher, writer, editor, bishop, and teacher. Fortunately for Harmon, only a handful in the church remembered him as a recipient of Martin Luther King's blistering criticism in the "Letter from Birmingham Jail."[12]

Criticism in general never seemed to bother the good-natured Charles Carpenter. In his annual bishop's address, Carpenter had spoken of such matters at the 1962 Diocesan Convention when he urged those present to be "critics of criticism," learning what criticism to accept or reject. "If criticism is unfair, we must keep from irritation," he exhorted; if untrue, ignore it; if well-founded, "profit by it." He also warned the delegates that criticism was causing disunity in the church and had become "not only a popular pastime but also a mighty force that can be used like dynamite—carefully to aid, carelessly to destroy."[13]

When Carpenter saw the "Letter from Birmingham Jail" for the first time, he simply disregarded what he viewed as careless criticism. After reading the document, Carpenter turned to George Murray and aptly described the frustration of many tempered white southerners. "This is what you get when you try to do something," he said. "You get it from both sides. George, you just have to live with that." Carpenter and most of the eight white clergy found little profit, only hardship, in King's public criticism.[14]

For Charles Carpenter, civil disobedience was a terrible transgression against genteel southern society. Two years later, during the Selma demonstrations of 1965, the bishop publicly urged all Alabama Episcopalians not to participate in a proposed Selma-to-Montgomery march scheduled for Sunday, March 21. The march was "a foolish business and sad waste of time" in which misguided souls would indulge a "childish instinct to parade" and Alabama would suffer the consequences. Carpenter resented the presence of "outside agitators," who he hoped would soon depart and would let the state move on with the progress "for which we feel a special responsibility."[15]

Many of those outsiders were scores of northern Episcopal clergy and laypersons. The Right Reverend C. Kilmer Myers, suffragan bishop of

Michigan, informed Carpenter of his plans to conduct a worship service in the sanctuary at Selma's prestigious Episcopal church St. Paul's, on the Saturday before the march. Under the canon laws of the Protestant Episcopal Church, visiting clergy had to receive permission to conduct worship services in another bishop's diocese. Myers never asked for Carpenter's consent—typical of the crusading mentality and sense of moral superiority of many white northerners. Consequently, Carpenter barred the visiting Episcopalians from using the church, but Myers proceeded with his plans for the prayer service anyway. In turn, Carpenter ordered the doors locked at St. Paul's. Not deterred, Myers held the service at the dividing line between white and black Selma. "Your crude and rude action in this matter," Carpenter scolded Myers, "makes me doubt the sincerity of your motives in coming to Selma where you did damage to the life and work of the church, particularly at a time when we are trying to work through a very difficult situation." Carpenter advised Myers to "learn some manners" if he ever came back to Alabama.[16]

Once again, Alabama's Episcopal bishop emerged as a target of intense criticism from around the country. An outspoken clergyman in Myers's diocese, the Reverend Carl Sayre, called for Carpenter's resignation. The rector of St. Stephen's Episcopal Church in Birmingham, Michigan, Sayre blasted Carpenter during a memorial service for Viola Liuzzo, a white Detroit civil rights worker who was murdered near Selma. He later wrote Carpenter an open letter. "As bishop of Alabama, you have been to the flock of Christ, a wolf and not a shepherd," Sayre wrote, "you have devoured them and not fed them, by making common cause with Governor Wallace's defiance of his nation and church. As the Governor stood wrongly in the school house door, you have stood wrongly and symbolically" in the doorway of God's house. Carpenter announced that he did not plan to resign and dismissed Sayre as a "little fellow" who wanted publicity.[17]

Other northerners were even less hospitable than Sayre. A New Yorker described Carpenter as an "inquisitional bishop" and scolded him for his snobbery and "ritualistic concept" of Christianity. Alabama's Episcopal bishop, he believed, was no better than Robert Shelton of the Ku Klux Klan, George Wallace, or Selma sheriff Jim Clark. "You are a fit shepherd for such wolves and an unfit shepherd for sheep." Carpenter needed to show courage and defend his concept of Christianity as well as Martin Luther King Jr., "or admit that your miter and crozier are in the wrong hands, un-Christian hands, defiling hands." The bishop had dragged his feet for years in racial matters. "I cannot respect you as either a churchman or a Christian—nor can I respect a church or religion which tolerates you. . . . Will you please see to it that I do not miss your obituary? It will be such pleasant reading."[18]

Much of the civil rights discontent during the Selma upheaval would focus on St. Paul's Episcopal Church. The Gothic Revival church building in downtown Selma had one of the most powerful, wealthy, and influential congregations in the diocese. It was also among the most conservative and reactionary. Dominated by a vocal group of elitist segregationists, the vestry struggled to prohibit those blacks and whites interested in "agitating racial strife and discord" from attending services. Early in March, a large group of whites and blacks, accompanied by television cameras and reporters, attempted to attend services at the Selma church. The vestry questioned the group's motives and turned them away. Other groups returned the next two Sundays and were again barred from entering the church. "Segregation," one parishioner later explained, "keeps Christians of each race separated where each race can develop their special racial qualities at all levels of society without the real possibility of intermarriage."[19]

Finally, Bishop Carpenter and Rector Frank Mathews convinced the church vestry to tolerate an interracial group, including students from the Episcopal Theological School at Cambridge, on Sunday, March 28. Tensions, however, continued to simmer during the following days, and Carpenter made a special trip to Selma to meet with the vestry. He affirmed the national church's open-door policy, but behind the scenes, Carpenter expressed his deep sympathy for the difficulties inflicted upon the church by the interracial groups. In a letter to Annette McCullough, the wife of a rich vestryman and a member of the right-wing John Birch Society, Carpenter noted that the local situation had been handled well and wished before long the unwanted "visitors" would all return home.[20]

On Easter Sunday, April 18, ushers seated an interracial group in the back of the sanctuary behind several empty rows of pews. Because of these seating arrangements, they also received the sacrament last. Carpenter and Mathews's rather conservative compromise provoked attacks from all sides of the race question. One parishioner questioned the wisdom of allowing segregated seating "in an obscure corner where they will not contaminate God's elite." On the other hand, while other church members protested the admission of the visitors, the visitors criticized Carpenter for the seating arrangements that they described as the "old slave gallery" in the church. The visitors believed it was ironic that in the state where blacks fought back-of-the-bus seating, the Episcopal Church sought to maintain traditional racial patterns. "We cannot let this devious maneuver go unchallenged," they charged. "The Carpenter of Birmingham must not be allowed to forever deny the Carpenter of Nazareth."[21]

By the end of April, a few of the interracial visitors at St. Paul's picketed diocesan headquarters. Several protesters carried signs proclaiming "Bishop Sanctions Segregated Seating in Selma Church" and "Slave Gallery Revived." The day of the picketing, however, Carpenter had chosen not to come to the office. One of the protesters was a twenty-six-year-old Episcopal Theological School student, Jonathan Myrick Daniels. A New Hampshire native, Daniels had moved to Selma to "encourage and uplift" local blacks by showing that someone cared enough to live and work in their community. Daniels also worked to open communication between the residents of the black and white communities. "Sometimes we confront the posse," Daniels wrote, "and sometimes we hold a child. Sometimes we stand with men who have learned to hate, and sometimes we must stand a little apart from them."[22]

Daniels consistently attended St. Paul's with several interracial groups. "Our life in Selma is filled with ambiguity, and in that we share with men everywhere," he surmised. "Selma, Alabama is like all the world"; the city needed the life and witness of "militant saints," he added. In late spring, Daniels returned to seminary for a brief stay to finish his final exams. He would make a fateful return during the summer months.[23]

As Daniels made his way back to New Hampshire, Charles Carpenter complained about Episcopal leaders coming to Alabama at the national church's expense—namely members of the Executive Council. "When the people of Alabama realize," Carpenter wrote, "that the money they are striving to give . . . is being used to buy free trips to Alabama for men who are not wanted there and served no purpose there . . . they will not like it." Alabama's bishop asked for a tighter control of the money spent by the church. George Murray, a member of the Executive Council, asked that the money spent to send five staff members be reimbursed from the voluntary Church and Race Fund. After a lengthy discussion, the council defeated the motion at their May meeting in Greenwich, Connecticut. The council, however, expressed regret to Carpenter that they had "added to the burden of the Church in Alabama, while endeavoring to support it in the bearing of that burden." Regardless, several of the churches in the diocese resented the "arrogant and cavalier treatment" of Alabama's bishops. The vestry of one Episcopal church passed a resolution praising Carpenter and Murray and expressing pity for those church leaders who had followed the example of the Pharisees and "succumbed to the siren call to come to Selma, Alabama, and display their religion by standing, marching and praying, not only on the street corners, but in the streets and highways to be seen of men."[24]

Later that summer Jonathan Daniels returned to the streets of Selma as a representative in a "continuing ministry of presence." On August 14, Daniels participated in a Student Nonviolent Coordinating Committee (SNCC) demonstration in Fort Deposit in Lowndes County, Alabama. Local police arrested the demonstrators "for their own protection" and placed them in the cramped Fort Deposit Jail. The prisoners were soon transferred to a bigger facility in nearby Hayneville. The group sang freedom songs as they rode to the jail in the back of a garbage truck. In an equally "wretched" facility, Daniels shared a cell with veteran SNCC activists' Stokely Carmichael and Chris Wildy. The trio spent time talking, singing, and worshiping God. On August 20, police unexpectedly released the entire group. With no transportation, Daniels and three others walked to a small grocery store for a bottle of Coke. Lowndes County deputy sheriff Thomas Coleman ordered them off the property and shouted "get the hell out of here or I'll blow your head off" as he shot and mortally wounded Daniels.[25]

Two days before Daniels's arrest, Carpenter wrote to the Reverend Frank Mathews at St. Paul's about Daniels. "If he is hanging around causing trouble, I think I will just have to write to his Bishop and tell him to take him on back to Seminary," Carpenter maintained, "but I will be awaiting word from you as to just how he is behaving himself." When Carpenter learned of Daniels's death, the bishop issued a brief response. He termed Daniels's death as "deplorable," believing that the event was another example of the "current wave of lawlessness sweeping our country."[26]

Police later arrested Thomas Coleman. At his trial for manslaughter, Coleman claimed Daniels had waved a knife, and that he (Coleman) had fired the gun in self-defense. After deliberating for one hour and forty-three minutes, a jury of twelve white men acquitted Coleman. John E. Hines, the presiding bishop of the Episcopal Church, deplored the verdict. Defense attorneys had "assassinated the character of a man already dead," Hines contended. The life of Jonathan Daniels was "no more and no less valuable than that of any other man in the sight of God." The bishop believed the cause in which Daniels laid down his life was "dear to everyone who breathes the air of free men."[27]

Many Episcopal leaders urged Bishop Carpenter to make a strong statement deploring the verdict. However, he again responded in ambivalent fashion. "Disagreement with another person's actions or even disapproval of his sin is no justification for attacking his person or taking his life," Carpenter affirmed. He called on Alabama Christians to pray that the acquittal of Thomas Coleman would not be interpreted "as a license to kill or injure those with whom we disagree or whose behavior we disapprove."[28]

Through the years, Bishop Carpenter's failure to comprehend racial injustice proved to be a source of personal anguish for the handful of Alabama's black Episcopalians. Following the Selma campaign, Luther H. Foster, the president of Tuskegee Institute, believed the official position of the Alabama church during the critical days of the civil rights movement was to "dampen the aspirations" of black citizens rather than to provide real solutions. Foster could no longer "harmonize" his views on the racial situation with Carpenter's. The state was in an uproar, and the people of Alabama needed Carpenter's "forthright and constructive leadership" to help the state "turn around to a new and finer day." The situation was desperate, Foster added, and Carpenter had to act in a prompt and bold fashion; "anything short of dramatic reversal will be totally inadequate." In the past, the black Episcopalian believed that he had been ineffective in convincing Carpenter of the sense of urgency for racial justice in Alabama. "Somehow," he continued, "I have failed at a terribly crucial point of contact—with my church, and that my church has failed me."[29]

The Reverend Vernon Jones, Foster's rector at St. Andrew's in Tuskegee, believed southern traditions had blinded Carpenter. "I think time had passed him by in approaching things realistically," Jones later recalled. "He would term himself as a moderate, but his actions did not support that." Carpenter believed change could come gradually, but Jones and Foster never witnessed the bishop taking any steps toward real progress. "He was part of his generation," Jones continued, "out of touch and only willing to make haste very slowly." Another of Jones's parishioners in the 1960s prayed that the "sinful scale" would fall from

Carpenter's eyes. "We forgive you," he wrote, "and pray for you now as we have for a long time for your failure to advance Christian brotherhood in the diocese." If Carpenter would only confess his belief in the sin of separation, then black Episcopalians from throughout Alabama would come to Birmingham "to pray with you to overcome this weakness."[30]

The civil rights battles in Alabama during the mid-1960s left Carpenter broken in body and spirit. The constant stress during a time of great social unrest made Carpenter, in George Murray's words, an "old man before his time." The upheaval took a heavy toll on Carpenter, he added, as it "took a toll on me." Tired, frail, and overworked, Carpenter was plagued by chronic illness during his few remaining years. Yet he determined to finish out thirty years of service as leader of the diocese of Alabama. When he retired in 1968, he was the senior bishop of the Protestant Episcopal Church. Carpenter lived only a few more months and died on June 29, 1969.[31]

Many Episcopalians in Alabama have fond memories of Charles Colcock Jones Carpenter, the titanic bishop with the "four-cylinder name," and his three decades of leading the diocese. They recall his imposing stature, his "hands as big as hams," his genteel manner, and his quick wit. Throughout the state, when the "big bishop" came for a parish visit, little children flocked to him. Carpenter filled his pockets with tiny toy kangaroos, which he gave to children and adults alike. "I induct you into the Order of the Kangaroo," he would say as he bestowed the figure. "Remember who you are and what you represent." Although the gift had no real significance, hundreds of people around the state of Alabama still cherish the memory and the memento.[32]

Carpenter will also be remembered as representing a generation of white southerners that fearfully watched the old order collapse around them. For the bishop, change came too quickly. Carpenter and his generation witnessed many positive changes in race relations from the Depression into the 1950s and 1960s. Yet the bishop lacked a forward vision to see the problems that remained. Much in the same way as his grandfather had viewed the passing of the agrarian South many years before, Carpenter focused upon the past and the end of a way of life that he believed had worked well. The bishop romanticized the South's past and enjoyed traveling to rural parishes in Alabama's Black Belt, where he could portray a similar role to that of his great-grandfather, Charles Colcock Jones Sr. Carpenter was also a child of pride.

*   *   *

Perhaps Martin Luther King's "Letter from Birmingham Jail" describes the attitudes of Charles Carpenter and Nolan Harmon more than the attitudes of the other eight ministers. "I guess I should have realized," King wrote in the letter, "that few members of a race that has oppressed another race can understand the deep groans and passionate yearning of the oppressed race, and still fewer have the vision to see that injustice must be rooted out by strong, persistent, and determined action."[33]

Time had passed by Carpenter and Harmon, and they were unable to envision a future without Jim Crow. During the civil rights era, few people understood the difficult time southerners of this generation had in dealing with the racial crisis. With age, adapting to change in the social order became increasingly difficult for even the most enlightened southerners. The best Harmon and Carpenter could hope for was to delay the inevitable, work hard as peacemakers, and condemn perceived opponents of law and order. Regardless, their efforts brought intense criticism from all sides of the racial issue. No peacemakers, not even those who failed to turn the corner toward racial enlightenment, avoided the wrath of radical segregationists.

9 "This City Isn't Dead Yet"

Soon after the "Letter from Birmingham Jail" appeared in the mass media, Rabbi Milton Grafman began receiving scores of impassioned letters from all over the country. One writer from New York suggested that the rabbi had turned his back on the spirit of the Passover and the Jews of the Holocaust. He hoped Grafman would reconsider his misguided position and, despite the difficult atmosphere of the Deep South, would positively lead his congregation and his neighbors in the "directions illuminated by our heritage both as Jews and Americans." Another writer was completely "ashamed and disgusted" with Judaism after she read the statement by the "supposed" white religious leaders. "How can you dare to give religious teaching to others when you yourself are untrue to God and his teachings?" she asked. The writer supposed Grafman's values had been so distorted from living in the South that he remained unable to distinguish good from bad. She believed the white ministers' praise of the Birmingham police for their "calm manner" was akin to "thanking the Gestapo for efficiently carrying out Hitler's orders." Other correspondents described their shame at being a member of a religion in which Rabbi Grafman "pretended" to be a spiritual leader. "Your agreement with and participation in this official attitude is a disgrace to your temple, to your religion and, if it makes any difference to you, to your God," one enraged Jew wrote. Deeply offended by these offerings, Grafman thought it was quite ironic that these "so-called Jews and advocates of nonviolence" were writing such violent letters.[1]

Each of the eight white ministers received such letters through the years. Few Americans understood that among this group of clergy were several men who "turned the corner" and embraced an enlightened racial viewpoint. In the years following Martin Luther King's "Letter from Birmingham Jail," Milton Grafman, Joseph Durick, George Murray, and Paul Hardin broadened their efforts to further racial justice.

During a 1963 sermon, Grafman described the "Letter from Birmingham Jail" as a beautiful yet vicious document. "He [King] did us an injustice," Grafman continued, "and said things that hurt us." Years later, in a hyperbolic moment, the rabbi still believed anyone reading the composition would think the white ministers were eight bigots. The letter enraged and embittered Grafman—it was a burden he carried the rest of his life. He resented the way King exposed the white clergy to ridicule, abuse, and dishonor before the public. The document placed the eight men, the rabbi added, in the position of appearing, "to posterity," as if they had opposed King's goals rather than the timing of the demonstrations. Regardless, as King argued, freedom long delayed was the same as freedom denied.[2]

One Birmingham minister described Milton Grafman as an Old Testament prophet with tireless energy, keen insight, and the courage to stand for justice and righteousness. In many ways, Grafman identified with the forsaken biblical prophets traveling a lonely road through a period of strife and unrest. He walked this secluded path, he once told his congregation, because he wanted justice and equality for blacks in the South, as well as fairness and decency for whites. Old Testament prophets Amos, Jeremiah, and Hosea never hid from controversial issues or cowered in fear of losing "fringe benefits" or social prestige. "They went where the action was," the rabbi said. Nevertheless, Rabbi Grafman traveled his lonely road at a gradual pace. "I have had the courage to remain in Alabama," he wrote in 1963, "and to try, in my humble way to meet our problems."[3]

The rabbi preferred living and working in the South during the racial turmoil and resented those northerners who traveled to the region for cameo appearances. During the height of the civil rights campaigns in 1963, nineteen rabbis, mostly northern, left a rabbinical conference and took a red-eye flight to Birmingham to, as they claimed, assert a "unique and highly imaginative" influence in the "arena of American social conflict." Their efforts caused a great deal of resentment in the local Jewish community.[4]

These well-intentioned but misguided rabbis had agreed to enter the city secretly, without informing anyone in Birmingham's Jewish community. When several local Jewish leaders discovered their plans, a small group of representatives (including Grafman) met the rabbis at the Birmingham Municipal Airport at 2:15 A.M. on May 8, 1963. The local group hoped to persuade the northerners to leave the city or at least not participate in the civil rights demonstrations. When the plane arrived, several of the rabbis were belligerent, angry, and uncooperative toward the local delegation. They had previously decided that the Jews of Birmingham were all segregationists and opponents of racial justice. The group of nineteen paid little heed to the fears of the local Jewish leaders, who believed the visit might provoke an anti-Semitic backlash from terrorist groups.[5]

That evening, the nineteen entered John Porter's Sixth Avenue Baptist Church and marched down the aisles like pilgrims on a holy crusade. Wearing rabbinical garb, they taught a crowd of black worshipers a Hebrew song of brotherhood. "I have never been moved more deeply in my life," Rabbi Alex Shapiro proclaimed. Inspired by the black struggle for freedom, the rabbis had embraced the spirit of the Holocaust to help end oppression in Birmingham. "We shall do what you ask," he said. "Our people are your people." Regardless, that was the extent of their aiding the civil rights cause; they quickly left Birmingham and returned to the safety of the north as heroes of a fanciful crusade.[6]

Rabbi Grafman resented the sense of moral superiority many northerners had about the South. When a longtime friend, fellow clergyman, and part-time journalist made a public stand in favor of the rabbis' visit and praised King's letter as a "glorious literary document," Grafman responded with a powerful rejoinder. "Frankly," he wrote, "I am a little sick and tired of news coverage by ear instead of by verification." Grafman's old friend knew nothing about the letter's background or the events that led up to it. "There is a story behind the Birmingham story that evokes a different reaction from unbiased people who hear it for the first time," Grafman wrote.[7]

In addition, he added, the story behind the flight of the rabbis to Birmingham was much more complex. "I would be much more impressed with you Prophets if you were to implement your Prophetism," Grafman wrote. For six months the pulpit at Birmingham's conservative Jewish temple remained vacant. "I find it quite strange that not one of the nineteen rabbis . . . to my knowledge applied for the local pulpit." In addition, the reform pulpit in Gadsden, Alabama, some sixty miles east of Birmingham, had also remained vacant. Grafman invited his friend to do his preaching in Alabama, rather than in his northern synagogue. "I would likewise be much more impressed if the men who have all the answers to this tragic problem which confronts the entire nation, not only the South, were to take pulpits in Alabama, Mississippi, and other areas of genuine tension instead of sublimating and expiating their failure to tackle problems in their own communities by indulging in homiletical heroics at a safe distance."[8]

While he described segregation in the South as dismal, obstinate, and stupid, Grafman blasted the revolting hypocrisy of the racial climate in the North. He believed the South had openly acknowledged its preference for segregation, while the North never admitted to de facto segregation. He often borrowed a quip from Dr. Lucius Pitts, president of Birmingham's historically black Miles College, to explain the difference in the two regions: southern politicians gave blacks rat poison and said it was rat poison, while their northern counterparts handed blacks rat poison and called it cake.[9]

Perhaps one day, Grafman believed, he would write a history of the Birmingham campaign and tell the complete story. "I might be encouraged to do so," he wrote in 1963, "if I did not have a sense of frustration that it would not be believed, because people . . . do not want to believe it." Most northerners simply wanted to assume that only Martin Luther King and his associates were "always right, always just, always played the game fair and square, whereas those who dared to question his tactics were on the side of bigotry and injustice."[10]

By working for a gradual solution to the racial crisis, Grafman considered himself trapped between the bigots on the right and the "bigoted liberals" on the left. Just as the rabbi vigorously opposed "whipping up hatred" against blacks, he pleaded with supporters of civil rights to stop inciting malice against those whites trying to help. Civil rights activists and the national press had created a "Roman Circus" atmosphere in Birmingham, the rabbi maintained, and he found this sickening. Grafman firmly believed the movement and the media were fostering a national hatred of Alabama's largest city, while the white ministers were fighting to "whip up love" in the community.[11]

*   *   *

Even with the end of organized street demonstrations in Birmingham in May 1963, tensions in the city remained high throughout the spring and summer. On Saturday, May 12, bombs exploded at the Gaston Motel and at the home of King's brother, A. D. King. Although no one was seriously injured, frustrated and angry blacks rioted in the streets for several hours. Individually, the eight clergy pleaded for calm in the city. Bishop Joseph Durick condemned the bombing as a gross injustice to the victims and an insult to all citizens of good will. "May the wisdom of God guide us all to a true spirit of justice," the Catholic leader prayed.[12]

Despite the actions of belligerents, the city's slow and sometimes painful process of dismantling the old system began. On May 23, the Alabama Supreme Court ruled that Albert Boutwell and the new city council were Birmingham's rightful government. With legitimate authority, the council asked Boutwell to appoint a special advisory committee to ease the transition from a segregated to an integrated society. The department stores in downtown Birmingham integrated fitting rooms by May 14 and removed "colored only" signs over restrooms and water fountains during June (unfortunately the signs remained in City Hall for several more months). By July, the city council unanimously repealed all of Birmingham's segregation ordinances, effectively ending the legal wall of separation between the races. By the end of the month, downtown merchants began serving blacks at lunch counters.[13]

By the fall of 1963, the city faced a federal court order to desegregate three public schools—Ramsey, West End High, and Graymont Elementary. With the school year rapidly approaching during the first week of September, five black children were preparing to attend classes at the various schools. Tensions in the city were on the rise. In response, leaders of the city and county law enforcement agencies asked the local clergy to help Birmingham's citizens "face up to the realities of the public school crisis." In a public statement, Bishop Joseph Durick encouraged the city's adults to provide a good example and for the children to "heed this example." Now was a fitting time, he added, to remember the Bible passage "Suffer the little children to come unto Me and forbid them not, for of such is the kingdom of heaven." Christians must seek Christ in their daily lives. "Is this not the time to imitate his love for the young by giving them an example of charity for all men, respect for all men, and a sense of dignity that befits us as creatures made in the image and likeness of God?" This was a testing period for Birmingham, the bishop believed, and a time for citizens to show the world that the city of fear, violence, and hatred was now "clothed in dignity, charity, and justice."[14]

On Wednesday, September 4, two young black boys, Dwight and Floyd Armstrong, registered at Graymont. As the children met with principal Fagan Canzoneri inside, a crowd of nearly two hundred whites gathered outside and began shouting, "Two, four, six, eight, we don't want to integrate." That same evening, dynamite rocked the home of local civil rights attorney Arthur Shores, touching off a series of demonstrations and riots. Under pressure from Governor George Wallace, the board of education closed the schools on a temporary basis.[15]

Once more the eight clergy called for calm in the city. On Saturday, September 7, they issued another public statement, again pleading for "law and order and common sense" in dealing with the racial crisis in Birmingham. The ministers believed the bombing of Shores's home was a "dastardly act" which had endangered the safety of the community and "rekindled anew a potentially explosive situation." Integration was a reality, and the clergy called for citizens and public officials of "good will, intelligence, and respect" to resolve the crisis with dignity and in compliance with the will of the courts. Everyone must cooperate to restore peace and ensure the continuity of public education, they added. God would judge the defiant actions of those not acting peacefully and prayerfully in Birmingham, "Let us all remember," warned the ministers, "that Almighty God will judge us for all of our actions: For each day is a judgment day."[16]

The schools reopened the following Monday, but Governor Wallace sent National Guard troops to the three Birmingham schools to prevent integration. Alabama's director of public safety, Al Lingo, stood in the schoolhouse door at Graymont Elementary flanked by a contingent of state troopers. Lingo told the Armstrong children and their escorts to "leave immediately." As the group turned to walk away, Dwight and Floyd smiled at one another, jubilant over another day of summer vacation. By the following day, President Kennedy federalized the National Guard, and the Armstrongs returned to school without an incident.[17]

On September 13, the white clergymen sent a letter of support to Robert Arthur, president of Birmingham's Board of Education. The clergy had great confidence in Arthur and his work for the "educational welfare" of the city. "[We] assure you of our desire to help in any way possible in your effort to keep our schools open and orderly," they emphasized.[18]

Watching and brooding over this "race-mixing" was Graymont resident Robert Chambliss. A Klansman with an affinity for dynamite, Chambliss told his niece the following Saturday, "Just wait until after Sunday morning, and they'll beg us to let them segregate." The next morning, a powerful explosion rocked the Sixteenth Street Baptist Church, killing four young black girls. The event shook the nation and made for another week of extremely negative media coverage for the city.[19]

The tragedies touched the lives of most everyone in the state, even those with a less progressive racial view. Archbishop Thomas Toolen denounced the bombing and pleaded with all Catholics to "pluck hatred out of their hearts and remember that all men are created equal." Joseph Durick invited the city's pastors, priests, and rabbis to meet and then attend three of the girls' funerals en masse at Sixth Avenue Baptist Church. Pastor John Porter met the ministers at a southside church and led the group on an impromptu march to his church some two blocks away. The irony of the event was not lost on Durick, who realized the white ministers, many dressed in robes and regalia, were marching just like the "unwise and untimely" civil rights demonstrators. The eight white ministers joined eight hundred city pastors of both races at the funeral—the largest interracial gathering of clergy in the city's history. "I felt great joy in seeing the togetherness of leaders of the religious community," recalled Porter, "but great sadness that it took this event to bring us together."[20]

Martin Luther King returned to deliver the eulogy. The civil rights leader called the young girls "martyred heroines of a holy crusade for freedom and human dignity." As in the "Letter from Birmingham Jail," King continued to attack the forces of moderation, complacency, and gradualism in the white and black communities. The young girls' lives had something to say to every minister who had "remained silent behind the safe security of stained glass windows." All blacks and whites must substitute courage for caution. The four little girls "say to us," King continued, "that we must be concerned not merely about WHO murdered them, but about the system, the way of life and the philosophy which PRODUCED the murders." Their death announced to the country that everyone must work "passionately and unrelentingly" to fulfill the American dream.[21]

Rabbi Milton Grafman had attended the funeral, not to be a hero or to appear on television. "I'm no martyr," he explained to his congregation. "I don't want to get killed. I don't want this Temple bombed and I don't want my home bombed. I don't want to be knocked off gangster style." Four children had died in a senseless act of violence. "All we wanted to do was to go there and express our grief and our sorrow," Grafman continued, "to show these Negro families that we felt the depth of their sorrow; that we shared it. All we wanted to do was to say to the Negro community that you are not alone. There are white people who care. This was all."[22]

On September 19, the day following the funeral, Birmingham's Jewish community prepared to observe Rosh Hashanah, the Jewish new year. Rabbi Grafman stood in the pulpit of Temple Emanu-El with a disquieted spirit. Every rabbi owed his best to his congregation, Grafman believed, and a good sermon should be the result of 95 percent preparation and perspiration and 5 percent inspiration. "His best may not be good enough for them," the rabbi said, "but at least it should be the best that he was capable of that week." The week's events and a heavy heart had prevented the rabbi from preparing adequately for his sermon. "I feel a sense of trepidation," he told the assembly in a loud and clear voice, "because the first time in all my years as a student and rabbi, I stand before a high holy day congregation unprepared."[23]

In the quiet of the crowded synagogue, Grafman's impromptu message unfolded. He was taking a calculated risk, he told the gathering, because of the uncertainty of what might flow from his mouth. "But there are certain things that have to be said," he added,

> and I'm going to say them. Very frankly, this has been a horrible summer. This has been a horrible year. These are troublous times. Very frankly I hardly knew that Rosh Hashanah was about to begin tomorrow night. There has been no time for thinking and preparation and outlines. There was no opportunity to make certain that I would stay within the respectable twenty minutes. There are things that are upon my heart that I want to say to you. There are many things I have been accumulating for thirty years as a rabbi and twenty-three years in this congregation.

The rabbi had a burdened soul. "I've been sick about it for years," he said, adding that anybody with even a shred of humanity within him could not but be horrified at what happened that Sunday. Grafman was troubled not only for those people responsible for the death of the four little girls and for those responsible for Birmingham's horrible image, but also for the attitude of many "nice people" at Temple Emanu-El.

"The people that sneer at everything that happens in this city," Grafman continued, "who point the finger at everyone, beginning with the rabbi; who want to put the blame on everyone but themselves." Grafman had grown weary of these prideful Jews, who were more concerned with the rabbi's actions than their own. "If I had the time I might tell you what your rabbi's been doing," he said. "I answer to my conscience. You'll have to answer to yours."[24]

As a rabbi, Grafman continued, he stood firm on two convictions. "I have never been unmindful of my responsibility to God," he said, "and the obligation that belief in God places upon me and my fellow man." He was also aware of his duty to his congregation. "I cannot speak for you," Grafman continued. "My name may go on a thousand documents or statements. I cannot commit you." A rabbi, he added, must be responsible for the safety and welfare of his temple, and must not say or do anything that will "in any way bring shame or disgrace, or God forbid, destruction to you as a congregation, to this Jewish community, or this beautiful house of God."[25]

Grafman believed he had done his part; now was the time for the congregation to act. "You're going to have to put up or you're going to have to shut-up," he declared. "You're either going to have to put up or stop talking and acting like liberals." The people of Temple Emanu-El had to do more than sit in quiet horror behind closed blinds and whisper their disgust to a lifeless circle of friends. "I'm not asking you to go out and lead a crusade," Grafman added, "but in heaven's sake can't you at least do what I've done and . . . join with other Christians?"[26]

Grafman chided his congregation for not doing more to ease racial tensions. "What's the matter?" he asked. "Haven't you got the guts to do it? You afraid you might have harassing calls?" Grafman had received plenty, and they went with the territory. Birmingham needed to change, and the nice people had to start making bold stands. "Are you willing to take the risk?" the rabbi inquired. "Are you willing to be harassed? Are you willing to be threatened?" Until they were ready, the city was in the hands of extremists. Grafman encouraged the worshipers at Temple Emanu-El to help rebuild the Sixteenth Street Baptist Church. "The question is: are you ready to pay the price?" he asked. "If you are not, God help this city. This city isn't dead yet, not by a long shot. It's almost dead. You and decent Christians can revive this city."[27]

That evening during the Rosh Hashanah Kaddish, the time in the service to remember those who had died the previous year, Grafman recited the names of the four girls killed in the church bombing. They had been brutally murdered, wantonly killed, and insanely slain, he proclaimed. "Whose death we mourn," the rabbi continued. "Whose families we would comfort. The shame of whose murder we would and we must have our city atone."[28]

Deeply moved, the people of Temple Emanu-El, regardless of age, sent money and letters of support to Rabbi Grafman. "I want with all my heart to help rebuild the church," wrote one little girl to Grafman. "I'm not ashamed to say what I believe and think these three dollars may not help a long ways, but at least I know I did something useful and I hope it will help." The rabbi found encouragement in the outpouring of support. "If you could read the letters that have come to me," he wrote to one friend, "you would know that there is a tremendous reservoir of goodness in Birmingham and a genuine desire to correct this horrible situation."[29]

Until his death in 1995, Rabbi Milton Grafman played an energetic role in building Birmingham's future. He was among leaders who actively protested the presence of a Ku Klux Klan exhibit at the Alabama State Fair during the fall of 1964. The KKK's display included a Klansman on horseback and stacks of racist and anti-Semitic books and literature. Grafman called the Klan an "organization devoted and dedicated to spreading hate." Local citizens and especially children "should not be exposed to this type of virus." In turn, lawyers for the Klan filed a $1 million defamation suit against Grafman and several others. The defendants had conspired to strip the organization of its "good name, credit and reputation and to bring it in disrepute among the people in the State of Alabama, and in the United States of America." The criticisms had also caused the Klan to lose many members and suffer great disrepute. The suit, however, never went too far; defending the "good name" of the Klan proved impossible.[30]

In 1975, Grafman retired as the Temple Emanu-El's rabbi, but he remained dedicated to an active public life for the next twenty years. "It's bothered me very much to see some people in this city do so much and then retire and fade away," he once said. "They should give more since they are free of the responsibility of a specific job and have more time to give to the community."[31]

Since he remained in Birmingham for so many years, the negative media portrait from Martin Luther King's "Letter from Birmingham Jail" continued to haunt Grafman. Through the years, Grafman often received letters from curiosity seekers, asking if he was still a segregationist and a bigot. White gradualists were a lonely, misunderstood group. Grafman believed he had to "play the game" and say what the media and the movement expected or face being labeled a bigot or a reactionary. "They were not interested in what the truth was," the rabbi insisted. "There were efforts being made," Grafman said, "and decent people here."[32]

During September 1963, soon after the bombing at the Sixteenth Street Baptist Church, Rabbi Milton Grafman, the Reverend Earl Stallings, Father Joe Allen, and Bishops Joseph Durick, George Murray, and Nolan Harmon traveled to Washington, D.C., to discuss the racial situation in Birmingham with President John F. Kennedy. Bishop Carpenter declined the invitation, telling George Murray he was too old to do any good. Assistant Attorney General Burke Marshall had invited two other groups to meet with the president (at different times), black civil rights leaders (including King), and representatives of the white economic elite.[33]

On Monday afternoon, September 23, 1963 the group assembled at the G Street Episcopal Church in Washington, where Harmon's friend Charles Kean served as rector. Kean had been called away from the church, but his secretary welcomed the clergymen into the minister's study. Durick rubbed his face and realized he needed a shave after the long trip. He borrowed the rabbi's razor and went to a small basin in the back of the study and shaved. Harmon chuckled at the strange ecumenical sight: a Catholic leader shaving with a rabbi's razor in an Episcopalian's basin, while a Southern Baptist preacher and a Methodist bishop watched. Afterwards, the nervous group walked down the street to the White House for the 6:50 P.M. meeting.[34]

The clergy gathered in a semicircle around President Kennedy, as he swayed gently in his rocking chair. Kennedy encouraged the ministers to further racial progress in Birmingham and to bring the "moral strength of religion to bear on this issue." Each of the ministers conveyed to the president their ideas for easing tensions in the city. Bishop Murray spoke first and described the difficulty in supporting improved race relations in the face of harassing midnight phone calls, hate-filled letters, and other forms of persecution. Several white Birmingham ministers had to contend with divided congregations and the loss of an effective leadership role in the community. The majority of white citizens in Birmingham were law abiding and intended to obey court decisions. Nevertheless, a "lawless minority" remained so vocal and used such extreme measures that the law-abiding majority remained silent. Murray blamed both Governor Wallace and the civil rights demonstrators for fostering a climate of mistrust between blacks and whites.[35]

After Murray finished, the president turned to Durick and said: "Okay bishop, you're next." In the seating arrangement, Durick should have been last to make comments. "I thought it was a nice gesture," remembered Durick. "Of course, he was Catholic and so was I, and I'm sure that didn't hurt any, but I thought it was a nice gesture just the same." The Catholic leader asked President Kennedy to send black FBI agents to Birmingham to improve relations between the black community and law enforcement officials. The bishop also encouraged Kennedy to use his influence with the Reverend Billy Graham to organize an ecumenical, interracial revival in the city. During the 1964 Easter season, Graham preached to a large interracial gathering at Birmingham's Legion Field. Bishop Durick told the president how each of the white ministers believed that racial discrimination was wrong, "whenever and wherever" practiced. The Catholic leader placed much of the blame for racial problems in Birmingham upon the youthful shallowness of the city. Entrepreneurs founded the city only ninety years before, and this, the bishop believed, accounted for the failure to appraise the social, political, and economic problems of segregation. Perhaps Birmingham was too young to admit a reluctance to "embrace the challenge of integration." The city desperately needed an infusion of new magic and a miracle of renewal for the Magic City's black citizenry.[36]

During the demonstrations, Earl Stallings explained to the president, Birmingham was "in the midst of a void without leadership. King, with children as his troopers, rushed into this void." The city's white religious community attempted to provide leadership during the crisis, Stallings added, but these efforts were "countered and made inadequate" by Martin Luther King and his demonstrations. The Baptist pastor encouraged Kennedy to help "us settle our own problems" and stabilize the community by removing from the scene "those who keep us from marshaling the forces for obedience."[37]

Harmon and Grafman each took turns explaining their views of the racial situation in Birmingham. When the rabbi complained of Martin Luther King's continued pressure and threats of more demonstrations, Kennedy stopped Grafman in mid-sentence. "You have no idea what's waiting in the wings," he said. "If King fails, you won't have much of a city to save." King, JFK emphasized, was much better than the militancy of those activists in SNCC. The clergy were scheduled to visit with the president for thirty minutes, but they stayed over an hour.[38]

When the six clergy emerged from the White House, a flock of reporters asked for a public statement. Suspicious of the national press, the group had selected the eloquent and unflappable Bishop Murray to speak on everyone's behalf. Murray told the reporters that he and his fellow clergy met from time to time to "consider racial problems in our city" and often issued public statements "which we thought might be helpful." The ministers had a pleasant meeting with President Kennedy, the bishop added, and he hoped that "some good may come of it." When asked for more specifics, the Episcopal leader stonewalled and told the media representatives that it was not his place to reveal what the president had discussed in the Oval Office. After badgering the ministers for a few minutes, the reporters finally gave up in disgust. One reporter hoped that the religious leaders' actions in Birmingham would be "more eloquent" than their "words at the White House door."[39]

After the White House gathering, the group agreed to eat dinner at a local Washington restaurant. A still-trembling and sweat-soaked Earl Stallings, however, remained so overwrought from meeting the president, he excused himself and took a shower in his hotel room to cool off. On social occasions, Durick and his sidekick Father Joe Allen often enjoyed sharing a scotch and soda and discussing eclectic topics ranging from University of Alabama football to banal poetry. But on this trip, Durick and Allen, out of respect for the other men in the group, decided in advance not to order alcohol at dinner. When the waiter queried the group about drink orders, however, each man turned down the offer, except Allen, who thought he really needed a drink after the excitement of the day. The double-cross really surprised Durick and the Protestant onlookers. Harmon, the seasoned Prohibitionist, leaned over and quietly told Allen he had never dined with anyone drinking an alcoholic beverage. "You're lucky you didn't live in Christ's Day," Allen responded. "You couldn't have attended the Last Supper." Flabbergasted by the young priest, Harmon slid back in his chair as Allen sipped his refreshment and flashed a wry grin and a wink at Durick.[40]

In December 1963, Pope Paul VI promoted Joseph Durick to the post of Coadjutor Bishop of Nashville (the diocese then covering the entire state of Tennessee) with right of succession to the aged Bishop William Adrian.[41] On March 3, 1964, one thousand people filled Nashville's Cathedral of the Incarnation for the installation service. Bishop Fulton Sheen spoke at the ceremony and described Durick as "one who will be responsive" to "all Catholics" regardless of their "light of . . . conscience." Remembering Durick's days as a humble street preacher, Sheen asked the audience to take "advantage of this man who will not stress his authority, but stress his service."[42]

Several months before, Durick had first read the "Letter from Birmingham Jail" and was upset that King "wasn't going to give us more time to work things out." It was a matter of logistics, the bishop argued. "Our clergy committee had asked for postponement and not cancellation of his nonviolent demonstration." At the time, Durick recognized that the civil rights leader was using the ministers as a "sounding board" to justify his tactics and to rebuke a wide variety of critics. "I felt certain," Durick wrote in 1971, "that he had a much broader scope of intended readers than my fellow clergymen and myself." Regardless, the bishop also claimed the letter made a significant impact upon his racial outlook. King had written in a language that was "gentle with us," he later reflected; "loving, but his soft words were painful to me. I had seen segregation as wrong, but not as he had portrayed it." The powerful message of the letter helped persuade Durick to take a more active role in the fight for racial justice.[43]

Another decisive moment for Durick came in the wake of the sweeping reforms initiated by Pope John XXIII in the Second Vatican Council. Durick participated in several sessions of the council between 1962 and 1965 and embraced the spirit of ecumenism, the modern liturgy, and the clear commands on equality. These new ideas emerged in "perfect synchrony" with Durick's evolving racial attitude, especially the pope's encyclical proclaiming that "all men are equal by reason of their natural dignity. . . . Hence racial discrimination can in no way be justified."[44] These directives, Durick later said, had to turn more than the "altar around"; they had to "turn the hearts of Catholics around"—no easy task in the South. The message of Vatican II, the bishop emphasized, compelled him to "go out in the world and restore the dignity of man," something Durick did with the same intensity he had displayed as a youthful revivalist. The winds of change, he once said, had forewarned the church of the abundant social ills that prevailed throughout the world. One of the greatest afflictions, Durick recognized, was racial injustice.[45]

For Durick, a rise in "greater consciousness" had occurred during the early 1960s, and he realized that segregation was not a mere political problem but an immense moral dilemma. The gradualist approach to racial justice gave way to a new sense of urgency. As Durick's racial attitudes evolved, he set out on a course to "make up for lost time." The paradigm shifted, remembered Durick's assistant in Alabama, Father Joe Allen. "Once it shifts," Allen said, "all of its relationships are now different. . . . He saw something had to be done." The bishop later thanked God that he, and the South, "had the courage and will to cross the Rubicon" from one way of thinking to another. "I had to be, as it were, converted to a greater understanding of humanity," Durick added; the idea that God "made us all his children regardless of color, race, or creed."[46]

During the spring of 1964, Durick began his ministry in Nashville "full of energy and hope for the future." Three days after the fanfare of his ordination, the new coadjutor spoke before a group of Catholic lay people in Nashville. One of the first questions asked was "How do you feel about the race question?" Durick responded with a simple answer. "I stand with the Church," he told the gathering. "Under God, every man is equal." Integration, the new bishop emphasized, was a "moral question." From that day forward, in Catholic and Protestant minds, Durick believed he had been branded "enemy number one" in Tennessee.[47]

This stand on race and reform put Durick at odds with the senior bishop in the diocese, William Lawrence Adrian. By the 1960s, Adrian was vocal in his opposition to dramatic changes, an opinion he consistently expressed in a weekly column for the *Wanderer*, a privately owned right-wing Catholic newspaper. As Durick grew increasingly active in confronting racial injustice, Adrian warned a convention of Catholic women to "beware of bishops and priests who were leading the laity astray."[48]

Still, like Thomas Toolen, Charles Carpenter, and so many of that generation of white southern religious leaders, Adrian was an enigma. Since becoming the leader of the diocese in 1936, he had provided opportunities for quality education and health care for black Tennesseans. He had taken the lead in integrating Catholic schools soon after the *Brown* decision. "This is the law of the land," he said in 1954, "and it must be obeyed." That same year Father Ryan High School in Nashville integrated with little fanfare.[49] Ten years later, however, Adrian stood in direct contrast to his forty-nine-year-old coadjutor. "Bishop Adrian," one newspaper editor later recalled, "was more than a little uncomfortable with the changes that came from the Second Vatican Council." What Adrian brushed aside with a cold detachment, Durick embraced with youthful enthusiasm.[50]

By setting in motion the Vatican II mandates, Durick not only challenged the wall of separation between the races, he also spearheaded a move for unity between Catholics and non-Catholics in Tennessee. "What we share with Protestants," Durick once said, "is far more important than what divides us. We have the same Lord, substantially the same faith, and the same baptism." In keeping with these ideals, the young "upstart" bishop shocked old-time Catholics by becoming an honorary Shriner and riding in an open convertible during a Shriners' parade in Nashville. Durick, however, pointed to a "new age of ecumenism" in the South and pledged to "help that spirit grow."[51]

Durick urged Catholics to "look beyond denominational self-interests" and to strive for a broader impact in the South. The bishop emphasized the Vatican II decrees on church unity and broadened the concept of ecumenism beyond building bridges from church to church to a "secular ecumenism," one "directed toward a more effective service of God in the world, and for the world—and ultimately for the sake of the Kingdom." All Christians must work "here and now," Durick said in a sermon, "to alleviate the afflictions and injustices of our times, to reconcile, to bind up wounds, to heal."[52]

The bishop also looked to fight anti-Semitism "tooth and nail" and establish close bonds with the Jewish community. "The Catholic Church . . . has a profound love and respect for the Jews," he emphasized. "They are a people dear to the heart of God." For the rest of his ministry, the bishop worked diligently for a spirit of cooperation among the three major religions in the state: Protestant, Catholic, and Jewish.[53]

In January 1966, Pope Paul VI relieved the declining Bishop Adrian of his administrative obligations and appointed Bishop Durick the apostolic administrator of the diocese. Almost immediately, Durick began a "whirlwind of activities" that transformed the Catholic Church in Tennessee. He held advising sessions to discuss how best to implement the Vatican II directives with a group of advisers that he called the "Kitchen Cabinet." These advisers included some of the state's most influential Catholic laymen and several distinguished priests.[54]

The "brainstorming sessions" with the Kitchen Cabinet, remembered former Nashville *Tennessean* editor John Seigenthaler, were often lengthy, noisy, and rowdy. Every six weeks or so, as many as twenty people would jam themselves into Seigenthaler's recreation room in the basement of his house. Everyone had an opportunity to voice their opinions on the state of the church in Tennessee. Durick listened and often accepted the advice, but he was no simple figurehead. He had learned from his mentor Thomas Toolen to rule a diocese with an authoritarian and autocratic style, and Durick did. Tennessee's new bishop possessed a supreme self-confidence and was bold, blunt, and more than a little outspoken. When one layman reminded Durick of the modest size of the Catholic Church in Tennessee and the lack of "clout" to make a difference in the state, Durick retorted that clout came from a possession of the "high moral" ground. "If we set an example as Catholics," he said, "others will find it easier to follow."[55]

Through these brainstorming sessions, Durick decided to introduce Project Equality, an ecumenical program designed to use the moral suasion of the church to achieve equal employment opportunities for black Tennesseans. Despite charges of "economic blackmail," the bishop gathered Nashville business leaders to discuss the lack of black employment. He explained the Catholic Church in Tennessee would provide "affirmative action of encouragement against unconscious discrimination" without blacklists or boycotts. The first of its kind in the South, the project emphasized a "positive approach," Durick said, and provided aid and recognition to the businesses that cooperated and gave that "extra effort as fair employers." Project Equality encouraged companies to end discrimination and provide a "good job at good pay" to help lift people out of poverty. This idea, the bishop emphasized, preserved dignity, confidence, and self-respect.[56]

While Bishop Durick called upon all priests to use Project Equality as an "effective weapon to fight injustice in the crucial area of employment opportunity," many Catholics remained skeptical. Several advisers urged Durick to delay implementing this religious affirmative-action enterprise until after the completion of a major diocesan fund-raising effort. The bishop warned his advisers against overlooking unemployment to make "money-raising easier." Immediately, some church contributors withheld support as a response to Durick's stand.[57]

With the growing militancy of many blacks in the civil rights movement, Durick emphasized that gradualist policies had grown outdated.

Blacks would no longer "settle for moderate progress." Time was "slipping by," he warned in 1968, and the country needed the fastest progress available to achieve equal opportunity. The bishop called for the business community to initiate an "American Power" to counter the "voices of fantasy and hatred" raised in the name of "Black Power." Business leaders in America had the money, experience, know-how, and power to provide a program uplifting and supporting the disadvantaged and cooling the smoldering embers of the inner cities. Durick believed Project Equality "nudged" business into helping achieve this goal. The bishop, however, terminated the program in 1968 because of the lack of support, "either financial or in concern from other communions."[58]

Despite intense criticism, Durick forged ahead with his agenda to further racial justice in Tennessee. During 1968, he played an active role during the strike of black sanitation workers in Memphis. As the black community rallied around the strikers, Durick donated one thousand dollars from his discretionary funds to help feed the families of the strikers. "For the poor among you," he said. It was the first gift of money from a white religious denomination—leading Memphis mayor Henry Loeb to make nasty remarks about Durick. Several Catholics in Memphis wrote Durick in disgust over his contribution to the strikers. The bishop, scolded one parishioner, must remain devoted to "our own people" and not to the "rabble rousers" in the street.[59]

A strike support group organized a boycott of downtown stores, and commenced daily marches and rallies. All Catholic participants in the marches went forth with Durick's blessings—in marked contrast to the condemnation by other white religious leaders in the state. The "needs of Christ in his people must be served," Durick later reflected, and service to people equaled service to Christ. It was never "beneath priestly dignity" for a religious leader to march and demonstrate against racial injustice. The apostles had been "prophets to the world" and remained unafraid to rebuke in order to lead the world to a "Christian Ethic of love, justice, and brotherhood."[60]

While in Memphis to support the strikers, Martin Luther King Jr. was cut down by an assassin's bullet on the balcony of the Lorraine Motel on April 4, 1968. Two days later, Durick flew to Memphis and led a memorial Mass at the Immaculate Conception Church. Flanked by Jewish, Protestant, and Catholic clergymen, Durick honored King as the prophet of a black "crusade for dignity and freedom." The bishop characterized King as the black community's voice (encouraging his people

to strive unyieldingly), their arms ("pointing out the way to the promised land"), their feet ("in his walk blazing a trail for freedom"), their
heart (by teaching and practicing nonviolence), their eloquence ("in
humiliation"), and their mind ("as he forged for them weapons of nonviolence that withstood and blunted the ferocity of segregation"). In
conclusion, Durick read a particularly self-abasing passage from King's
"Letter from Birmingham Jail" that condemned the white moderate as
the "great stumbling block in the stride toward freedom." Prayerfully,
the bishop pleaded with God to "examine our individual conscience—to
assess my part of the blame in the death of Dr. King—may I resolve to a
greater dedication and work to make our morality meaningful—as with
greater vigor we translate it into the social power structure and into living laws and social institutions."[61]

In the shadows of a hundred flickering candles, mourners sang
"Kumbaya" as they slowly moved toward the Communion rail to honor
the slain civil rights leader. On Monday, April 8, the Catholic leader participated in a tense memorial march through the streets of Memphis. A
crowd estimated at thirty thousand to forty thousand jammed City Hall
Plaza to hear King's eulogizers, including Durick. The bishop humbly
asked the crowd to join "in a spirit of true love" to enable those "in this
weary world to instill some reality into the dream of Martin Luther
King."[62]

Durick returned to Memphis a year later to join in a Good Friday
memorial march and rally honoring King. Many Catholics condemned
Durick's participation on a solemn holiday and the comments he made
about King—especially the paraphrase of a famous Bob Dylan song:
"For the spirit of Martin King, my friend, is blowin' in the wind. His
spirit is blowin' in the wind."[63]

Following the ceremony, several priests in Memphis began "quietly"
criticizing Durick to parishioners. One communicant contended that
most Catholics in the state had never understood the bishop's vision of
equating political and social concerns with the responsibility of ministering to the "spiritual needs of those souls entrusted to him." The bishop's
Good Friday march had been a "sad day" for all Catholics, wrote one
Nashville resident. Durick had grown "so obsessed with contemporary
fads" that he had been compelled to "selfishly prance down public
streets in honor of a racial demagogue and communist sympathizer."
Consequently, the bishop had exalted a "man over the crucified Jesus"
instead of offering a Good Friday Mass in a Catholic cathedral. An odd

demand, since no mass is offered on Good Friday, even in the unreformed liturgy.[64]

To call the Tennessee Catholic reaction to Durick a backlash was the understatement of the century, wrote one angry Memphis resident. "Wholesale disgust and outright renunciation" had emerged as the prevailing and most "fitting terms." When one Catholic confronted Durick on why he participated in marches, he replied: "I suppose it was because others don't—or won't." Durick told Catholics the church had to emerge as the "conscience of society" and no longer remain a "chameleon." Society would be doomed if the church remained silent on the "vital issues" of human rights and human needs. "We cannot hide the pulpit today behind the Gothic facades of ancient buildings and let the rest of the world go by," Durick said. Religious leaders needed to physically serve the people and that often included marching in the streets. Clergymen, the bishop emphasized, made many "nice statements" from behind a desk or a pulpit, but until the people witnessed their physical involvement in confronting injustices, they were "just not going to listen." Humbly and apologetically, Durick urged his flock to get involved in the fight for social justice. "Please do not misconstrue my remarks as righteous rhetoric," he explained after a lengthy exhortation, "but accept them as a plea for your individual and intelligent involvement."[65]

In September 1969, Bishop Adrian resigned and Pope Paul VI gave Durick the title bishop of Nashville. Durick announced he had "redoubled" his commitment to "seek human dignity" for all men regardless of race, political views, or church affiliation. He believed that a strong commitment to racial justice was the "best way" to serve "my God, my Church and my state." He had not always found involvement in social justice the "easiest course" except in the recesses of his own mind and in the loyalty to his "episcopal vow of being shepherd to the whole flock in Tennessee."[66]

A month later a strike by hourly employees at the Catholic St. Joseph's Hospital in Memphis demonstrated Durick's deep commitment to justice and identification with the underdog in society. The bishop called on both sides in the fight for union recognition to "swallow a little pride" and to work out their differences. The hospital administration, however, remained defiant, as demonstrations spread throughout the city following the NAACP's decision to link the strike to a dispute with the Memphis Board of Education. While the strike continued for some twelve weeks, Durick quietly urged the hospital to recognize the union—

much to the derision of St. Joseph's board of administrators. Powerful Catholic laymen on the hospital board demanded a meeting with Durick, and the bishop complied.[67]

The bishop arrived in Memphis a few days before Christmas. Instead of immediately meeting with the hospital board, Durick entered the Shelby County Jail and visited several black ministers jailed during the demonstrations. Durick spoke briefly with Southern Christian Leadership Conference president Ralph Abernathy and secured the civil rights leader's support for a proposed compromise. "This is my bishop!" Abernathy shouted when Durick entered the jail. (Six years earlier they had been on opposing sides in Birmingham.) "My bishop! Yes, praise the Lord, my bishop."[68]

Durick then proceeded to demonstrate to the hospital board that he commanded the power and respect of a bishop. When he arrived at St. Joseph's the bishop had changed from his simple black clerical shirt and collar into a house cassock, a sash, the zucchetto of a bishop, and a gold pectoral cross. Durick later said that he knew many of the board members were older Catholics with a "deep respect" for the office of bishop. By wearing the vestments, he had "made sure" they were unable to "take their minds off the fact" that a bishop had interceded. "They had me outnumbered," Durick said, "but I had them out dressed."[69]

On the same day, Durick called a news conference at St. Peter's Church in Memphis and proposed an end to demonstrations and "in fair turn" for St. Joseph's to reinstate all workers "without reprisal in the spirit of Christian reconciliation." He also praised the five ministers who were jailed during the demonstrations and had learned to "identify with the imprisoned poor of this city and this nation." Within a few days, the union and the administrators reached an agreement.[70]

During the early 1970s, Durick increasingly turned his attention to prison reform. As an outspoken opponent of the death penalty, the bishop believed that killing was an "unconscionable" act of immeasurable immorality. "If Jesus told us anything," Durick once said, "he told us to turn the other cheek, to forgive." In 1972, he hailed the "enlightened" U.S. Supreme Court decision ruling capital punishment unconstitutional. "Let us treasure life, not gamble with it," the bishop told a group of state officials seeking to reinstate the death penalty in Tennessee. Prison reform was a "critical social need," Durick believed as he worked to develop "broad concern" among Tennesseans for humane and functional prison facilities and for a more comprehensive ministry to prisoners and their families. This concern for the lives and souls of prisoners led Durick to become an advocate of prison ministries.[71]

In March 1973, Durick called for sweeping prison reforms in a pastoral letter entitled "Humanity Demands It." Often societies overlooked the "basic human rights" of prisoners in the judicial process, he pointed out. The bishop called for more funding for rehabilitation programs that rebuilt lives, restored hopes, and developed skills for former prisoners to live "peacefully and productively" in society. As the spiritual leader of the Diocese of Nashville, Durick urged fellow Tennesseans to utilize the "Gospel of brotherly love" in demanding immediate changes in the prison system. He designated several "moral imperatives" as priorities for reform: ending racial, economic, and religious discrimination; providing adequate health care and access to professional counselors, educators, and spiritual advisers; updating correctional facilities; and maintaining a complete ban on the death penalty. The bishop also advocated conjugal visits for husbands and wives as a way to reduce sexual maladjustments among prisoners.[72]

Later in the year, Durick spent Christmas morning visiting, playing the piano, and singing songs with a group of prisoners at the Tennessee State Prison in Nashville. The bishop thought it was fitting to spend part of Christmas with men who had been "legally judged" criminals by society, as society "once legally judged the Savior to be a criminal." The prisoners' enthusiastic response "whet" Durick's interest to become more physically involved in prison reform.[73]

Durick had grown weary of the heavy demands of a bishop. After eleven years of leading and sometimes dragging the Diocese of Nashville into the modern era, the bishop longed for a quiet assignment. The immense criticism and the responsibilities of shepherding a diocese during a period of social unrest had taken a toll. He suffered from an acute back problem, drank much more than he should, and only fitfully watched his diet. He was only sixty years old, but he felt older. In 1975, on the twentieth anniversary of his ordination as bishop, Durick retired to devote full-time to a prison ministry. The complete account of his retirement, however, remains a mystery. So many documents are sealed in Nashville and in papal offices in Washington and Rome that it is impossible to tell the full story of his decision to step aside. Apparently, alcohol and liberal activism had forced him from his position.[74]

In his 1975 farewell statement to his fellow "pilgrims" of the Nashville diocese, Durick noted that he had "simply tried to take seriously the teachings of the church." He knew he had "failed many times," but he always had a "Christian discontent" that drove him to try to "constantly improve" himself and society. He had decided to enter this new ministry after witnessing the "heart shattering despair" and estrangement of prisoners. "Saddest of all," Durick noted, "so many of us" who were free brought little solace to those inside the prisons.[75]

During December 1975, Durick arrived in Fort Worth, Texas, to serve as temporary Catholic chaplain in the Federal Correction Institution. "I came to do a little time myself," Durick explained to his new parishioners, perhaps feeling like he was doing penance for his own sins. He described the prison as "just like a parish," except for the "walls and towers," and he held mass in the basement of the religious ministry building known by the convicts as the "Fish House" and invited a Southern Baptist "resident" (his term for inmate) to play the organ while Durick led the singing. After only three months, Durick moved onto another temporary assignment in a federal prison in Pleasanton, California. In addition to his Catholic duties, Durick had to conduct a weekly Protestant service in the absence of a Protestant pastor. He told a reporter that he was "quite at home" preaching to Protestants, having worked as a revivalist years before.[76]

After six years of ministering to prisoners in various locations, a severe heart problem and subsequent surgery forced the prison chaplain into semi-retirement. He was a much different Joseph Durick from the one who had ruled the Diocese of Nashville. The brazen peacemaker and activist seemed meek, humble, and poor in spirit as he moved back to his parents' home on Sixth Avenue in Bessemer, Alabama, less than a block from his boyhood parish of St. Aloysius. Despite a mild stroke in 1986, Durick continued to play an active role in the Catholic Church until the early 1990s, traveling much like the early days and preaching almost every Sunday at rural mission parishes in the State.

In 1990, Durick celebrated his fiftieth year as a priest. "Ah, those were the days," Durick often remembered. He hoped it had been the "spirit of God" that guided him down the road from passivist to activist. "I know it certainly was the right thing." In reflection, the editor of the Catholic *Tennessee Register* praised Durick for revolutionizing the Catholic Church in Tennessee. His fearless stands for civil rights, labor relations, and the rights of the poor placed him in the forefront of progressive Catholic leadership. Durick had also experienced many "painful moments," because these issues had been "land mines waiting to blow up, both within the church and without." He had been "praised as a visionary" and "criticized by those fighting any change in society's status quo." Time, however, had "proven him right."[77]

In the final weeks of his life, Durick said, he had been granted a "quiet peace" and was quite prepared for the "journey ahead." He felt grateful for the "good" God had given him and the "ability to try to make changes for the better." He quietly passed away in his sleep during the night of June 26, 1994. "He always made me feel that I was a Catholic," remembered noted Southern Baptist minister Will D. Campbell. "Boundaries drawn by society—racial, religious, regional, citizen of the free world or citizen locked away by the state—were not of him. So in his presence we were all catholic, if not Catholic, for to him the universe was one."[78]

No other Catholic bishop in Tennessee, and perhaps the South, endured such a steady stream of criticism. Durick never sought a reputation as a controversial social activist, for that was "only vain glory," he thought. God had been everything in Tennessee, Durick emphasized, and he had been nothing. Regardless, the bishop had ignited a period of unrest in the state, but all of his stands had "moral overtones" and a function of the church was to "speak up where moral issues were concerned."[79]

The "Letter from Birmingham Jail," the events in Birmingham, and the reforms of the Second Vatican Council each had an enormous influence on Durick's liberal activism. On a personal level, Durick experienced an intellectual awakening rare among white southerners. As his role in the Catholic Church grew in prominence, he realized the injustice of segregation and began to advocate gradual change. The brutality of segregation in Birmingham in the early 1960s shook the foundation of the bishop's culture-based beliefs. The blinders fell off his eyes and he could no longer wait passively with other southern gradualists. With freedom of spirit and office, Durick broke loose from the "paralyzing chains of conformity," emerged from behind stain-glass windows, and aggressively worked for civil rights. Durick emerged as the most liberal of the eight white clergy. The letter had helped transform him, and he too paid a high price for his outspoken ministry.[80]

After reading the "Letter from Birmingham Jail" for the first time, George Murray was perplexed. To Murray, King was unjustified in addressing the clergy in his letter, because the white ministers' statement had specifically addressed local black leaders. Here was a very smart man, the bishop later recalled, quoting scripture against us and answering a statement written to someone else. At the White House meeting in the fall of 1963, Murray had told the president that the civil rights leader had "seriously misconstrued both our statement and our intention."[81]

In the letter, King attributed motives to the eight clergymen which Murray insisted they never had and in turn created "straw men" out of them. King and the SCLC had recognized the weakness of the white clergy's position, especially after the violent clashes in the streets, and exploited the innocuous group as adversaries. Murray argued that King saw only what he wanted in Birmingham: white religious leaders opposed to all change.[82]

Nonetheless, after much reflection, the bishop was glad King achieved his goal in Birmingham. "They were my objectives too," he said, "but I would still object to the tactics used."[83] For months, Murray had moderated lengthy negotiations between black and white community leaders at the Episcopal headquarters in Birmingham. "I wonder if groups in opposition really try to understand one another," he pondered at the time. "I think the church ought to perform this reconciling function—to provide a place and opportunity for these groups to come together and talk." The discussions, however, proved to be a source of tremendous frustration for Murray and other white negotiators. King apparently declined to meet with Murray's group and instead sent emissaries, namely Andrew Young and Fred Shuttlesworth, to communicate the SCLC's position. The bishop argued that King had "no interest in conferences with us unless we would accept his leadership and come to march with him." One of King's representatives told him that the only way to lend support was to join the demonstrations. "If we would do that," Murray said, "that was great. They'd welcome us." Compromise was out of the question. Ironically, Murray noted that many of these men asking for negotiations at the beginning of campaign were later involved in the "Birmingham settlement." King claimed that only the pressure of the demonstrations had made these whites "willing at last to talk with him."[84]

It took several months to implement each point of the settlement, especially the establishment of a biracial commission. Finally in the fall of 1963, Boutwell announced the formation of the Committee on Group Relations, made up of nine blacks and sixteen whites. Bishop Carpenter was selected chairman; Rabbi Grafman and Bishop Durick served as committee members, along with several black ministers: J. L. Ware (serving as vice chairman), Edward Gardner, and Abraham Woods. During the organizational meeting, Bishop Carpenter told the committee to park their prejudices at the door and make every effort to gain a mutual understanding. He further charged the group with the "instant goals of improving racial communications and understanding." Regardless, Carpenter still looked to an ultra-gradualist solution to the racial problems in the city. "Come on fellows," he told the committee, "let's get in here and kick the ball around a little bit, but I don't want any of you picking it up and running with it."[85]

At one of the committee's first meetings, held in City Hall, J. L. Ware complained of "For White Men Only" signs hanging on the restroom doors. Ware said he looked for the "colored" facility, but found none. The black minister considered going through the white-only door, but feared what the police might do if they found him in there. The committee passed a unanimous resolution calling for all "white" and "colored" signs to be removed from City Hall. These symbols of the old system were finally removed by the end of 1963.[86]

The committee continued the push for an upgrade in black employment opportunities and the hiring of Birmingham's first black police officer. "We were trying to be helpful any way we could," asserted Rabbi Grafman. "It wasn't easy to be helpful at the time." Mayor Boutwell and the city council, however, had given the committee no real authority to bring about effective change. The committee criticized Boutwell and the council for their "hands off attitude" toward the recommendations. Bishop Durick pleaded with Mayor Boutwell to push for the hiring of blacks on the police force. Black employment on the force had taken on a symbolic importance and was perhaps the key to long-awaited progress and an "ultimate solution to our problems."[87]

With no power to make effective change, the Committee on Group Relations limped along for some time and ultimately dissolved without seeing any of its recommendations enacted by the city. The city council didn't appoint a black to an independent board or agency until December 1964, and it took two more years for Birmingham to hire a black police officer.[88]

The civil rights battles were taking their toll on George Murray. The bishop looked gaunt, suffered from stomach ulcers, and had a general feeling of helplessness and bitterness. "These are difficult days in Alabama," Murray wrote at the time. "I must confess to some discouragement under the heavy fire from both sides of [the] raging controversy. I do not have a very thick skin." Events in Alabama during 1964 and 1965 proved just as frustrating as 1963 for the two Episcopal leaders.[89]

Pressure from segregationist laity in the diocese remained intense. A sore point for Alabama's white Episcopalians, and for many white southerners in general, was the involvement of the National Council of Churches of Christ in the United States of America (NCC) in civil rights activities in the region. During the summer of 1964, the NCC's Commission on Religion and Race provided training and counseling for volunteers to the Mississippi Freedom Summer Project—an incursion of hundreds of college students to lead voter-registration drives and literacy training in Alabama's neighboring state. The whole prospect of an invasion of northern students distressed Charles Carpenter. "I very much hope that none of them will come to Alabama," he wrote in 1964, "where I assure you no encouragement has been given to any groups who wish to come down and 'do us good' during the summer months."[90]

This was the summer of the passage of the Civil Rights Act of 1964, and tensions were running high in Mississippi and throughout the South. George Murray questioned the wisdom of "adding fuel to the fire" during this time of uncertainty and exposing young people to danger. NCC involvement was "unwise, because some of the leaders of civil rights seemed to expect violence and seemed to hope for federal troops to enter Mississippi," he added.[91]

Nevertheless, Murray refused to condemn the student participants or the Commission on Religion and Race. "I do grant these people the right to offer their lives if they desire to do so," he concluded. Jesus Christ had stood firm for "what he thought was right" and suffered through a painful death on a wooden cross. The students had the right to enter Mississippi and help others to learn to read, write, and register to vote. "We are one nation," Murray wrote in 1964, "and it has always been my feeling that citizens of this nation are welcome any place in this nation. We do not need passports or permission to cross state lines." A remarkable statement in light of Murray's opposition to King entering Birmingham a year before.[92]

When the Episcopal laity in the state realized that a portion of their tithes was going to the NCC, money in the collection plates began to dwindle. "The Glory of God is not diminished by the unworthiness of those who serve Him," wrote one parishioner. "Nevertheless, I have withdrawn personal and financial contributions to the Episcopal Church until such a time as it severs this undesirable alliance."[93] The church had weathered financial storms before, like the Great Depression, and these lean years were a time of testing, Murray concluded, in which true believers would be separated from "those who hold no Christian commitment." Murray promised that this economic intimidation would not work, vowing to cut programs and salaries, like other dioceses had done, to meet the national quota of giving.[94]

Organized in 1950, at the height of the post-war red scare, the National Council of Churches provided an ecumenical umbrella organization for twenty-nine denominations coordinating efforts in foreign and home missions, evangelism, education, and social action. The NCC's focus on civil rights issues and other social concerns led many white southerners to brand the organization a "Communist front." One outraged Alabamian scolded Murray's superior, Charles Carpenter, for following the directives of the NCC and failing to "see the fine finger of Communism working for the down fall of America." The Freedom Summer literacy schools were nothing more than a Communist training ground, another parishioner suggested. Why did these northern students come to Mississippi when the state already had public schools? Illiterates in Mississippi were probably illiterate because they were too lazy to "take advantage of the educational opportunities available to them," he added. When three civil rights workers disappeared that summer, one Episcopalian suggested that the trio were "living it up" in Cuba or some other Communist country. This might just be a conspiracy, he suggested, to disgrace the great state of Mississippi. The bodies of the three men were later discovered buried in an earthen dam.[95]

When parishioners charged the NCC with Communist activities, Murray invited the accusers to provide proof. "Both I and the F.B.I. must know at once," Murray wrote in 1964. The coadjutor bishop demanded that the accuser provide definitive proof and be prepared to testify before criminal and ecclesiastical courts. "Slurs and smears are constantly made," he continued, "but they are not backed up." If these charges had sufficient evidence, Murray promised to personally rid the NCC of the Communist infiltrators. The tendency of some southerners to see a Communist conspiracy behind all social and economic outreach programs irritated Murray. He saw a logical fallacy in assuming that people who attacked the same problems shared the same principles. The proposition that since Communists opposed racial discrimination, then

Christians who opposed this injustice were "aiding and abetting the Communist cause" was simply wrong. "I am personally convinced," he added, "that unless Christians are able to effectively combat racial discrimination and injustice, the nonwhite peoples of the world will turn toward Communism."[96]

While Murray and Charles Carpenter had the daunting task of keeping radical segregationists within the church placated, the national Episcopal governing body made the Alabama church leaders' jobs increasingly difficult by making public pronouncements in favor of civil disobedience. At the General Convention of the Protestant Episcopal Church in October 1964, the House of Bishops adopted a resolution calling on Christians to obey laws except in "extreme circumstances" where a conscience demanded "obedience to God rather than man." The church recognized the right of any individual or group to legally pressure, even through peaceful demonstrations, the government to repeal unjust laws. If these actions failed, then a person had the right to disobey the unjust laws, as long as they accepted the legal repercussions, used nonviolent tactics, and demonstrated "severe restraint" because of the possibility of undermining the rule of law.[97]

In response, Murray appeared before the bishops and pointed out that the measure undercut efforts moderate southern leaders had been making. The bishops of the Deep South had appealed to people to obey the law, because the court decisions and congressional laws were moving in the right direction. "And now here you are, all you northern bishops saying disobey the law," Murray proclaimed. "If you're not careful you're going to drive the South out of the church." Northern church leaders treated the southern bishop as if he were a "Klansman who had just left his sheet in the hotel room" while he came to the meeting.[98]

Murray considered this portrait somewhat amusing, since many radical Alabama segregationists thought him a wide-eyed liberal bent on "burning the stars and stripes and banishing motherhood." He feared the wrath of these hostile whites and soon took several personal precautions by removing his boldly lettered name from his shiny black mailbox and relocating his children's beds to the center of the house to protect them from a bomb blast. "I am considered by some in this country to be a rightist reactionary," he wrote in 1964. "A great many more consider me to be very conservative. Many others consider me to be liberal, and I am sure there are some who believe me to be a Communist sympathizer."[99]

While many white Alabamians saw Murray as a liberal activist, the bishop maintained a tempered approach to civil rights. He was "unwilling to go all out" and participate in the demonstrations; if he did, he would be forced to leave Alabama. "One can never be sure what is right," he wrote. The only times he believed his work became unbearable was when he felt "hated by my brothers in other parts of the country who feel that I should join the revolution in a way which would automatically end my ministry here."[100]

Like all of the eight white ministers, Murray detested non-Birmingham residents, such as King, coming to town for a few weeks, criticizing, confronting, and then going elsewhere. The bishop believed Alabama needed people to move to the state to bridge gaps between the races and build relationships. "We could not use men who are only interested in integration," he wrote one northern clergyman in 1965, "and would not have any interest in the other needs of the people." During the civil rights protests, Murray offered a position, including outstanding pay and housing allowances, to a northern priest participating in the demonstrations. "Come down here and work with us," Murray entreated. The young priest refused. "Bishop, you got me," he confessed. Murray then asked the priest to stop complaining about the South and the "sorry outfit" governing the Episcopal Church in Alabama. "You know I'm going back [North] and I don't think I'm going to say anything about the South," the young priest told Murray. "I think I'm going to talk to my parishioners about their own sins."[101]

Following the Selma demonstrations and as Charles Carpenter's health failed, George Murray took an increasingly active role in the affairs of the diocese. During the spring of 1965, Murray suffered through "days of real resentment" in the wake of the events in Selma. "I saw the planning and work I had been doing, and the relationship I had been building," he said, "swept away by a sudden revolutionary convulsion which now leaves some of us behind to pick up the pieces and start building again."[102]

Self-doubt and uncertainty overwhelmed Murray—believing that his years of planning, negotiating, and mediating had been "mighty puny and almost irrelevant." The bishop found it difficult to see the civil rights cause advanced through the improper tactics of others. "But I realize all of us must learn to accept it," he added. Justice had been advanced but at the expense of order and love. Revealing the differences between himself and Martin Luther King, Murray argued that justice, order, and love had to work together—with love working within order to attain justice. "I tried to work through persuasion," he added, but now the civil rights movement had pushed justice ahead of order and love. "Perhaps that is the way it should be," he concluded.[103]

The easiest response to this frustration and bitterness, Murray maintained, would be to pack his bags and leave Alabama. "But I feel I am called to minister here," he wrote in 1965, "and to try to carry forward this ministry of reconciliation." The activist phase of the civil rights movement ended with Selma and the passage of the Voting Rights Act of 1965, and Murray believed he had to "reconcile people to living these laws and obeying them." Among the most pitiful people in the South, he argued, was the "defeated rabid segregationist." Southern leaders had to find some way to help these people "live in the new society rather than to end up in mental hospitals."[104]

When Bishop Murray succeeded Carpenter as the Episcopal bishop of Alabama in 1968, he continued to press for open communication between the races, as he had during the Birmingham crisis. "The world around us is involved in change at a near unbelievable rate," Murray said in 1969. "The church's job is to help people live with change, and with one another in change." As with most white, southern, moderate religious leaders, Murray believed the church's role was not to create change but to serve as a "guiding and reconciling agent" for a society in flux.[105]

Murray, however, did radically change the Episcopal Diocese of Alabama. The bishop proposed dividing the state with Birmingham the headquarters for a north Alabama diocese and Mobile the headquarters for a south Alabama–northwest Florida diocese. When the Alabama diocese was divided in 1971, Murray jumped at the opportunity to leave Birmingham and move to Mobile. That south Alabama port city was far away from the bad memories and difficult times in Birmingham. He served as bishop until he retired in 1981 and continued to play an active role in church affairs from his retirement home in Fairhope, Alabama, in 2000.

Even after leaving Birmingham in 1964, Paul Hardin continued his fight to ease racial tensions in the Methodist Church. As he returned to full-time duties as the bishop of South Carolina, Hardin was annoyed by the misrepresentation of his ministry and racial outlook while in Alabama. Regardless, he had no regrets for the white clergy's stand against the Birmingham demonstrations. Hardin maintained that the ministers had only asked King to postpone the protests and wait for the new city government to make good on election promises. King chose the names of the eight clergy, Hardin added, and addressed the "Letter from Birmingham Jail" to the only religious leaders in Alabama bold enough to act openly to "make the situation better." A surprising move, he believed, since there was not a "single segregationist" in the group. Hardin said he initially thought the letter was a joke and never had a "twinge of conscience" about King's arguments. The bishop insisted that his entire ministry in Birmingham and in South Carolina contradicted the impression the document gave. "I don't think that he meant to take advantage of a situation," Hardin reflected, "but he saw . . . the names of men who were prominent in the religious life of Birmingham and the state of Alabama and he wanted to address that letter to that type of person, people who were well known. In a measure, I never really felt badly toward him for it."[106]

As he worked to change the racial climate among Methodists in South Carolina, Hardin also hoped his actions would prove that King's portrait was wrong. The nagging tensions over the all-black Central Jurisdiction came to a head. The Central Jurisdiction's South Carolina Conference had the largest membership of any black conference, with over forty-five thousand members. In 1964, the black bishop, C. F. Golden, and the white bishop, Hardin, began discussing a formal merger of the two conferences. "We are quietly and deliberately going about the business of setting things right," Hardin said. The walls of prejudice were "quietly but definitely" crumbling, with better communication and understanding "creeping in" to change attitudes. "The status quo of yesterday," the bishop added, "was not that of today, nor will today's be that of tomorrow."[107]

Almost immediately a vocal group of belligerent segregationists began pressuring Hardin to halt the drive toward merger. When one angry layman confronted the bishop, Hardin responded: "You know, if I were you, and felt as you do toward the black race, I'd be afraid to die." The bishop continued to provide moderate leadership, despite additional pressure from black activists, who thought the process for merger remained too slow.[108]

By the late 1960s, both conferences came under Hardin's episcopal leadership, and the bishop ordered both Annual Conferences to meet together for the first time. "I don't know whether it was legal or not," he said. "I didn't care." At the meeting, the black conference sat on one side of the aisle and the white conference on the other. Hardin sat before them in a squeaky swivel chair answering questions about the merger. The tension was thick, and when a white delegate asked how long it would be before the bishop assigned a black preacher to a white church, a hushed silence fell over the room. With a wide grin, Hardin answered: "Brother, I . . . can't hardly get you to take a white one." The auditorium exploded in laughter, and the delegate pulled a white handkerchief from his back pocket and waved it in the air, surrendering to the will of the bishop. Afterwards, the two sides slowly came to accept the merger. After several years of heated debate and squabbling over details, both conferences adopted a formal merger plan on January 27, 1972. Hardin retired that year and moved to a Methodist retirement area near Asheville, North Carolina, remaining active in the affairs of the church until his death in 1996.[109]

In later years, Hardin often paused to reflect on Martin Luther King's "Letter from Birmingham Jail." "You know," he mused in the early 1990s, "I think most of his [King's] arguments were right. White ministers should have taken a more active role during the crisis. However, I'm not certain his letter accurately describes the personal convictions of this particular group of clergymen."[110]

Most people that read the letter assumed that the eight white ministers were a monolithic group of obstructionists. While Nolan Harmon and Charles Carpenter emerged as the most conservative, Paul Hardin, Milton Grafman, Joseph Durick, and George Murray maintained an enlightened commitment to racial progress. Durick and Grafman, as members of minority religious groups in the region, remained especially sympathetic to racial injustices. Regardless, their reactions to the "Letter from Birmingham Jail" remained as diverse as the men themselves.

10   The Unpardonable Sin

Most churchgoing radical segregationists embraced the faithful spirit of racial separation over the Holy Spirit of God. Blinded by ignorance and social tradition, they watched the old social older die. As the walls of segregation tumbled down all over the South, they determined to preserve Jim Crow in their last bastion of control, the churches. Even if a minister made veiled pronouncements of Christian unity or brotherly love, segregationists interpreted these remarks as integrationist rhetoric. As journalist Ralph McGill noted during the racial crisis of the 1950s and 1960s, white southern religious leaders that proposed even modest solutions faced "ostracism and obstruction, repeated telephone calls in the dead of night, ugly whispered filth, threats of violence and death inspired by minds, stewing with God alone knows what evil."[1]

Throughout the era, journalists, liberals, and civil rights activists condemned the do-nothing white ministers of the South. This was a central theme in Martin Luther King's "Letter from Birmingham Jail." Yet this criticism often ignored those white clergy who had spoken out and faced the wrath of hardline segregationists. These weary white southern pastors, like Edward Ramage and Earl Stallings, bore a heavy burden during the racial crisis.

For years, Ed Ramage looked to escape the stresses of his job by traveling to his farm a few miles north of Birmingham near Argo, Alabama. At every opportunity he loaded his wife, Katherine, their kids, and

Snowball the dog into the family station wagon for a quick retreat away from the pressures of his ministry. "I basically love the country," Ramage once wrote. "It helps more than anything else to untangle the tight strands that the city weaves." The farm freed Ramage from intellectual pursuits ("after all, I make my living with my head") and allowed him to use his hands as a gardener, carpenter, painter, plumber, and mechanic. Mounting racial tensions in Birmingham and in his church prevented the Ramages from traveling to the farm during much of 1963. A small pastor's study at the church served as the minister's only retreat.[2]

On a warm day in late spring 1963, the postman stuffed the bundled mail through the tarnished brass door slot at First Presbyterian Church. The stately old Birmingham church was quiet this day, often the case during the long summer, allowing Ramage time to catch up on his readings and melancholy reflections. Assistant Pastor William Ford heard the clanking sound of the mail slot's metal door and strolled down the hallway to retrieve the morning mail.[3]

In the mail was an envelope addressed to Ramage. Ford handed the correspondence to his mentor and quietly returned to his office. Sent by an acquaintance, the envelope contained a copy of the Quakers' printing of the "Letter from Birmingham Jail." Alone in his study, Ramage quietly read the document for the first time. When he finished, he summoned Ford. "Read this," he said as he tossed the pamphlet across his desk toward Ford. After the young assistant pastor finished scanning the pamphlet, Ramage proclaimed that King's composition seemed "just about like getting a letter from St. Paul." After a moment of quiet introspection, Ramage reflected on his long service to First Presbyterian and his career ahead. "But you know," he told Ford, "I suppose this letter will be the one thing in my life I will be remembered for."[4]

The racial tensions that surfaced at First Presbyterian during the spring of 1963 greatly distressed Ramage, and he felt caught in the middle of a multi-sided argument. After meeting with Ramage and other white Birmingham ministers, Dr. William H. McCorkle, the top elected official of the Presbyterian Church in the United States (PCUS), announced that the city's ministers were damned if they took steps toward integration and damned if they did not. "I will not sit in judgment," McCorkle told a Presbyterian gathering. "I ask you to pray earnestly for them and not to sit in judgment. We don't know what we would do there."[5]

One former church member at First Presbyterian recognized Ramage's precarious middle-of-the-road position. "Please forgive those of us who ran away to safer fields," she entreated, "and those of us who condemned your silence, as well as those who now attack you." Others in the church suggested Ramage should leave town for his own safety and the protection of his family. "I fear," wrote one member, "we have put upon you a burden requiring superhuman strength and I would urge you to consider your own welfare in this continuing crisis."[6]

As the focal point of the congregation's outspoken critics, Ramage grew concerned that his presence and the continued unrest might precipitate a split in the church. Throughout the summer of 1963, Ramage stood in the pulpit at times bewildered and bothered. "I stand up there and look out over the congregation," he told his wife, Katherine, one evening, "and I know everything about everybody in those seats. I know all about their relatives; all about their problems; and all their joys. I think maybe it is just time to try something new." The Ramages had hoped to stay at First Presbyterian until Ed's retirement, but the long-time minister had decided that the church would heal quicker under different leadership. In the fall of 1963, Ramage resigned and accepted a position at St. Paul's Presbyterian in Houston, Texas—far away from the racial volatility in Alabama. When he made the final decision, he simply scrawled on his calendar, "I quit."[7]

A few weeks later, following Sunday-morning services, Ramage announced his impending departure at a congregational meeting. Before action was taken to dissolve the pastoral relation between Ramage and First Presbyterian, William Rushton requested permission to speak to the congregation. A solemn Rushton described Ramage as a splendid pastor and leader. "He has had the courage of his convictions," he told the crowd, "and has been forthright and outspoken about them." Some church members and elders had disagreed with him at times. "I am confident," Rushton added, "none have disagreed with him on as many subjects, nor on any more occasions, than I have." Regardless, Colonel Rushton, who had clashed with Ramage over the race issue a few months earlier, now concluded that the termination of Ramage's ministry was "a great loss to this church and to this community."[8]

Other church leaders recognized the quality leadership Ramage had provided during his transitional period at First Presbyterian. Elder Harold Walker noted that in times of change, Ramage was "acutely sensitive to our problems in balancing the circumstances and obligations which required response to change" while he maintained with "corresponding insistence the witness of the church to the fundamental Christian message." The *Birmingham News* echoed these sentiments in an editorial lamenting the loss of such a "creative religious force" in the city. "His service, his guidance, his contribution toward enlightenment and his steady hand on our shoulders in time of considerable crisis, have been a very great benefit."[9]

The years of work as a minister in Birmingham had left their scars on Ramage. He had served as a pastor at various churches for more than thirty years and had grown disillusioned and frustrated. At his Houston church he began questioning his ability to minister to the spiritual needs of the congregation. "Are they any better off?" he wondered. Ramage longed to build deep meaningful relationships with his church members, but he never seemed to move beyond artificial bonds. He hoped to minister to the needs of these people, but he could never even recognize their real wants. "I am a product of an order," Ramage concluded a few years after leaving Birmingham, "a society, an establishment that made me what I didn't want to be."[10]

To keep a ministry afloat in the South, a preacher had to avoid controversial subjects from the pulpit. The quickest way to end a ministry, Ramage believed, was to "get out of line" in theological or social issues. Christianity offered so much more, he thought, than this sterile feelgood religion and these "man-made" dogmas. Like King Solomon in the book of Ecclesiastes, Ramage pondered the futility of human wisdom, the mortality of his own calling, and the confining spirituality of the church. Playing it safe in a comfortable pulpit had come back to haunt Ramage. "How did I ever get so deluded?" he pondered. "I have played the game. I have said the right things in the right way. . . . I have far more of this world's good, according to some standards, than a preacher ought to have, and yet there is an emptiness, a vacuum, a longing for something never fulfilled. There is a longing to pull off all the trimming and just be a real, everyday garden variety person; to quit using the [words] . . . that sound pious but have no real meaning; to relate to real people in a real way."[11]

The burden of the racial crisis in Birmingham and the stress of adapting to a new ministry had taken a toll on Ramage's physical health as well, and not long after arriving in Houston he suffered a mild heart attack. Serving a new church after eighteen years proved a difficult and at times frustrating task. Unlike the eclectic mix of familiar faces at the

urban "Old First" in Birmingham, transient oil workers and their families filled the membership rolls at the suburban St. Paul's. They had little
interest in building a strong community, sinking roots in a church, or
forming long-lasting relationships with church members or the pastor.
"Everything was just so different" Katherine Ramage later recalled. "It
was a whole new world, and I think that added to his disillusionment."
Nevertheless, Ramage offered his melancholy service to the Houston
church for nine years, until his retirement on his sixty-fifth birthday,
October 2, 1973.[12]

Preachers find no retirement from the service of the Lord, and when
the sixty-member First Presbyterian Church in Sealy, Texas, offered
Ramage the temporary position of "stated supply" pastor, he jumped at
the opportunity. Located a few miles west of Houston on the road to San
Antonio, Sealy had a population of only four thousand people, but
Ramage attracted some forty new members to the small church during
the four years he "filled in." In 1977, he accepted a three-month position
as the interim pastor at the First Presbyterian Church of Pine Bluff,
Arkansas. Subsequently he "retired" again, but the Ramages decided to
stay in Arkansas and purchased a big rambling house near the church.
Despite a steady decline in his health, Ed Ramage spent his remaining
years substitute preaching around the state until his death from a rup-
tured aorta in 1981. During these later years, as he spent more time
reflecting on his life's work, Ramage lamented that his only "claim to
fame" had been Martin Luther King's "Letter from Birmingham Jail."[13]

When the letter first came to the attention of Ramage's colleague Earl
Stallings, the Southern Baptist minister had no substantive reaction.
Under so much pressure from segregationists at First Baptist, Stallings
had little time to reflect on the essay. "I felt he had made a clear presentation of what he thought were the facts," Stallings said. He was the
only one of the eight white ministers mentioned by name in the text of
the document: King commended the Baptist minister for allowing black
visitors to worship at First Baptist on a nonsegregated basis. Regardless,
Stallings later concluded that the overall tone of the letter did not accurately describe his racial convictions or the inclusive nature of his ministry.[14]

Widely printed and read, the document only served to draw more
public attention to the Baptist minister, something he hoped to avoid,
especially following the scrutiny he received after his picture appeared

on the front page of the April 15, 1963, *New York Times*. Regardless, racial tensions in Birmingham compelled Stallings to continue speaking out. In the days following the May 10 truce, Stallings publicly blamed Birmingham's white churches for much of the climate of unrest in the city. By choosing to remain silent in the wake of increasing violence, the white churches had now become part of the racial problem, he believed—a point that King made in his letter. Stallings rebuked white Christians and Jews for providing little meaningful leadership during the crisis. The Southern Baptist minister also condemned the black community for contributing to the rising tensions by submitting to outside and irresponsible leadership, presumably King and the SCLC. "Let us pray earnestly for all men, and ask Almighty God for peace and understanding," he said. Ironically, Stallings would find neither within his own congregation.[15]

Even as the organized street demonstrations came to a conclusion and blacks stopped attending First Baptist, the pressure on Stallings continued to increase. The presence of blacks at the church served to unite segregationists in a fight to the end. They began collecting information on Stallings's "liberal" activities in an effort to sway other members that the open-door visitor policy must be changed, just in case the blacks returned in the future. Stallings had not initiated the policy of openness, which he saw as basic and right; he had just enforced it. Regardless, in the minds of many, the two had become synonymous.[16]

On May 15, the deacons held a special meeting to consider a change in the seating policy. Invited by chairman W. R. Cottrell Jr. to address the group, Stallings appeared before the thirty-one deacons and made a personal plea as one "whose heart was not embarrassed and whose mind was not distressed" by the policy. The issue had never been about examining the motives of church visitors, Stallings emphasized, but whether the church would "do the Christian thing" and seat blacks who attended worship services. The congregation needed strong unified leadership from the deacons in this time of crisis, so the pastor pleaded for a unanimous reaffirmation of the open-door policy. Youth minister Billy Allen, who witnessed the passionate appeal, believed Stallings had a "clear vision" of the future at First Baptist Church. "He was striving to right a wrong," Allen later recalled, "and make Christianity consistent in practice and in theory. He never once backed down on his position that the church was open for all people, regardless of race."[17]

Stallings, however, had not convinced all the deacons; far from unanimous, they voted sixteen to ten in favor of keeping the open-door policy. On May 22, the deacons called a special church conference to obtain churchwide approval of the reaffirmation. Stallings served as moderator and opened the conference with prayer for the church's sick and bereaved. Afterwards, he announced that the deacons, through "exhaustive deliberations and earnest prayers," had reached a decision on seating black visitors that Stallings had "approved wholeheartedly." Chairman W. R. Cottrell read the resolution to the congregation.[18]

Cottrell reminded the audience that for nearly a decade, the church had maintained a policy of admitting "all who seek to worship with us regardless of race, color, creed, or social position." Regardless, in recent weeks blacks had violated the "established social customs of our community" and put the principle to a "severe test." The controversy had divided the congregation between those who supported the policy and those who demanded an immediate end to open-door worship. Finding a reasonable compromise, Cottrell added, proved impossible. "A reversal of our present stand," he continued, "would not only embarrass our denomination but would satisfy one group of our people only to antagonize another." The deacons had concluded that "sudden drastic changes" in the principle were unwise and unjustified. "We realize, that some of our members have feelings to the contrary," he continued, "but we feel that more than anything else, we need to stand united in Christian fellowship."[19]

For many in the congregation, however, social traditions took precedence over Christian unity. When Cottrell finished, a mixture of sighs of relief and gasps of frustration filled the sanctuary. In turn, Stallings asked for a response from church members. One by one they came to the microphone and expressed their support for or disappointment with the measure. "The harm done to the fellowship in the church," declared A. F. Longshore Jr., "would outweigh any possible good derived from seating Negroes in the church." On the other hand, one member praised the church policy for its "tremendous impact for the missionary cause at home and abroad." The two sides debated back and forth until one of the deacons suggested the discussion be limited to ten more minutes. When the discussion ended, the congregation voted, and the deacons counted hands row by row to get an accurate total. Stallings compiled the votes and announced that the church had voted 182 to 136 in favor of retaining open admission.[20]

The defeat only inflamed segregationists, and Stallings received a constant stream of threatening letters and harassing telephone calls. At times, the phone would ring all night long and keep him awake. Stallings, however, refused to turn off the phone ringers, because he feared someone in the congregation "might really need me." Callers, many of them church members, shouted obscenities or branded him a race traitor, an integrationist, or a Judas. Other segregationists attempted less direct methods of intimidation by calling the church and impersonating the SCLC's Ralph Abernathy. "We appreciate what your church is doing," the person told the church secretaries, "and we want to bring 750 black folks next Sunday morning to worship with you." Minister of education William Simmons later discovered that the caller was one of the segregationist deacons hoping to create enough fear to prompt a change in the open-door principle.[21]

Stallings, however, stood firm, and prayed for God to soften segregationist hearts. "The most difficult thing," he wrote a friend in 1963, "is to break through the hard barrier of resentment and prejudice that keeps so many people from being responsive to the leadership of the Holy Spirit." Stallings had chosen to minister to the hard hearts at First Baptist and pledged to "say what I think needs to be said." He transcended the confines of the basic salvation message and encouraged churchgoers to make a deeper spiritual commitment to justice, brotherhood, and equality. With almost each Sunday morning sermon, the pastor's message made segregationists in the congregation angry. "If we are going to be Christian," Stallings proclaimed from the pulpit, "then we cannot determine or designate who can come and worship and who cannot." Always in control while preaching, he never resorted to browbeating his audience; rather he carefully, tactfully, and systematically, through prayer and preparation, presented a blunt message that heralded the equality of all persons or encouraged moderation.[22]

In late May, Stallings preached a blistering sermon entitled "Pilate's Wash Bowl." In the New Testament, Roman prelate Pontius Pilate had washed his hands of any "personal responsibility for righteousness and justice" and sent Jesus to his death. "Pilate preferred the status quo," Stallings told the congregation. "He wanted nothing to upset his little kingdom. But are we any different?" Not at all, the pastor concluded, this generation of churchgoers were characterized by much moral "two timing, political buck-passing, mink-coated five-per-centing-rule by influence" that ignored social injustice and racial prejudice. "Aren't we afraid to look at our freedoms, our privileges, to ask again if we really believe that these things are for all men?" The people of First Baptist Church had to "choose between truth and the prejudices which bolster racial pride." It was a difficult choice. "Even the minister must choose between truth and the possibility of losing his popularity, even his position," Stallings added. "Ah, Pilate, we condemn you because your position, your security, meant more to you than truth. But, are we any better? We hear the call of truth, of righteousness, of justice, but we are not men enough to heed its challenge. Selfishness, caution, expediency, opportunism, all together slam shut the doors and we never cross the threshold of truth, of freedom, of justice."[23]

In this time of change, people were marching for justice in Africa, Asia, and in the United States. "They march out of the doors of Negro churches in our Southland," Stallings continued. "We may deplore their methods. We may question their motives. We may be shocked at their shock-troops consisting of elementary-age children, but still they march. Shall the Christian remain alarmingly indifferent?" The pastor encouraged the congregation to reexamine the meanings of American citizenship and ask if these privileges and freedoms were for all people. "Our day, our city, our Southland need men willing to pay the price to be moral and spiritual heroes," the pastor believed. "Without such courage given of God, man marks time and time moves forward." Stallings asked God to provide young men and women who embraced truth rather than praise and love rather than prejudice. "Even if it means to be bound, even if it means to be spat upon, even if it means to be ignored, even if it means to be betrayed, even if it means to be rejected, yes even if it means to be crucified."[24]

Seated on the platform during these straightforward sermons, Billy Allen often witnessed the response of some church members. "I could see clinched fists," he recalled, "and I could see gritted teeth and heads shaking no." After dropping bombs in the morning worship, Stallings spent evening services "salvaging the fellowship" and explaining his position.[25]

Those that tired of hearing such messages stopped coming and joined the ranks of the behind-the-scenes agitators. Parents that favored racial separation stopped speaking to their children that supported an inclusive church. In September 1963, hard-liners distributed a petition to compel the church to once again reconsider the policy of seating blacks. "We're not trying to wreck the church," one announced at a deacon's meeting on September 11, "but . . . straighten out trouble." A committee of segregationists had circulated the appeal to three hundred members and had "heard protests from nearly all." In turn, one deacon scolded the committee for expending energy acquiring petition signatures instead of winning souls for Christ. The majority of the deacons rejected the segregationist proposal.[26]

Determined, these hard-liners vowed to never be outvoted again in a church conference, and they recruited marginal members to build a segregationist majority at First Baptist. They had become increasingly desperate. Public facilities had integrated; Bull Connor had been replaced; the walls of separation were falling down all around. They lost on every front. The last citadel of segregation was their church, and they determined to never see that tradition end. In their minds, Earl Stallings stood as a symbol of enforced integration.[27]

The actions of these segregationists only served to increase pressure on racial moderates in the congregation and further isolate Stallings and the church staff. These clandestine pro-segregation committees held secret meetings in the homes of church members and plotted strategy to preserve racial separation. They also worked quietly to sow seeds of mistrust against Stallings and encouraged an insurrection among the staff. A segregationist deacon urged Billy Allen to break ranks, and as a reward Allen would be hired as Stallings's replacement. "We want to get you into position to be our next pastor," he told the stunned youth minister. Allen refused and later retold the story to a dismayed Stallings. On another occasion, with the pastor out of town one week, a group asked Bill Simmons to join their forces, and he too refused. "I wasn't about to be enlisted against Earl," Simmons later recalled. "To be perfectly frank," he continued, "they were just beating the hell out of him emotionally. He was not only my pastor, he was my friend. I didn't relate well to that."[28]

These were difficult days, Stallings remembered some years later, but the Lord had never promised "us any easy times." During the crisis, he found strength in daily prayers, loyalty from his staff, and encouragement from two local Southern Baptist ministers, Dotson Nelson at Mountain Brook and Darold Morgan at Hunter Street. Stallings later claimed they were the only two white Baptist ministers in the state that actively supported his stand for racial inclusiveness. A friend since seminary days in Fort Worth, Morgan spent countless hours listening to Stallings, praying for him, and helping him emotionally deal with the trauma. "I've never seen any pastor that had to literally pay the price of being abandoned, of being ignored and mistreated as much as he was in that vicious setting back in the mid-sixties," Morgan later recalled.[29]

Still, the pastor continued to plan for better days at First Baptist. In 1964 he recommended long-overdue capital improvements in church facilities. A committee presented a plan to the congregation that would remodel the library and church offices; expand parking, dining, recreation, fellowship, and education facilities; and install air conditioning and other modern conveniences. On April Fools' Day, the members approved the $150,000 Vital Improvement Program (VIP). The plan, however, never got too far. Any program or ministry associated with Stallings had been stained with the sin of integration.[30]

By 1965, segregationist discontent had nullified Stallings's leadership and his ability to minister effectively to the congregation. The warring factions in the church considered "agreeing to disagree" and splitting the congregation to start a new church. Ironically, however, some members bristled at the proposal, because in their minds separation was an "un-Christian" act. Maintaining a dying social order had blinded segregationists to the inherent contradictions in their arguments.

Stallings never dreamed when he accepted the job in 1961 that this would happen. Most southern church congregations afford preachers a tremendous amount of respect and deference—Christianity and regional gentility demand such etiquette. On the other hand, like shepherds leading sheep, clergymen expect their flocks to submit and follow their leadership. At First Baptist, however, some lay leaders and church members treated preachers like hired hands and expected complete submission to their whims. When the resolute Earl Stallings stood for Christian unity, those same members that had called him to lead the congregation now condemned him as an integrationist.

Southern gentility compelled most members to avoid direct confrontations with Stallings. Instead they quietly refused to submit to his leadership, harassed him anonymously, subtly sabotaged his ministry, and incited rebellion when he left town. One Sunday evening following services, Stallings reached out to shake hands with a visitor and in turn was greeted with a solid punch in the mouth. The shaggy-looking man, one of the drifting homeless that pass through downtown each day, had apparently slipped in the back of the church for the evening service, and something Stallings said in his sermon touched off the violent response. Witnesses claimed that the visitor had no connection to any of the problems at First Baptist, he just served as another symbol of Stallings's tribulation. Some in the congregation whispered that the "nigger-loving preacher" had finally received his just reward. They hoped he might soon depart and the church would hire a segregationist preacher or at least a pastor that would keep his mouth shut.[31]

The shock of being treated with such disdain became too traumatic for Stallings to deal with. He continued, however, to humbly serve the church, but each week became a struggle to emotionally survive. On less volatile Sundays the pastor would ask Bill Simmons to sit nearby during worship services. "I'm not sure I can make it today," he would tell Simmons. As one former First Baptist member later noted, the malicious segregationists in the church had "crucified his soul." But despite the trials, Stallings always found the strength to place the spiritual needs of his congregation first.[32]

One by one, the young, dynamic staff at First Baptist, with the encouragement of Stallings, found opportunities to minister elsewhere. "There was just no point in staying," Bill Simmons remembered, "because we were not getting anything done." A pastor cannot serve people that do not wish to be served.[33]

In August 1965, Earl Stallings himself accepted a pastorship at the First Baptist Church of Marietta, Georgia. He could at least physically leave the trauma of the Birmingham church behind and work in much more congenial surroundings. The Marietta congregation embraced the new pastor and his ministry, and the once-forlorn preacher spent twelve happy years at this thriving church near Atlanta.[34]

In the mid-1970s, through the encouragement of denominational leaders, Stallings and the Marietta congregation launched a two-year study to determine the types of ministries needed for the growing numbers of senior adults. During these same years, Ruth Stallings had developed a rare form of arthritis that required her to live in a dry climate. So when the Southern Baptist Convention Home Mission Board offered to appoint the couple missionaries in Arizona to develop a statewide program for senior adults, they jumped at the opportunity. In March 1977, Stallings left Georgia to become the director of Christian Social Ministries for the Arizona Southern Baptist Convention.[35]

Arizona had become a popular retirement spot for many Americans, and Ruth and Earl discovered a fruitful mission field. Many senior adults had reached their later years with an "empty place" in their hearts and a "lack of purpose and fulfillment." The Stallingses began encouraging Baptists throughout the state "to break through the doors" and reach seniors. For the next eighteen years, Ruth and Earl conducted seminars on senior adult ministries in Arizona and throughout the United States. "I have no record, no way to conceive of how many places we went and how many things we did as God opened doors of service," Stallings recalled. In 1990 the couple coauthored *Seniors Reaching Seniors,* a groundbreaking book in the field of senior adult evangelism.[36]

Even in faraway Arizona, the memories of those uncharitable times in Birmingham haunted Stallings, and he found the topic too traumatic to discuss with anyone. "I can only come to the conclusion that it was something God wanted me to do," Stallings said in 1998. "I had a mission to carry out while I was there and when he was finished with me, he moved me." The scars, however, will always remain.[37]

Driving Stallings from the pulpit solved none of First Baptist's problems in confronting the race question, and the church continued to struggle with the dilemma for years to come. On April 1, 1966, Dr. James H. Landes, the former president of Hardin-Simmons University in Abilene, Texas, began his tenure as the pastor of the troubled church. On the surface, tensions seemed to ease with Stallings out of the picture, but this would only be the calm before the storm.[38]

Under Landes's leadership, the church began making "exciting plans" for expanded ministries and capital improvements. The social and economic diversity of a downtown congregation, the pastor believed, offered Christians the truest example of the early apostolic church. "Each segment enriched the other by experience and in relationships in the fellowship of Christ," Landes emphasized. The new pastor hoped to diversify the church's ministries so that First Baptist could "serve all groups." Although the congregation seemed to respond to this optimistic program, Landes resigned on February 25, 1968, to accept a pastorate of a church in Richardson, Texas. Several First Baptist members tried to persuade Landes to stay by offering to move the church out of the inner city to the elite suburb of Mountain Brook. It seemed a strange offer in light of the pastor's enthusiasm in leading a downtown church.[39]

Regardless, as Landes departed, First Baptist entered a period of introspection over its mission to a rapidly changing demographic area in the inner city. The Central City housing project across the street from the sanctuary had integrated and the congregation had reached a crossroads over whether to remain downtown or move to a new location. Following a lengthy self-study, a church committee drew up a series of proposals for congregational approval. Unanimously approved by members at a church conference in the summer of 1968, the "Commitments," as they came to be called, reaffirmed First Baptist's "primary obligation" to ministering in downtown Birmingham. "We are maintaining here a small part of God's great democracy," they concluded, "and we ask courtesy and tolerance for all alike. On these stern terms, we invite all who will, whether they be young or old, proud or plain, rich or poor, to partake with us of the love of God, and to give themselves to the task that is before us."[40]

The following fall, First Baptist hired the theologically liberal and highly controversial J. Herbert Gilmore Jr. as the new pastor. Gilmore embraced the "Commitments" and announced that the church would "care about all people regardless of condition or color." As he launched outreach efforts in the housing project nearby, a handful of blacks began attending worship services and sending their children to Sunday school classes. Under Gilmore's direction, the church also began a literacy ministry to disadvantaged black youths. One child in attendance had difficulty understanding why some members of First Baptist were reaching out. "You are white," she told one of the math tutors, "you are not supposed to love me."[41]

By 1970, many members of the congregation had grown uncomfortable with this apparent march toward integration. Segregationists opposed all ministries targeting blacks, and once again a First Baptist pastor became the focal point of intense criticism. Adding to this problem was another faction within the church that began grumbling at the same time about Gilmore's theological liberalism. In the spring of that year these two factions united in what Gilmore later termed an "unholy alliance." For months to come, the bickering between the segregationists, theological conservatives, and Gilmore's supporters raged.[42]

Dissension rose to the kindling point in June 1970 when two blacks, Winifred Bryant and her daughter, Twila Fortune, applied to the church for membership. The applications touched off a firestorm of controversy, and the congregation quarreled over whether to accept blacks as members. In July, before the church had resolved the issue, Gilmore left town for a long-planned journey to the Baptist World Alliance meeting in Tokyo and a subsequent six-week world tour. With the pastor so far away from home, segregationists and theological conservatives began a campaign to rally the "fringe of the membership" to dismiss Gilmore. A quarterly church conference on July 22 attracted a group of inactive members, including a few transported from local nursing homes. A vote to declare the pulpit vacant "as of this date" failed by only two votes, 188–186. Hobart H. Grooms Sr. condemned the attempted coup in Gilmore's absence as an "unseemly thing to do." Regardless, the motion to dismiss would be considered again at a special church conference in August.[43]

In Hong Kong, Gilmore cut his trip short and returned to Birmingham. At a churchwide conference on August 19, members quarreled from 6:45 P.M. until 2:30 A.M. over whether to fire the church staff. A vote to dismiss failed by only four votes, 241–237. On Sunday morning, September 27, 1970, the congregation finally voted on whether to accept Bryant and Fortune as members. The pair failed to receive the necessary two-thirds acceptance votes from members—a mere formality for white aspirants. Immediately, Gilmore walked to the pulpit and announced that he would not pastor a "racist church" and resigned along with most of the church staff. Layman Byrn Williamson stood up and told Gilmore that "many of us feel the way you do about this. I would like to ask all those who feel a sense of moral repugnance at what has been done to stand now and leave the congregation as a moral protest." Nearly three hundred members walked out. "Some of us," Gilmore declared soon after, "when we have the opportunity, have got to drive some nails in the casket of racism." Within weeks this group formed the Baptist Church of the Covenant, with Gilmore as pastor, and held services in Rabbi Milton Grafman's Temple Emanu-El. A physical split at the First Baptist Church of Birmingham had been a long time coming.[44]

During the weeks that followed, the controversy at First Baptist became a topic of intense debate among many of the city's leading white clergy, especially members of the Ministerial Association of Greater Birmingham. Believing this to be an exclusively Christian matter, Rabbi Grafman simply folded his arms and remained silent during the sometimes heated discussions. When one pastor noticed the usually outspoken Grafman merely listening, he asked the Jewish leader for his observations. With a voice that was both powerful and composed, Grafman told the Christian leaders that they must act boldly and confront the racial issue with all biblical authority. As a hush and a calming spirit fell across the room, Grafman asked the clergy, How many had read the "series of little books" called the New Testament? "I have!" he proclaimed. "How many of you ever walked in the footsteps of Jesus Christ? I have! When you read these books and when you walk in his path, you will have your answer. He has settled this matter Gentlemen!" Following Grafman's passionate plea, the ministers quietly and unanimously passed a resolution supporting racial inclusiveness in all Birmingham churches.[45]

With the departure of another pastor and a large segment of its membership, First Baptist struggled for two years to find a new permanent minister. Andrew W. Tampling assumed the pulpit in 1972, but stayed only a little more than three years. Other pastors followed for short tenures, adding to the instability of the dwindling downtown congregation. In 1980 pastor Samuel R. Jones Jr. resigned after three troublesome years of "having to continually secure my ministry" at First Baptist. His program to revive the church had been received with little enthusiasm by members. As he resigned, Jones described his time at the church as analogous to a physician who had failed to resuscitate a dying patient. The next year, two-thirds of the church's members again failed to vote in favor of a black membership application. As Birmingham's inner-city housing became almost exclusively black by the early 1980s, the church retreated even further behind its fortress-like walls into a near siege state.[46]

Finally, in 1984, the congregation turned its back on the inner city and voted to sell the church property to a local bank. First Baptist Church selected a new location in an affluent and mostly white suburb near the city's Southern Baptist university—far away from the troubles of the past. Workers carefully removed the majestic stained-glass windows from the old building for use in the new sanctuary and replaced the kaleidoscopic panes with sheets of knotty-pine plywood. The old church remained vacant for several years, but eventually the thick stone walls came tumbling down to make way for a ground-level parking lot. The discontent in the troubled church that began in the early 1950s, intensified following the 1954 *Brown* decision, boiled over in 1963 with Earl Stallings's stand for openness, and exploded under Herbert Gilmore, finally seemed to end over a generation later.

Like many white southern pastors, Earl Stallings and Ed Ramage faced the wrath of white segregationists. The two city pastors had committed the unpardonable sin in the minds of many hard-liners by allowing blacks to worship in the last bastion of segregation, the white church. Stallings and Ramage stood firm on their convictions of Christian unity and an inclusive church, but that was little consolation. Their ministries withered under the segregationist onslaught, and they left Birmingham for safer and more fruitful pastures.

Conclusion

In 1992, almost thirty years after the publication of Martin Luther King's "Letter from Birmingham Jail," the new Birmingham Civil Rights Institute opened across the street from the Sixteenth Street Baptist Church. Dedicated as a "testament to building bridges of understanding among all people," the institute proudly displays a replica of King's 1963 Birmingham jail cell, including the original door—removed years before during jail renovations. The moving words of the "Letter from Birmingham Jail" are printed on the walls surrounding the cell. Over a loudspeaker, King can be heard reading passages from the letter. Across from the jail cell door is a copy of the white ministers' Good Friday statement. Missing, however, are their names.[1]

So obvious a part of the letter, but so seldom discussed, the eight clergymen found their place in the chronicle of the civil rights struggle in Birmingham by being written out of history and deemed irrelevant figures. The stories of these white ministers are the missing part of the history of the letter. For right or for wrong, history should remember them—not as misguided opponents of Martin Luther King, but as individuals with diverse ideas on the volatile segregation issue who struggled with social change the way all people do one way or the other. Their lives, careers, and convictions reveal a great deal about the role the church and synagogue played during the civil rights crisis of the 1950s and 1960s.

As the mood of hysteria grew during the era, most of their religious colleagues in Alabama and throughout the South remained silent and did precious little to alleviate tensions. In the years following the *Brown* decision, positions hardened and even terminology seemed to be redefined. As one historian later noted, a moderate became someone who "dared open his mouth," and an "extremist" one who favored obedience to the law; even the term *compliance* "took on the connotations of treason." This wall of silence seems to explain why King and other integrationists dismissed the eight when they spoke out in 1963.[2]

In the years following the publication of the "Letter from Birmingham Jail," the American public, its scholars, and its journalists never understood the eight white clergymen. Many misinformed northern liberals concluded that the eight were reactionary spokesmen of the segregated South. On the other side of the issue, impulsive southern segregationists characterized these clergymen as liberals and race traitors. Most thoughtful readers of the letter, however, understood that King was attacking a group of "moderates" or "gradualists." Nevertheless, these interpretations assume these religious leaders were all like-minded and possessed a collective conscience on the race problem in the South.

On an individual basis, they expressed strong personal opinions about the racial upheaval of the era. Their ideas were just as diverse as the judgments against them. Few outside the region understood this complexity of thought, because the media had portrayed a solid, one-dimensional South. In Birmingham, opinions concerning the racial crisis varied widely in the black and white communities. For a nation and a region that thrives on the principles of individualism and freedom of expression, the notion of a corporate response to the race question is inaccurate. A study of the eight clergymen, as representatives of a variety of southern religious traditions, reveals the diversity of opinions in the white community, even among self-described moderates and gradualists.

As advocates of racial moderation and gradualism, these clergymen shouldered a heavy burden. They struggled to find an appropriate response to the massive changes in southern society, as did countless other racial moderates. "Like the rest of the South," one moderate wrote during the racial crisis, "I am confused . . . a southerner slowed down by racial fog but determined to find a way out."[3]

Self-styled moderates ultimately played a pivotal role in the transformation of the South. "It will be the moderate and the practical man," one journalist predicted in 1958, "who will see the South through this period which is to many one of agonizing readjustment far more acute than can be imagined by those whose liberal position is based entirely on principle without any corollary experience."[4]

This prediction seemed all too accurate in Birmingham. Meaningful change in the Magic City occurred only at a gradual and moderate pace. Inevitably, it was the citizens of the Magic City, both black and white, and not Martin Luther King and the SCLC, that brought about the real transformation of the city. As the white clergy argued, moderation and the push for change had been in process several months before King arrived on the scene. The Freedom Rides, the park controversy, and the excesses of Bull Connor and the city commission had rallied the reform forces in the white community.

Nonetheless, the intensity of the civil rights era changed forever the lives of the eight clergy. Fresh opportunities, retirements, ill-health, and retribution from segregationists compelled most of these men to leave Birmingham after 1963. Within eighteen months of the demonstrations, only three of the eight religious leaders remained, and by 1971 only one continued to work in the city. No matter how much or how little they said on the racial issue, each clergyman paid a price for speaking out during the volatile civil rights era.[5]

The events in Birmingham during the spring of 1963 also had a powerful impact upon the mood of the nation. "It was the year of Birmingham," Martin Luther King later recalled, "when the civil rights issue was impressed on the nation in a way that nothing else before had been able to do." The demonstrations and subsequent violence in Alabama's largest city brought civil rights to the forefront of the nation's conscience and even prompted President John F. Kennedy to call the issue a moral dilemma. Within months, the federal government had taken legislative action to safeguard the rights of all Americans.[6]

The year 1963 and on into 1964 emerged as Martin Luther King's finest hours. He had succeeded in his quest to focus the nation's attention upon the injustices of southern segregation, as well as to gain publicity for himself, the movement, and the Southern Christian Leadership Conference. King had won a tremendous public relations victory in Birmingham. From the beginning to the end of the campaign, the movement had focused on securing media coverage. Most often, King and other SCLC officials had carefully planned and staged confrontations for media consumption. On a local level, the movement applied economic pressure through boycotts and sit-ins to force the business community to end discriminatory practices. Those methods were only part of the plan to end segregation. At the national level, the short-term goal of the SCLC wing of the civil rights movement was obtaining extensive media coverage to reveal the injustices of segregation, to sway public opinion, to raise much-needed funding for the cash-starved movement, and to promote King's image.

The overarching goals remained the destruction of segregation and the establishment of racial justice; however, civil rights advocates acknowledged that the use of the media was the primary means to that end. As activist Andrew Young emphasized, the SCLC had a plan to use the media to achieve victory, and the whole movement had focused on "getting publicity." Fred Shuttlesworth added that the civil rights movement "would not have succeeded as it did" without the press.[7]

Many movement leaders had their eyes on the press as a way of gaining the prize of freedom. The "Letter from Birmingham Jail" played a pivotal role in this strategy. The story of the letter reveals a great deal about the search for peace and justice during the civil rights era. It shows how the Southern Christian Leadership Conference used the media to promote both King's image and the movement in general; using the media also helped in fund-raising activities. The fabled accounts of the essay's creation and the letter's mass appeal masked a more pragmatic tale: the document was a press release. The media and the American public were the real targets, not the eight white clergymen.

At times the singular focus on the media seemed to blind SCLC officials to the broader goal of racial justice. With the Birmingham accord of May 10, 1963, King had accepted a symbolic victory over concrete gains. The terms of the truce, the Southern Regional Council reported in 1963, "were not the all-out capitulation of Birmingham which Dr. King had predicted would crack the remaining solidarity of the South, or even agreement to previous demands."[8]

King had settled for much less than the original goals of Shuttlesworth's local group. At the time, SCLC officials realized they had not achieved a substantive victory in Birmingham. Two weeks after the accord, King's closest adviser, Stanley Levison, urged the civil rights leader to delay publication of an expanded version of the "Letter from Birmingham Jail" or any "definitive interpretation of Birmingham" until "the beginning of something that indicated that the victory was won." On May 27, Ralph Abernathy's secretary was still keeping the civil rights leader's schedule open until "the crisis had been resolved in Birmingham."[9]

Regardless, the lack of a substantive victory had little impact on the Southern Christian Leadership Conference and Martin Luther King. With the bonanza of publicity, money, and prestige, King walked away from Birmingham and proclaimed his mastery of the moment. The media and most of the American public seemed to agree.

Only a few weeks following the Birmingham movement, the SCLC's quest for money, prestige, and justice moved up the road to Virginia. Eyeing the struggle for civil rights in Danville, King promised to bring his "task force" to the southern Virginia town to help mobilize people and attract national attention. As in Birmingham, and earlier in Albany, the symbolic rhetoric began anew. "Virginia is really the leader of the southern segregationist forces," Ralph Abernathy added. "As Virginia goes, the South will go."[10]

Despite the diligent efforts of hundreds of grassroots volunteers, the excesses and successes of Birmingham were not duplicated to the same degree in Danville. The campaign there and subsequent campaigns in St. Augustine and Chicago never captured the imagination of a national audience. Only in Selma, Alabama, did King and the SCLC once again confront a belligerent southern lawman and garner the attention of the news media and the public.

In the Selma campaign of 1965, King and the SCLC hoped to reproduce one of the greatest successes of the Birmingham movement, the prison cell letter. While the civil rights leader was under arrest in Selma, the *New York Times* printed a large SCLC advertisement entitled "A Letter from MARTIN LUTHER KING from a Selma, Alabama Jail." As activist John Lewis later recalled, SCLC officials hoped this letter would "arouse the same interest in a federal voting rights bill" that the Birmingham Jail document had enkindled in a civil rights act.[11]

"Our people are eager to work, to sacrifice, to be jailed," King emphasized in the brief, three-hundred-word essay, "but their income, normally meager, is cut off in these crises." If someone was so moved, they could clip the coupon on the ad and mail a contribution to "advance human dignity" in the United States. "Your help can be a message of unity which the thickest jail walls cannot muffle," King concluded.[12]

The Selma epistle, however, provoked little interest. By 1965, Americans had grown to depend even more on the visual images created by television news more than the written words of the print media. Perhaps this was the reason the SCLC released such a paltry prison letter and targeted the document to such a specific audience. Regardless, the movement, the media, and their relationship with one another were changing.

Following Selma, the struggle for civil rights shifted: urban riots, the cry of Black Power, and internal differences led to the introduction of more complex ideas and symbols. The old formula reporting of good versus evil in a sensational Western shoot-out no longer worked. Clearly defined roles were less distinctive. "While peaceful southern marchers had been 'good guys' and brutal southern lawmen 'bad guys,' " one writer later concluded, "angry urban blacks burning and looting became 'bad guys' just as much as harassed northern policemen were seen as 'good guys.'"[13]

When Martin Luther King clashed with younger and more militant black activists over the use of the Black Power slogan, the media focused on the sensational aspects of the story. King, who always believed the national media was an important ally, criticized the press for diverting attention from white southern injustice to internal divisions within the movement. "This debate might well have been little more than a healthy internal difference of opinion," King later wrote, "but the press loves the sensational and it could not allow the issue to remain within the private domain of the movement." Ironically, King scolded the media for creating heroes and villains, something that had worked so well for him in Birmingham and Selma. "In every drama there has to be an antagonist and a protagonist," he wrote, "and if the antagonist is not there the press will find and build one."[14]

From these differences, one SCLC associate recognized, many in the civil rights establishment came to view the press as another white institution seeking to "use and abuse the black struggle" by concentrating exclusively on conflict. With riots, Black Power, and militancy shifting the media's focus from direct action, love, and nonviolence, white reporters sensed a shift in black attitudes as well. "I found the same kind of hostility toward the press which I had experienced in the [white] South," one newsman commented in 1967. He heard from blacks many of the same arguments that he had heard from segregationists. "You guys are distorting the news"; "Why don't you tell the story right"; "If it weren't for guys like you . . ."[15]

The mood of the nation had changed. The American public seemed much more concerned with maintaining law and order than any more acts of civil disobedience. Entering the fray, the U.S. Supreme Court, which in 1967 upheld King's conviction for violating the court order and proceeding with a march on Good Friday 1963. The high court's ruling in a narrow 5–4 decision required the civil rights leader to return to Birmingham and serve five days in the city's jail. Writing the majority opinion, Justice Potter Stewart seemed to echo the white ministers' law-and-order and "unwise and untimely" arguments. One may sympathize with civil rights activists' "impatient commitment to their cause," Stewart wrote, but respect for the legal process was a "small price to pay for the civilizing hand of law, which alone can give abiding meaning to constitutional freedom." Stewart emphasized that King and the other marchers had no right to bypass an "orderly judicial review of the injunction before disobeying it."[16]

On the other hand, Justice William J. Brennan wrote a particularly forceful dissent, arguing that convictions for contempt-of-court orders which abridged the First Amendment "must be condemned." Clearly, Brennan recognized the symbolism and the public relations motives King and the civil rights activists had in marching. The justice believed the activists had effectively dramatized the quest for racial justice by choosing to march on Good Friday, April 12, 1963. The civil rights demonstrators had hoped "to gain the attention to their cause which such timing might attract," he wrote.[17]

The decision disappointed King. "I am sad," King told reporters, "that the Supreme Court could not uphold the rights of individual citizens in the face of deliberate use of oppression." Nevertheless, Wyatt Walker, Ralph Abernathy, King, and other SCLC associates returned to Birmingham during early November 1967 to finally serve out the five-day sentence ordered by Judge Jenkins some four and a half years before. King again wore his prison uniform: a denim shirt, blue work pants, and a sweater. He brought three books: the Bible, John Kenneth Galbraith's *The New Industrial State,* and William Styron's *The Confessions of Nat Turner.* Birmingham police officials placed King and the others in a less accessible facility, in Bessemer, thwarting plans to focus national attention on the infamous Birmingham Jail. Walker brought his camera and snapped several striking pictures of a reflective King staring through the bars of a jail cell. City officials released the group twenty-four hours early.[18]

By the next spring, King was dead. In the hours following his April 4, 1968, assassination, waves of violence spread throughout the nation's urban areas. Birmingham, however, remained quiet that evening and in the days to come. On April 7, nearly four thousand citizens, both black and white, gathered outside the Sixteenth Street Baptist and marched silently down Fifth Avenue North to Twentieth Street and then up to the Jefferson County Courthouse for a memorial service. George Murray opened the service with a solemn prayer. While billowy rain clouds circled over head, the mourners sang hymns; many wept. Leaders from throughout the community eulogized the slain civil rights leader. Birmingham's new mayor, Republican George Seibels, praised citizens for "the peace and order that has prevailed in the city since the death of Dr. Martin Luther King." He pledged to serve all of the city's residents, regardless of race. "Through unity, understanding, and concern for our fellow man," Seibels added, "we shall have peace and unity in our city, in our nation, and across the world."[19]

Birmingham's racial climate quietly transformed. At the end of the 1960s, some five thousand black children were attending formerly all-white schools; in 1963, only seven blacks were in integrated classrooms. Registered black voters had increased dramatically, and blacks held important positions on the planning commission, the Chamber of Commerce, the board of education, and all the major civic organizations. During the elections of 1969, civil rights attorney Arthur Shores became the first black elected to the nine-member City Council.[20]

Despite the rising political fortunes of Birmingham's black community, the city's image remained tied to the events of 1963. At the signing of the truce between the SCLC and the city's business leaders in May 1963, King proclaimed that Birmingham stood on the "threshold of becoming a great enlightened symbol, shining the radiance of its example throughout the entire nation."[21] Despite these optimistic pronouncements and vast changes, Birmingham remained the symbol of racial intolerance.

In the years following the movement, selling Birmingham to prospective businesses proved a near-impossible task. "You'd finish speaking at some convention up North," said one Birmingham business leader, "and the first question they'd ask you was 'How many niggers did you get before breakfast?'" The city's image was so bad at times, leaders even considered changing Birmingham's name. In a twist of irony, just as Martin Luther King had often turned to New Yorkers to help his publicity campaigns, Birmingham officials hired a New York public relations firm to "show that the good folk down here don't have horns."[22]

By 1971, *Ebony* magazine hailed Birmingham for not being "the ham it used to be." Regardless, much work remained: the city suffered from choking air pollution, a decaying inner city, and whites fleeing to the suburbs. Negative images of the past and present continued to haunt the city. A decline in steel production in the late seventies prompted U.S. Steel officials to send a stinging letter to all employees in the Birmingham area. The company publicly blamed "sloppy work habits" and "laziness and inefficiency" for the financial loss; just another black eye for the city.[23]

In 1979, however, Birmingham citizens elected the city's first black mayor, Richard Arrington, and continued reelecting him the next sixteen years. Arrington emerged as a tremendous symbol of the empowerment of the black community and a shining example of the many changes in the city since 1963. Through the years, extensive revitalization efforts transformed Birmingham's business district from a gritty, industrial center into a symbol of New South progress.

Yet despite this outward facelift, race relations remain polarized. The old steel mills no longer belch black smoke into the air of the city, but a heart of darkness remains in Birmingham. An underlying bitterness and subtle animosity still seeps through the city as a lingering reminder of the long years of racial separation. De jure segregation has been replaced by a de facto apartheid mentality by both races. Few whites and blacks, to borrow a quip from Bull Connor, "segregate together." Whites continue to push farther into suburbs and embrace the old "us versus them" mentality. Few in the city have the courage to pursue meaningful dialogue about mutual problems. Only a handful of interracial churches exist in the city, and blacks would be no more welcome in many of the area's white congregations than they would have been in 1963. The peace that Martin Luther King sought and that the eight white clergy advocated has remained an elusive dream.[24]

Epilogue to the 2021 Edition

Pastors Who Paid the Price

She told me he was dead. When I asked the woman who answered the phone at First Baptist Church of Birmingham for information on their former pastor, Earl Stallings, the pleasant-sounding voice who answered the phone went silent. After an awkward pause, she spoke again in a cold, unforgiving tone. "He died many years ago," she explained, and scolded me for trying to "dig up the past." Disappointed, I thanked her for her time and hung up the telephone. As one of the eight white ministers addressed by Martin Luther King Jr. in his "Letter from Birmingham Jail," the Reverend James Earl Stallings was an essential part of the story. He was the only Southern Baptist of the eight and the only one that King singles out in the body of the "Letter."

King wrote of his disappointment in the white church, its leadership, and racial moderates, but he also highlighted "some notable exceptions": individuals who he believed took "significant stands" in the fight against segregation. The only minister he mentioned was Earl Stallings. "I commend you, Reverend Stallings," King wrote, for the "Christian stand" in permitting blacks to worship at First Baptist Church on a "non-segregated basis." History remembered Stallings and the other seven ministers as little more than religious mouthpieces for the segregationist status quo in Birmingham, but Stallings's stand for integration at an all-white church told a different story. Here was a white preacher in the heart of the Jim Crow South; a pastor of the most visible Southern Baptist congregation in Birmingham, Alabama; a city synonymous with racism, violence, and defiance; a minister who was commended by the most important black leader of the civil rights movement. I assumed that with his death, the full story of Stallings's praiseworthy stand and racial views were lost to history.[1]

In contrast, the racial perspectives of the other seven white clergymen whom King addressed were detailed, nuanced, and complicated. Although the men were united in issuing public statements—speaking out against racist rhetoric, "untimely" demonstrations, and violent activities—their thoughts on segregation and race varied from individual to individual, providing a much more sophisticated look at not only their own viewpoints, but also those of the whites they represented. "White southerners' doubts about segregation," one historian wrote, "were both more extensive and more complex than either zealous segregationists or civil rights advocates initially appreciated." The civil rights movement transformed the lives of white southerners in countless ways, and their reactions to these changes were just as numerous. As an observer of the South explained, "Even in those cases where the civil rights movement succeeded in changing whites' attitudes and altering their lives, nothing was simple or straightforward about those transformations." The same was true of the movement's impact on the eight clergymen, who in many ways were dehumanized and oversimplified by those reading King's "Letter." This book aimed to humanize, or as historian Jim Cobb once said to me, "recomplexify," the history of both the ministers and the "Letter from Birmingham Jail."[2]

But with Earl Stallings's thoughts, words, and deeds missing, the only substitute was to focus on the people at First Baptist Church of Birmingham. Their racial views, I soon learned, were equally complicated and diverse. As author Jason Sokal wrote in his broad study of white southern reactions to the civil rights movement: "For some, the law forced changes in practices, but it could not touch the recesses of hearts and minds. Others began to question deeply held views even though their lives looked much the same as before. . . . And for still others, change in any form—in law, mind-set, or lifestyle—was something to fear and resist, with denial and bitterness, all the way to the grave." At First Baptist, this last group of bitter resisters caused most of the upheavals. During the 1950s and 1960s, Birmingham's economic downturn, demographic changes, and racial unrest impacted First Baptist much more deeply than the other downtown churches. From 1952 to 1972, First Baptist hired seven pastors (with an average tenure of less than three years) and saw a significant drop in its membership.[3]

Before the civil rights era, however, the church experienced consistent growth and steady leadership through several dramatic shifts. Only three ministers served the church between the turn of the twentieth century and the post–World War II era, and both pastor and congregation adapted to changing demographic and social conditions in the surrounding neighborhoods. When the Reverend Alfred J. Dickinson became pastor in 1901, private homes lined the streets near the church, but over the next decade, families moved to outlying areas and joined other Baptist churches. By 1913, one observer noted, the demographics had changed so much in the community that Dickinson preached to an "almost new congregation." Nonetheless, the church continued to prosper throughout the period, with the theologically liberal Dickinson making the church's evangelistic outreach, in his words, "more social than individual." A preacher at a downtown church, he added, "must be more of a missionary than a pastor. He must speak to a cosmopolitan congregation with all their diversities and incongruities."[4]

By the time Dickinson resigned as pastor in 1918, the residential areas around the church were filled with impoverished people living in boarding houses, apartments, and tenements. Vice and violence were widespread, but Dickinson convinced his congregation that a "gospel of social redemption" was the will of God. The pastor envisioned "dry bones coming to life under the prophesying of the messengers of God . . . to plant hope for all the despairing." Under Dickinson's successor, James Randolph Hobbs, church membership boomed to almost 2,800 by the time he stepped down in 1938. Following Hobbs's resignation, during the Reverend John Lawrence Slaughter's pastorate, the tosspot areas around the church were cleared and the federal government built the vast white-only Central City housing project—the largest low-income housing in Birmingham. When the project opened in 1940, evangelistic outreach was a high priority for the church—although many of their efforts were interrupted by World War II. Following the war, however, membership increased to over 3,500 at its peak around 1950. Following Slaughter's departure in 1952, church attendance began its steady decline.[5]

While the church suffered from dissension prior to the civil rights era, the situation became much more pronounced following the 1954 *Brown* decision when Pastor James Thomas Ford initiated an open-door policy for any visitors, regardless of race. Like other southern churches, the hard-core segregationists at First Baptist grew more agitated and cantankerous after 1954. As an Alabama churchgoer said, "I'll roast in hell before I'll agree to let Negroes in my church." Some members of First Baptist pressured each subsequent pastor to end the open-door policy. One woman wrote in 1963 that church members, and not the pastor, decided which visitors to welcome and which to shun, and which new members to accept and which to reject. Nonetheless, each pastor who followed Thomas reaffirmed the guiding principle that all were welcome in First Baptist's house of worship. The leading segregationists only grumbled louder about the man in the pulpit.[6]

These evolving attitudes revealed a dramatic change in the fundamental relationship between pulpit and pew in Protestant churches throughout the South. Most white southerners showed a certain amount of deference to preachers—holding them in high esteem and considering them above reproach. But that changed following *Brown.* "It is alarming," one layman wrote in 1958, "how the masses are losing confidence in preachers and churches, and I have lost just about all I had."[7]

For many churchgoing segregationists, the white preacher, especially in churches like First Baptist, was nothing more than a "hired man" who served at the whims and pleasures of the church membership. "This is the truth of it," a segregationist wrote in 1963, "all this talk about Christian 'duty' is meaningless." While other denominations maintained "hierarchical protections" for ministers, Baptist congregations could fire a pastor just as quickly as they could "take a vote." One laymen wrote in 1957 that there were "more preachers being cast out of church than devils." One estimate put the numbers in the hundreds.[8]

Historian David L. Chappell argued that most segregationists wanted to "keep the churches as apolitical as possible," and indeed many churchgoers at Birmingham's First Baptist only wanted a safe place to worship and to remain "at ease in Zion"—unconfronted by difficult questions regarding race and equality. Other, more restless and confrontational whites, however, saw their church as the last "bulwark of segregation" and the place to make the final stand against integration. As a keen observer noted in 1963, the pastors at churches like First Baptist had three options: "He either adjusts, is fired, or suffers some sort of breakdown." The fourth option was to watch the life choked out of your ministry to the point you have no other choice but to quit.[9]

The Reverend James Thomas Ford resigned from the pulpit in July 1955 citing his weariness in reconstructing his "pastoral relationship with the church." Over forty years later, Ford was still reluctant to discuss his brief time at the church. "There's nothing else to say about those days," Ford remarked. "God led us there and then called us elsewhere." When Grady C. Cothen resigned his pastorate in February 1961, after just sixteen months in the pulpit, he called his time at First Baptist among the "happiest fellowships" of his ministry. Looking back decades later, Cothen believed he was in the pulpit "too briefly" to run into any major problems with the factions in the church. When he left Birmingham, he recommended that the pulpit committee visit his friend Earl Stallings in Ocala, Florida—a recommendation that he later regretted. "I knew there were elements in that congregation that were difficult; those type people were in every church," Cothen said, "but if I [had] realized that they were so cruel, I never would have mentioned the name Earl Stallings to that committee."[10]

When I asked Reverend Cothen for more information about Stallings's ministry, he paused and then replied: "Have you talked to Earl?" No, I answered. "I thought he died years ago." No, Cothen said, "I talked to him last week." He told me that Stallings and his wife led a vibrant program for senior adults in Arizona. I was thrilled to receive Stallings's address and telephone number but annoyed that the woman at First Baptist misled me. After listening to a few of Reverend Cothen's anecdotes about the congregation, though, I realized why she discouraged me from looking at First Baptist's past. The story was growing dark.[11]

After I hung up with Cothen, and in a moment of youthful enthusiasm, I cold-called Stallings. It was a mistake. His wife, Ruth, picked up the telephone, and I asked to speak to Reverend Stallings. When he answered, I gave him a fast introduction and told him that I wanted to interview him about his ministry in Birmingham. After a long pause, he said, "That is something that I never talk about." I dared to ask him why. In an angry, booming voice he told me that it was none of my business and hung up the phone.[12] I decided to write him a letter and apologize for my impulsive call. Over the next few months, we exchanged letters, and he explained that the memories of Birmingham were still so painful that he promised his wife to never revisit those years with anyone. But he tried. Stallings sent me copies of his sermons and a tape recording covering the early years of his life and ministry. In subsequent conversations and correspondence, the most he ever said or wrote about Birmingham was that he had a mission to carry out while he was there, and when God was finished with his ministry at First Baptist, he moved him elsewhere. Even with all the care I took in building a meaningful relationship with Reverend Stallings, I knew that those years in Birmingham were too torturous to discuss with anyone. I moved on and completed my dissertation and revised my manuscript without Earl Stallings's full story.

Just a few weeks after Louisiana State University Press published *Blessed Are the Peacemakers* in March 2001, Samford University, a onetime Southern Baptist school in Birmingham, invited the Reverend Earl Stallings and the Reverend John Thomas Porter to receive honorary degrees. From 1962 to 1965, they were pastors of two of the most prestigious Baptist churches in Birmingham, but they never met each other—coexisting strangers, separated by what W. E. B. Du Bois described as a "vast veil" between the races.[13]

A month before the ceremony, Ruth Stallings died. She was eighty-five. Heartbroken over her death, Earl Stallings still flew to Birmingham. "As soon as my plane landed," he later wrote, "I felt the bitterness of 37 years begin to lift from my soul." John Porter's soul, however, was weighed down from the loss of his son who had died a few hours before graduation. On the morning of May 26, 2001, Porter and I sat in the robing room as a spry Stallings walked through the door. As soon as he saw Stallings, and despite aching knees that made rising difficult, Porter said: "I'm going to stand up for this man." He stood and the two men embraced. They sat down and offered each other words of comfort in the sorrow that they both shared. Following a prayer, Stallings told Porter, "I wish we were able to pray with each other all those years ago." He reminded Porter that he had been in his church once for the funeral of three of the four girls murdered in the Sixteenth Street Baptist Church bombing. "I drove by your church," Porter recalled. "I never went inside." Ironically both of their churches were torn down—one a victim of urban "renewal" and the other a casualty of white flight. When Stallings received his honorary degree, the resolution described him as a "Southern Baptist prophet who pursued truth rather than praise, embraced love rather than prejudice."[14]

The following morning, the Reverend Stallings preached a sermon entitled "The Name of Jesus" at the Baptist Church of the Covenant—the breakaway congregation that split from First Baptist Church of Birmingham during the racial crisis. Following his sermon, one by one, older members approached Stallings, apologized for how he was treated at "our former church," and thanked him for ministering to the people in Birmingham. "You'll always be," one elderly woman told Stallings, "my pastor."

That Sunday afternoon, Stallings and I spent several hours talking about his visit to Birmingham. I quietly asked him if he felt like he could revisit those painful years as minister at First Baptist Church. He told me that he was ready to "lay that burden down," and he told his story.[15]

What first attracted Stallings to the job at First Baptist was the church's commitment to evangelistic outreach. Early in his ministerial career, Stallings had developed a passion for evangelistic work. At the rural Dumplin Creek Baptist Church in the 1940s, he often set out on a Gospel-sharing journey by walking miles through remote areas around the French Broad River and over the foothills of the Great Smoky Mountains—places so isolated that healthy mules found the traveling difficult. Throughout the area, Stallings followed dirt paths through the woods to simple log cabins where he stood on the porch steps and preached the Gospel message. When young people from the church accompanied him on the journey, they sang hymns, which brought much delight to residents—especially an old infirmed man who watched and listened through the open door of his cabin. When he died, friends and neighbors placed his body in a pine box, loaded it onto a wagon, drove his remains down the creek bed to the Baptist church, and asked Stallings to preach the funeral. It was Stallings's first. To assist the young minister, the Reverend Thomas C. Wyatt traveled from nearby Knoxville for the service. Following the funeral, the gathering began the procession down a long, winding footpath to the graveyard. As they walked, Wyatt opened his Bible and began reading Isaiah 43: "Fear not, for I have redeemed you; I have called you by name, you are mine. When you pass through the waters, I will be with you; and through the rivers, they shall not overwhelm you; when you walk through fire you shall not be burned, and the flame shall not consume you." Wyatt read the chapter all the way to the graveside. The prophet Isaiah's words so moved Stallings that he embraced the verses as a guide for his ministry and evangelistic efforts. The passage played an essential role for Stallings during the crisis in Birmingham.[16]

Stallings grew up with the same narrow racial views as other white southerners of his generation—a cultural segregationist who never really gave much thought to the social order. While attending Southwestern Baptist Theological Seminary, however, he came under the influence of Christian ethicist Thomas Buford (T. B.) Maston, who had just published his book *Of One: A Study of Christian Principles and Race Relations*. Maston saw the "race problem" as a moral issue that "moral forces" should "take the lead" in solving. It was the "church's business" to be at the vanguard in solving the problem and transforming culture. "It will be a tragedy of tragedies," Maston added, "for the churches of Christ to surrender their moral leadership."[17]

In T. B. Maston's Christian ethics course and in chapel services, Stallings was exposed to these ideas, which shaped the way he thought about race. Maston forced him to become "painfully aware" that he was not "relating well" to the culture in which he lived. "It made me search my own soul," Stallings said, never dreaming that his transformed convictions on racial equality would compel him to take a stand in Birmingham almost two decades later.[18]

In December 1961, Earl Stallings arrived as the pastor of the First Baptist Church of Birmingham and visited every member—active or not. The minister's good faith efforts were well received by the congregation, and Stallings's evangelism and ministry flourished. But that changed in January 1963, when he joined with other Birmingham ministers to sign the anti-segregationist statement. Episcopal bishop George Murray and Catholic bishop Joseph Durick contacted Stallings about meeting with other ministers and issuing a public statement in the wake of Governor George Wallace's inaugural address. "They didn't have to convince me," Stallings said. When the statement appeared in the papers, the problems started. The segregationists at First Baptist were "very unhappy about me being on that committee," he recalled. The issue continued to simmer throughout the winter and into the spring of 1963.[19]

But Murray and Durick pushed Stallings to make even bolder moves on the racial issue. As a pastor in the largest denomination in the state and of the most prestigious Southern Baptist church in the city, Stallings would make a dramatic impact with his public actions. "Their deep convictions about the moral structure of society," he recalled, helped refine his own thinking on the immorality of racial segregation. A new sense of "moral urgency" in Stallings, combined with the influence of T. B. Maston's ideas, compelled the pastor to reaffirm the open-door policy and to explain to the deacons that if blacks wanted to come to the church, he wanted them to come; and if blacks wanted to join the church, he wanted that too. "I could pastor black people just like I could white people," he told them. When black worshipers showed up on Easter Sunday 1963, however, those words meant little to hard-line segregationists in the congregation.[20]

Following the service, Stallings was shocked to see both sides of Twenty-second Street North filled with police, sheriff's deputies, highway patrolmen, and the news media. "They all expected racial trouble at the Baptist church," he recalled, "but there wasn't any." He warmly greeted Andrew Young and the two black women as they exited the sanctuary. "That was satisfying to me," Stallings added. But the segregationists in the church were anything but satisfied and began acting out. A large number of members and some of the deacons wanted to revoke the church's open-door policy, but Stallings disagreed. By a narrow margin, the deacon board upheld the policy, but one infuriated deacon slammed Stallings up against a wall and told the minister to never oppose him again or he would get "even rougher." Stallings was, after all, nothing but a hired hand.[21]

Those racists at First Baptist were "mean as hell," Stallings said. "I mean they were MEAN. I tried to love those that I didn't like, but it was pretty hard. . . ." He recalled members standing up at Wednesday night business meetings castigating him for his racial stand and calling him appalling names. In May 1963, in the days following the end of the demonstrations and Eugene "Bull" Connor's violent responses, Stallings further incensed the hard-core segregationists in the church by preaching his fearless sermon "Pilate's Washbowl." Echoing the influences of T. B. Maston, Stallings blasted his congregation for washing their hands of moral responsibility for the racial dilemma in Birmingham. The congregation must choose between truth and prejudice no matter the cost: "Even if it means to be bound, even if it means to be spat upon, even if it means to be ignored, even if it means to be betrayed, even if it means to rejected, yes even if it means to be crucified." When Birmingham civil rights leader the Reverend Fred Shuttlesworth read the text of Stallings's sermon three decades later, he responded with a loud whoop and said, "I never thought I would hear those words out of the mouth of a white Baptist minister in Birmingham. I want to shake his hand."[22]

Segregationists at First Baptist, however, had a different response to Stallings's sermons. The death threats and harassment intensified and became daily events. It took a toll—especially on Ruth Stallings. "It was harder on her than me," Earl Stallings recalled. Every morning when he left for work, Ruth worried for his safety. "I don't know what it's like for a wife to have her husband leave," Stallings said, "not knowing if he might not come back at night." And she lived that way for the rest of their time in Birmingham. While Earl faced his own "personal Calvary" at First Baptist, the stress and the strain led directly to Ruth's developing painful fibromyalgia, with which she struggled until her death in 2001. Stallings blamed himself for her nervous condition and vowed never to discuss those terrible years in Birmingham with anyone while she remained living. Ruth paid the "penalty of the price" of ministering at the First Baptist Church of Birmingham. Stallings said that he was able to endure the pain, but it was devastating to "your companion, your bride, your wife, the mother of your child. The girl who was doing more to shape my life. She was the peacemaker. She grieved for me and she prayed for me and she stood by me."[23]

To cope with the emotional pain of harassment, Stallings hoped for support from some of the thousand or so Baptist pastors in Alabama, but only two contacted him. "That's pretty lonely," he said. Stallings received more encouragement from non-Baptists (including several of the white ministers with whom he signed the statements) and his former professor T. B. Maston, who offered heartening words of assistance throughout the crisis. Still, Stallings felt that his ministry was failing. "I've been a good pastor," he said. "God gave me a pastoral heart and gave my wife a pastoral heart, and we've always found joy in helping people and challenging people. I think I'd become so heavily burdened about what it was, and my mind was not clear."[24]

Stallings also developed physical ailments related to stress that landed him in the hospital, but it was the psychological toll that was most severe. He visited a psychiatrist at the Medical College of Alabama who urged Stallings to get away from the stress. The doctor took a pragmatic approach: "If you're going through all this trauma, why haven't you done something about it?" Stallings explained God's calling in his life and how he could not just leave his ministry. Yes, you can, responded the psychiatrist. "I want you to leave tomorrow. Don't wait another week." So, Earl, Ruth, and son James packed their car and drove to Destin, Florida, for a three-week respite and renewal. Stallings said that the crisis at the church left him "emotionally and mentally disturbed." For the first ten days of their vacation, the minister walked around in a fog. "All I did was read, study, pray, and walk on the beach," he said. Finally, the fog lifted.[25]

Returning home, Stallings read Martin Luther King's "Letter from Birmingham Jail" for the first time. Although he disagreed with King's characterization of the white clergymen, Stallings thought that King was right—because most white ministers did nothing to guide their congregations through the racial crisis. "The average pastor in a southern state," wrote the Reverend Robert Paul Sessions in 1961, was "damned if he did and damned if he didn't." To illustrate his point, Sessions described a group of psychiatrists who probed the psychological differences in three white southern ministers: an outspoken integrationist, an ardent segregationist, and one who lacked convictions either way. Their analysis discovered that the outspoken integrationist had no brain, the ardent segregationist had no heart, and the uncommitted had no backbone. "I've been greatly disappointed in my fellow pastors," Earl Stallings said. Some did try to make a difference, but what was a minister to do if he was pastoring a 300-member church and 285 of them were rabid segregationists. "You just don't have a chance," he added.[26]

In September 1963, segregationists at First Baptist lashed out at Earl Stallings for his trip to Washington, D.C., to meet with President John F. Kennedy. The church budget included a line item for a pastor's fund of a few hundred dollars that Stallings could use at his discretion for travel costs or other expenses. At the next business meeting, segregationists berated Stallings, with one woman demanding to know if he used any of the church's money to pay for an airline ticket to fly to Washington and meet with "those" Kennedys. "That just wasn't pleasant," Stallings said, but he continued to minister to the congregation in hopes of leading them through the difficult period of social change. But a pastor can't lead people to a place they're unwilling to go. It was obvious to Stallings and the others on the church staff that the hard-liners were committed to preserving segregation at First Baptist at any cost—preferring to see the church die rather than integrate. "I've never been unhappy at a church," Stallings said, "but I was troubled in Birmingham." He often drove home from downtown asking God, "How much longer?" And, as one member of the church staff said, "There was just no point in staying."[27]

Earl and Ruth Stallings sold their house and moved into an apartment closer to downtown in anticipation of being called to minister elsewhere. That call came in 1965 to the First Baptist Church of Marietta, Georgia. Stallings left Birmingham, he said, with no regrets. "I wasn't angry, even if I did think that many of the people at First Baptist were evil." His bitterness was more like a dull ache that never faded away. He added: "I look back on it and I know that God sent me to that place for that time. I found spiritual satisfaction in my own ministry because I had done what I felt God had led me to do. I found satisfaction from the response that I got from people. It gave me a great sense of accomplishment. I think it further developed my compassion for the needs of people whether it was an individual with a social problem or a community problem." As Stallings also once said, "Sometimes the Lord uses us in unique ways if we're open to his prompting."[28]

When Earl Stallings died on February 23, 2006, newspapers remembered him with a wide range of perspectives. The Associated Baptist Press called him a white preacher who was "made both famous and infamous" by King's letter. The *Los Angeles Times* wrote that Stallings was a white minister "who was praised" by King in the letter. The *New York Times* described Stallings as a prominent Baptist minister who "risked the rejection of his own white congregation, and worse, by seating African-American worshipers among them at his Easter service and urging reconciliation amid the city's erupting racial antagonisms." The *New York Times* highlighted that Stallings was one of the eight ministers addressed in Martin Luther King's "Letter from Birmingham Jail," in which King justified his actions in the city and expressed his hope that the white church would embrace the civil rights movement as a just and moral cause. "I had hoped that each of you would understand," King wrote in 1963. "But again I have been disappointed." Nonetheless, the *New York Times* emphasized, King "singled out" Stallings "by name as one of the few who took the side of justice." The result for the Reverend Stallings was "antagonism" from both civil rights supporters and segregationist devotees—an issue that resulted in a congregational split at First Baptist Church following his departure.[29]

As one minister said in 1970, before a church made a physical split, the congregation had already separated the "purpose of the church from the purpose of Christ." This was also true of First Baptist Church of Birmingham. For Earl Stallings, the racial dilemma that ultimately led to the physical split at the church in 1970 was a simple Biblical precept: love your neighbors as yourself. For segregationists, the issue was a deep-seated cultural edict: maintain segregation at any cost. In other words, these whites chose to cast off their neighbors, separate the church from Christ, and embrace a white-only civil religion based on racial segregation. While Stallings and most of the other preachers left and established fruitful pastorates elsewhere, First Baptist remained divided—spiritually and physically—over the race question. By the 1970s and 1980s, the deep division within the congregation led to a physical separation as the church denied membership to blacks at least twice—before closing its doors, selling its building, and retreating to the white suburbs "over the mountain."[30]

This was the opposite of what Martin Luther King hoped to see from a white church in the Deep South. King told an audience at the Southern Baptist Theological Seminary in Louisville, Kentucky, in April 1961 that the church should be at the forefront of opening avenues of communication between the races. "I'm absolutely convinced that men hate each other because they fear each other," he added. "They fear each other because they don't know each other. They don't know each other because they are separated from each other." King emphasized that "no greater tragedy can befall society" than to live on in "monologue rather than dialogue." The church had a duty to foster racial unity.[31]

During King's visit to the seminary—two years before he composed the "Letter from Birmingham Jail"—his sermons, lectures, and class discussions foreshadowed his words and themes in the letter. King justified his use of nonviolent direct action, his breaking of unjust laws, and his embracing extremism. "I'm an extremist," he told students in Professor Henlee Barnette's Christian ethics class, one who embraced "extreme love and goodwill."[32]

Barnette was a renowned Christian ethicist and one of the most outspoken Southern Baptist voices in favor of integration and equal rights for blacks. He helped invite King to speak at the seminary. During the 1946–47 academic year, Barnette had taught at Birmingham's all-white Southern Baptist school, Howard College. His interracial activities with black preachers and educators so deeply troubled the college's administration that they refused to renew his contract for the following year. After a short tenure teaching at Stetson University in Florida, Barnette joined the faculty of Southern Seminary in 1951—sending him to the forefront of Southern Baptist thought on race and social issues. He died in 2004, at age ninety-three, following a prolific career of influence and controversy.[33]

A few months following his death, Henlee's son, Jim Barnette, stopped by my office at Samford University carrying an accordion folder bulging with files. A valued friend and colleague in the Department of Religion, Jim told me that the last book his father read before his death was *Blessed Are the Peacemakers*. "He liked it very much," Jim said, as he placed the folder on my desk. "Henlee would have wanted you to have this," he added. On the outside of the folder, Henlee had scribbled in bold letters: PASTORS WHO PAID THE PRICE. Inside were dozens of files on white southern ministers—of all denominations—who "paid the price" by losing their positions or pulpits in the 1950s and 1960s. Henlee collected the materials from the 1950s to the 1990s and apparently intended to write a book about those white ministers who, in one way or another, supported racial equality and experienced the wrath of hard-core segregationists. Their stories provide a more complicated picture of white southern racial views during the civil rights era.

In 1961, the congregation at First Christian Church (Disciples of Christ) in Jackson, Mississippi, voted to enforce a strict all-white attendance policy. The policy went untested until June 16, 1963, four days after the murder of civil rights leader Medgar Evers, when two black women (one being activist Anne Moody) were barred from entering the church. One usher told the pair that First Christian was a "church of Christ, not a place for publicity." An older church member intervened and invited the young women to sit with her family, but the ushers refused, prompting the older woman to say: "God is the judge of us all. Who else can judge where we worship?" The incident occurred unbeknownst to the church's pastor, Roy Hulan, who was preparing to preach on Christian unity and brotherhood. He ended his sermon by telling the congregation: "To deny any person, on account of race or color, access to the House of God—not my house, not your house, not First Christian's house, but God's House—is an unchristian act." When Hulan found out after the service that the ushers turned away the two black women, he said, "I no longer consider myself a minister of a Christian church because the Christian church does not have bars at its doors." By August, he was dismissed by a vote of 172 to 92.[34]

In September 1963, the bombing of the Sixteenth Street Baptist Church deeply moved the Reverend Lucius DuBose, a Presbyterian minister in Mullins, South Carolina. A Birmingham native, DuBose preached a sermon entitled "My Home Town" in which he told his congregation that as "participants in a segregated society," he and the church were "all corporately involved" in the tragedy. After the sermon, one elder confronted DuBose, saying, "You accused me of being a murderer." The pastor left town the next day, and when he returned, he was told by the elders that he was fired. "It's a terribly lonely feeling," DuBose said at the time, "an isolated feeling."[35]

Tattnall Square Baptist—the campus church for Mercer University in Macon, Georgia—presented a spiritual dilemma for segregationists. The church supported missionaries in Africa, but when the fruit of that mission's work, Ghana native Sam Oni, attended Tattnall Square in 1966, the segregationist response was visceral. The majority of the church members refused to integrate, with a 289–109 vote to close their doors to Oni and all blacks—which led Oni to proclaim that "their segregationist policy was torpedoing their own mission program to Africa." When he returned to the church again, Oni was dragged away by police before entering; one Southern Baptist described the incident as an "act of savagery" and a "denial of the relevancy of Jesus Christ." The pastor, Thomas J. Holmes, said at the time that he could not be part of a church that turned away "anyone who wants to worship." Within weeks, the church voted 259–189 to fire Holmes and other members of the church staff. "I saw the true church emerge from our tragedy. I saw the nobility of Christian fellowship shining in the lives of suffering people."[36]

In 1967, Martin Luther King said he was convinced that segregation was "as dead as a doornail in its legal sense" and he supposed the only uncertainty about Jim Crow was "how costly some of the segregationists who still linger around will make the funeral." The costs in the white churches were staggering. In 1969, the congregation at Union Grove Baptist Church in Huntsville, Alabama, voted by a narrow margin to dismiss pastor James England. His "most serious crime," fellow Huntsville minister Harold Shirley wrote, was the observance of "Race Relations Sunday" once a year. "Even though this is the Tennessee Valley in north Alabama," he added, "we are still afflicted with a certain George Wallace mentality." Shirley wrote Professor Page H. Kelley at Southern Seminary to help England find another position and not leave the ministry. "I do not think," Shirley stated, "that we Southern Baptists can afford to lose many more men of Jim's caliber, integrity, and serious dedication."[37]

In rural Manchester, Georgia, the Reverend Lawson Jolly Jr. regularly told his congregation that Northside Baptist Church had an open-door policy for black worshipers. Supported by the deacons and other lay leaders, no one at the church ever questioned the policy until blacks started attending worship services. In January 1970, when a young black woman presented herself for church membership on a profession of faith, one white man stood and voted against her joining Northside. Following the service, the man told Jolly, "You are no better than a dirty nigger yourself." The pastor later wrote, "Thank the Lord! Someone finally understood my preaching." That was the message of Christian unity and equality that he tried to explain to the congregation. "That was the gospel," Jolly added, "in its purest form."[38]

Nonetheless, the most active members of Northside supported Jolly with a "spiritual maturity" that recognized the contradiction of supporting missions to Africans while excluding Americans from church membership. When the black woman asked to be baptized, opposition in the church grew. Marginal members took a more vocal role in opposing both her baptism and the open-door policy, but Jolly still immersed the woman at a regular baptismal service with other candidates. The opposition only grew, and Jolly began asking his congregation difficult questions: What is the church? Who does it belong to? How is the church governed? Will you be led by scripture or your peers? Do you choose "worldly security over personal integrity?" On February 22, 1970, the church fired Jolly effective immediately. "No word of accusation," the pastor wrote a few weeks later, "was said about race or theology." He was told that he was fired for "failing to cooperate with the deacons." Perhaps, Jolly suggested, they confused "cooperate" with "compromise." His stand could "never be determined by any majority or minority vote, but by the spirit of our Christ." Until congregations embraced the purpose Christ had for the church, Jolly added, they will continue to split. Until church members let the spirit of Christ "prevail through their lives, we will not meet the crisis and need of our day." Until pastors preach, practice, and stand on God's word, he continued, the church will never resolve the racial divide. "Until Christians begin to grow," Jolly emphasized, "pastors will continue to be fired" or choose to leave the flock they shepherded.[39]

Over 150 miles west of Lawson Jolly's former church, the congregation at First Baptist Church of Birmingham struggled with many of the same issues. Each pastor at the church, before and after Stallings, were Gospel-sharing evangelists who were zealous about ministering to the "lost" in Birmingham—especially to the poor whites living near the church. But throughout the post–World War II era, each pastor's evangelistic program failed—even with the support of like-minded laypeople in the church. Ironically, growing racial tensions in the church and the community played a key role in undermining evangelism efforts at First Baptist. This was especially true following the 1968 passage of the Fair Housing Act, which outlawed racial discrimination in public housing. Integration quickly began at the Central City housing project. Many whites at First Baptist wondered if their church's ministries would extend to blacks. Traditionally, white evangelistic outreach toward blacks, as historian Samuel S. Hill Jr. argued, was to convert souls, befriend them within the paternalistic framework of segregation, but to never mention changes in the social structure. But the civil rights movement and the federal government transformed the social order, so the church needed a new evangelistic program. Many whites at First Baptist, however, grew increasingly hostile to simple evangelistic outreach to blacks living in the project, much less any type of effort that went beyond ministering to an individual's soul. By definition, the First Baptist Church of Birmingham was a "southern church in crisis," torn asunder by those members who adhered to the ideology of Jim Crow rather than a theology that embraced evangelism and neighborly love. "It is not just a problem for laity or clergy," wrote one observer in 1957, "but an agony of soul for thousands."[40]

Following the hiring of J. Herbert Gilmore Jr. in 1968, the agony at First Baptist deepened as the new pastor and staff began outreach programs to blacks living in the Central City housing project. In 1970, two blacks—a mother and daughter—began attending the church, but when they walked the aisle to join First Baptist, they failed to receive the necessary votes for membership. In protest, Gilmore, most of the church staff, and almost three hundred members walked out of the church and soon formed the interracial Baptist Church of the Covenant. On February 24, 1971, deacons and members of First Baptist issued a public statement announcing that "race was not the main issue" in the church's split. "The church was severely divided about Dr. Gilmore before the black persons ever came forward for membership." They cited financial mismanagement, lack of visitation, weak children's ministries, personnel resignations, "liberal and humanistic preaching," and "failure to promote evangelism"; everything but race. Gilmore admitted to many shortcomings, but none of those had anything to do with the split. "The church voted to exclude blacks," he said. "That was the issue." Until First Baptist received blacks as members, Gilmore added, then no one would "take seriously the charge that the issue was not race." A decade later, in 1981, blacks again tried to join the church, and again the all-white congregation rejected them—unable to find enough votes to allow Christians with a different skin color to become members.[41]

In the thirty years between 1952 and 1982, the church lost over 70 percent of its membership, and attendance at Sunday services decreased over 85 percent. In 1984, when those who remained at First Baptist decided to sell their historic downtown building and join the white flight to the suburbs, only 143 (13 percent) of 1,100 members showed up to cast a vote. After 112 years in downtown Birmingham, First Baptist was unable to minister to the spiritual needs of the inner city. Even in their new and affluent location, far from urban decay and black people, First Baptist continued to struggle for members and an identity—despite being just down the road from Samford University. During the forty years following the 1970 split, a dozen or so ministers and supply pastors came and went—among them a white South African and a Presbyterian. In 2012, after the departure of the Reverend Stan Lewis, the church asked seventy-five-year-old retired preacher Charles T. Carter to serve as interim pastor.[42]

In a touch of irony, First Baptist chose the white minister who helped write the Southern Baptists' apology to blacks for the denomination's past sins of slavery and segregation—repenting of the "racism of which we have been guilty." Adopted by a nearly unanimous vote, the resolution lamented and repudiated "historic acts of evil such as slavery from which we continue to reap a bitter harvest, and we recognize that the racism which yet plagues our culture today is inextricably tied to the past." At its 1995 annual meeting, the Southern Baptist Convention asked for "forgiveness from our African-American brothers and sisters, acknowledging that our own healing is at stake." When one prominent black pastor read the statement, he said: "If there's a fitting response to the 'Letter from Birmingham Jail,' this is it."[43]

Conservative theologically and powerful rhetorically, Carter began his journey toward what writer Fred Hobson called a "racial conversion experience" forty years earlier. In 1956, as a nineteen-year-old preacher at Providence Baptist Church in rural Chilton County, Alabama, Carter encountered racial intimidation after allowing a black pastor to give a closing prayer at a youth rally. Two weeks later at another Saturday-night youth gathering, ten hooded Klansmen marched into the church, walked down the center aisle, lined up in the front of the congregation, kneeled, and offered a "white supremacist prayer"; they then stood, dropped ten dollars in the offering, and marched back out the door. The youth were terrified, but Carter seethed with anger. After the rally ended, Carter stayed up most of the night preparing a sermon that he entitled "God Is No Respecter of Persons," based on the second chapter of James—emphasizing that Christians should not show partiality to or discrimination against others. As for any white minister who even mentioned race in those days, death threats followed, but Carter stood his ground.[44]

Fifteen years later, in 1971, the pulpit committee at Shades Mountain Baptist Church near Birmingham invited Carter to preach a trial sermon and interview for the pastorate. During a question-and-answer session with church members, Carter expected that he would be asked about his own racial views. Even with all the racial tension at First Baptist and other white churches in the area, no one asked him a single question, and so he decided to bring up the issue. He told the gathering if he were called as pastor and a black person "walked the aisle" at Shades Mountain, he would embrace that person as a member. Carter said that he refused to be "party to rejecting anybody" based upon the "pigmentation of their skin." When he asked the gathering if they had any questions about his racial views, he was met with cold silence. But then an elderly man stood and said, "We would not want anyone to be our pastor who didn't feel the way you feel." Carter received a unanimous call to the pastorate of Shades Mountain. Less than two years later, Rufus Adetona, an African student who was led to Christianity by a missionary supported by the church, asked Carter if he could become a member. "Absolutely!" Carter proclaimed. But, Adetona said, "I don't see any black people here." The pastor responded: "Well, you can be the first one." The church accepted Adetona as a new member unanimously.[45]

In 1995, following the passage of the resolution at the Southern Baptist Convention's annual meeting, Charles Carter realized that the words were not enough. "The easy thing to do was to pass a resolution," he said. The more difficult thing was "what can we do to demonstrate [that] we are really serious about this?" Pastor Carter and many of his church members worked with black pastors and congregations to minister to the Central City housing project (rebranded Metropolitan Gardens)—the place that the whites at First Baptist Church feared and abandoned in the rush to the suburbs.[46]

When First Baptist asked Charles Carter to serve as temporary pastor in 2012, his presence, however transitional, was part of the church's long struggle to move beyond their tragic racial past. In 2015, Carter's successor in the pulpit, Jim Cooley, said that the church embraced the idea that the Gospel message was for anyone and that the church was open for everyone. First Baptist's problems, Cooley argued, "happened to different people a long time ago," when the church's "relationship with Dr. King . . . reflected the divisiveness of a difficult time in American history." The congregation now embraced Martin Luther King's "vision of a multiracial church," he added, and few, if any, churchgoers even remembered Earl Stallings or what he did. Yet the *Alabama Baptist* still wrongly described Stallings as the church's pastor whom King criticized in 1963 for "contributing to the 'silent—and often—vocal sanction' of racial segregation."[47]

*   *   *

African-American journalist Edward Gilbreath wrote in 2013 that many who read the eight white ministers' statement still "peg the signatories as racists, at worst, or white religious snobs, at best." Evaluating the statement without understanding the "complex environment" in which they lived was unfair, Gilbreath continued, because the eight "paid a high price for their commitment to racial equality and their opposition to King's disruptive tactics." They were strawmen who served as "little more than symbols" and "historical foils" for Martin Luther King's evolving literary masterpiece.[48]

King embraced what he called the "fierce urgency of now," but the struggle to destroy the foundations of segregation, obtain the right to vote, and realize the promise of integration took time. In the span of one decade (1955–65), the dedicated work of King and countless others forced local, state, and federal governments to dismantle the Jim Crow system. But once all the legal underpinnings were gone, the more difficult task came: integrating society and destroying systemic racism. The vestiges of Jim Crow wormed their way into institutions and systems throughout the country: government, real estate, finance, justice, education, agriculture, law enforcement, industry, entertainment, churches, etc. To untangle and remove that intricate web of systemic racism—tied to at least 350 years of slavery and Jim Crow—was not going to happen in the course of one or two generations. King understood that changing laws was much easier than changing hearts.

Afterword

JAMES C. COBB

One of the most critical challenges embedded in the otherwise mundane duties of a dissertation director lies in counseling a Ph.D. candidate who shows up with an absolute killer of a topic that also stands to contest an otherwise straightforward, compelling, and widely embraced narrative. Though it was roughly a quarter of a century ago, I recall having precisely that conversation with Jonathan Bass about the dissertation that would become this splendid book. I felt obliged to suggest that, however diplomatic and restrained his approach might be, he should expect some blowback against what was still likely to be construed in some quarters as an effort to chip away at the monumental legacy of the Reverend Martin Luther King Jr. In his typically quiet and unassuming way, Jonathan gave me to understand that he was fully mindful of the sensitivity of his topic, even though he envisioned no critical examination of King himself beyond exploring the motives and circumstances behind his fabled "Letter from Birmingham Jail." Besides that, I quickly perceived, he was, if anything, more interested in the project as an opportunity to do justice to the troubled, near-tragic stories of the eight ministers known to few outside Birmingham as anything more than the faceless men whom King had rebuked in his letter. Fully persuaded of not only Jonathan's passion for the project but also his capabilities as both a historian and storyteller, I had only to wave the green flag and then stay out of the way, save for giving an occasional "atta boy" to let him know I was around, if needed. Suffice it to say, that was seldom the case. Yet, if my primary contribution to this undertaking consisted of little more than standing by while Jonathan did his thing, I am nonetheless grateful for even that slender connection to a book whose meticulous scholarship is rivaled only by the fortitude of its author.

One of my criteria for determining the true significance of any historical work is its capacity, after many years in print, to inspire readers to reflect further upon the broader issues that it raises. On this score, *Blessed Are the Peacemakers* leaves little room for doubt. One thought that came to me immediately upon rereading Bass's assessment of the eight white clergymen is that when considered in historical context, their reluctance to make a clean and immediate break with racial segregation is not so difficult to fathom. For the better part of the seventy years leading up to 1963, the South's most racially tolerant whites had generally regarded segregation as the most feasible and humane approach to assuring peace, order, and progress in a biracial society. In the 1890s, Episcopal priest Edgar Gardner Murphy saw it affording blacks at least some measure of protection by shielding them, insofar as possible, from the direct contact with whites that put them at greater risk of falling victim to the racial passions so easily incited by hate-mongering politicians like South Carolina's Benjamin Tillman and Mississippi's James K. Vardaman. Beyond putting the lives and safety of black southerners at risk, lynchings, race riots, and other acts of terrorism triggered by the fulminations of these demagogues also threatened the stability and order deemed vital to the region's economic progress. In this sense, the Jim Crow laws of the 1890s reveal a distinct kinship with the host of subsequent Progressive Era measures regulating behavior in the workplace and restricting the consumption of alcohol.

The more moderate white advocates of segregation may have anticipated that the Supreme Court's 1896 *Plessy v. Ferguson* decision, stipulating that facilities set aside for blacks should be equal to those reserved for whites, would surely mitigate some of the harsher aspects of the Jim Crow system. Yet, with the overwhelming majority of southern blacks stripped of the vote by 1910, and in most cases sorely deficient in economic leverage as well, they were in no position to coerce whites into giving them access to schools and public accommodations, much less jobs, even remotely equivalent to those available only to whites. Thus, more than fifty years after *Plessy*, what one historian called "separate-but-equal liberals" like journalists Hodding Carter and Ralph McGill were still vainly imploring their fellow white southerners simply to live up to the letter of the court's stipulation that separate must be equal. In retrospect, that state of affairs foreshadowed what lay in store some sixty years later, when the headlines offered almost daily reminders that judicial or legal mandates matter little in the absence of the requisite will to enforce them. Both then and now, anyone demanding adherence to the law could expect a constant barrage of threats and invective in which "liberal" was likely to be the epithet of choice. "In the South," observed sociologist Gunnar Myrdal in 1944, "a person may be ranked as liberal . . . merely by insisting that the law shall be adhered to in practice." In reality, the question of whether "liberal" or "moderate" was the more opprobrious reference was pretty much a toss-up. In his 1959 gubernatorial campaign, Mississippi segregationist Ross Barnett decided that the most damning malediction he could fling at his archenemy Hodding Carter was the charge that he was "a moderate by his own admission."[1]

The death threats elicited by efforts to demonize white moderates in print and public discourse in those years simply left them even more persuaded that, as Mississippi writer David Cohn put it in 1944, any attempt to implement immediate racial integration in the South virtually guaranteed that "every southern white man would spring to arms, and the country would be swept by civil war." At this point, historian Morton Sosna observed, white moderates in the South found themselves almost muzzled by a "genuine dread that an all-out race war was impending."[2]

Surely no white moderates of the civil rights era had better reason to find warnings of widespread racial conflict entirely plausible or to foresee blacks accounting for an inordinate share of its casualties than the eight clergymen whose stories Bass tells. Like their predecessors of generations past, they were steeped in the faith that the key to resolving the "race problem" in the South lay in keeping the peace until regional economic and educational progress took its presumably inevitable toll on white hostility to black advancement. Any violent disruption of this orderly progression promised to set it back severely, if not halt it altogether. "If we can put off violence in the present," Hodding Carter assured a friend in 1956, "time is on the side of integration."[3]

Many black southerners had clearly lost their patience with the seemingly inexhaustible patience of white moderates by the time the eight white clergymen pled their case on Good Friday 1963 against the "unwise and untimely" demonstrations in their city led by the Reverend Martin Luther King Jr. and his SCLC colleagues. Nearly six decades later, it might well appear that these white ministers had stubbornly positioned themselves squarely in the path of an irresistible force at that point. Yet, as is so often the case, what seems so readily apparent in hindsight was anything but in real time. While their commendation of the "calm manner" in which local law enforcement officials had handled the demonstrations to date seemed like a textbook example of low expectations run amok, the clergymen's claim that such demonstrations had failed thus far to contribute "to the resolution of our local problems" was not entirely unfounded. Earlier nonviolent protests elsewhere, like the lunch-counter sit-ins in Greensboro, North Carolina, in 1960, had brought some localized gains, but similar efforts in Birmingham had largely come to naught at that point. The 1961 Freedom Rides had done little more than make Birmingham the staging ground for a carefully choreographed unleashing of white racial savagery that managed to further darken an already indelible stain on the city's image and ramp up racial tensions in the bargain. A series of boycotts by black college students in the fall of 1962 had successfully pinched the cash flow of some downtown businesses and prompted the temporary removal of some gratuitously demeaning "Whites Only" signs here and there. The city commission had retaliated, however, by slashing the funds for a surplus food program geared to serve low-income black families.[4]

Meanwhile, King and his cohort arrived in Birmingham in early 1963 still smarting from what appeared to be a thoroughly embarrassing, potentially discrediting failure to achieve much of anything in Albany, Georgia. Even King's arrest there had not energized the campaign or captured significant media coverage in the face of tactically astute local police chief Laurie Pritchett's overtly restrained approach to jailing hundreds of protestors. On the national scene, meanwhile, the Kennedy administration had repeatedly made it clear to anyone paying much attention that it was less concerned with eliminating the racial injustices behind the civil rights demonstrations than with simply making the demonstrations themselves go away. All of this is to say that, even before King's Birmingham campaign seemed to be faltering in April 1963, the eight white clergymen had some justification for their doubts—shared by a sizable contingent of local black ministers as well—that the demonstrations themselves would ultimately benefit the people in their respective congregations. Conversely, of course, despite the eights' fortitude in lending their names to a forthright rebuttal to Governor George C. Wallace's defiant "segregation forever" inaugural address three months earlier, their city's past—recent and otherwise—offered little to suggest that their "appeal for law and order" stood to accomplish even that, much less lead to progress for the great majority of its black citizens.

Formidable as the challenge awaiting King and his associates in Birmingham might be, however, they believed they might have found an unwitting ally in someone not just inside, but at the forefront of, enemy ranks. In the parlance of journalist Calvin Trillin, Albany's Laurie Pritchett was a "smart seg" who, like the Birmingham clergymen, sensed that regardless of the setting, the ultimate success of King's nonviolent demonstrations depended on provoking precisely the opposite response from local white leaders. Fortunately for King's purposes, there was no shortage of less astute "dumb segs," as Trillin put it, especially in Alabama, which he saw as the reigning "world headquarters for dumb segs." Although he would eventually face stiff competition in Dallas County sheriff Jim Clark—who presided over the bloodbath at Selma two years later—in April 1963, Birmingham's commissioner of public safety Eugene "Bull" Connor was still securely ensconced at the top the states' otherwise hotly contested dumb-seg hierarchy. When local black minister Fred Shuttlesworth invited King to come to Birmingham, where, he argued, a victory would largely vaporize the lingering fallout from the Albany fiasco, Shuttlesworth knew that, unlike the shrewd and disciplined Pritchett, in Connor, King would be facing off against a more volatile and less calculating adversary who should be more susceptible to his strategy.[5]

King had come to Birmingham, then, looking to exploit Connor's mercurial temper and proclivity for violence. This is precisely what the eight clergymen hoped to forestall, and their reference in their Good Friday statement to ostensibly "peaceful" demonstrations that nonetheless incited "violence and hatred" suggested they were under no illusions about what King was up to in their city. The debacle in Albany had forced King to face up to a deeply disheartening reality and to plan his Birmingham approach accordingly. His impassioned speeches and appeals to the consciences of white Americans outside the South had failed thus far to capture or maintain their attention or guarantee their political or financial support. Achieving that would require more graphic, real-life representations of what he and his followers and the powerless masses of black southerners were truly up against on a daily basis. In practical terms, this meant scenes of peaceful, polite black demonstrators seeking nothing more than recognition of their duly constituted rights as Americans only to meet with horrific, near-homicidal white violence. These images would then be disseminated by mass media to a vast national audience, thereby generating sufficient public pressure to force Congress and the president to intercede on their behalf, while hopefully wringing concessions from recalcitrant local officials as well.[6]

As Bass and others have shown, a frustrated King and his SCLC associates had failed to generate such dramatic, media-worthy footage in Birmingham prior to King's arrest on the same day that the eight ministers' statement appeared in print. Ironically, however, amid indications that the white clergymen's skepticism about the efficacy of civil rights protests might be on the rise nationwide, their statement was to be the catalyst for an eloquent and compelling rebuke of such skepticism and a reaffirmation of the legitimacy and urgency of the civil rights cause. As Bass notes, King's letter would not be released publicly in time to affect the demonstrations or to grab much notice in the press for several weeks. Birmingham would not feel the full glare of the media spotlight until SCLC strategist James Bevel's success in filling the streets with hundreds of black teenagers finally goaded Bull Connor into a tactically disastrous decision whose ramifications would effectively reinvigorate the entire civil rights movement. With no end in sight to the ghastly scenes of teenagers knocked upside down by massive jets of water or attacked by snarling dogs, cooler white heads than Connor's finally acknowledged that their city was in economic free fall and perhaps even on the brink of a race war. Only then did they grudgingly agree to a plan, announced on May 9, 1963, for what amounted, in most respects, to little more than token desegregation of downtown businesses.

The true significance of what historian Numan V. Bartley and others saw as "the civil rights movement's most important victory" lay not in its actual substance but in the indelible imagery of what had to be overcome to achieve it. The symbolic importance of the breakthrough in Birmingham helped to unloose an unprecedented flood of civil rights protests across the South throughout the remainder of the year and beyond. The Birmingham demonstrations also exposed the raw human reality of the brutal repression of black southerners in scenes so compelling that President John F. Kennedy realized he could no longer avoid immediate and forceful action to end these injustices once and for all. On June 11, 1963, scarcely a month after the Birmingham settlement had been reached, Kennedy went on television to call on Congress to enact sweeping new legislation that ultimately became the Civil Rights Act of 1964.[7]

Meanwhile, the significance of the "Letter from Birmingham Jail" was slower to sink in. It was just making its debut in major publications when Kennedy delivered his address, and the first print outlets to run it catered overwhelmingly to white readers. Morally compelling as its superbly crafted message might be, its claim on the consciences and sensibilities of those whites at that point was still secondary to the searing real-life scenes from ground zero in Birmingham. The letter's lofty status as what a King associate hailed a modern "Magna Carta for human rights" would be accorded primarily in retrospect, although as Bass shows, this was not long in coming to pass. King's treatise would soon be drawing comparisons with Lincoln's Gettysburg Address and rubbing shoulders with the writings of Thomas Jefferson and Henry David Thoreau in several anthologies that were required reading for students in a variety of college courses, including history, literature, ethics, philosophy, rhetoric, and religion.[8]

The annals of American oratory offer few instances of a speaker rising more triumphantly to the magnitude of the occasion than King's "I Have a Dream" speech at the culmination of the March on Washington in August 1963. Even so, the statement he had begun to compose in the isolation of a Birmingham jail cell some four months earlier had also become the stuff of legend in its own right well before *Blessed Are the Peacemakers* appeared in 2001. At the core of that legend lay the improbable tale of the "Letter from Birmingham Jail" as a spontaneous outpouring of impassioned genius rushing uninterruptedly from King's brain and heart through his pen and into print without need of further editing. However unlikely this version of the letter's genesis might appear upon serious reflection, on its face, it seemed no less a testament to King's brilliance and passion than the carefully crafted remarks he would soon deliver in Washington.

Other historians had already noted King's efforts to manipulate media coverage of his campaigns and other activities, and Bass's meticulously assembled case for the letter as a calculated and collaborative composition, nipped, tucked, and fluffed in certain spots to enhance its media appeal, proved difficult to dispute. Yet, as anticipated, his book appeared nonetheless to trigger a certain, almost reflexive defensiveness in at least a couple of reviewers who saw it as an implicit attempt to demean not just a sacred historical document but the man who composed it as well. One of these reviewers charged Bass with playing down "the ethical and moral dimensions of King's words and actions," though these virtues had already been extolled and expanded upon in numerous other works by that point. Moreover, Bass's references to it as "the most important written document of the civil rights era" and "a tangible account of the long road to freedom" hardly suggest someone bent on downplaying its significance. Bass had made it clear at the outset that he was exploring the impact of the letter on the eight ministers to whom it was addressed. Yet a second reviewer accused him not only of pursuing the dubious "subterranean goal" of showing that the clergymen named in King's letter "deserve a more elevated position" than they had thus far been accorded, but also of undertaking on his own part to boost their standing at King's expense.[9]

Bass clearly showed more empathy for these men than anyone who has written on them before or since, but he hardly presented them as flawless or uniformly appealing. Whatever good intentions he may have harbored, for example, it is hard to imagine Episcopal bishop Charles Carpenter cringing in the least at the effusive tributes to the Lost Cause churned out by his grandfather, Charles Colcock Jones Jr., nearly a century before. Nor, for that matter, did any of the clergymen escape revelations of personal limitations, resentments, and occasional pettiness. In truth, Bass was not out to refurbish their reputations so much as to simply rescue them from loss of individual identity that comes of being reduced to a stereotype (think Ralph Ellison's *Invisible Man*), as they had been in King's letter. In this, Bass succeeded most dramatically with the emotionally gripping story of the courageous, though deeply traumatized Baptist minister Earl Stallings, who endured several years of vicious emotional persecution by diehard segregationists within his own congregation. Though he was finally forced to resign his pastorate, Stallings managed to hang on longer than most of the hundreds, perhaps even thousands, of racially moderate white ministers driven from their pulpits in the South during the civil rights era.

For King, meanwhile, his letter to the eight ministers, only one of whom he addressed by name, was by and large a means of upbraiding all white moderates, ministerial and otherwise, for prizing order over justice in direct contradiction to the teachings and actions of Jesus himself. Understandably, the Birmingham ministers were stung by this criticism, though perhaps no more so than by King's suggestion that the moderate mindset was in some respects more injurious to the cause of racial justice than the extremism of the Klan. This characterization may have made some sense within the parameters of King's own tactical approach to advancing that cause, but otherwise it seemed calculated primarily to shock and shame the white moderates. Frustrated with the gradualism of those moderates as they surely were, blacks in Birmingham, who had years of experience in dealing with the extremism of the Klan and bore the scars to prove it, might have begged to differ ever so slightly with King on this point. Nor is there any indication that, when the time came, King or his associates sought to negotiate with Klansmen rather than moderates.

Because, as Bass reiterates, the eight ministers themselves were actually not the primary intended targets of King's letter, insofar as he may have considered its demeaning effects on them personally, they might have struck him as collateral damage incidental to a struggle for the greater good. Such a calculation might seem wholly out of character for so humane a figure as King. Once again, however, it is important to note he was at that particular moment on the front line of a moral conflict of surpassing importance in which, at the time he penned the letter, the prospect of victory seemed to be growing more distant by the day. Even his arrest had failed to reenergize support for the campaign, and it would be more than a week after his release before James Bevel managed to catch lightning in a bottle with the so-called children's crusade. Hippocrates's reputed observation about desperate times calling for desperate measures might not do full justice to the intricacies of King's dilemma at this critical juncture, but it is not hard to see why he may have felt such measures were necessary.

Meanwhile, rather than approach complexities such as the letter's consequences for its titular addressees, subsequent commentary has largely continued to hew to a less-cluttered, more cut-and-dried narrative, expanding further on the salience of the document and the undeniably brilliant achievement it represents. If Bass's treatment of the eight ministers and the composition of the letter itself ruffled a few feathers twenty years ago, then what sort of reaction might be anticipated if it were making its print debut today? The murder of George Floyd and other controversial slayings of blacks by law enforcement officers that fueled the explosive revival of the "Black Lives Matter" movement have led many Americans to reconsider not only how they view the present but the way they construe the past as well. For all that such surges of moral fervor stand to contribute to the betterment of contemporary society, their effect on how we approach our history may not be altogether salutary. By applying the anointed moral standards of our moment to people operating under very different standards in a very different moment, historians take it upon themselves not simply to judge these people but to label them for good or ill, as opposed to helping us to actually understand them and the times in which they lived. Bass's meticulous and forthright scholarship surely warns us of the pitfalls of blurring the distinctions between those struggling earnestly to do the right thing and those fighting just as fiercely to assure the right thing is never done. In doing so, we risk populating our past so exclusively with heroes and villains that we can perceive that past only as a reflection of the moral polarities of our own day. All the more reason, then, to welcome the updated edition of *Blessed Are the Peacemakers* as a vital and timely reminder of how history should be written and understood.

Appendix 1

The White Ministers' Law and Order Statement, January 16, 1963

"An Appeal for Law and Order and Common Sense"

In these times of tremendous tensions, and change in cherished patterns of life in our beloved Southland, it is essential that men who occupy places of responsibility and leadership shall speak concerning their honest convictions.

We the undersigned clergymen have been chosen to carry heavy responsibility in our religious groups. We speak in a spirit of humility, and only for ourselves. We do not pretend to know all the answers, for the issues are not simple. Nevertheless, we believe our people expect and deserve leadership from us, and we speak with firm conviction for we do know the ultimate spirit in which all problems of human relations must be solved.

It is clear that a series of court decisions will soon bring about desegregation of certain schools and colleges in Alabama. Many sincere people oppose this change and are deeply troubled by it. As southerners, we understand this. We nevertheless feel that defiance is neither the right answer nor the solution. And we feel that inflammatory and rebellious statements can lead only to violence, discord, confusion and disgrace for our beloved state.

We therefore affirm, and commend to our people:

1. That hatred and violence have no sanction in our religious and political traditions.

2. That there may be disagreement concerning laws and social change without advocating defiance, anarchy and subversion.

3. That laws may be tested in courts or changed by legislatures, but not ignored by whims of individuals.

4. That constitutions may be amended or judges impeached by proper action, but our American way of life depends upon obedience to the decisions of courts of competent jurisdiction in the meantime.

5. That no person's freedom is safe unless every person's freedom is equally protected.

6. That freedom of speech must at all costs be preserved and exercised without fear of recrimination or harassment.

7. That every human being is created in the image of God and is entitled to respect as a fellow human being with all basic rights, privileges, and responsibilities which belong to humanity.

We respectfully urge those who strongly oppose desegregation to pursue their convictions in the courts, and in the meantime peacefully to abide by the decisions of those same courts.

We recognize that our problems cannot be solved in our strength nor on the basis of human wisdom alone. The situation which confronts us calls for earnest prayer, for clear thought, for understanding love, and for courageous action. Thus we call on all people of goodwill to join us in seeking divine guidance as we make our appeal for law and order and common sense. Signed by: Bishop Nolan B. Harmon, Bishop of the North Alabama Conference of the Methodist Church; Bishop Paul Hardin, Bishop of the Alabama–West Florida Conference of the Methodist Church; C. C. J. Carpenter, D.D., LL.D., Bishop of Alabama; Joseph A. Durick, D.D., Auxiliary Bishop, Diocese of Mobile-Birmingham; Earl Stallings, Pastor, First Baptist Church, Birmingham, Alabama; George M. Murray, D.D., LL.D., Bishop Coadjutor, Episcopal Diocese of Alabama; Rabbi Milton L. Grafman, Temple Emanu-El, Birmingham, Alabama; Edward V. Ramage, D.D., Moderator, Synod of the Alabama Presbyterian Church in the United States; Rev. Soterios D. Gouvellis, Priest, Holy Trinity–Holy Cross Greek Orthodox Church; Rabbi Eugene Blackschleger, Temple Beth-Or, Montgomery, Alabama; J. T. Beale, Secretary-Director, Christian Churches of Alabama

Appendix 2

The White Ministers' Good Friday Statement, April 12, 1963

We the undersigned clergymen are among those who, in January, issued "An Appeal for Law and Order and Common Sense," in dealing with racial problems in Alabama. We expressed understanding that honest convictions in racial matters could properly be pursued in the courts, but urged that decisions of those courts should in the meantime be peacefully obeyed.

Since that time there had been some evidence of increased forbearance and a willingness to face facts. Responsible citizens have undertaken to work on various problems which cause racial friction and unrest. In Birmingham, recent public events have given indication that we all have opportunity for a new constructive and realistic approach to racial problems.

However, we are now confronted by a series of demonstrations by some of our negro citizens, directed and led in part by outsiders. We recognize the natural impatience of people who feel that their hopes are slow in being realized. But we are convinced that these demonstrations are unwise and untimely.

We agree rather with certain local negro leadership which has called for honest and open negotiation of racial issues in our area. And we believe this kind of facing of issues can best be accomplished by citizens of our own metropolitan area, white and negro, meeting with their knowledge and experience of the local situation. All of us need to face that responsibility and find proper channels for its accomplishment.

Just as we formerly pointed out that "hatred and violence have no sanction in our religious and political traditions," we also point out that such actions as incite to hatred and violence, however technically peaceful those actions may be, have not contributed to the resolution of our local problems. We do not believe that these days of new hope are days when extreme measures are justified in Birmingham.

We commend the community as a whole, and the local news media and law enforcement officials in particular, on the calm manner in which these demonstrations have been handled. We urge the public to continue to show restraint should the demonstrations continue, and the law enforcement officials to remain calm and continue to protect our city from violence.

We further strongly urge our own negro community to withdraw support from these demonstrations, and to unite locally in working peacefully for a better Birmingham. When rights are consistently denied, a cause should be pressed in the courts and in negotiations among local leaders, and not in the streets. We appeal to both our white and negro citizenry to observe the principles of law and order and common sense. Signed by: Bishop Nolan B. Harmon, Bishop of the North Alabama Conference of the Methodist Church; Bishop Paul Hardin, Bishop of the Alabama–West Florida Conference of the Methodist Church; C. C. J. Carpenter, D.D., LL.D., Bishop of Alabama; Joseph A. Durick, D.D., Auxiliary Bishop, Diocese of Mobile-Birmingham; Rabbi Milton L. Grafman, Temple Emanu-El, Birmingham, Alabama; George M. Murray, D.D., LL.D., Bishop Coadjutor, Episcopal Diocese of Alabama; Edward V. Ramage, D.D., Moderator, Synod of the Alabama Presbyterian Church in the United States; Earl Stallings, Pastor, First Baptist Church, Birmingham, Alabama.

Appendix 3

A Documentary Edition of the "Letter from Birmingham Jail"

Statement of Textual Method: In the following documentary edition of the "Letter from Birmingham Jail," bracketed text is text which appeared in the earliest-known versions of the letter but which was changed or omitted in later versions. Underscored text is text which appeared in later versions either as an addition or augmentation to the text or as an emendation of wording, punctuation, or capitalization in an earlier version. Emphasis, represented by italics, is in all cases that of Martin Luther King Jr.

The versions of King's letter compared here are earliest-known typed transcripts of the letter, dating from May 1963, and the edited version that appeared in King's book Why We Can't Wait *(New York: Harper and Row, 1964).*

[Martin Luther King, Jr.
Birmingham City Jail]
April 16, 1963

[Bishop C. C. J. Carpenter
Bishop Joseph A. Durick
Rabbi Milton L. Grafman[1]
Bishop Nolan B. Harmon
The Rev. George H. Murray
The Rev. Edward V. Ramage
The Rev. Earl Stallings]

*AUTHOR'S NOTE: This response to a published statement by eight fellow clergymen from Alabama (Bishop C. C. J. Carpenter, Bishop Joseph A. Durick, Rabbi Hilton L. Grafman, Bishop Paul Hardin, Bishop Holan B. Harmon, the Reverend George M. Murray, the Reverend Edward V. Ramage and the Reverend Earl Stallings) was composed under somewhat constricting circumstances. Begun on the margins of the newspaper in which the statement appeared while I was in jail, the letter was continued on scraps of writing paper supplied by a friendly Negro trusty, and concluded on a pad my attorneys were eventually permitted to leave me. Although the text remains in substance unaltered, I have indulged in the author's prerogative of polishing it for publication.

My [d]Dear Fellow Clergymen,

While confined here in the Birmingham City Jail, I came across your recent statement calling [our] my present activities "unwise and untimely." Seldom [, if ever,] do I pause to answer criticism of my work and ideas. If I sought to answer all [of] the criticisms that cross my desk, my secretaries would [be engaged in little else] have little time for anything other than such correspondence in the course of the day, and I would have no time for constructive work. But since I feel that you are men of genuine [goodwill] good will and that your criticisms are sincerely set forth, I [would like to] want to try to answer your statements in what I hope will be patient and reasonable terms.

I think I should [give the reason for my being] indicate why I am here in Birmingham, since you have been influenced by the [argument of] view which argues against "outsiders coming in." I have the honor of serving as president of the Southern Christian Leadership Conference, an organization operating in every [S]southern state, with headquarters in Atlanta, Georgia. We have some eighty-five [affiliate] affiliated organizations [all] across the South [—one being], and one of them is the Alabama Christian Movement for Human Rights. [Whenever necessary and possible] Frequently we share staff, educational and financial resources with our affiliates. Several months ago [our local] the affiliate here in Birmingham [invited] asked us to be on call to engage in a nonviolent [direct action] direct-action program if such were deemed necessary. We readily consented, and when the hour came we lived up to our [promises] promise. So I [am here], along with several members of my staff, am here because [we were] I was invited here. I am here because I have [basic] organizational ties here.

[Beyond this,] But more basically, I am in Birmingham because injustice is here. Just as the [eighth century prophets] prophets of the eighth century B.C. left their [little] villages and carried their "thus saith the Lord" far beyond the boundaries of their home towns[;], and just as the Apostle Paul left his [little] village of Tarsus and carried the gospel of Jesus Christ to [practically every hamlet and city] the far corners of the Greco-Roman world, [I too am] so am I compelled to carry the gospel of freedom beyond my [particular] own home town. Like Paul, I must constantly respond to the Macedonian call for aid.

Moreover, I am cognizant of the interrelatedness of all communities and states. I cannot sit idly by in Atlanta and not be concerned about what happens in Birmingham. Injustice anywhere is a threat to justice everywhere. We are caught in an inescapable network of mutuality, tied in a single garment of destiny. Whatever affects one directly, affects all indirectly. Never again can we afford to live with the narrow, provincial "outside agitator" idea. Anyone who lives inside the United States can never be considered an outsider anywhere [in this country] within its bounds.

You deplore the demonstrations taking place in Birmingham. But [I am sorry that] your statement, I am sorry to say, [did not] fails to express a similar concern for the conditions that brought about the demonstrations [into being]. I am sure that [each of] none of you would want to [go beyond] rest content with the superficial kind of social [analyst] analysis [who looks] that deals merely [at] with effects[,] and does not grapple with underlying causes. [I would hesitate to say that it] It is unfortunate that [so-called] demonstrations are taking place in Birmingham [at this time], but [I would say in more emphatic terms that] it is even more unfortunate that the city's white power structure [of this city] left the Negro community with no [other] alternative.

In any nonviolent campaign there are four basic steps: [(1)] [C]collection of the facts to determine whether injustices [are alive] exist[.]; [(2)] [N]negotiation[.]; [(3)] [S]self-purification; and [(4)] [D]direct [A]action. We have gone through all these steps in Birmingham. There can be no gainsaying [of] the fact that racial injustice engulfs this community. Birmingham is probably the most thoroughly segregated city in the United States. Its ugly record of [police] brutality is [known in every section of this country] widely known. [Its unjust treatment of] Negroes have experienced grossly unjust treatment in the courts [is a notorious reality]. There have been more unsolved bombings of Negro homes and churches in Birmingham than in any other city in [this] the nation. These are the hard, brutal [and unbelievable] facts of the case. On the basis of these conditions, Negro leaders sought to negotiate with the city fathers. But the [public leaders] latter consistently refused to engage in [good faith] good-faith negotiation.

Then [came the opportunity], last September, came the opportunity to talk with [some of the] leaders of [the] Birmingham's economic community. In [these negotiating sessions] the course of the negotiations, certain promises were made by the merchants—[such as the promise] for example, to remove the stores' humiliating racial signs [from the stores]. On the basis of these promises, [Rev. Shuttlesworth] the Reverend Fred Shuttlesworth and the leaders of the Alabama Christian Movement for Human Rights agreed to [call] a moratorium on [any type of] all demonstrations. As the weeks and months [unfolded] went by, we realized that we were the victims of a broken promise. [The signs remained.] A few signs, briefly removed, returned; the others remained.

[Like[2] so many experiences of the past we were confronted with blasted hopes,] As in so many past experiences, our hopes had been blasted, and the [dark] shadow of [a] deep disappointment settled upon us. [So we] We had no alternative except [that of preparing] to prepare for direct action, whereby we would present our very bodies as a means of laying our case before the conscience of the local and the national community. [We were not unmindful] Mindful of the difficulties involved[.], [So] we decided to [go through] undertake a process of self-purification. We [started having] began a series of workshops on nonviolence, and we repeatedly asked ourselves [the questions,]: "Are you able to accept blows without retaliating?" "Are you able to endure the ordeal[s] of jail?" We decided to [set] schedule our [direct action] direct-action program [around] for the Easter season, realizing that [with the exception of] except for Christmas, this [was the largest] is the main shopping period of the year. Knowing that a strong economic-withdrawal program would be the by-product of direct action, we felt that this [was] would be the best time to bring pressure to bear on the merchants for the needed change[s].

Then[3] it occurred to us that [the March election was ahead] Birmingham's mayoral election was coming up in March, and [so] we speedily decided to postpone action until after election day. When we discovered that [Mr. Connor was in the run-off,] the Commissioner of Public Safety, Eugene "Bull" Connor, had piled up enough votes to be in the run-off we decided again to postpone action until the day after the run-off so that the demonstrations could not be used to cloud the issues. [At this time we agreed to begin our nonviolent witness the day after the run-off. This⁴ reveals that we did not move irresponsibly into direct action. We too wanted to see Mr. Connor defeated;] Like many others, we waited to see Mr. Connor defeated, [so we went through] and to this end we endured postponement after postponement [to aid in this community need.]. [After this] Having aided in this community need, we felt that our direct-action program could be delayed no longer.

You may well ask: "Why direct action? Why sit-ins, marches [, etc?] and so forth? Isn't negotiation a better path?" You are [exactly] quite right in [your call] calling for negotiation. Indeed, this is the very purpose of direct action. Nonviolent direct action seeks to create such a crisis and [establish such] foster such a [creative] tension that a community [that] which has constantly refused to negotiate is forced to confront the issue. It seeks so to dramatize the issue that it can no longer be ignored. [I just referred to] My citing the creation of tension as part of the work of the [nonviolent resister] nonviolent-resister[. This] may sound rather shocking. But I must confess that I am not afraid of the word "tension." I have earnestly [worked and preached against] opposed violent tension, but there is a type of constructive, nonviolent tension [that] which is necessary for growth. Just as Socrates felt that it was necessary to create a tension in the mind so that individuals could rise from the bondage of myths and half-truths to the unfettered realm of creative analysis and objective appraisal, [we must] so must we see the need [of having] for nonviolent gadflies to create the kind of tension in society that will help men [to] rise from the dark depths of prejudice and racism to the majestic heights of understanding and brotherhood.

[So⁵ the] The purpose of [the] our direct-action program is to create a situation so crisis-packed that it will inevitably open the door to negotiation. [We,] I therefore[,] concur with you in your call for negotiation. Too long has our beloved Southland been bogged down in [the] a tragic [attempt] effort to live in monologue rather than dialogue.

One of the basic points in your statement is that [our acts are] the action that I and my associates have taken in Birmingham is untimely. Some have asked[,]: "Why didn't you give the new city administration time to act?" The only answer that I can give to this [inquiry] query is that the new Birmingham administration must be prodded about as much as the outgoing one, before it will act[s]. We [will be] are sadly mistaken if we feel that the election of [Mr.] <u>Albert</u> Boutwell <u>as mayor</u> will bring the [millenium[6]] <u>millennium</u> to Birmingham. While Mr. Boutwell is <u>a</u> much more [articulate and] gentle <u>person</u> than Mr. Connor, they are both segregationists, dedicated to [the task of maintaining] <u>maintenance of</u> the status quo. [The hope I see in] <u>I have hope that</u> Mr. Boutwell [is that he] will be reasonable enough to see the futility of massive resistance to desegregation. But he will not see this without pressure from devotees of civil rights. My friends, I must say to you that we have not made a single gain in civil rights without determined legal and nonviolent pressure. [History is the long and tragic story of the] <u>Lamentably, it is an historical</u> fact that privileged groups seldom give up their privileges voluntarily. Individuals may see the moral light and voluntarily give up their unjust posture; but, as Reinhold Niebuhr has reminded us, groups [are] <u>tend to be</u> more immoral than individuals.

We know through painful experience that freedom is never voluntarily given by the oppressor; it must be demanded by the oppressed. Frankly, I have [never] yet <u>to</u> engage[d] in a direct-action [movement] <u>campaign</u> that was "well timed[,]" [according to the timetable] <u>in the view</u> of those who have not suffered unduly from the disease of segregation. For years now I have heard the word "Wait!" It rings in the ear of every Negro with [a] piercing familiarity. This "Wait" has almost always meant "Never." [It has been a tranquilizing thalidomide, relieving the emotional stress for a moment; only to give birth to an ill-formed infant of frustration.] We must come to see, with [the] <u>one of our</u> distinguished jurists, [of yesterday], that "justice too long delayed is justice denied."

We[7] have waited for more than [three hundred and forty] <u>340</u> years for our constitutional and God-given rights. The nations of Asia and Africa are moving with jet[-]like speed toward [the goal of] <u>gaining</u> political independence, [and] <u>but</u> we still creep at [horse and buggy] <u>horse-and-buggy</u> pace toward [the] gaining [of] a cup of coffee at a lunch counter. [I guess] <u>Perhaps</u> it is easy for those who have never felt the stinging [facts[8]] <u>darts</u> of segregation to say, "Wait." But when you have seen vicious mobs lynch your mothers and fathers at will and drown your sisters and brothers at whim; when you have seen hate-filled policemen curse, kick [, brutalize] and even kill your black brothers and sisters [with impunity]; when you see the vast majority of your twenty million Negro brothers smothering in an [air tight] <u>airtight</u> cage of poverty in the midst of an affluent society; when you suddenly find your tongue twisted and your speech stammering as you seek to explain to your [six-year old] six-year-old daughter why she can't go to the public amusement park that has just been advertised on television, and see tears welling up in her [little] eyes when she is told that Funtown is closed to colored children, and see [the depressing] ominous clouds of inferiority beginning to form in her little mental sky, and see her [begin] beginning to distort her personality by [unconsciously] developing [a] an unconscious bitterness toward white people; when you have to concoct an answer for a [five-year old] five-year-old son [asking in agonizing pathos] who is asking: "Daddy, why do white people treat colored people so mean?"; when you take a [cross country] cross-country drive and find it necessary to sleep night after night in the uncomfortable corners of your automobile because no motel will accept you; when you are humiliated day in and day out by nagging signs reading "white" and "colored[;]"; when your first name becomes "nigger," [and] your middle name becomes "boy" (however old you are) and your last name becomes "John," and your wife and mother are never given the respected title "Mrs.[;]"; when you are harried by day and haunted by night by the fact that you are a Negro, living constantly at tip[-]toe stance, never quite knowing what to expect next, and are plagued with inner fears and outer resentments; when you are forever fighting a degenerating sense of "nobodiness[;]"—then you will understand why we find it difficult to wait. There comes a time when the cup of endurance runs over, and men are no longer willing to be plunged into [an] the abyss of [injustice where they experience the bleekness of corroding] despair. I hope, [S]sirs, you can understand our legitimate and unavoidable impatience.

You express a great deal of anxiety over our willingness to break laws. This is certainly a legitimate concern. Since we so diligently urge people to obey the Supreme Court's decision of 1954 outlawing segregation in the public schools, [it is rather strange and] at first glance it may seem rather paradoxical [to find] for us consciously [breaking] to break laws. One may well ask: "[how] How can you advocate breaking some laws and obeying others?" The answer [is found] lies in the fact that there are two types of laws: [There are *just*] just and [there are *unjust*] unjust [laws]. I would be the first to advocate obeying just laws. One has not only a legal but a moral responsibility to obey just laws. Conversely, one has a moral responsibility to disobey unjust laws. I would agree with St. Augustine that "[An] an unjust law is no law at all."

Now, what is the difference between the two? How does one determine [when] <u>whether</u> a law is just or unjust? A just law is a man-made code that squares with the moral law or the law of God. An unjust law is a code that is out of harmony with the moral law. To put it in the terms of [Saint] <u>St.</u> Thomas Aquinas[,]<u>:</u> [an] <u>An</u> unjust law is a human law that is not rooted in eternal <u>law</u> and natural law. Any law that uplifts human personality is just. Any law that degrades human personality is unjust. All segregation [statues⁹] <u>statutes</u> are unjust because segregation distorts the soul and damages the personality. It gives the segregator a false sense of superiority[,] and the segregated a false sense of inferiority. [To use the words of Martin Buber, the great Jewish philosopher,] [s]<u>Segregation, to use the terminology of the Jewish philosopher Martin Buber,</u> substitutes an "I-it" relationship for [the] <u>an</u> "I-thou" relationship[,] and ends up relegating persons to the status of things. [So] <u>Hence</u> segregation is not only politically, economically and sociologically unsound, [but] it is morally wrong and [sinful] <u>awful.</u> Paul Tillich has said that sin is separation. Is not segregation an existential expression of man's tragic separation, [an expression of] his awful estrangement, his terrible sinfulness? [So] <u>Thus it is that I can urge men to obey the 1954 decision of the Supreme Court, for it is morally right; and</u> I can urge them to disobey segregation ordinances [because]<u>, for</u> they are morally wrong.

Let us [turn to] <u>consider</u> a more concrete example of just and unjust laws. An unjust law is a code that a [majority] <u>numerical or power</u> [inflicts] <u>group compels</u> [on] a minority group [that is not] <u>to obey but does not make</u> binding on itself. This is [difference] <u>*difference*</u> made legal. [On the other hand] <u>By the same token,</u> a just law is a code that a majority compels a minority to follow <u>and</u> that it is willing to follow itself. This is [sameness] <u>*sameness*</u> made legal.

Let me give another explanation. [An unjust law is a code] <u>A law is unjust if it is</u> inflicted [upon] <u>on</u> a minority [which] that [minority]<u>, as a result of being denied the right to vote,</u> had no part in enacting or [creating] <u>devising</u> [because they did not have the unhampered right to vote] <u>the law.</u> Who can say that the legislature of Alabama which set up [the] <u>that state's</u> segregation laws was democratically elected? Throughout [the state of] Alabama all [types of conniving] <u>sorts of devious</u> methods are used to prevent Negroes from becoming registered voters, and there are some counties [without a single Negro registered to vote despite the fact that the] <u>in which, even though</u> [Negro] <u>Negroes</u> constitute[s] a majority of the population[.]<u>, not a single Negro is registered.</u> Can any law [set up in such a state] <u>enacted under such circumstances</u> be considered democratically structured?

[These are just a few examples of unjust and just laws.] [There are some instances when] <u>Sometimes</u> a law is just on its face and unjust in its application. For instance, I [was] <u>have been</u> arrested [Friday] on a[10] charge of parading without a permit. Now, there is nothing wrong [with] <u>in having</u> an ordinance which requires a permit for a parade[,]. [b]But [when the] <u>such an</u> ordinance <u>becomes unjust when it</u> is used to [preserve] <u>maintain</u> segregation and to deny citizens the First Amendment privilege of peaceful assembly and [peaceful] protest [then it becomes unjust].

I hope you [can] <u>are able to</u> see the distinction I am trying to point out. In no sense do I advocate evading or defying the law, as <u>would</u> the rabid segregationist [would do]. [This] <u>That</u> would lead to anarchy. One who breaks an unjust law must do [it] <u>so</u> [*openly*] <u>openly,</u> [*lovingly*] <u>lovingly,</u> [(not hatefully as the white mothers did in New Orleans when they were seen on television screaming "nigger, nigger, nigger")] and with a willingness to accept the penalty. I submit that an individual who breaks a law that conscience tells him is unjust[,] and <u>who</u> willingly accepts the penalty [by staying in jail] <u>of imprisonment in order</u> to arouse the conscience of the community over its injustice, is in reality expressing the highest respect for law.

Of course, there is nothing new about this kind of civil disobedience. It was [seen] <u>evidenced</u> sublimely in the refusal of Shadrach, Meshach and Abednego to obey the laws of Nebuchadnezzar [because], on the ground that a higher moral law was [involved] <u>at stake.</u> It was practiced superbly by the early Christians, who were willing to face hungry lions and the excruciating pain of chopping blocks[, before submitting] <u>rather than submit</u> to certain unjust laws of the Roman Empire. To a degree, academic freedom is a reality today because Socrates practiced civil disobedience. <u>In our own nation, the Boston Tea Party represented a massive act of civil disobedience.</u>

We [can] <u>should</u> never forget that everything <u>Adolf</u> Hitler did in Germany was "legal" and everything the Hungarian freedom fighters did in Hungary was "illegal." It was "illegal" to aid and comfort a Jew in Hitler's Germany. [But] <u>Even so,</u> I am sure that [if I], had <u>I</u> lived in Germany [during that] <u>at the</u> time, I would have aided and comforted my Jewish brothers [even though it was illegal]. If <u>today</u> I lived in a [c]Communist country [today] where certain principles dear to the Christian faith are suppressed, I [believe I] would openly advocate disobeying [these] <u>that country's</u> [anti-religious] <u>antireligious</u> laws.

I must make two honest confessions to you, my Christian and Jewish brothers. First, I must confess that over the [last] <u>past</u> few years I have been gravely disappointed with the white moderate. I have almost reached the regrettable conclusion that the Negro's great stumbling block in [the] <u>his</u> stride toward freedom is not the White Citizen's Council[-]er or the [Klu¹¹)] <u>Ku</u> Klux Klanner, but the white moderate, who is more devoted to "order" than to justice; who prefers a negative peace which is the absence of tension to a positive peace which is the presence of justice; who constantly says: "I agree with you in the goal you seek, but I [can't] <u>cannot</u> agree with your methods of direct action[;]"; who paternalistically [feels that] <u>believes</u> he can set the time[-]table for another man's freedom; who lives by [the myth] <u>a mythical concept</u> of time and who constantly advises the Negro to wait for a "more convenient season." Shallow understanding from people of good will is more frustrating than absolute misunderstanding from people of ill will. Lukewarm acceptance is much more bewildering than outright rejection.

I had hoped that the white moderate would understand that law and order exist for the purpose of establishing justice[,] and that when they fail [to do this] <u>in this purpose</u> they become the dangerously structured dams that block the flow of social progress. I had hoped that the white moderate would understand that the present tension in the South is [merely] a necessary phase of the transition from an obnoxious negative peace, [where] <u>in which</u> the Negro passively accepted his unjust plight, to a [substance-filled] <u>substantive and</u> positive peace, [where] <u>in which</u> all men will respect the dignity and worth of human personality. Actually, we who engage in nonviolent direct action are not the creators of tension. We merely bring to the surface the hidden tension that is already alive. We bring it out in the open, where it can be seen and dealt with. Like a boil that can never be cured so long as it is covered up but must be opened with all its [pus-flowing] ugliness to the natural medicines of air and light, injustice must [likewise] be exposed, with all [of] the tension its [exposing] <u>exposure</u> creates, to the light of human conscience and the air of national opinion before it can be cured.

In your statement you assert[ed] that our actions, even though peaceful, must be condemned because they precipitate violence. But [can this assertion be logically made?] <u>is this a logical assertion?</u> Isn't this like condemning a robbed man because his possession of money precipitated the evil act of robbery? Isn't this like condemning Socrates because his unswerving commitment to truth and his philosophical [delvings] inquiries precipitated the act by the misguided [popular mind to make] populace in which they made him drink hemlock? Isn't this like condemning Jesus because [His] his unique God-[C]consciousness and never-ceasing devotion to [His] God's will precipitated the evil act of crucifixion? We must come to see[,] that, as the federal courts have consistently affirmed, [that] it is [immoral] wrong to urge an individual to [withdraw] cease his efforts to gain his basic constitutional rights because the quest may precipitate violence. Society must protect the robbed and punish the robber.

I had also hoped that the white moderate would reject the myth [of] concerning time in relation to the struggle for freedom. I have just received a letter [this morning] from a white brother in Texas [which said:]. He writes: "All Christians know that the colored people will receive equal rights eventually, but it is possible that you are in too great [of] a religious hurry. It has taken Christianity almost [2000] two thousand years to accomplish what it has. The teachings of Christ take time to come to earth." [All that is said here grows out of] Such an attitude stems from a tragic misconception of time[.], [It is] from the strangely rational notion that there is something in the very flow of time that will inevitably cure all ills. Actually, time itself is neutral[.]; [It] it can be used either [distructively12] destructively or constructively. More and more I [am coming to] feel that the people of [ill-will] ill will have used time much more effectively than have the people of good will. We will have to repent in this generation not merely for the [vitriolic] hateful words and actions of the bad people[,] but for the appalling silence of the good people. [We must come to see that h]Human progress never rolls in on wheels of inevitability[.]; [I]it comes through the tireless efforts [and persistent work] of men willing to be co-workers with God, and without this hard work, time itself becomes an ally of the forces of social stagnation. We must use time creatively, [and forever realize] in the knowledge that the time is always ripe to do right. Now is the time to make real the promise of democracy[,] and transform our pending national elegy into a creative psalm of brotherhood. Now is the time to lift our national policy from the quicksand of racial injustice to the solid rock of human dignity.

You [spoke] speak of our activity in Birmingham as extreme. At first I was rather disappointed that fellow clergymen would see my nonviolent efforts as those of [the] an extremist. I [started] began thinking about the fact that I stand in the middle of two opposing forces in the Negro community. One is a force of complacency, made up in part of Negroes who, as a result of long years of oppression, [have been] are so [completely] drained of self-respect and a sense of "somebodiness" that they have adjusted to segregation[,]; and[,] in part of a few [Negroes in the middle class] middle-class Negroes who, because of a degree of academic and economic security[,] and because [at points] in some ways they profit by segregation, have [unconsciously] become insensitive to the problems of the masses. The other force is one of bitterness[,] and hatred, and it comes perilously close to advocating violence. It is expressed in the various black nationalist groups that are springing up [over] across the nation, the largest and [best known] best-known being Elijah Muhammad's Muslim movement. [This movement is] [nourished] Nourished by the [contemporary] Negro's frustration over the continued existence of racial discrimination[.], [It] this movement is made up of people who have lost faith in America, who have absolutely repudiated Christianity, and who have concluded that the white man is an [incurable] incorrigible "devil."

I[13] have tried to stand between these two forces, saying that we need [not follow] emulate neither the "do-nothingism" of the complacent [or] nor the hatred and despair of the black nationalist. For [There] there is the[14] more excellent way of love and nonviolent protest. [I'm] I am grateful to God that, through the influence of the Negro church, the [dimension] way of nonviolence [entered] became an integral part of our struggle.

If[15] this philosophy had not emerged, [I am convinced that] by now many streets of the South would, I am convinced, be flowing with [floods of] blood. And I am further convinced that if our white brothers dismiss as "rabble-rousers" and "outside agitators" those of us who [are working through the channels of] employ nonviolent direct action, and if they refuse to support our nonviolent efforts, millions of Negroes will, out of frustration and despair, [will] seek solace and security in [black nationalist] black-nationalist ideologies[,] a development that [will] would inevitably lead to a frightening racial nightmare.

Oppressed people cannot remain oppressed forever. The [urge] yearning for freedom [will] eventually [come.] manifests itself, and [This] that is what has happened to the American Negro. Something within has reminded him of his birthright of freedom[;], and something without has reminded him that [he can gain it] it can be gained. Consciously or unconsciously, he has been [swept in by what the Germans call] caught up by the [Zeitgeist] Zeitgeist, and with his black [brother] brothers of Africa[,] and his brown and yellow brothers of Asia, South America and the Caribbean, [he] the United States Negro is moving with a sense of [cosmic] great urgency toward the promised land of racial justice. [Recognizing] If one recognizes this vital urge that has engulfed the Negro community, one should readily understand why public demonstrations are taking place. The Negro has many [pent up] pent-up resentments and latent frustrations[. He has to get them out], and he must release them. So let him march [sometime]; let him make prayer pilgrimages to the city hall; [understand why he must have sit-ins and freedom rides] let him go on freedom rides—and try to understand why he must do so. If his repressed emotions [do] are not [come out] released in [these] nonviolent ways, they will [come out in ominous] seek expression[s of] through violence[.]; [T]this is not a threat[; it is] but a fact of history. So I have not said to my people ["get]: "Get rid of your discontent." [But] Rather, I have tried to say that this normal and healthy discontent can be [channelized through] channeled into the creative outlet of nonviolent direct action. And [N]now this approach is being [dismiss[16]] termed extremist. [I must admit that I was initially disappointed in being so categorized.]

But though I was initially disappointed at being categorized as an extremist, as I continue[d[17]]d to think about the matter I gradually gained a [bit] measure of satisfaction from [being considered an extremist] the label. Was not Jesus an extremist [in] for love[—]: "Love your enemies, bless them that curse you, do good to them that hate you, and pray for them [that] which despitefully use you, and persecute you." Was not Amos an extremist for justice [—]: "Let justice roll down like waters and righteousness like [a mighty stream] an ever-flowing stream." Was not Paul an extremist for the Christian gospel [of Jesus Christ—]: "I bear in my body the marks of the Lord Jesus." Was not Martin Luther an extremist [—]: "[h]Here I stand; [I can do none other] I cannot do otherwise, so help me God." [Was not] And John Bunyan [an extremist—]: "I will stay in jail to the end of my days before I make a butchery of my conscience." [Was not] And Abraham Lincoln [an extremist—]: "This nation cannot survive half slave and half free." [Was not] And Thomas Jefferson [an extremist—]: "We[18] hold these truths to be self-evident, that all men are created equal. . . ." So the question is not whether we will be extremists, but what kind of extremists [will] we will be. Will we be extremists for hate or [will we be extremists] for love? Will we be extremists for the preservation of injustice [—] or [will we be extremists for the cause] for the extension of justice? In that dramatic scene on Calvary's hill[,] three men were crucified. We must [not] never forget that all three were crucified for the same crime[.]—[T]the crime of extremism. Two were extremists for immorality, and [thusly] thus fell below their environment. The other, Jesus Christ, was an extremist for love, truth[,] and goodness, and thereby rose above his environment. [So, after all, maybe] Perhaps the South, the nation and the world are in dire need of creative extremists.

I had hoped that the white moderate would see this need. [Maybe] Perhaps I was too optimistic; [Maybe] perhaps I expected too much. I [guess] suppose I should have realized that few members of [a] the [race that has oppressed another race] oppressor race can understand [or appreciate] the deep groans and passionate yearnings of [those that have been oppressed] the oppressed race, and still fewer have the vision to see that injustice must be rooted out by strong, persistent and determined action. I am thankful, however, that some of our white brothers in the South have grasped the meaning of this social revolution and committed themselves to it. They are still too few in quantity, but they are big in quality. Some [like]—such as Ralph McGill, Lillian Smith, Harry Golden, [and] James McBride Dabbs, Ann Braden and Sarah Patton Boyle—have written about our struggle in eloquent[,] and prophetic[, and understanding] terms. Others have marched with us down nameless streets of the South. They have languished in filthy, roach-infested jails, suffering the abuse and brutality of policemen who [see] view them as "dirty nigger lovers." [They, u]Unlike so many of their moderate brothers and sisters, they have recognized the urgency of the moment and sensed the need for powerful "action" antidotes to combat the disease of segregation.

Let me [rush on to mention] take note of my other major disappointment. I have been so greatly disappointed with the white church and its leadership. Of course, there are some notable exceptions. I am not unmindful of the fact that each of you has taken some significant stands on this issue. I commend you, [Rev.] Reverend Stallings, for your Christian stand on this past Sunday, in welcoming Negroes to your worship service on a non[-]segregated basis. I commend the Catholic leaders of this state for integrating [Springhill] <u>Spring Hill</u> College several years ago.

But despite these notable exceptions, I must honestly reiterate that I have been disappointed with the church. <u>I do not say this as one of those negative critics who can always find something wrong with the church.</u> I say [it] <u>this</u> as a minister of the gospel, who loves the church; who was nurtured in its bosom; who has been sustained by its spiritual blessings and who will remain true to it as long as the cord of life shall lengthen.

[I had the strange feeling w]<u>W</u>hen I was suddenly catapulted into the leadership of the bus protest in Montgomery, <u>Alabama,</u> [several years ago] <u>a few years ago, I felt</u> [that] we would [have the support of] <u>be supported by</u> the white church. I felt that the white ministers, priests and rabbis of the South would be among our strongest allies. Instead, some have been outright opponents, refusing to understand the freedom movement and misrepresenting its leaders; all too many others have been more cautious than courageous and have remained silent behind the anesthetizing security of stained-glass windows.

In spite of my shattered dreams [of the past], I came to Birmingham with the hope that the white religious leadership of this community would see the justice of our cause[,] and<u>,</u> with deep moral concern, <u>would</u> serve as the channel through which our just grievances could [get to] <u>reach</u> the power structure. I had hoped that each of you would understand. But again I have been disappointed.

I have heard numerous <u>southern</u> religious leaders [of the South call upon] <u>admonish</u> their worshipers to comply with a desegregation decision because it is the [*law,*] <u>law,</u> but I have longed to hear white ministers [say,] <u>declare:</u> "[f]<u>F</u>ollow this decree because integration is morally [*right*] <u>right</u> and <u>because</u> the Negro is your brother." In the midst of blatant injustices inflicted upon the Negro, I have watched white [churches] <u>churchmen</u> stand on the sideline and mouth pious [irrelevances] <u>irrelevancies</u> and sanctimonious trivialities. In the midst of a mighty struggle to rid our nation of racial and economic injustice, I have heard [so] many ministers say[,]<u>:</u> "[t]<u>T</u>hose are social issues, with which the gospel has no real concern["],]<u>."</u> [a]<u>A</u>nd I have watched [so] many churches commit themselves to a completely other[-]worldly religion which [made] <u>makes</u> a strange<u>,</u> <u>un-Biblical</u> distinction between body and soul, <u>between</u> the sacred and the secular.

[So here we are moving toward the exit of the twentieth century with a religious community largely adjusted to the status quo, standing as a taillight behind other community agencies rather than a headlight lead-ing men to higher levels of justice.]

I have [travelled] <u>traveled</u> the length and breadth of Alabama, Missis-sippi and all the other southern states. On sweltering summer days and crisp autumn mornings I have looked at [her] <u>the South's</u> beautiful churches with their lofty spires pointing heavenward. I have beheld the impressive [outlay] <u>outlines</u> of her massive religious-education buildings. Over and over [again] I have found myself asking: "What kind of people worship here? Who is their God? Where were their voices when the lips of Governor Barnett dripped with words of interposition and nullifica-tion? Where were they when Governor Wallace gave a clarion call for defiance and hatred? Where were their voices of support when bruised and weary Negro men and women decided to rise from the dark dun-geons of complacency to the bright hills of creative protest?"

Yes, these questions are still in my mind. In deep disappointment I have wept over the laxity of the church. But be assured that my tears have been tears of love. There can be no deep disappointment where there is not deep love. Yes, I love the church[; I love her sacred walls]. How could I do otherwise? I am in the rather unique position of being the son, the grandson and the great-grandson of preachers. Yes, I see the church as the body of Christ. But, oh! How we have blemished and scarred that body through social neglect and <u>through</u> fear of being non-conformists.

There was a time when the church was very powerful[.]— [It was during that period] <u>in the time</u> when the early Christians rejoiced [when they were] <u>at being</u> deemed worthy to suffer for what they believed. In those days the church was not merely a thermometer that recorded the ideas and principles of popular opinion; it was a thermostat that trans-formed the mores of society. Whenever the early Christians entered a town, the [power structure got] <u>people in power became</u> disturbed and immediately sought to convict [them] <u>the Christians</u> for being "disturb-ers of the peace" and "outside agitators." But [they went] <u>the Christians pressed</u> on, [with] <u>in</u> the conviction that they were "a colony of heaven["‚]‚" [and had] <u>called to</u> obey God rather than man. [They were s]<u>S</u>mall in number [but], <u>they were</u> big in commitment. They were too God-intoxicated to be "astronomically intimidated." <u>By their effort and example</u> [T]<u>t</u>hey brought an end to such ancient evils as infanticide and gladiatorial contest<u>s</u>.

Things are different now. <u>So often</u> [T]the contemporary church is [so often] a weak, ineffectual voice with an uncertain sound. [It is s]<u>S</u>o often [the arch supporter] <u>it is an archdefender</u> of the status quo. Far from being disturbed by the presence of the church, the power structure of the average community is consoled by the church's silent—and often even vocal—sanction of things as they are.

But the judgment of God is upon the church as never before. If [the] <u>today's</u> church [of today] does not recapture the sacrificial spirit of the early church, it will lose its [authentic ring,] <u>authenticity,</u> forfeit the loyalty of millions, and be dismissed as an irrelevant social club with no meaning for the twentieth century. [I am meeting] <u>Every day I meet</u> young people whose disappointment with the church has [risen to] <u>turned into</u> outright disgust.

[Maybe again I have been] <u>Perhaps I have once again been</u> too optimistic. Is organized religion too inextricably bound to the [status-quo] *status quo* to save our nation and the world? [Maybe] <u>Perhaps</u> I must turn my faith to the inner spiritual church, the church within the church, as the true [*ecclesia*] *ekklesia* and the hope of the world. But again I am thankful to God that some noble souls from the ranks of organized religion have broken loose from the paralyzing chains of conformity and joined us as active partners in the struggle for freedom. They have left their secure congregations and walked the streets of Albany, Georgia, with us. They have gone [through] <u>down</u> the highways of the South on tortuous rides for freedom. Yes, they have gone to jail with us. Some have been [kicked out of] <u>dismissed from</u> their churches, [and] <u>have</u> lost <u>the</u> support of their bishops and fellow ministers. But they have [gone with] <u>acted in</u> the faith that right defeated is stronger than evil triumphant. [These men have been the leaven in the lump of the race.] Their witness has been the spiritual salt that has preserved the true meaning of the [G]gospel in these troubled times. They have carved a tunnel of hope through the dark mountain of disappointment.

I hope the church as a whole will meet the challenge of this decisive hour. But even if the church does not come to the aid of justice, I have no despair about the future. I have no fear about the outcome of our struggle in Birmingham, even if our motives are [presently] <u>at present</u> misunderstood. We will reach the goal of freedom in Birmingham, and all over the nation, because the goal of America is freedom. Abused and scorned though we may be, our destiny is tied up with [the destiny of

America] America's destiny. Before the pilgrims landed at Plymouth, we were here. Before the pen of Jefferson etched [across the pages of history] the majestic words of the Declaration of Independence across the pages of history, we were here. For more than two centuries our [fore-parents] forebears labored [here] in this country without wages; they made cotton king; [and] they built the homes of their masters [in the midst of brutal] while suffering gross injustice and shameful humilia-tion—and yet out of a bottomless vitality they continued to thrive and develop. If the inexpressible cruelties of slavery could not stop us, the opposition we now face will surely fail. We will win our freedom because the sacred [herigage[19]] heritage of our nation and the eternal will of God are embodied in our echoing demands.

[I must close now. But b]Before closing I [am] feel impelled to men-tion one other point in your statement that has troubled me profoundly. You warmly commended the Birmingham police force for keeping "order" and "preventing violence." I [don't believe] doubt that you would have so warmly commended the police force if you had seen its [angry violent] dogs [literally biting six] sinking their teeth into unarmed, nonviolent Negroes. I [don't believe] doubt that you would so quickly commend the policemen if you [would] were to observe their ugly and [inhuman] inhumane treatment of Negroes here in the city jail; if you [would] were to watch them push and curse old Negro women and young Negro girls; if you [would] were to see them slap and kick old Negro men and young boys; if you [will] were to observe them, as they did on two occasions, refuse to give us food because we wanted to sing our grace together. [I'm sorry that] I [can't] cannot join you in your praise [for the] of the Birmingham police department.

It is true that [they have been rather] the police have exercised a degree of discipline[d] in [their public] handling [of] the demonstrators. In this sense they have [been rather publicly] conducted themselves rather ["nonviolent."] "nonviolently" in public. But for what purpose? To preserve the evil system of segregation. Over the [last] past few years I have consistently preached that nonviolence demands that the means we use must be as pure as the ends we seek. [So] I have tried to make clear that it is wrong to use immoral means to attain moral ends. But now[20] I must affirm that it is just as wrong, or perhaps even more so, to use moral means to preserve immoral ends. [Maybe] Perhaps Mr. Con-nor and his policemen have been rather [publicly] nonviolent in public, as <u>was</u> Chief Pritchett in Albany, Georgia[,] but they have used the moral means of nonviolence to maintain the immoral end of [flagrant] racial injustice. <u>As</u> T. S. Eliot has said [that there is no greater treason than to do the right deed for the wrong <u>reason.</u>]: "<u>The last temptation is the greatest treason: To do the right deed for the wrong reason.</u>"

I wish you had commended the Negro sit-inners and demonstrators of Birmingham for their sublime courage, their willingness to suffer and their amazing discipline in the midst of [the most in human] <u>great</u> provocation. One day the South will recognize its real heroes. They will be the James Merediths, [courageously and with a majestic] <u>with the noble</u> sense of purpose[, facing] <u>that enables them to face</u> jeering and hostile mobs, and with the agonizing loneliness that characterizes the life of the pioneer. They will be old, oppressed, battered Negro women, symbolized in a [seventy-two year old] <u>seventy-two-year-old</u> woman [of] <u>in</u> Montgomery, Alabama, who rose up with a sense of dignity and with her people decided not to ride segregated buses, and [respond to one who inquired about her tiredness] <u>who responded</u> with ungrammatical profundity <u>to one who inquired about her weariness:</u> "[m]<u>My</u> feets is tired, but my soul is [rested] <u>at rest.</u>" They will be the young high school and college students, the young ministers of the gospel and a host of their elders, courageously and nonviolently sitting[-]in at lunch counters and willingly going to jail for conscience sake. One day the South will know that when these disinherited children of God sat down at lunch counters, they were in reality standing up for [the] <u>what is</u> best in the American dream and <u>for</u> the most sacred values in our Judeo-Christian heritage, [and thusly, carrying] <u>thereby bringing</u> our [whole] nation back to those great wells of democracy which were dug deep by the founding fathers in [the] <u>their</u> formulation of the Constitution and the Declaration of Independence.

Never before have I written so long a letter[, (or should I say a book?)]. I'm afraid [that] it is much too long to take your precious time. I can assure you that it would have been much shorter if I had been writing from a comfortable desk, but what else [is there to] <u>can one</u> do when [you are alone for days in the dull monotony of] <u>he is alone in</u> a narrow jail cell, other than write long letters, think [strange] <u>long</u> thoughts[,] and pray long prayers?

If I have said anything in this letter that [is an overstatement of] <u>over-states</u> the truth and [is indicative of] <u>indicates</u> an unreasonable impatience, I beg you to forgive me. If I have said anything [in this letter] that [is an understatement of] <u>understates</u> the truth and [is indicative of] <u>indicates</u> my having a patience that [makes me patient with] <u>allows me to settle for</u> anything less than brotherhood, I beg God to forgive me.

I hope this letter finds you strong in the faith. I also hope that circumstances will soon make it possible for me to meet each of you, not as an integrationist or a civil rights leader but as a fellow clergyman and a Christian brother. Let us all hope that the dark clouds of racial prejudice will soon pass away and the deep fog of misunderstanding will be lifted from our fear-drenched communities, and in some not too distant tomorrow the radiant stars of love and brotherhood will shine over our great nation with all their scintillating beauty.

Yours for the cause of Peace and Brotherhood,

Martin Luther King, Jr.
[MLK:wm]

Appendix 4

The White Ministers' Anti-Violence Statement, September 7, 1963

Once again we feel bound to issue a solemn call for law and order and common sense in dealing with our racial problem in Birmingham. Violence has broken out. Life has been taken.

We condemn anew the dastardly act of bombing which has not only imperiled human life but has also enkindled anew a potentially explosive situation.

We reaffirm our trust, however, in the citizens and public officials of Birmingham, and believe that there is enough good will and intelligence and respect for law and order on the part of people of both races in our city for this present situation to be resolved in dignity and in obedience to the orders of the courts of our land.

Let all cooperate with our city officials and law enforcement officers in restoring peace and assuring at all costs the continuance of public education. We beseech the prayers of all children of God and men of good will in this mutual crisis.

Let all remember that Almighty God will judge us for all our actions; for each day is a judgment day. Let us, therefore approach all our actions prayerfully, seeking to do as well as to accept God's will for and for our community. Signed by: Bishop Nolan B. Harmon, Bishop of the North Alabama Conference of the Methodist Church; Bishop Paul Hardin, Bishop of the Alabama–West Florida Conference of the Methodist Church; C. C. J. Carpenter, D.D., LL.D., Bishop of Alabama; John M. Crowell, Moderator, Synod of the Alabama Presbyterian Church in the

United States; Joseph A. Durick, D.D., Auxiliary Bishop, Diocese of Mobile-Birmingham; Earl Stallings, Pastor, First Baptist Church, Birmingham, Alabama; George M. Murray, D.D., LL.D., Bishop Coadjutor, Episcopal Diocese of Alabama; Rabbi Milton L. Grafman, Temple Emanu-El, Birmingham, Alabama.

Notes

Introduction

1. Newspaper Clipping Files, Birmingham Jail File, Tutwiler Collection of Southern History and Literature, Birmingham Public Library, Birmingham, Alabama (hereinafter referred to as Tutwiler Collection); Newspaper Clipping Files, "Birmingham Jail" folk song, Tutwiler Collection.

2. Rabbi Milton Grafman to Kivie Kaplin, June 14, 1963, Rabbi Milton Grafman Papers, in possession of Stephen Grafman, Potomac, Md.

3. *Birmingham News,* January 17, 1963.

4. *Alabama Baptist,* March 18, 1993.

5. David Halberstam, *The Fifties* (New York: Villard Books, 1993), 691–92; Daniel Boorstin, *The Image: A Guide to Pseudo-Events in America* (New York: Atheneum, 1961), 10–12.

6. Milton Grafman, interview by author, tape recording, Birmingham, Ala., March 22, 1995.

7. Grafman to Kivie Kaplin, June 14, 1963, Grafman Papers.

8. John Marion, "An Overview of the Desegregation Controversy," in *Southern Churches and Race Relations: Report of the Second Interracial Consultation Held at the College of the Bible, July 18–22, 1960,* ed. Lewis S. C. Smythe (Lexington, Ky.: College of the Bible, 1960), 21–22.

9. Samuel S. Hill Jr., *Southern Churches in Crisis* (New York: Holt, Rinehart, and Winston, 1966), 5; Samuel S. Hill Jr., ed., *Encyclopedia of Religion in the South* (Macon: Mercer University Press, 1984), 604, 468–69.

10. Hill, *Encyclopedia,* 361.

11. Grafman to Kivie Kaplin, June 14, 1963, Grafman Papers.

Chapter 1

1. James McBride Dabbs, quoted in George R. Osborne, "Boycott in Birmingham," *Nation,* May 5, 1962, p. 399.

2. Kyle Haselden, *Mandate for White Christians* (Richmond: John Knox Press, 1966), 62; Martin Luther King Jr., *Why We Can't Wait* (New York: Harper and Row, 1964), 89.

3. Ralph McGill, "The Southern Moderates Are Still There," in *No Place to Hide: The South and Human Rights* (Macon: Mercer University Press, 1984), 2:283; Erskine Caldwell, *In Search of Bisco* (New York: Farrar, Straus, and Giroux, 1965), 26.

4. Hoke Norris, ed. *We Dissent* (New York: St. Martin's Press, 1962), v.

5. *Alabama Baptist,* March 18, 1993; Milton Grafman, untitled sermon, January 18, 1963, tape recording in possession of author.

6. Samuel Southard, "Are Southern Churches Silent?" *Christian Century* 80 (November 20, 1963): 1430.

7. Numan V. Bartley, *The Rise of Massive Resistance: Race and Politics in the South during the 1950's* (Baton Rouge: Louisiana State University Press, 1978), 295–96; Frank E. Smith, *Look Away from Dixie* (Baton Rouge: Louisiana State University Press, 1965), 80.

8. Bartley, *Massive Resistance,* 295–96; William Peters, *The Southern Temper* (Garden City, N.Y.: Doubleday, 1959), 95, 98, 102; Kenneth K. Bailey, *Southern White Protestantism in the Twentieth Century* (New York: Harper and Row, 1964), 148–49.

9. Minutes of the Executive Committee of the Ministers' Association of Greater Birmingham, Protestant Pastors Union Papers, BPLDAM, Birmingham, Ala.

10. *Ibid.*; Wayne Flynt, *Alabama Baptists: Southern Baptists in the Heart of Dixie* (Tuscaloosa: University of Alabama Press, 1998), 472; Bartley, *Massive Resistance,* 297–99.

11. Terry Lawrence Jones, "Attitudes of Alabama Baptists toward Negroes, 1890–1914" (master's thesis, Samford University, 1968), 20, 21, 28, 52, 53.

12. *Birmingham News,* December 26, 1999; Wayne Flynt, "Alabama," in *Religion in the Southern States: A Historical Study,* ed. Samuel S. Hill Jr. (Macon: Mercer University Press, 1981), 21; James Williams Marshall, *The Presbyterian Church in Alabama* (Montgomery: Presbyterian Historical Society of Alabama, 1977), 450; Marion Elias Lazenby, *History of Methodism in Alabama and West Florida* (Birmingham: North Alabama Conference and West Florida Conference of the Methodist Church, 1968), 750.

13. Protestant Pastors Union et al. to Franklin D. Roosevelt, June 6, 1933; Announcement, n.d., Protestant Pastors Union Papers.

14. Birmingham Ministers' Association to James E. Folsom, December 1, 1947, Protestant Pastors Union Papers.

15. Ministers' Discussion Group Papers, SUSC, Birmingham, Ala.

16. Wilson Fallin Jr., *The African American Church in Birmingham, Alabama, 1815–1963: A Shelter in the Storm* (New York: Garland Press, 1997), 98.

17. *Ibid.*, 133–34.

18. Leon McBeth, "Southern Baptists and Race since 1947," *Baptist History and Heritage* 7 (July 1972): 158; Frank Stagg, "Henlee Hulix Barnette: Activist," in *Perspectives in Religious Studies: Essays in Honor of Henlee Hulix Barnette,* ed. Rollin S. Armour (Macon: Mercer University Press, 1991), 34–35.

19. James E. Davidson, *South Avondale Baptist Church, Birmingham, Alabama: Its Pastors, People, and Program, 1887–1974* (Birmingham: South Avondale Baptist, 1977), 83–91; Susan Ingram Hunt Ray, *The Major: Harwell G. Davis, Alabama Statesman and Baptist Leader* (Birmingham: Samford University Press, 1991), 157; "The Witness" (Birmingham Baptist Association), October 1947–October 1948, SUSC. As a result of these efforts, white Southern Baptists also organized an underfunded and ineffective Negro Baptist Mission Center the following year and rented office space at Sixteenth Street Baptist.

20. George R. Stewart, "Birmingham's Reaction to the 1954 Desegregation Decision" (master's thesis, Samford University, 1967), 89; *Pulpit Digest,* December 1958, 13. Bartley noted that the poll "may have exaggerated pro-integrationist sentiment, but there seems little reason to dispute the basic point that a substantial majority of denominational clergymen approved of the principle of the *Brown* decision." See Bartley, *Massive Resistance,* 295 n. 6; Peters, *The Southern Temper,* 209.

21. Martha Louise Lanier, "Alabama Methodists and Social Issues, 1900–1914" (master's thesis, Samford University, 1969), 142; Bailey, *Southern White Protestantism,* 150.

22. Robert Gaines Corley, "The Quest for Racial Harmony: Race Relations in Birmingham, Alabama, 1947–63" (Ph.D. diss., University of Virginia, 1979) 202. The Southern Institute of Management, Inc., conducted the "Audit."

23. *Ibid.*, 202–203, 242.

24. Newspaper Clipping Files, Tutwiler Hotel, Tutwiler Collection. The original Tutwiler Hotel was located at 2001 Fifth Avenue North in Birmingham. The hotel was razed in 1974. The "new" Tutwiler (a converted apartment building) is located at Park Place and Twenty-first Street North.

25. Wesley Phillips Newton, "Lindbergh Comes to Birmingham," *Alabama Review* 26, No. 2 (April 1973): 119; *Birmingham Post,* September 1, 1937.

26. *Birmingham News,* July 18, 1948. For a comprehensive examination of the incident and the life and times of Connor, see William A. Nunnelley, *Bull Connor* (Tuscaloosa: University of Alabama Press, 1991).

27. George M. Murray to Milton L. Grafman, January 9, 1963, Grafman Papers.

28. George C. Wallace, "Inaugural Address," in *Black, White and Gray:*

Twenty-one Points of View on the Race Question, ed. Bradford Daniel (New York: Sheed and Ward, 1964), 180.

29. C. C. J. Carpenter et al., "Appeal for Law and Order and Common Sense," Bishop Charles Colcock Jones Carpenter Papers, BPLDAM.

30. A. E. Joffrion to John Patterson, October 16, 1962, Carpenter Papers; A. E. Joffrion, telephone conversation with author, June 17, 1998.

31. Carpenter et al., "Appeal," Carpenter Papers.

32. *Ibid.*

33. *Ibid.*

34. *Ibid.*; Carpenter to Moreland Griffith Smith, January 21, 1963, Carpenter Papers; Corley, "The Quest," 241–42.

35. Milton Grafman, untitled sermon, January 18, 1963, tape recording in possession of author.

36. *Birmingham Methodist Christian Advocate,* January 29, 1963, February 12, 1963.

37. *Birmingham Post-Herald,* January 17, 18, 1963; *Birmingham News,* January 17, 20, 1963; E. L. Holland Jr. to Earl Stallings, January 22, 1963, Earl Stallings Papers, Southern Baptist Archives, Nashville, Tenn. The statement also appeared in numerous religious papers throughout the country, including the *Boston Pilot,* and in various other daily papers, like the *Jackson (Miss.) Clarion Ledger.*

38. Carpenter to Moreland Griffith Smith, January 21, 1963, Carpenter Papers; Anonymous to Stallings, January 22, 1963, Stallings Papers; Anonymous to Stallings, January 17, 1963, Stallings Papers; Mrs. Newman Hubbard to Stallings, January 17, 1963, Stallings Papers; Laurie Reaves to the Editor, *Montgomery Advertiser,* January 21, 1963, Stallings Papers.

39. Grafman to James R. Beard, January 21, 1963, Grafman Papers; Maurice Rogers to Grafman, January 16, 1963, Grafman Papers; newspaper clipping, n.d., Grafman Papers.

40. Peters, *The Southern Temper,* 41–42, 279; James Sellers, *The South and Christian Ethics* (New York: Associated Press, 1962), 111.

41. Ralph McGill, *The South and the Southerner* (New York: Little, Brown, 1963), 273–78; Bailey, *Southern White Protestantism,* 149–51; Corley, "The Quest," 182; David Bowen, *The Struggle Within: Race Relations in the United States* (New York: W. W. Norton, 1965), 109; Bartley, *Massive Resistance,* 297–99; Anonymous to Stallings, January 19, 1963, Stallings Papers.

42. Bartley, *Massive Resistance,* 296–97; Benjamin Muse, *Ten Years of Prelude: The Story of Integration since the Supreme Court's 1954 Decision* (New York: Viking Press, 1964), 166.

43. George McMillan, "Silent White Ministers of the South," *New York Times Magazine,* April 5, 1964, p. 114; John Lee Eighmy, *Churches in Cultural Captivity: A History of the Social Attitudes of Southern Baptists* (Knoxville: University of Tennessee Press, 1987), 197.

44. Marion, "An Overview of the Desegregation Controversy," 27; Peters, *The Southern Temper,* 94, 209; Tom P. Brady, "Black Monday," pamphlet, SUSC (see also Bartley, *Massive Resistance,* 296–97); Brooks Hays, *A Southern Moderate Speaks* (Chapel Hill: University of North Carolina Press, 1959), 211–12; Eighmy, *Churches in Cultural Captivity,* 197; Southard, "Are Southern Churches Silent?" 1430; Smith, *Look Away from Dixie,* 80.

45. McMillan, "Silent White Ministers," 114.

46. For a look at the gap between the national movement and the local movement for civil rights in Birmingham, see Glenn T. Eskew, *But for Birmingham: The Local and National Movements in the Civil Rights Struggle* (Chapel Hill: University of North Carolina Press, 1997).

47. Muse, *Ten Years of Prelude,* 263.

48. Nolan Harmon, *Ninety Years and Counting: Autobiography of Nolan B. Harmon* (Nashville: Upper Room, 1983), 294–302.

49. Typed sermon notes are in the Nolan B. Harmon Papers, Pitts Theological Library Archives and Manuscripts, Emory University; Harmon, *Ninety Years,* 298–301; Milton Grafman, interview by author, tape recording, Birmingham, Ala., March 1, 1991.

50. Grafman, interview, March 22, 1995.

51. *Birmingham News,* April 13, 1963; *Birmingham Post-Herald,* April 13, 1963; C. C. J. Carpenter et al., White Ministers' Statement, April 12, 1963, Carpenter Papers.

52. Carpenter et al., White Ministers' Statement.

53. Judith D. Hoover, "Reconstruction of the Rhetorical Situation in 'Letter from Birmingham Jail,' " in *Martin Luther King, Jr., and the Sermonic Power of Public Discourse,* ed. Carolyn Calloway-Thomas and John Louis Lucaites (Tuscaloosa: University of Alabama Press, 1993), 51.

54. Hoover, "Reconstruction," 59; George Murray, interview by author, tape recording, Fairhope, Ala., March 21, 1995.

55. George Murray, telephone interview by author, tape recording, Fairhope, Ala., October 20, 1992, in possession of author; Bishop Joseph A. Durick to Dr. Thomas J. Elliott, January 26, 1971, Bishop Joseph A. Durick Papers, in possession of author; Grafman, interview, March 22, 1995; Joseph A. Durick, interview by author, tape recording, Bessemer, Ala., February 21, 1992, in possession of author.

Chapter 2

1. Howard W. Odum, *The Way of the South: Toward the Regional Balance of America* (New York: Macmillan, 1947), 116; James McBride Dabbs, *The Southern Heritage* (New York: Alfred A. Knopf, 1959), 11.

2. Joel Williamson, *The Crucible of Race: Black-White Relations in the*

American South since Emancipation (New York: Oxford University Press, 1984), 486–87.

3. Morton Sosna, *In Search of the Silent South: Southern Liberals and the Race Issue* (New York: Columbia University Press, 1977), 206.

4. Caldwell, *In Search of Bisco,* 29.

5. Fred Shuttlesworth, telephone interview by author, Cincinnati, Ohio, April 23, 1992; Eighmy, *Churches in Cultural Captivity,* 204; George Murray to C. Kilmer Myers, April 30, 1965, Carpenter Papers.

6. *New York Times,* December 5, 1921; Murray, interview, March 21, 1995; Doug Carpenter, interview by author, tape recording, Birmingham, Ala., January 27, 1991; *Alabama Churchman,* December 1968.

7. *Alabama Churchman,* December 1968.

8. *Alabama Churchman,* May and June 1938. Bishop William George McDowell (1882–1938) had served the diocese from 1922 until his death in 1938. Clergymen elected Carpenter on the eleventh ballot and the laity on the seventh ballot. Other nominees included R. Bland Mitchell, James Stoney, R. A. Kirchhoffer, Noble Powell, Willis Clark, and A. R. McKinstry.

9. Carpenter to Will Scarlett, December 12, 1961, Carpenter Papers; *New York Times,* March 21, 1960.

10. W. J. Cash, *The Mind of the South* (New York: Vintage Books, 1941), 185.

11. Andrew E. Murray, *Presbyterians and the Negro: A History* (Philadelphia: Presbyterian Historical Society, 1966), 58. The best source on the Jones family is Robert Manson Myers, *Children of Pride: A True Story of Georgia and the Civil War* (New Haven: Yale University Press, 1972).

12. George Murray, letter to the author, April 5, 1991; Murray, telephone interview, October 20, 1992.

13. Princeton University "30-Year Book," Princeton University Archives, Princeton, N.J.; C. C. J. Carpenter, interview by David Lowe, "Who Speaks for Birmingham?" Columbia Broadcasting System, May 18, 1961, transcript, Tutwiler Collection; Coordinating Council of Social Forces Papers, BPLDAM; Corley, "The Quest," 63. Carpenter served as chairman from 1951 to 1954 and remained an active member until 1956. Other, lower-priority goals of the committee included improvement of schools, elimination of police brutality, investigation of bombings and arson, dealing with problems of "shootings and cutting scrapes," improvement of church and ministerial relations, black participation on public boards, stopping loan sharks, and improvement of the parking problems in downtown.

14. Statement of the Interracial Committee of the Jefferson County Coordinating Council, March 1, 1956, Carpenter Papers.

15. Murray, telephone conversation, February 8, 1991; Doug Carpenter, interview, January 27, 1991.

16. John O. Deman to Carpenter, March 14, 1956, Carpenter Papers.

17. Statement, April 13, 1956, Coordinating Council of Social Forces Papers.

18. Carpenter to James T. Williams Jr., January 18, 1957, Carpenter Papers.

19. Murray, telephone interview, October 20, 1992; Francis X. Walter, interview by author, tape recording, Birmingham, Ala., March 1, 1991.

20. William Stough, conversation with author, June 23, 1997. By 1963 the diocese had built a new headquarters adjacent to the Church of the Advent and named the building Carpenter House. The bishop had a large, comfortable office overlooking a landscaped courtyard.

21. *Alabama Churchman,* May 1956.

22. *Ibid.,* January 1958.

23. *New York Times,* March 21, 1960.

24. Carpenter to Officers and Members of the National Council, April 7, 1960, Carpenter Papers; Newspaper clipping, n.d., Carpenter Papers; *Mobile Register,* April 6, 1960.

25. Carpenter to the National Council, April 7, 1960, Carpenter Papers.

26. Memo, March 30, 1960, Carpenter Papers; *Birmingham News,* n.d., Carpenter Papers; *New York Times,* April 19, 29, 1960.

27. Taylor Branch, *Parting the Waters: America in the King Years, 1954–1963* (New York: Simon and Schuster, 1988), 742; Will Scarlett to Carpenter, July 22, 1960, Carpenter Papers.

28. Carpenter to Will Scarlett, October 6, 1960, Carpenter Papers; Will Scarlett to Carpenter, n.d., Carpenter Papers.

29. Carpenter to Will Scarlett, December 12, 1961, Carpenter Papers.

30. *Alabama Churchman,* April 1961.

31. "Who Speaks for Birmingham?" Tutwiler Collection.

32. *Ibid.*

33. *Alabama Churchman,* June 1961.

34. *Ibid.*

35. Unknown to Carpenter, May 30, 1961, Carpenter Papers.

36. H. Nesheim to Carpenter, May 18, 1961, Carpenter Papers; Nancy Jo Boyd to Carpenter, May 22, 1961, Carpenter Papers.

37. Doug Carpenter, interview; Carpenter to J. P. Mitchell, May 29, 1963, Carpenter Papers.

38. William R. Cannon, "Bishop Nolan B. Harmon," Memorial Service Eulogy, Harmon Papers; Harmon, *Ninety Years,* 295–96.

39. J. Tyra Harris, "Alabama Reaction to the *Brown* Decision 1954–1956: A Case Study in Early Massive Resistance" (Ph.D. diss., Middle Tennessee State University, 1978), 143–51; Flynt, "Alabama," 22. For a look at the Association of Methodist Ministers and Laymen and its successor organization, the Methodist Layman's Union, see Corley, "The Quest," 179–209.

40. Cannon, "Bishop Nolan B. Harmon," Harmon Papers; Harmon, *Ninety Years,* 16–17.

41. Nolan B. Harmon, "Prohibition and the Churches Duty," sermon presented on July 15, 1923, Harmon Papers; Harmon, *Ninety Years,* 16–29. Mescal is a liquor distilled from fermented juice from the maguey plant.

42. Nolan B. Harmon, untitled sermon presented on April 27, 1924, Harmon Papers; Harmon, *Ninety Years,* 30–78.

43. Harmon, *Ninety Years,* 84–86.

44. Harmon, *Ninety Years,* 109, 114. See Nolan B. Harmon, "Talk on Lee's Birthday," 1940, Harmon Papers. While in Maryland, Harmon married Rebecca Lamar on June 20, 1923. See Harmon, *Ninety Years,* 88–101.

45. Nolan B. Harmon, untitled "Sunday" sermon, February 16, 1936, Harmon Papers.

46. Nolan B. Harmon, "Prohibition and the Churches Duty" sermon presented on July 15, 1923, Harmon Papers; Harmon, *Ninety Years,* 124.

47. Nolan B. Harmon, "Our Duty to the Negro" (sermon presented on August 12, 1928), Harmon Papers.

48. Nolan B. Harmon, "Many Churches—One Church," sermon presented at Washington Street Methodist Church, Columbia, S.C., September 20, 1962, Harmon Papers; Nolan B. Harmon, "We Have Become Too Contemporary," *Christian Advocate,* April 23, 1942, clipping in Harmon Papers.

49. Harmon, "Many Churches—One Church," Harmon Papers.

50. *Ibid.*

51. Harmon, *Ninety Years,* 251.

52. Ibid., 253–55; Peter C. Murray, "The Racial Crisis in the Methodist Church" *Methodist History* 26 (October 1987): 4–5. According to Harmon, the southern bishops had drafted the plan and "found" a northern lay delegate to present the proposition to the General Conference.

53. Harmon, "Many Churches—One Church," Harmon Papers.

54. Harmon, *Ninety Years,* 251–53; Nolan B. Harmon, *Encyclopedia of World Methodism* (Nashville: United Methodist Publishing House, 1974), 1712.

55. Nolan B. Harmon, statement, n.d., Harmon Papers.

56. Harmon, *Ninety Years,* 297.

57. Nolan B. Harmon, "The Methodist Church and Race," paper presented at Race Forum, Charlotte, N.C., February 1, 1964, Harmon Papers; *Greensboro Daily News,* February 2, 1964.

58. Harmon, statement, n.d., Harmon Papers.

59. Samuel S. Hill Jr., in Eighmy, *Churches in Cultural Captivity,* 204; Caldwell, *In Search of Bisco,* 18; Ralph Creger, *A Look Down the Lonesome Road* (New York: Doubleday, 1964), 85.

Chapter 3

1. George Murray to C. Kilmer Myers, April 30, 1965, Carpenter Papers; Murray to George L. Cadigan, April 5, 1965, Carpenter Papers.

2. Murray to Myers, April 30, 1965; Williamson, *Crucible of Race*, 486–87.

3. Hardin spent most of his Birmingham career, from 1949 to 1960, as pastor of First Methodist Church. In 1963, he was a bishop.

4. Murray to Myers, April 30, 1965; George M. Murray, interview, tape recording, Fairhope, Ala., March 21, 1995. Around the diocese, Carpenter was referred to as the "big bishop" and Murray the "little bishop."

5. Murray to Myers, April 30, 1965; Murray, interview, March 21, 1995.

6. *Alabama Churchman*, March 1969; *Mobile Press-Register*, May 26, 1961; George Murray, telephone conversation with author, February 8, 1991; Murray to J. C. Hodges Jr., May 26, 1964, Carpenter Papers.

7. Murray, telephone interview, October 20, 1992; Murray to Mrs. J. S. Meriwether, December 21, 1964, Carpenter Papers; Murray to J. C. Hodges Jr., May 26, 1964, Carpenter Papers.

8. *Alabama Churchman*, March 1969; Murray, interview, March 21, 1995.

9. Murray, interview, March 21, 1995.

10. *Ibid.*

11. *Ibid.*

12. *Ibid.*

13. *Ibid.*

14. John Morris to Murray and Carpenter, September 2, 1961, Carpenter Papers.

15. *Ibid.*; Murray and Carpenter to John Morris, August 30, 1961, Carpenter Papers; Murray to John Morris, September 6, 1961, ESCRU Papers, Martin Luther King Center for Nonviolent Social Change, Inc., Archives (hereinafter referred to as King Center), Atlanta, Ga.

16. Murray to the Reverend Albert T. Mollegen, May 7, 1962, Carpenter Papers.

17. ESCRU Staff to the Clergy of the Diocese of Alabama, May 1, 1965, ESCRU Papers; Carpenter to John Morris, December 4, 1961, Carpenter Papers; Morris to Carpenter, December 5, 1961, Carpenter Papers.

18. *Business Week*, May 12, 1962, pp. 130, 132; Benjamin Muse, memorandum: "Dangerous Situation in Birmingham: General Observations," January 11, 1962, Southern Regional Council Papers, BPLDAM; Corley, "The Quest," 223–31.

19. Muse, "Dangerous Situation"; Benjamin Muse, memorandum: "Visit to Birmingham—September 22–24 and Alabama Plans," September 30, 1960, Southern Regional Council Papers; Corley, "The Quest," 177.

20. Murray, untitled Holy Week sermons, 1962, copies in possession of author.

21. Murray to Albert T. Mollegen, May 7, 1962, Carpenter Papers.

22. Murray, Holy Week sermons; *Alabama Churchman*, September 1960.

23. *Alabama Churchman*, March 1969; L. H. Pitts to Grafman, February 22, 1962, Grafman Papers.

24. Murray, telephone interview, October 20, 1992; Andrew Young, *An Easy Burden: The Civil Rights Movement and the Transformation of America* (New York: Harper Collins, 1996), 190; Fred Shuttlesworth, quoted in Enrique DuBois Rigsby, "A Rhetorical Clash with the Established Order: An Analysis of Protest Strategies and Perceptions of Media Responses, Birmingham, 1963" (Ph.D. diss., University of Oregon, 1990), 165.

25. Joseph A. Durick, interview by author, tape recording, Bessemer, Ala., May 8, 1992; Durick, interview, February 21, 1992.

26. Durick, untitled public speech, 1963, Durick Papers; Durick, background notes for public statement issued May 25, 1963, Durick Papers; *Catholic Week,* May 31, 1963.

27. *Tennessee Register,* July 4, 1994; Durick, interview, May 8, 1992.

28. Wayne Flynt, "Religion in the Urban South: The Divided Religious Mind of Birmingham, 1900–1930." *Alabama Review* 30 (April 1977): 108–34. Father James E. Coyle, pastor of St. Paul's Catholic Church in Birmingham, had been shot to death by the Reverend E. R. Stephenson. Hugo Black later acted as his defense council and won an acquittal.

29. Daniel Savage Gray, *Alabama: A Place, a People, a Point of View* (Dubuque, Iowa: Kendall/Hunt, 1977), 216; William Warren Rogers et al., *Alabama: The History of a Deep South State* (Tuscaloosa: University of Alabama Press, 1994), 430.

30. *Tennessee Register,* July 4, 1994; Durick, interview, February 21, 1992; *The Western Star,* March 4, 1992.

31. *Tennessee Register,* July 4, 1994; *Our Sunday Visitor,* April 20, 1975.

32. Joseph A. Durick, "Curriculum Vitae," n.d., Durick Papers; *Tennessee Register,* July 4, 1994; Durick, interview, February 21, 1992.

33. Joseph A. Durick, interview by Sister Rose Sevenich, October 2, 1992, October 23, 1992, Catholic Diocese of Birmingham, Alabama, Archives.

34. Joseph Durick, sermon, n.d., Durick Papers; *Tennessee Register,* July 4, 1994; Durick, interview, May 8, 1992.

35. "Outdoor Apostolate Instructional Pamphlet," n.d., Durick Papers.

36. Joseph A. Durick, "Results of Street Preaching," Durick Papers; *Catholic Week,* September 21, 1945; Durick, interview, May 8, 1992; Durick, interview, February 21, 1992; Joseph A. Durick, "Street Preaching Outline," n.d., Durick Papers. In 1956, Durick preached five nights at a revival. His sermons included "The Purpose in Life," "Life of Jesus," "The Church," "Two Great Powers," and "Church and Bible."

37. Durick, interview, February 21, 1992; Durick, "Street Preaching Outline."

38. *Catholic Week,* September 21, 1945; Durick, "Street Preaching Outline"; Durick, interview, May 8, 1992.

39. Durick, "Results of Street Preaching"; *Catholic Week,* September 21, 1945; Durick, interview, May 8, 1992.

40. *Tennessee Register*, March 19, 1990. The churches included St. Margaret's (Birmingham), St. Francis Church (West Blocton), St. Thomas (Montevallo), St. Edward's (Gardendale), St. Alice (Edgewater), and St. Michael's (Brookside).

41. Durick, interview, May 8, 1992; *Catholic Week,* March 19, 1955. Ironically, Durick's road crew so impressed Sheen that the noted Catholic radio and television orator traveled with the group for a week-preaching eighteen times.

42. "Solemn Observance of the Fortieth Episcopal Anniversary and the Fifty-seventh Sacerdotal Anniversary of the Most Reverend Thomas Joseph Toolen," 1967, Durick Papers.

43. Durick, interview by Sevenich.

44. *Catholic Week,* January 8, 1955.

45. *Catholic Week,* March 26, 1955.

46. *Ibid.* Durick, interview, May 8, 1992.

47. *Birmingham News,* December 6, 1976; Durick, interview, May 8, 1992.

48. Muse, "Dangerous Situation"; Durick, interview, May 8, 1992.

49. Rogers et al., *Alabama,* 547–48.

50. Durick, interview by Sevenich; "Solemn Observance," Durick Papers.

51. Grafman to Albert Vorspan, March 1, 1956, Grafman Papers.

52. Mark H. Elovitz, *A Century of Jewish Life in Dixie: The Birmingham Experience* (Tuscaloosa: University of Alabama Press, 1974), 86–87.

53. John Egerton, *Speak Now against the Day: The Generation before the Civil Rights Movement in the South* (New York: Alfred A. Knopf, 1994), 561.

54. Robert P. Ingalls, "Antiradical Violence in Birmingham during the 1930s," *Journal of Southern History* 47 (November 1981): 522–24; Egerton, *Speak Now,* 529; Robin D. G. Kelley, *Hammer and Hoe: Alabama's Communists during the Great Depression* (Chapel Hill: University of North Carolina Press, 1990), 227.

55. Connor, quoted in Michael Cooper Nichols, " 'Cities Are What Men Make Them': Birmingham, Alabama, Faces the Civil Rights Movement, 1963" (Senior honors thesis, Brown University, 1974), 66; Haselden, *Mandate,* 47–48; Robert Paul Sessions, "Are Southern Ministers Failing the South?" *Saturday Evening Post,* May 13, 1961 p. 82; Wayne Flynt, "The Ethics of Democratic Persuasion and the Birmingham Crisis," *Southern Speech Journal* 35 (fall 1969): 49–50.

56. David M. Chalmers, *Hooded Americanism: The History of the Ku Klux Klan* (New York: New Viewpoints, 1976), 350–51.

57. Southern Shofar, December 1991; Elovitz, *A Century of Jewish Life,* 166–67; *New York Times,* April 12, 1961.

58. *Time,* February 27, 1956; J. D. Williams to Grafman, February 20, 1956, Grafman Papers; Grafman to J. D. Williams, February 6, 1956, Grafman Papers.

59. George Chancy et al., "Statement," n.d., Grafman Papers.

60. Joshua Trachtenberg to Grafman, February 21, 1956, Grafman Papers; Carl I. Miller to Grafman, March 7, 1956, Grafman Papers.

61. Terry Barr, "Rabbi Grafman and Birmingham's Civil Rights Era," paper presented at symposium on Southern Rabbis' Involvement in Black Civil Rights, Memphis, Tenn., April 1995, p. 7; "A neighbor" to Grafman, February 22, 1956, Grafman Papers; anonymous to Grafman, February 24, 1956, Grafman Papers.

62. "1924 Firth Avenue High School Yearbook, Pittsburgh, Pennsylvania," Grafman Papers; Grafman, quoted in Stephen W. Grafman, letter to author, October 3, 1995.

63. Stephen Grafman, letter to author, October 3, 1995; Milton Grafman, interview by Birmingham Public Library, tape recording, August 19, 1977, BPLDAM.

64. Stephen Grafman, letter to author, October 3, 1995.

65. *Birmingham News,* n.d., clipping in Grafman Papers.

66. Stephen Grafman, letter to author, August 18, 1997.

67. Elovitz, *A Century of Jewish Life,* 153; *Birmingham News,* February 19, 1949.

68. See Mark Cowett, *Birmingham's Rabbi: Morris Newfield and Alabama, 1895–1940* (Tuscaloosa: University of Alabama Press, 1986).

69. Grafman, interview, March 22, 1995.

70. Grafman, untitled sermon preached at Rosh Hashanah service, Temple Emanu-El, Birmingham, Ala., September 19, 1963, tape recording in possession of author.

71. Paul Hardin, "A Plea for a Militant Church," sermon, n.d., Paul Hardin Jr. Papers, WMA, Lake Junaluska, N.C.

72. *Ibid.*

73. Paul Hardin, "The Sin of Prejudice," sermon presented at the First Methodist Church of Birmingham, Birmingham, Ala., January 29, 1956, Hardin Papers; Paul Hardin, "Slaves in a Free Country," sermon presented at First Methodist Church of Birmingham, Birmingham, Ala., July 1, 1951, Hardin Papers.

74. Paul Hardin, "The Sin of Hating," sermon presented at the First Methodist Church of Birmingham, Birmingham, Ala., January 15, 1956, Hardin Papers; Paul Hardin III, telephone conversation with author, July 30, 1997.

75. Corley, "The Quest," 136; Paul Hardin, interview by Elliott Wright, tape recording and transcript, Indianapolis, Ind., April 18, 1980, WMA.

76. Paul Hardin, "Race and the Methodist Church—The Southeastern Jurisdiction," report presented to the Council of Bishops, April 1965, Hardin Papers.

77. *Ibid.*

78. Hardin interview by Wright; Hardin, "Sin of Prejudice."

79. Hardin, interview by Wright.

80. Sellers, *The South and Christian Ethics,* 152.

81. Robert B. McNeill, *God Wills Us Free: The Ordeal of a Southern Minister* (New York: Hill and Wang, 1964), 198.

Chapter 4

1. Earl Stallings, "Where Shall I Begin: Reminiscences of Earl Stallings," tape recording, 1998, in possession of author.

2. *The Messenger* April 11, 1963, in John Chandler Papers (copy in possession of author).

3. Stallings, "Where Shall I Begin."

4. *Ibid.*

5. *Ibid.*

6. *Ibid.*

7. O. W. Taylor, *Early Tennessee Baptists, 1769–1872* (Nashville: Executive Board of Tennessee Baptist Association, 1957), 22, 226–28; *Ibid.*

8. Earl Stallings, conversation with author, August 17, 1998.

9. *Ibid.*; Stallings, "Where Shall I Begin"; Earl Stallings, "Biographical Sketch," copy in possession of author.

10. Stallings, "Where Shall I Begin"; "A General Report on Reverend Earl Stallings," November 22, 1961, FBCB Papers, SUSC.

11. Timothy Scott McGinnis, "The Controversy and Division of First Baptist Church, Birmingham, Alabama, 1968–1970" (senior honors thesis, Samford University, May 1990), 19, 21; William Simmons, telephone interview by author, August 6, 1998.

12. Newspaper Clipping Files, Churches, First Baptist, Birmingham, Tutwiler Collection.

13. McGinnis, "Controversy," 21.

14. *Ibid.*, 19; McGill, *The South and the Southerner,* 276.

15. McGinnis, "Controversy," 20; Church Conference and Deacon Minutes, January 7, 1953, June 10, 17, September 9, 1953, January 13, 1954, FBCB Papers.

16. Church Conference and Deacon Minutes, January 13, 1954, FBCB Papers.

17. *Ibid.*, July 15, 1955.

18. Report of the Special Committee, July 27, 1955, FBCB Papers. Questionnaires were mailed in July 1955 to the 1,850 active members of the congregation. Of those, only 314 returned the questionnaire to the committee.

19. Minutes of Special Church Conference, September 2, 1959, FBCB Papers.

20. Simmons, telephone interview; T. R. "Swede" Lawson and Mrs. Ernest S. Story, "First Baptist Church Centennial, 1872–1972," SUSC.

21. Earl Stallings, letter to the author, July 7, 1995; *Cleveland Call and Post,* April 20, 1963.

22. John Chandler, conversation with author, September 8, 1995; Andrew Manis, *A Fire You Can't Put Out: The Civil Rights Life of Birmingham's Rever-*

end Fred Shuttlesworth (Tuscaloosa: University of Alabama Press, 1999), 358. Young's reminiscences of events in Birmingham during the summer of 1963 are at best inconsistent. He also claimed to have been "turned away at the door" of First Baptist—an event that never happened. See Andrew Young, "There's a New World Coming," *Bulletin of the Peace Studies Institute* (August 1971): 9. *Bulletin of the Peace Studies Institute* was a publication of Manchester College in North Manchester, Ind.

23. Letter (n.d., n.p.), Chandler Papers.

24. "Excerpts from Deacons' Meetings," Chandler Papers; Chandler, conversation.

25. Baptist Press News Release, April 20, 1963, Stallings Papers; *Alabama Baptist,* March 18, 1993; Simmons, telephone interview; *New York Times,* April 15, 1963.

26. John L. and Margaret Slaughter to Stallings, April 23, 1963, Stallings Papers; Grady Cothen to Stallings, May 17, 1963, Stallings Papers.

27. Helen Bullard to Stallings, April 15, 1963, Stallings Papers; Robert Sherer to Stallings, April 16, 1963, Stallings Papers; Ralph H. Langley to Stallings, April 16, 1963, Stallings Papers; James A. Sawyer to Stallings, April 18, 1963, Stallings Papers.

28. Juliette Mather to Stallings, April 17, 1963, Stallings Papers; William M. and Martha Gilliland to Stallings, April 15, 1963, Stallings Papers.

29. Betty Thomas to Stallings, April 28, 1963, Stallings Papers; Laurella Owens to Stallings, April 17, 1963, Stallings Papers; Alma Hunt to Stallings, April 17, 1963, Stallings Papers; Elaine Dickson to Stallings, June 4, 1963, Stallings Papers.

30. Blue Print Class to Stallings, May 26, 1963.

31. Members of the Visitation Class to Stallings, April 16, 1963, Stallings Papers.

32. Willie Mae Bartlett to Stallings, April 21, 1963, Stallings Papers.

33. Lamar Thompson to Stallings, April 15, 1963, Stallings Papers; anonymous to Stallings n.d., Stallings Papers; anonymous to Stallings, April 15, 1963, Stallings Papers.

34. *Washington Post,* April 22, 1963.

35. Church Conference and Deacon Minutes, April 24, 1963; "Excerpts," Chandler Papers; Earl Stallings, telephone conversation with author, May 4, 1992.

36. *Birmingham Post-Herald,* January 16, 1960; Edward V. Ramage, "Some Hae Meat," unpublished article, n.d., Edward V. Ramage Papers, copies in possession of author.

37. Ramage, "Some Hae Meat." It is unclear whether Ramage ever obtained a degree. According to officials at Columbia Theological Seminary, Ramage completed his senior year of study, but the seminary had no record of an actual degree conferred.

38. *Ibid.*

39. Birmingham *Post-Herald,* January 16, 1960. Ramage later pastored churches in Elberton, Georgia (1936–38), Decatur, Alabama (1938–42), and Oklahoma City (1942–46), before coming to Birmingham in 1946.

40. *Ibid.*; William Ford, telephone conversation with author, September 6, 1995; Hill, *Encyclopedia of Religion in the South,* 604.

41. Clarence M. Kilian, ed., *"The Old First" of Birmingham, Alabama: From the Founding in 1873 to the Year of Our Lord 1952* (Birmingham: Birmingham Publishing, 1952), 4–10; Catherine Marshall, *A Man Called Peter: The Story of Peter Marshall* (New York: McGraw-Hill, 1951), 26–31. The Vanguard Class at First Presbyterian paid for Marshall's seminary training.

42. Katherine Ramage Love, telephone conversation with author, August 9, 1998.

43. J. Tyra Harris, "Alabama Reaction to the *Brown* Decision," 141–42.

44. Corley, "The Quest," 178.

45. Minutes of the Session, July 23, 1961, First Presbyterian Church, Birmingham, Records, BPLDAM.

46. Love, telephone conversation, August 9, 1998; Ann Fleming Deagon to Ramage, June 30, 1963, Ramage Papers.

47. "Order of Worship," April 14, 1963, Ramage Papers; Notes for sermon, April 1963, Ramage Papers; Katherine Ramage Love, telephone interview by author, tape recording, Pine Bluff, Ark., February 28, 1992; *Cleveland Call and Post,* April 20, 1963.

48. Love, telephone interview, February 28, 1992; "Order of Worship," April 14, 1963, Ramage Papers; sermon notes, April 1963, Ramage Papers; *Cleveland Call and Post,* April 20, 1963; Tennant McWilliams, conversation with author, January 21, 1998.

49. Love, telephone interview, February 28, 1992; "Order of Worship," April 14, 1963, Ramage Papers; sermon notes, April 1963, Ramage Papers; Ford, telephone conversation.

50. Katherine Ramage Love, interview by author, tape recording, Pine Bluff, Ark., February 2, 1995; Ford, telephone conversation; Cleveland *Call and Post,* April 20, 1963.

51. Love, interview, February 2, 1995; Ann Fleming Deagon to Edward Ramage, June 30, 1963, Ramage Papers; McNeill, *God Wills Us Free,* 197.

52. Ann Fleming Deagon to Ramage, June 30, 1963, Ramage Papers.

53. First Presbyterian Records; McNeill, *God Wills Us Free,* 197–98.

Chapter 5

1. Charles S. Johnson, *Patterns of Negro Segregation* (New York: Harper and Brothers, 1943), 139.

2. Joel Williamson, ed., *The Origins of Segregation* (Lexington, Mass.: D. C. Heath, 1968), v.

3. Jack Temple Kirby, *Darkness at the Dawning: Race and Reform in the Progressive South* (Philadelphia: J. B. Lippincott, 1972), 18; Vernon Lane Wharton, *The Negro in Mississippi, 1865–1890* (Chapel Hill: University of North Carolina Press, 1947), 230; Johnson, *Patterns,* 139, 143; Jesse Walter Dees Jr. and James S. Hadley, *Jim Crow* (Westport, Conn.: Negro Universities Press, 1951), 24.

4. Johnson, *Patterns,* 137.

5. Blaine A. Brownell, "Birmingham, Alabama: New South City in the 1920s." *Journal of Southern History* 38 (February 1972): 48.

6. George R. Leighton, "Birmingham, Alabama: The City of Perpetual Promise," *Harpers Magazine,* August 1937, pp. 225–27; Flynt, "Religion in the Urban South," 109; Irving Beiman, "Birmingham: Steel Giant with a Glass Jaw," in *Our Fair City,* ed. Robert S. Allen (New York: Vanguard Press, 1947), 101; Hanes, quoted in David Cort, "The Voices of Birmingham," *Nation,* July 27, 1963, p. 47.

7. Carl V. Harris, "Reforms in Government Control of Negroes in Birmingham, Alabama, 1890–1920," *Journal of Southern History* 28 (November 1972): 570–71; Corley, "The Quest," 24–25.

8. C. Vann Woodward, *Thinking Back: The Perils of Writing History* (Baton Rouge: Louisiana State University Press, 1986), 96.

9. Johnson, *Patterns,* 306, 125, 127, 285.

10. Newspaper clippings, n.d., Durick Papers.

11. James C. Cobb, *The Selling of the South* (Baton Rouge: Louisiana State University Press, 1983), 128–41.

12. Carl V. Harris, *Political Power in Birmingham, 1871–1921* (Knoxville: University of Tennessee Press, 1977), 13; Leighton, "Birmingham, Alabama," 227; Brownell, "Birmingham," 31.

13. Leighton, "Birmingham, Alabama," 225; Neal R. Peirce, "The Southern City Today" in *Dixie Dateline: A Journalistic Portrait of the Contemporary South,* ed. John B. Boles (Houston: Rice University Studies, 1983), 106.

14. Connor, quoted in Nichols, "Cities," 135.

15. *New York Times,* April 12, 1960.

16. *Ibid.*

17. *Ibid.,* April 12, 13, 1960.

18. Grafman, quoted in newspaper clipping, n.d., Grafman Papers; *New York Times,* July 7, 1993.

19. Grafman, quoted in newspaper clipping, n.d.

20. "Birmingham: Brinkmanship in Race Relations," *Christian Century,* May 29, 1962, p. 689.

21. *New York Times,* May 4, 1960.

22. *New York Times,* May 10, 1960.

23. Nunnelley, *Bull Connor,* 89–90. The U.S. Supreme Court would ultimately overturn the lower court and rule in favor of the *Times.* See *New York Times v. Connor,* 365F.2d 567 (5th Cir 1966). This court case and the *New York Times v. Sullivan* ruling provided another ironic example of the way Alabama resistance helped the civil rights movement achieve its goals.

24. Creger, *A Look Down,* 72.

25. Karl Fleming, quoted in Jack Lyle, *The Black American and the Press* (Los Angeles: Ward Ritchie Press, 1968), 32; Hodding Carter III, quoted in Lyle, *The Black American and the Press,* 40.

26. Lewis M. Killian, *White Southerners* (New York: Random House, 1970), 40; Halberstam, *The Fifties,* 440; Claude Sitton, "Racial Coverage: Planning and Logistics" in *Race and the News Media,* ed. Paul L. Fisher and Ralph L. Lowenstein (New York: Frederick A. Praeger, 1967), 77–78.

27. King, quoted in Glenn Thomas Eskew, "But for Birmingham: The Local and National Movements in the Civil Rights Struggle" (Ph.D. diss., University of Georgia, 1993), 369.

28. King, *Why We Can't Wait,* 50; Eskew, "But for Birmingham," 354; *Washington Post,* May 13, 1963; Martin Luther King, "Eulogy for the Martyred Children," in *A Testament of Hope: The Essential Writings and Speeches of Martin Luther King, Jr.,* James Melvin Washington (San Francisco: HarperSanFrancisco, 1986), 222; Fred Shuttlesworth, "Birmingham Shall Be Free Some Day" *Freedomways,* winter 1964, 16; David Cort, "The Voices of Birmingham," 47.

29. *Newsweek,* April 15, 1963, p. 29; Connor, quoted in Arthur M. Schlesinger Jr., *Robert Kennedy and His Times* (Boston: Houghton Mifflin, 1978), 328.

30. David Garrow, *Bearing the Cross: Martin Luther King, Jr., and the Southern Christian Leadership Conference* (New York: William Morrow, 1986), 228; Walker, quoted in Henry Hampton, Steve Fayer, and Sarah Flynn, *Voices of Freedom: An Oral History of the Civil Rights Movement from the 1950s through the 1980s* (New York: Bantam Books, 1992), 125.

31. Branch, *Parting the Waters,* 299; Wyatt T. Walker, interview by author, tape recording, New York, N.Y., January 7, 1997.

32. Willie Pearl Mackey King, letter to author, March 18, 1997; Willie Pearl Mackey King, telephone interview by author, October 25, 1998, transcript in possession of author.

33. Walker, interview, January 7, 1997.

34. *Ibid.*

35. *Ibid.*

36. E. Culpepper Clark, "The American Dilemma in King's 'Letter from Birmingham Jail' " in *Martin Luther King, Jr., and the Sermonic Power of Public Discourse,* ed. Carolyn Calloway-Thomas and John Louis Lucaites (Tuscaloosa:

University of Alabama Press, 1993), 37; Richard Lentz, *Symbols, the News Magazines, and Martin Luther King* (Baton Rouge: Louisiana State University Press, 1990), 64, 68. In addition, competition for publicity and money with the Student Nonviolent Coordinating Committee (SNCC) and local civil rights leaders was also a factor in the debacle in Albany.

37. Eskew, "But for Birmingham," 289; Shuttlesworth, quoted in Hampton, *Voices of Freedom,* 125; Nunnelley, *Bull Connor,* 130; Garrow, *Bearing the Cross,* 669 n. 9.

38. Lentz, *Symbols,* 84; Pat Watters, *Down to Now: Reflections on the Southern Civil Rights Movement* (New York: Pantheon Books, 1971), 266; Garrow, *Bearing the Cross,* 228; Nichols, "Cities," 28.

39. Garrow, *Bearing the Cross,* 228; Nichols, "Cities," 286; Walker, interview, January 7, 1997.

40. Mary-Helen Vick, "A Survey of the Governing Body of Birmingham, Alabama, 1910–1964" (master's thesis, Alabama College, 1965), 86–87, 92.

41. Joe David Brown, "Birmingham, Alabama: A City in Fear" *Saturday Evening Post,* March 2, 1963, p. 16; Boutwell, quoted in Nunnelley, *Bull Connor,* 134.

42. Connor, quoted respectively in *Newsweek,* April 15, 1963, p. 29, and Nunnelley, *Bull Connor,* 134–35. The *News* was owned by Newhouse in New York and the *Post-Herald* by Scripps-Howard in Cleveland, Ohio.

43. *Washington Post,* May 13, 1963; Connor, quoted in *Birmingham World,* April 6, 1963. Wallace Terry reported in the *Post* (May 13, 1963) that a "solid Negro vote" of over seven thousand ballots was the margin of victory for Connor's defeat.

44. *Birmingham News,* April 3, 1963; Garrow, *Bearing the Cross,* 236; Branch, *Parting the Waters,* 722.

45. King, quoted in Nunnelley, *Bull Connor,* 139.

46. King, *Why We Can't Wait,* 43–44, 70–71. King believed Connor could have used the protests as an "emotion-charged" issue to rally white support.

47. Bloomer, quoted in Nunnelley, *Bull Connor,* 145.

48. D. B. Grace, "Official Life of George B. Ward," 74–82, Tutwiler Collection; Leah Rawls Atkins, *The Valley and the Hills: An Illustrated History of Birmingham and Jefferson County* (Birmingham: Windsor Publications, 1981), 141.

49. Connor, quoted in *Washington Post,* April 5, 1963; *Birmingham News,* April 4, 1963.

50. *Washington Post,* April 5, 9, 1963; Nunnelley, *Bull Connor,* 122, 132.

51. *Birmingham News,* April 3, 1963. Many of the department stores in downtown Birmingham had lunch counters with names; for example: the Tea Room inside Loveman's and Britt's inside J. J. Newberry's. Britt's should not be confused with a local cafeteria chain, Britling's.

52. *Birmingham News,* April 3, 1963.

53. *Birmingham News,* April 4, 1963; *Birmingham Post-Herald,* April 15, 1963.

54. *Birmingham News,* April 5, 1963.

55. James Forman, *The Making of Black Revolutionaries: A Personal Account* (Seattle: Open Hand, 1985), 312. Forman, who witnessed Walker's outburst, said: "It was a disgusting moment for me for it seemed very cold, cruel, and calculating to be happy about police brutality coming down on innocent people . . . no matter what purpose it served." Wyatt Walker later called Forman's account a lie. See Walker, interview, January 7, 1997; Garrow, *Bearing the Cross,* 239–40.

56. Graham, quoted in *New York Times,* April 17, 1963; Branch, *Parting the Waters,* 737.

57. *Washington Post,* April 5, 14, 1963; *Time,* April 19, 1963.

58. Peters, *The Southern Temper,* 181.

59. *Birmingham World,* April 10, 17, 1963.

60. *Birmingham World,* April 10, 17, 1963.

61. *Birmingham World,* April 10, 1963; Branch, *Parting the Waters,* 703, 726, 737. Gaston, however, later provided some vocal and financial support. King, *Why We Can't Wait,* 65; Garrow, *Bearing the Cross,* 240; Adam Fairclough, *To Redeem the Soul of America: The Southern Christian Leadership Conference and Martin Luther King, Jr.* (Athens: University of Georgia Press, 1987), 119.

62. Garrow, *Bearing the Cross,* 240–42; *Washington Post,* April 5, 7, 1963; Fairclough, *To Redeem,* 119.

63. Abernathy, quoted in Birmingham Police Department Inter-Office Communication, April 10, 1963, Report of Meeting at First Baptist Church of Ensley, April 8, 1963, Eugene "Bull" Connor Papers, BPLDAM, Birmingham, Ala.; April 11, 1963, Report of Meeting at Sixteenth Street Baptist Church, April 9, 1963, Connor Papers; King, quoted in Garrow, *Bearing the Cross,* 240; Willie Morris, ed., *The South Today: 100 Years after Appomattox* (New York: Harper and Row, 1965), 265.

64. *Birmingham News,* April 11, 1963; see also Howell Raines, *My Soul Is Rested: The Story of the Civil Rights Movement in the Deep South* (New York: Penguin Books, 1977), 143; Shuttlesworth, quoted in Alan F. Westin and Barry Mahoney, *The Trial of Martin Luther King* (New York: Thomas Y. Crowell, 1974), 76–77; King, *Why We Can't Wait,* 70; Shuttlesworth, telephone interview, April 23, 1992. Fred Shuttlesworth had insisted that if "any judge" issued an injunction "we would not stop . . . because a court injunction could kill the movement."

65. King, quoted in Westin and Mahoney, *Trial,* 78–79, and *Washington Post,* April 12, 1963.

66. Abernathy, quoted in William Kunstler, *Deep in My Heart* (New York: William Morrow, 1966), 185; Shuttlesworth, quoted in *Birmingham News,* January 19, 1986.

67. *Walker v. City of Birmingham,* 388 U.S. 307 16 (1967).

68. Abernathy, quoted in Birmingham Police Department Inter-Office Communication, April 12, 1963, Report of Meeting at Sixth Avenue Baptist Church, April 11, 1963, Connor Papers.

69. King, *Why We Can't Wait,* 71.

70. *Cleveland Call and Post,* April 20, 1963; Newspaper Clipping Files, A. G. Gaston, Tutwiler Collection.

71. *Cleveland Call and Post,* April 20, 1963; King, quoted in Garrow, *Bearing the Cross,* 242.

Chapter 6

1. Walker, interview, January 7, 1997. Several historians identified the Sixteenth Street Baptist Church as the beginning of King's march to jail, but television footage, newspaper accounts, and court documents all identify the Zion Hill Church.

2. "Warden's Docket (Avenue "F" Prison)," Birmingham, Ala., BPLDAM; Young, *An Easy Burden,* 207.

3. Stephen B. Oates, *Let the Trumpet Sound: The Life of Martin Luther King, Jr.* (New York: Mentor Press, 1982), 213.

4. "Birmingham City Directory, 1963," Tutwiler Collection.

5. *Call and Post,* April 20, 1963.

6. "Birmingham City Directory, 1963."

7. *King: A Film Record from Montgomery to Memphis* (Martin Luther King Film Project, 1970), videocassette.

8. Garrow, *Bearing the Cross,* 242; King, quoted in Walker, interview, January 7, 1997; Walker, quoted in *Walker v. City of Birmingham,* 208.

9. *Walker v. City of Birmingham,* 161.

10. *Chicago Tribune,* April 13, 1963; *Washington Post,* April 13, 1963.

11. *King: A Film Record*; Nunnelley, *Bull Connor,* 142–43.

12. Newspaper Clipping Files, Birmingham Jail File, Tutwiler Collection; *Birmingham News,* November 18, 1974.

13. Garrow, *Bearing the Cross,* 243, 670; King, *Why We Can't Wait,* 73.

14. *Walker v. City of Birmingham,* 18.

15. Walker, interview, January 7, 1997.

16. Norman Amaker, "De Facto Leadership and the Civil Rights Movement: Perspective on the Problems and Role of Activists and Lawyers in Legal and Social Change," *Southern University Law Review* 16 (1989): 27; Garrow, *Bearing the Cross,* 242–44.

17. Moore, quoted in Nunnelley, *Bull Connor,* 144; Ralph David Abernathy, *And the Walls Came Tumbling Down* (New York: Harper and Row, 1989), 253;

Amaker, "De Facto Leadership," 28; Norman Amaker, telephone interview by author, tape recording, July 22, 1998.

18. Oates, *Let the Trumpet Sound*, 213–14; Garrow, *Bearing the Cross*, 243; Amaker, interview, July 22, 1998.

19. On April 13, the white ministers' statement appeared on page two of the *Birmingham News* and on page ten in the *Birmingham Post-Herald*; part of the white ministers' statement also appeared in the Sunday, April 14, *New York Times*.

20. Walker, quoted in Eugene P. Walker, "A History of the Southern Christian Leadership Conference, 1955–1965: The Evolution of a Southern Strategy for Social Change" (Ph.D. diss., Duke University, 1978), 140; Clark, "American Dilemma," 35.

21. *New York Times*, April 14, 1963; Harrison Salisbury, *Without Fear or Favor: The "New York Times" and Its Times* (New York: Times Books, 1980), 6. Salisbury called the Saturday deadline the "magic hour."

22. Keith D. Miller, *Voices of Deliverance: The Language of Martin Luther King, Jr., and Its Sources* (New York: Free Press, 1992), 162–63; Martin Luther King, Jr., *Stride toward Freedom: The Montgomery Story* (New York: Harper, 1958), 209.

23. Branch, *Parting the Waters*, 602.

24. *Birmingham News*, April 13, 1963; see Appendix 2.

25. King, *Why We Can't Wait*, 76; Abernathy, *And the Walls*, 253–54.

26. King, *Why We Can't Wait*, 74; Joan Daves phone call to Stanley Levison, April 19, 1963, in *The King-Levison File*, part 2 of *The Martin Luther King, Jr., FBI File* (Frederick, Md.: University Publications of America, 1987), microfilm, 2.

27. Mackey King, letter to author.

28. Ibid.

29. Branch, *Parting the Waters*, 738, 740.

30. Mackey King, interview; Mackey King, letter to author.

31. Mackey King, letter to author.

32. *Ibid.*; Walker, interview.

33. Mackey King, interview.

34. Branch, *Parting the Waters*, 740; Walker, interview.

35. Robert P. Fulkerson, "The Public Letter as a Rhetorical Form: Structure, Logic, and Style in King's 'Letter from Birmingham Jail,' " *Quarterly Journal of Speech* 65 (April 1979): 125–27.

36. Mia Klein, "The *Other* Beauty of Martin Luther King, Jr.'s 'Letter from Birmingham Jail,' " *College Composition and Communication* 32 (February 1981): 30; Malinda Snow, "Martin Luther King's 'Letter from Birmingham Jail' as Pauline Epistle," *Quarterly Journal of Speech* 71 (August 1985): 319–20.

37. Martin Luther King Jr., "Letter from Birmingham Jail," 1, Mayor Albert Boutwell Papers, BPLDAM. For a complete text of this early version of the letter, see Appendix 3.

38. James Strong, "Dictionary of the Greek Testament," in *The New Strong's Exhaustive Concordance of the Bible* (Nashville: Thomas Nelson Publishers, 1984), 15; King, "Letter from Birmingham Jail," 1–2, Boutwell Papers. Acts 16:9–10 New International Version.

39. King, "Letter from Birmingham Jail," 2, Boutwell Papers.

40. King also commended Catholic leaders for integrating Spring Hill College in Mobile.

41. The eight white clergy had indeed condemned Wallace for his statements, but Fred Shuttlesworth later called this a mere "pebble in the ocean." Shuttlesworth, interview.

Chapter 7

1. *Washington Post*, April 21, 1963; *Chicago Tribune*, May 21, 1963; *Birmingham News*, April 26, 1963; *Washington Post*, April 27, 1963.

2. Porter, quoted in Nichols, "Cities," 282.

3. Eskew, "But for Birmingham," 352; *Washington Post*, May 3, 1963.

4. Garrow, *Bearing the Cross*, 251; "The Change in Birmingham," *Newsweek*, December 8, 1969, p. 79; "Freedom—Now," *Time*, May 17, 1963, p. 25.

5. *Washington Post*, May 2, 1993.

6. Stanley Levison phone call to unknown, May 13, 1963, in *The King-Levison File*, 1; Stanley Levison said there were 187 journalists covering the Birmingham movement.

7. *Washington Post*, May 8, 1963.

8. Hampton, Fayer, and Flynn, *Voices of Freedom*, 133.

9. *Ibid.*; Walker, interview.

10. *New York Times*, May 7, 1963.

11. Martin Luther King, Jr. fund-raising letter, May 1963, attached to memorandum, SAC (Los Angeles) to Director FBI, May 23, 1963, *The King-Levison File*.

12. *Washington Post*, May 11, 1963; *New York Times*, May 11, 1963; Eskew, *But for Birmingham*, 292–96.

13. Mackey King, interview.

14. Branch, *Parting the Waters*, 744. The earliest excerpt from the "Letter from Birmingham Jail" was printed in the *New York Times*, May 5, 1963; the following quotation appeared in a story on Birmingham: "I stand alone in the middle of two opposing forces in the Negro community. One is the force of complacency. . . . The other force is one of bitterness and hatred and comes perilously close to advocating violence. It is expressed in the various black nationalist groups." This is slightly different from what appears even in the early typed versions of the letter. Although the quotation is attributed to King, it is unclear if it came from the document or another source.

15. Amaker, interview.

16. *Ibid.*

17. Anonymous to Martin Luther King, Jr., n.d., Southern Christian Leadership Conference (SCLC) Papers, King Center; King eliminated the quotation "We have come a long way, haven't we?" The letter writer further added: "Even so, a thousand years can be as only one day to God. We are all impatient—probably because we are Americans—but we have to allow God the necessary time to accomplish His purpose in the hearts of the people. May God help all of you to be extremely careful in your desire to carry out His wishes, by making you very alert in recognizing Him as your Leader. Yours, In Christ's Service."

18. Clark, "The American Dilemma," 35; Martin Luther King phone call to Stanley Levison, May 21, 1963, *The King-Levison File, 6.*

19. *Ibid.*

20. Hermine Popper phone call to Stanley Levison, January 24, 1964, *The King-Levison File,* 1. This editing apparently occurred before the letter received revisions for King's book on the Birmingham campaign, since no new additional passages were included in the book version.

21. *Ibid.,* King, "Letter from Birmingham Jail," 18, Boutwell Papers; King, *Why We Can't Wait,* 93.

22. Raines, *My Soul Is Rested,* 161. Regardless, Shuttlesworth added that King deserved "all the credit."

23. Branch, *Parting the Waters,* 744.

24. Walker, quoted in Earl and Miriam Selby, *Odyssey: Journey through Black America* (New York: G. P. Putnam's Sons, 1971), 285; Walker, interview. Of all the volumes written on the movement in Birmingham, only one writer, E. Culpepper Clark, has examined the circumstances surrounding the production of the "Letter from Birmingham Jail"; see Clark, "American Dilemma," 35.

25. Mackey King, interview; Walker, interview.

26. Clark, "American Dilemma," 40.

27. King, "Letter from Birmingham Jail," 19, Boutwell Papers; King, *Why We Can't Wait,* 94.

28. Robert P. Fulkerson, "The Public Letter," 132–33. The sentences have an average of 22 words, and the paragraphs have an average of 7 sentences and an average of 149 words.

29. Douglas Sturm, "Crisis in the American Republic: The Legal and Political Significance of Martin Luther King's 'Letter from a Birmingham Jail,' " in *Martin Luther King, Jr.: Civil Rights Leader, Theologian, Orator,* ed. David J. Garrow (New York: Carlson, 1989), 945; Fulkerson, "The Public Letter," 123, 132.

30. Miller, *Voices of Deliverance,* 150; Martin Luther King, Jr., "A Challenge to the Churches and Synagogues," paper presented at the National Conference on Religion and Race, Chicago, Ill., January 17, 1963, copy in Durick Papers.

31. King, "Transformed Nonconformist," in *Strength to Love* (New York: Harper and Row, 1963), 8–15. King said the white church had been called to "combat social evils," but had "remained silent behind stained-glass windows." King, "Letter from Birmingham Jail," 6, 15, Boutwell Papers.

32. King, "Transformed Nonconformist," 10, 12, 14; King, "Antidotes for Fear" in *Strength to Love* (New York: Harper and Row, 1963), 116; King, *Stride toward Freedom*, 10.

33. Miller, *Voices of Deliverance*, 5–6, 162, 164. Fosdick had written how Christianity had "stopped ancient curses like infanticide. It put an end to the . . . gladiatorial shows."

34. Martin Luther King phone call to Stanley Levison, May 23, 1963, *The King-Levison File*, 3–4.

35. Ibid.; *New York Post*, May 19, 1963; Martin Luther King Jr., "From the Birmingham Jail," *Christianity and Crisis*, May 27, 1963. King told Stanley Levison on May 23, 1963, that the *Times* had asked him to write another letter based on the section in the "Letter from Birmingham Jail," in which King expresses deep disappointment with the moderates and answers the charge of being an extremist. King phone call to Levison, May 23, 1963.

36. Memorandum by Barbara Moffett, May 8, 1963, AFSCA, Philadelphia, Pa.; memorandum by Fred Echelmeyer, May 13, 1963, AFSCA.

37. An accompanying press release noted that the letter had been written by King in "longhand on April 16 in his jail cell." Frederick Echelmeyer, American Friends Service Committee Press Release, May 28, 1963, AFSCA.

38. Martin Luther King Jr., *Letter from Birmingham Jail* (Philadelphia: American Friends Service Committee, 1963).

39. Harold Fey to Martin Luther King Jr., May 22, 1963, letter in possession of Dean Peerman, Chicago, Ill.

40. *Christian Century*, June 12, 1963; James F. Findlay, "Religion and Politics in the Sixties: The Churches and the Civil Rights Act of 1964," *Journal of American History* 77 (June 1990): 70 n.

41. Reese Cleghorn, "Martin Luther King, Jr.: Apostle of Crisis," *Saturday Evening Post*, June 15, 1963, pp. 15–19.

42. Martin Luther King Jr., "Letter from Birmingham City Jail," *New Leader*, June 24, 1963; "Between Issues," *New Leader*, April 4, 1988.

43. *Birmingham News*, July 30, 1963.

44. Martin Luther King Jr., "The Negro Is Your Brother," *Atlantic Monthly*, August 1963, 78; Martin Luther King, Jr., "A Letter from Birmingham Jail," *Ebony*, August 1963.

45. Stanley Levison phone call to Martin Luther King, May 18, 1963, *The King-Levison File*, 1; Martin Luther King phone call to Stanley Levison, May 19, 1963, *The King-Levison File*, 1–3; Jack O'Dell phone call to Stanley Levison, May 19, 1963, *The King-Levison File*, 1–2; Martin Luther King phone call to

Stanley Levison, May 21, 1963, *The King-Levison File*, 4–5; Martin Luther King phone call to Stanley Levison, May 23, 1963, *The King-Levison File*, 1–2.

46. Stanley Levison phone call to Clarence Jones, May 24, 1963, *The King-Levison File*, 1–2.

47. Martin Luther King phone call to Stanley Levison, May 23, 1963, *The King-Levison File*, 1–2.

48. Stanley Levison phone call to Martin Luther King, May 24, 1963, *The King-Levison File*, 1.

49. King, *Why We Can't Wait*, 78.

50. King, "Letter from Birmingham Jail," 2, Boutwell Papers; King, *Why We Can't Wait*, 79.

51. John Porter, interview by author, Birmingham, Ala., May 7, 1992, tape recording in possession of author.

52. Walker, interview; Flip Schultke and Penelope McPhee, *King Remembered* (New York: Pocket Books, 1986), 126; Young, *An Easy Burden*, 225.

53. Shuttlesworth, interview; Raines, *My Soul Is Rested*, 161; *Birmingham News*, April 17, 1988.

54. "*Playboy* Interview," in *A Testament of Hope: The Essential Writings and Speeches of Martin Luther King, Jr.*, ed. James Melvin Washington (San Francisco: HarperSanFrancisco, 1986), 351. Originally published in *Playboy*, January 1965.

55. Abernathy, quoted in *Birmingham News*, April 17, 1988; Abernathy, *And the Walls*, 254.

56. James A. Colaiaco, "The American Dream Unfulfilled: Martin Luther King, Jr., and the 'Letter from Birmingham Jail,'" *Phylon* 55 (spring 1984): 1; Haig A. Bosmajian and Hamida Bosmajian, *The Rhetoric of the Civil-Rights Movement* (New York: Random House, 1969), 16.

57. Charles Muscatine and Marlene Griffith, eds., *The Borzoi College Reader*, 3rd ed. (New York: Alfred A. Knopf, 1976); Taylor and Okada, eds., *The Craft of the Essay*, 310; Richard L. Lawson, *Rhetorical Guide to the Borzoi College Reader* (New York: Alfred A. Knopf, 1967), 84, 87.

58. Nicholas Wardey to King, June 19, 1963, SCLC Papers; Martin Gal to King, August 8, 1963, SCLC Papers. At a later date, Martin Luther King did record an audio version of the "Letter from Birmingham Jail."

59. Martin Luther King Jr., "Letter from a Birmingham Jail," music by Paul Reif (New York: Seesaw Music Corporation, 1963); John Scully, "Letter from Birmingham Jail: A Narrative for Soprano and Orchestra," 1994.

60. *Birmingham Post-Herald*, August 11, 1979.

61. Young, *An Easy Burden*, 224.

62. King, "Letter from Birmingham Jail," 20, Boutwell Papers.

63. Young, *An Easy Burden*, 190, 228; Walker, interview.

64. Carpenter et al., "White Ministers' Statement," January 16, 1963, Carpenter Papers.

65. Shuttlesworth, interview.

66. *Ibid.*

67. Shuttlesworth, quoted in Barr, "Rabbi Grafman and Birmingham," 25; Shuttlesworth, interview.

68. Barr, "Rabbi Grafman and Birmingham," 24.

69. Porter, interview; *Alabama Baptist,* March 18, 1993.

70. Abernathy quoted in *Birmingham News,* April 17, 1988; Abernathy, *And the Walls,* 256.

Chapter 8

1. Hardin, interview by Wright.

2. *Birmingham News,* April 2, 1972; Bishop Nolan Harmon, interview by author, tape recording, Atlanta, Ga., July 30, 1992.

3. Harmon, *Ninety Years,* 298-99.

4. *Ibid*; *Birmingham News,* June 5, 1989.

5. Harmon, *Ninety Years,* 298-99; *Methodist Christian Advocate,* June 11, 1963.

6. *Greensboro Daily News,* February 2, 1964.

7. *Ibid.*

8. Harmon, statement, n.d., Harmon Papers.

9. *Methodist Christian Advocate,* September 3, 1963.

10. *Ibid.* Harmon, *Ninety Years,* 299-300.

11. Harmon, *Ninety Years,* 310-11; *Atlanta Constitution,* June 10, 1993; Cannon, "Bishop Nolan B. Harmon," Harmon Papers.

12. Cannon, "Bishop Nolan B. Harmon."

13. *Alabama Churchman,* July 1962; *Birmingham News,* January 24, 1962.

14. Branch, *Parting the Waters,* 745.

15. Carpenter, Statement, n.d., Carpenter Papers.

16. Rt. Rev. C. Kilmer Myers to Carpenter, March 20, 1965, Carpenter Papers; Carpenter to C. Kilmer Myers, March 24, 1965, Carpenter Papers.

17. Newspaper clipping, n.d., Carpenter Papers; Carpenter to Richard S. Emrich, April 6, 1965, Carpenter Papers; *New York Times,* June 29, 1969.

18. Rabe Walters to Carpenter, n.d., Carpenter Papers.

19. Charles W. Eagles, *Outside Agitator: Jon Daniels and the Civil Rights Movement in Alabama* (Chapel Hill: University of North Carolina Press, 1993), 46-48.

20. Eagles, *Outside Agitator,* 46-47; Carpenter to Mrs. David N. McCullough, April 20, 1965, Carpenter Papers.

21. ESCRU Statement, April 29, 1965, Carpenter Papers; Eagles, *Outside Agitator,* 49-50.

22. Reverend John Morris to Directors, Chapter Chairman, and Members,

April 30, 1965, ESCRU Papers; ESCRU Staff to the Clergy of the Diocese of Alabama, May 1, 1965, ESCRU Papers; ESCRU brochure on Jonathan Daniels, Carpenter Papers; see also Eagles, *Outside Agitator.*

23. ESCRU brochure on Jonathan Daniels, Carpenter Papers.

24. Executive Council Press Release, May 1963, Carpenter Papers; Resolution of the Vestry of the Episcopal Church of the Nativity, Dothan, Ala., June 22, 1965, Carpenter Papers.

25. Jonathan Daniels, *The Jon Daniels Story* (New York: Seabury Press, 1967), 43.

26. Carpenter to T. Frank Mathews, August 12, 1965, Carpenter Papers; Carpenter to The Living Church, n.d., Carpenter Papers.

27. ESCRU brochure on Jonathan Daniels, Carpenter Papers; Daniels, *The Jon Daniels Story,* 48–50.

28. *Birmingham News,* October 2, 1965.

29. L. H. Foster to Carpenter, April 1, 1965, Carpenter Papers.

30. Vernon Jones, telephone conversation with author, June 17, 1998; Lewis Wade Jones to Carpenter, n.d., Carpenter Papers.

31. Peggy Rupp, interview by author, February 1, 1991, tape recording in possession of author; Murray telephone interview, February 8, 1991.

32. Murray, telephone interview, February 8, 1991; Carpenter, interview; *Alabama Churchman,* December 1968.

33. King, *Why We Can't Wait,* 89.

Chapter 9

1. Phillip L. Bereano to Grafman, May 19, 1963, Grafman Papers; Betty Norwind to Grafman, May 19, 1963, Grafman Papers; Gabe Sumner to Grafman, May 20, 1963, Grafman Papers; Grafman to Samuel Silver, June 26, 1963, Grafman Papers.

2. Grafman, Rosh Hashanah Sermon; Grafman, interview by Birmingham Public Library, August 19, 1977.

3. Dr. Lamar Jackson, quoted in Elovitz, *A Century of Jewish Life,* 151; Grafman, Rosh Hashanah Sermon; Grafman, interview by Birmingham Public Library, August 19, 1977; Grafman to Kivie Kaplan, June 14, 1963, Grafman Papers.

4. *New York Times,* May 9, 1963.

5. Karl B. Friedman to Stephen Grafman, October 17, 1995, copy in possession of author.

6. *Ibid.*; Branch, *Parting the Waters,* 785.

7. Grafman to Samuel Silver, June 26, 1963, Grafman Papers.

8. *Ibid.*

9. Grafman, notes, n.d., Grafman Papers.

10. Grafman to Samuel Silver, June 26, 1963, Grafman Papers.

11. Grafman, notes to untitled speech presented at the annual meeting of the Reform Jewish congregation, Columbus, Ohio, March 22, 1964, Grafman Papers; Grafman, Rosh Hashanah Sermon.

12. Edward LaMonte, *Politics and Welfare in Birmingham, 1900–1975* (Tuscaloosa: University of Alabama Press, 1995), 185–86; *Birmingham News,* May 13, 1963.

13. LaMonte, *Politics and Welfare in Birmingham,* 185–86; Corley, "The Quest," 276–78.

14. *Catholic Week,* September 3, 1963.

15. Branch, *Parting the Waters,* 888–89; *Birmingham News,* September 3, 4, 9, 1963.

16. *Catholic Week,* September 13, 1963. The new Presbyterian moderator, John M. Crowell, had replaced Ramage; see Appendix 4.

17. *Birmingham News,* September 9, 1963; *Catholic Week,* September 13, 1963.

18. C. C. J. Carpenter et al. to Robert Arthur, September 13, 1963, Grafman Papers.

19. Townsend Davis, *Weary Feet, Rested Souls* (New York: W. W. Norton, 1998), 84; see also Petric J. Smith, *Long Time Coming: An Insider's Story of the Birmingham Church Bombing That Rocked the World* (Birmingham: Crane Hill Publishers, 1994).

20. *Birmingham News,* September 21, 1963; Branch, *Parting the Waters,* 892; Paul Hemphill, *Leaving Birmingham: Notes of a Native Son* (New York: Viking Press, 1993), 162–63; Durick, interview, February 21, 1992; Porter, quoted in Barr, "Rabbi Grafman and Birmingham," 37.

21. King, "Eulogy for the Martyred Children," 221–23.

22. Grafman, Rosh Hashanah sermon.

23. *Ibid.*

24. *Ibid.*

25. *Ibid.*

26. *Ibid.*

27. *Ibid.*

28. Grafman, Rosh Hashanah Kaddish, September 19, 1963, tape recording in possession of author.

29. Julie Monsky to Grafman, September 19, 1963, Grafman Papers; Grafman to Irving Engel, October 7, 1963, Grafman Papers.

30. *Birmingham News,* October 10, 1964; *New York Times,* May 27, 1965; *United Klans of America, Incorporated, v. The Birmingham News et al.,* May 13, 1965, Tenth Judicial Circuit of Alabama, Jefferson County, Ala.; Stephen Grafman, letter to author, April 21, 1997.

31. Stephen Grafman, letter to author, April 21, 1997; *Birmingham News,* May 3, 1983.

32. Grafman, interview, March 1, 1991; Grafman, interview by Birmingham Public Library, July 27, 1977.

33. *Birmingham News,* September 24, 1963.

34. Harmon, *Ninety Years,* 299.

35. Durick, interview, February 21, 1992; Father Joseph Allen, telephone conversation with the author, Athens, Ala., January 28, 1993; Alabama File, Presidential Briefing Paper, Birmingham Crisis, Burke Marshall Papers, copies in BPLDAM. Earl Stallings scribbled down his impressions of the meeting. He noted that Kennedy wore a dark suit, a gray tie with spots, and a white shirt with stripes. The president was relaxed and gave "no suggestion of hurry." Stallings, "Interview with President," September 23, 1963, Stallings Papers.

36. Notes for White House Meeting, September 23, 1963, Durick Papers; Durick, interview, May 8, 1992; William Martin: *A Prophet with Honor: The Billy Graham Story* (New York: William Morrow, 1991), 312. Billy Graham held an integrated United Evangelistic Rally on Easter Sunday 1964. Threats of violence limited the crowd to thirty-five thousand in the sixty-thousand-plus Legion Field football stadium. The crowd, about fifty-fifty white-black, listened to Graham's sermon, "The Great Reconciliation."

37. Stallings, "Interview with President," September 23, 1963, Stallings Papers.

38. Garrow, *Bearing the Cross,* 296 and 678 n. 6; Murray, interview, March 21, 1995; Joseph Allen, interview by Sister Rose Sevenich, transcript, Catholic Diocese of Birmingham (Ala.) Archives, October 2, 1992.

39. Murray et al., statement, Durick Papers; *Birmingham News,* September 24, 1963.

40. Durick, interview, May 8, 1992; Joseph Allen, telephone interview.

41. Durick, interview, May 8, 1992. Bishop Durick always enjoyed telling a joke about the difference between an auxiliary bishop and a coadjutor. An auxiliary bishop shakes hands with the reigning bishop and asks, "What can I do for you?" While the coadjutor shakes hands with the reigning bishop and asks, "How are you feeling today?"

42. *Nashville Tennessean,* March 4, 1964.

43. Durick, interview, May 8, 1992; *New York Times,* November 11, 1969; Durick to Thomas J. Elliott, January 26, 1971, Durick Papers; *Tennessee Register,* July 4, 1994; *New York Times,* July 28, 1994.

44. Pope John XXIII, Encyclical, "Pacem in Terris," Durick Papers.

45. Bishop Joseph A. Durick, untitled sermon delivered at the Catholic Nurses' Convention Banquet at St. Joseph's Hospital, Memphis, Tenn., April 27, 1968, Durick Papers; *New York Times,* June 28, 1994; *Tennessee Register,* July 4, 1994.

46. Joseph Allen, telephone conversation; *Tennessee Register,* July 4, 1994; Durick interview, May 8, 1992.

47. *Nashville Tennessean*, May 4, 1969; Durick, interview, May 8, 1992.

48. *Nashville Tennessean*, May 4, 1969. Adrian never mentioned Durick by name.

49. Thomas Stritch, *The Catholic Church in Tennessee: The Sesquicentennial Story* (Nashville: Catholic Center, 1987), 333–36.

50. *Tennessee Register*, July 4, 1994.

51. *Nashville Tennessean*, September 11, 1964.

52. Durick, untitled sermon preached at Christ Church, place unknown, March 14, 1968, Durick Papers.

53. Durick, "A Council Summary," n.d., Durick Papers.

54. An obvious reference to the group of behind-the-scenes advisers used by President Andrew Jackson in the 1820s and 1830s.

55. *Tennessee Register*, July 4, 1994; John Seigenthaler, telephone conversation with author, June 22, 1998.

56. Durick, interview, May 8, 1992; *Memphis Commercial Appeal*, April 21, 1966; *Nashville Banner*, March 2, 1967.

57. *Nashville Tennessean*, May 4, 1969.

58. Joseph A. Durick, "Talk," paper presented at Project Equality Luncheon and Business Meeting, January 25, 1968, Durick Papers; *Fort Worth Star-Telegram*, December 1, 1975.

59. Joan Turner Beifuss, *At the River I Stand* (Memphis: St. Luke's Press, 1990), 273; Harriet Verrell to Durick, March 23, 1968, Durick Papers.

60. Durick, untitled homily presented at the Convention of Serra International, July 1, 1970, Durick Papers.

61. Durick, untitled sermon presented at Memorial Mass for Dr. Martin Luther King Jr. at Immaculate Conception Church, Memphis, Tenn., April 6, 1968, Durick Papers.

62. *Nashville Tennessean*, April 6, 1968; Beifuss, *At the River I Stand*, 416; *Memphis Commercial Appeal*, April 7, 1968. Durick also sent out a pastoral letter to be read at Sunday masses throughout the state.

63. Durick, untitled sermon presented at the Martin Luther King Memorial Service, Memphis, Tenn., April 4, 1969, Durick Papers; *Tennessee Register*, May 4, 1969.

64. *Memphis Press-Scimitar*, May 10, 1969; *Nashville Tennessean*, May 4, 1969.

65. Durick, interview, May 8, 1992; *Nashville Tennessean*, May 4, 1969 *National Register*, May 10, 1969; Durick, untitled "remarks" presented to Kiwanis International meeting in Memphis, Tenn., on February 11, 1970, Durick Papers.

66. Durick, Kiwanis remarks; *Nashville Banner*, September 10, 1969.

67. *Memphis Commercial-Appeal*, November 10, 1969.

68. *Tennessee Register*, July 4, 1994.

69. *Memphis Commercial-Appeal,* December 24, 1969; *Tennessee Register,* July 4, 1994.

70. *Memphis Commercial-Appeal,* December 24, 1969; *Tennessee Register,* July 4, 1994.

71. Newspaper clipping, n.d., Durick Papers; *One Voice,* April 11, 1975; Joseph Durick, "Jailhouse Blues," *Liguorian,* July 1974.

72. The Most Reverend Joseph A. Durick, "Humanity Demands It," n.d, Durick Papers.

73. Newspaper clipping, n.d., Durick Papers; Durick, interview, May 8, 1992.

74. The Reverend Monsignor Robert Trisco, letter to author, November 7, 1997; anonymous, telephone conversation with author, May 15, 1998. Durick relinquished his administrative duties, but he retained the title of bishop, although he was no longer the bishop of Nashville.

75. *Tennessee Register,* April 14, 1975; *Nashville Tennessean,* May 19, 1975; *Catholic Week,* April 11, 1975.

76. Clipping from *National Catholic Reporter,* n.d., Durick Papers.

77. *Tennessee Register,* March 19, 1990; Durick, interview, May 8, 1992.

78. Durick, conversation with author, May 25, 1994; *Birmingham News,* June 27, 1994; *Tennessee Register,* July 4, 1994.

79. *Fort Worth Star-Telegram,* December 1, 1975.

80. King, "Letter from Birmingham Jail," Boutwell Papers.

81. Alabama File, Presidential Briefing Paper, Birmingham Crisis, September 1963, Marshall Papers.

82. *Birmingham News,* April 17, 1988; Murray, interview, March 1, 1991.

83. Murray, interview, March 1, 1991; *Alabama Churchman,* March 1969; Barr, "Rabbi Grafman and Birmingham," 29.

84. Murray, interview, February 8, 1991; Murray to Kenneth J. Sharp, July 16, 1965, Carpenter Papers.

85. Grafman, Group Relations Committee Files, Grafman Papers; LaMonte, *Politics and Welfare,* 188; Doug Carpenter, interview.

86. Community Affairs Committee on Group Relations Minutes, October 25, 1963, Grafman Papers.

87. Grafman, interview, March 1, 1991; Durick to Mayor Albert Boutwell, October 12, 1963, Durick Papers.

88. LaMonte, *Politics and Welfare,* 189.

89. *Ibid.;* Murray to John Hines, July 27, 1965, Carpenter Papers.

90. Carpenter to Sam W. Pipes III, June 8, 1964, Carpenter Papers.

91. Murray to Patricia Houtz, June 25, 1964, Carpenter Papers; Murray to George A. Mattison Jr., July 20, 1964, Carpenter Papers; *Alabama Churchman,* August 1964.

92. Murray to Houtz, June 25, 1964; Murray to James M. Hackney, July 9, 1964, Carpenter Papers; Murray to Hackney, July 30, 1964, Carpenter Papers.

93. Mrs. Woodrow Ivey to Carpenter, September 2, 1964, Carpenter Papers.

94. Murray to Francis B. Wakefield Jr., July 29, 1964.

95. Martin, *A Prophet with Honor,* 294, 219; Mark Noll et al., *Eerdmans' Handbook to Christianity in America* (Grand Rapids: William B. Eerdmans, 1983), 429; Thelma Strange to Carpenter, August 15, 1964, Carpenter Papers; James Hackney to Murray, July 27, 1964.

96. Murray to James M. Hackney, June 27, 1964, Carpenter Papers; Murray to J. C. Hodges Jr., June 2, 1964, May 26, 1964, Carpenter Papers.

97. *Journal of the General Convention of the Protestant Episcopal Church in the United States of America,* St. Louis, Mo., October 12–23, 1964, pp. 59–60.

98. Murray, interview, February 8, 1991.

99. *Alabama Churchman,* March 1969; Barr, "Rabbi Grafman," 29; Murray to J. C. Hodges Jr., May 5, 1964, Carpenter Papers.

100. Murray to Henry Knox Sherill, April 2, 1965.

101. *Ibid.;* Murray, interview, March 1, 1991; Murray to James R. Gundrum, April 12, 1965.

102. Murray to George L. Cadigan, April 5, 1965, Carpenter Papers.

103. *Ibid.;* Murray to John E. Hines, March 25, 1965.

104. Murray to Cadigan, April 5, 1965; Murray to Hunter Flack, April 5, 1965; Murray to Charles Morgan Jr., September 13, 1965.

105. *Alabama Churchman,* March 1969.

106. Hardin, interview by Wright.

107. *Ibid.;* Charles H. Lippy, "Towards an Inclusive Church: South Carolina Methodism and Race, 1972–1982" in *Rethinking Methodist History: A Bicentennial Historical Consultation,* ed. Russell E. Richey and Kenneth E. Row (Nashville: Kingswood Books, 1983), 220–21; Hardin, "Race and the Methodist Church: The Southeastern Jurisdiction," April 1965, Hardin Papers.

108. Hardin, interview by Wright.

109. *Ibid.;* Lippy, "Towards an Inclusive Church," 221.

110. Paul Hardin Jr., telephone conversation with author, October 19, 1992.

Chapter 10

1. *New York Times,* September 27, 1959.

2. Edward Ramage, "Let's Go to the Farm," unpublished article, n.d., Ramage Papers.

3. Ford, telephone conversation.

4. *Ibid.*

5. *Nashville Tennessean,* October 7, 1963.

6. Ann Fleming Deagon to Ramage, June 30, 1963, Ramage Papers; illegible to Ramage, June 24, 1963, Ramage Papers.

7. Love, interview, February 2, 1995; Calendar for 1963, Ramage Papers.

8. Minutes of a Congregational Meeting, December 8, 1963, First Presbyterian Records.

9. Harold Walker to Thomas F. Williams Jr., January 24, 1964, First Presbyterian Records; newspaper clipping, *Birmingham News,* n.d., Ramage Papers.

10. Edward Ramage, "I Confess," n.d., Ramage Papers.

11. *Ibid.*

12. Love, telephone conversation, August 9, 1998.

13. *Ibid.*

14. Stallings, letter to author, July 7, 1995; Billy Allen, interview by author, August 9, 1998, transcript in possession of author.

15. *Birmingham News,* May 13, 1963.

16. Chandler, conversation; Darold Morgan, telephone conversation with the author, August 12, 1998; Stallings, letter to author, July 11, 1995.

17. Minutes from Deacons' Meeting, May 15, 1963, FBCB Papers; Notes from deacons' meetings, May 1963, Chandler Papers; Billy Allen, interview.

18. Minutes of a Special Church Conference, May 22, 1963, FBCB Papers.

19. *Ibid.*

20. *Ibid.;* Simmons, telephone interview.

21. Simmons, telephone interview; Billy Allen, interview.

22. Billy Allen, interview; Stallings to Bill Gaventa, October 8, 1963, Stallings Papers.

23. Stallings, "Pilate's Wash Bowl," sermon delivered at First Baptist Church, Birmingham, May 19, 1963, copy in possession of author.

24. *Ibid.*

25. Billy Allen, interview.

26. *Ibid.;* Minutes from Deacons' Meeting, September 11, 1963, FBCB Papers.

27. Billy Allen, interview; Simmons, telephone interview.

28. Billy Allen, interview; Simmons, telephone interview.

29. Stallings, conversation with author, May 4, 1992; Morgan, telephone conversation.

30. Lawson and Story, "First Baptist Church Centennial."

31. Simmons, telephone interview.

32. *Ibid.;* Marvin Spry, conversation with author, August 17, 1998.

33. Simmons, telephone interview.

34. *Ibid.* Billy Allen, interview.

35. Stallings, "Where Shall I Begin."

36. *Ibid.;* Earl Stallings, *Senior Adults: Finding Life's Meaning* (Nashville: Broadman Press, 1990); *Baptist Beacon,* September 15, 1977; *Vista,* winter 1996.

37. Stallings, "Where Shall I Begin."

38. Lawson and Story, "First Baptist Church Centennial," 26–27.

39. *Ibid.*; McGinnis, "Controversy," 23.

40. McGinnis, "Controversy," 58–59.

41. "First Baptist Church Invites You to Become Involved," FBCB Papers.

42. McGinnis, "Controversy," 28–34.

43. *Ibid.*; *Christian Century,* December 2, 1970.

44. McGinnis, "Controversy," 28–34; *Christian Century,* December 2, 1970.

45. *Southern Shofar,* July 1995; J. Herbert Gilmore, Jr., *They Chose to Live: The Racial Agony of an American Church* (Grand Rapids: William B. Eerdmans, 1972), 59.

46. Newspaper Clipping Files, Baptist Churches, Birmingham, First Baptist, Tutwiler Collection; Flynt, *Alabama Baptists,* 594; *Alabama Baptist,* August 7, 1980.

Conclusion

1. None of several people I asked who had been involved in designing the exhibits at the institute had any recollection of a conscious effort to leave the names of the eight off the display.

2. Woodward, *Strange Career,* 166.

3. Dabbs, *The Southern Heritage,* 3.

4. McGill, "The Southern Moderates," 245–46.

5. By 1965 only Carpenter, Murray, and Grafman remained. When Murray moved to Mobile in 1971, Grafman was the only clergyman left.

6. *Time,* January 3, 1964.

7. Young quote in Garrow, *Bearing the Cross,* 264; Shuttlesworth, quoted in Rigsby, "A Rhetorical Clash," 173.

8. "Birmingham and Beyond," *New South,* October-November 1963, 18.

9. Willie Hunter to William S. Thompson, May 27, 1963, SCLC Papers.

10. "Rev. King to Come to Danville," *Freedom Banner,* September 29, 1963, in possession of Avon Rollins, Knoxville, Tenn.

11. David Garrow, *Protest at Selma: Martin Luther King, Jr., and the Voting Rights Act of 1965* (New Haven: Yale University Press, 1978), 52–53; John Lewis, *Walking the Wind: A Memoir of the Movement* (New York: Simon and Schuster, 1998), 314.

12. Garrow, *Protest at Selma,* 52–53.

13. *Ibid.,* 164–65.

14. Martin Luther King Jr., *Where Do We Go from Here: Chaos or Community?* (Boston: Beacon Press, 1968), 32; Hamilton, "Blacks and Mass Media," 228–29.

15. Hamilton, "Blacks and Mass Media," 228–29; Lyle, *The Black American,* 30.

16. *Walker v. City of Birmingham* (1967).

17. Ibid.

18. "Birmingham Revisited," *Time,* November 10, 1967; Garrow, *Bearing the Cross,* 379-80.

19. *Birmingham News,* April 7, 8, 1968; "Can Birmingham Break with Its Past?" *Business Week,* March 15, 1969.

20. "The Change in Birmingham," *Newsweek,* December 8, 1969. Ironically, Bull Connor happened to visit the council chambers the day Shores was sworn in.

21. Corley, "The Quest," 271–72.

22. "The Change in Birmingham."

23. Fred L. Shuttlesworth, "Birmingham Revisited," *Ebony,* August 1971; *New York Times,* September 7, 1979.

24. "Bull at Bay," *Newsweek,* April 15, 1963.

Epilogue

1. *New York Times,* March 4, 2006.

2. J. Mills Thornton, *Dividing Lines: Municipal Politics and the Struggle for Civil Rights in Montgomery, Birmingham, and Selma* (Tuscaloosa: University of Alabama Press, 2002), 2; Jason Sokal, *There Goes My Everything: White Southerners in the Age of Civil Rights, 1945–1975* (New York: Vintage Press, 2007), 15.

3. Sokal, *There Goes My Everything,* 15; Flynt, *Alabama Baptists,* 594–95.

4. *Birmingham News,* February 2, 1913.

5. *Birmingham News,* October 16, 1911, April 23, 1942, May 6, 1941.

6. *Louisville Times,* May 22, 1963; Newspaper clippings, n.p., n.d., Henlee Hulix Barnette Papers, in possession of author.

7. David L. Chappell, *A Stone of Hope: Prophetic Religion and the Death of Jim Crow* (Chapel Hill: University of North Carolina Press, 2005), 132; Wesley Shrader, "Segregation in the Churches," *Esquire,* May 1, 1958.

8. *Louisville Times,* May 22, 1963; *Courier-Journal,* November 9, 1957.

9. Chappell, *A Stone of Hope,* 138; *Louisville Times,* May 22, 1963.

10. James Thomas Ford, telephone conversations with author, June 12, 1995, September 6, 1995; Grady Cothen, telephone conversation with author, June 16, 1995.

11. Cothen, telephone conversation, June 16, 1995.

12. Earl Stallings, telephone conversation with author, June 16, 1995.

13. W. E. Burghardt Du Bois, "Strivings of the Negro People," *Atlantic Monthly,* August 1897.

14. Earl Stallings to author, May 30, 2001, in possession of author; William Nunnelley, "I Felt the Bitterness of 37 Years Begin to Lift from My Soul," *Seasons* (Samford University), Summer 2001, p. 2.

15. Earl Stallings, interview by author, tape recording, Birmingham, Ala., May 26, 2001.

16. *Ibid.*

17. *Ibid.*; T. B. Maston, *Of One: A Study of Christian Principles and Race Relations* (Atlanta: Home Mission Board, Southern Baptist Convention, 1946), 9.

18. Stallings, interview, May 26, 2001.

19. *Ibid.*

20. *Ibid.*

21. *Ibid.*

22. *Ibid.*; Fred L. Shuttlesworth, interview by author, tape recording, Birmingham, Ala., March 20, 2003.

23. Stallings, interview, May 26, 2001.

24. *Ibid.*

25. *Ibid.*

26. *Ibid.*; Sessions, "Are Southern Ministers Failing the South?" 37, 82–88.

27. Stallings, interview, May 26, 2001.

28. *Ibid.*

29. Associated Baptist Press, March 6, 2006; *Los Angeles Times*, March 21, 2006; *New York Times*, March 4, 2006.

30. *Christian Century*, March 12, 1970.

31. Martin Luther King Jr., "The Church on the Frontier of Racial Tension," (address, Southern Baptist Theological Seminary, Louisville, Ky., April 19, 1961), https://digital.library.sbts.edu/bitstream/handle/10392/2751/King-ChurchOnFrontier.pdf?sequence=1&isAllowed=y

32. Henlee Hulix Barnette, "The Southern Baptist Theological Seminary and the Civil Rights Movement: The Visit of Martin Luther King, Jr., Part Two," *Review and Expositor* 93 (1996): 77–126.

33. Jeff Robinson, "Henlee Barnette, Southern Ethics Professor from 1952–77, Dies," baptistpress.com, October 22, 2004, https://www.baptistpress.com/resource-library/news/henlee-barnette-southern-ethics-professor-from-1952-77-dies/.

34. Carter Dalton Lyon, *Sanctuaries of Segregation: The Story of the Jackson Church Visit Campaign* (Oxford: University Press of Mississippi, 2017), 100–101.

35. Newspaper clipping, n.p., n.d., Barnette Papers.

36. *Christian Index*, August 4, 1966; *Atlanta Constitution*, September 27, 1966; Sam Oni, interview by Melody An, Sean Kennedy, Alden Moore, Megan Rutherford, and Diandra Walker, transcript, Macon, Ga., April 22, 2009, http://faculty.mercer.edu/davis_da/fys102/Sam_Oni.pdf; periodical clipping, n.p., ca. 1966, Barnette Papers.

37. Martin Luther King Jr., "America's Chief Moral Dilemma" (speech, Hungry Club Forum, Atlanta, Ga., May 10, 1967), https://www.theatlantic.com/magazine

/archive/2018/02/martin-luther-king-hungry-club-forum/552533/; Page H. Kelly to All Members of the [Southern] Seminary Faculty, March 21, 1969, Barnette Papers.

38. Newspaper clipping, n.p., ca. 1967, Barnette Papers.

39. *Christian Index,* March 12, 1970, Barnette Papers.

40. Hill, *Southern Churches in Crisis,* x; *Courier-Journal,* November 9, 1957.

41. Newspaper clipping, n.p., March 19, 1971, Barnette Papers.

42. Flynt, *Alabama Baptists,* 595.

43. *New York Times,* June 21, 1995.

44. Charles T. Carter, interview by Evan Musgraves, digital recording and transcript, Birmingham, Ala., September 13, 2013, Samford University Oral History Collection, Birmingham; Fred Hobson, *But Now I See: The White Southern Racial Conversion Narrative* (Baton Rouge: Louisiana State University Press, 1999), 1–17.

45. Hobson, *But Now I See,* 1–17.

46. Charles T. Carter, interview by Timothy George, Birmingham, Ala., June 4, 2019, Beeson Podcast (Episode 447), https://www.beesondivinity.com /podcast/2019/transcripts/beeson-podcast-episode-447-carter.txt; Carter, interview by Evan Musgraves, September 13, 2013.

47. *Alabama Baptist,* January 16, 2015.

48. Edward Gilbreath, *Birmingham Revolution: Martin Luther King Jr.'s Epic Challenge to the Church* (Downers Grove, Ill.: InterVarsity Press, 2013), 83–85.

Afterword

1. Gunnar Myrdal, *An American Dilemma: The Negro Problem and Modern Democracy* (New York: Harper and Bros., 1944), 440; James W. Silver, *Mississippi: The Closed Society* (New York: Harcourt, Brace and World, 1964), 44.

2. David L. Cohn, "How the South Feels," *Atlantic Monthly* 173 (January 1944): 48–51; Morton Sosna, *In Search of the Silent South: Southern Liberals and the Race Issue* (New York: Columbia University Press, 1977), 110.

3. Carter is quoted in Benjamin O. Sperry, "Caught Between Our Moral and Material Selves: Mississippi's Elite White Moderates and Their Role in Changing Race Relations, 1945–1956" (Ph.D. diss., Case Western Reserve University, 2010), 44n56.

4. See p. 236.

5. Calvin Trillin, "Reflections: Remembrance of Moderates Past," *The New Yorker* (March 21, 1977): 86.

6. See p. 236.

7. Numan V. Bartley, *The New South: 1945–1980* (Baton Rouge: Louisiana State University Press, 1995), 338.

8. See p. 145.

9. James W. Findlay, review of *Blessed Are the Peacemakers,* by S. Jonathan Bass, *Journal of American History,* 89 (September 2002): 722; see p. 145; Paul Griffin, review of *Blessed Are the Peacemakers,* by S. Jonathan Bass, *Anglican and Episcopal History,* 71 (December 2002): 584–85.

Appendix 3

1. Bishop Paul Hardin's name was missing from the early-version text.
2. No paragraph break in the early-version text.
3. No paragraph break in the early-version text.
4. New paragraph break in the early-version text.
5. No paragraph break in the early-version text.
6. *Sic.*
7. No paragraph break in the early-version text.
8. Handwritten alteration in the early-version text.
9. *Sic.*
10. Handwritten alteration in the early-version text.
11. *Sic.*
12. *Sic.*
13. No paragraph break in the early-version text.
14. Handwritten alteration in the early-version text.
15. No paragraph break in the early-version text.
16. *Sic.*
17. Handwritten alteration in the early-version text.
18. Quotation marks missing in early-version text.
19. *Sic.*
20. Handwritten alteration in the early-version text.

Bibliography

Manuscript Sources

American Friends Service Committee Collection. University Library, Special Collections, University of Illinois at Chicago, Chicago, Ill.

American Friends Service Committee. Papers. American Friends Service Committee Archives, Philadelphia, Pa.

Birmingham Ministers Discussion Group. Papers. Samford University Special Collection, Birmingham, Ala.

Barnette, Henlee Hulix. Papers. Copies in possession of author.

Boutwell, Albert Burton. Mayoral Papers. Birmingham Public Library Department of Archives and Manuscripts, Birmingham, Ala.

Carpenter, Charles Colcock Jones. Papers. Birmingham Public Library Department of Archives and Manuscripts, Birmingham, Ala.

Catholic Diocese of Birmingham Archives. Birmingham, Ala.

Chandler, John. Papers. Copies in possession of author.

Connor, Eugene "Bull." Papers. Birmingham Public Library Department of Archives and Manuscripts, Birmingham, Ala.

Coordinating Council of Social Forces. Papers. Birmingham Public Library Department of Archives and Manuscripts, Birmingham, Ala.

Durick, Joseph Aloysius. Papers. Copies in possession of author.

Episcopal Society for Cultural and Racial Unity (ESCRU). Papers. Martin Luther King Center for Nonviolent Social Change, Inc., Archives, Atlanta, Ga.

First Baptist Church, Birmingham. Church Conference and Deacon Minutes. Samford University Special Collection, Birmingham, Ala.

First Presbyterian Church, Birmingham. Records. Birmingham Public Library Department of Archives and Manuscripts, Birmingham, Ala.

Grafman, Milton L. Papers. In possession of Stephen Grafman, Potomac, Md.

Hardin, Paul, Jr. Papers. World Methodist Archives, Lake Junaluska, N.C.

Harmon, Nolan B. Papers. Pitts Theological Library, Archives and Manuscripts, Emory University, Atlanta, Ga.

Jefferson County Coordinating Council on Special Forces. Papers. Birmingham Public Library Department of Archives and Manuscripts, Birmingham, Ala.

King, Martin Luther, Jr. Papers. Martin Luther King Center for Nonviolent Social Change, Inc., Archives, Atlanta, Ga.

Marshall, Burke. Papers. Copies in Birmingham Public Library Department of Archives and Manuscripts, Birmingham, Ala.

Ministers' Discussion Group. Papers. Samford University Special Collection, Birmingham, Ala.

Newspaper Clipping Files. Birmingham Public Library Tutwiler Collection of Southern History and Literature, Birmingham, Ala.

Protestant Pastors Union. Papers. Birmingham Public Library Department of Archives and Manuscripts, Birmingham, Ala.

Ramage, Edward V. Papers. Copies in possession of author.

Southern Christian Leadership Conference. Papers. Martin Luther King Center for Nonviolent Social Change, Inc., Archives, Atlanta, Ga.

Southern Regional Council. Papers. Copies in Birmingham Public Library Department of Archives and Manuscripts, Birmingham, Ala.

Stallings, Earl. Earl Stallings to author, May 30, 2001. In possession of author.

Stallings, Earl. Papers. Southern Baptist Archives, Nashville, Tenn.

Temple Emanu-El. Papers. Birmingham Public Library Department of Archives and Manuscripts, Birmingham, Ala.

Books, Articles, Pamphlets, and Microfilm Editions

Abernathy, Ralph David. *And the Walls Came Tumbling Down.* New York: Harper and Row, 1989.

Alvis, Joel L., Jr. *Religion and Race: Southern Presbyterians, 1946–1983.* Tuscaloosa: University of Alabama Press, 1994.

Amaker, Norman. "De Facto Leadership and the Civil Rights Movement: Perspective on the Problems and Role of Activists in Legal and Social Change." *Southern University Law Review* 16 (1989): 1–54.

Ashmore, Harry S. *An Epitaph for Dixie.* New York: W. W. Norton, 1957.

———. *The Man in the Middle.* Columbia, Mo.: University of Missouri Press, 1966.

———. *Hearts and Minds: The Anatomy of Racism from Roosevelt to Reagan.* New York: McGraw-Hill, 1982.

Atkins, Leah Rawls. *The Valley and the Hills: An Illustrated History of Birmingham and Jefferson County.* Birmingham: Windsor Publications, 1981.

Bailey, Kenneth K. *Southern White Protestantism in the Twentieth Century.* New York: Harper and Row, 1964.

Baldwin, Lewis V. "'Let Us Break Bread Together': Martin Luther King, Jr., and the Black Church in the South, 1954–1968." In *Cultural Perspectives on the American South,* ed. Charles Reagan Wilson, 5:119–42. New York: Gordon and Breach, 1991.

Barr, Terry. "Rabbi Grafman and Birmingham's Civil Rights Era." Paper presented at symposium on Southern Rabbis' Involvement in Black Civil Rights, Memphis, Tenn., April 1995.

Barnette, Henlee Hulix. "The Southern Baptist Theological Seminary and the Civil Rights Movement: The Visit of Martin Luther King, Jr., Part Two." *Review and Expositor* 93 (1996): 77–126.

Bartley, Numan V. *The Rise of Massive Resistance: Race and Politics in the South During the 1950's.* Baton Rouge: Louisiana State University Press, 1978.

———. *The New South: 1945–1980.* Baton Rouge: Louisiana State University Press, 1995.

Bass, S. Jonathan. "Bishop C. C. J. Carpenter: From Segregation to Integration." *The Alabama Review* 45 (July 1992): 184–215.

———. "Not Time Yet: Alabama's Episcopal Bishop and the End of Segregation in the Deep South." *Anglican and Episcopal History* 63 (June 1994): 235–59.

Bedau, Hugo Adam, ed. *Civil Disobedience in Focus.* New York: Routledge, 1991.

Beifuss, Joan Turner. *At the River I Stand.* Memphis: St. Luke's Press, 1990.

Beiman, Irving. "Birmingham: Steel Giant with a Glass Jaw." In *Our Fair City,* ed. Robert S. Allen, 99–122. New York: Vanguard Press, 1947.

Boles, John B., ed. *Dixie Dateline: A Journalistic Portrait of the Contemporary South.* Houston: Rice University Studies, 1983.

Boorstin, Daniel. *The Image: A Guide to Pseudo-Events in America.* New York: Atheneum, 1961.

Bosmajian, Haig A. "Rhetoric of Martin Luther King's 'Letter from Birmingham Jail.'" *Midwest Quarterly* 8 (1967): 126–143.

Bosmajian, Haig A., and Hamida Bosmajian, eds. *The Rhetoric of the Civil-Rights Movement.* New York: Random House, 1969.

Bowen, David. *The Struggle Within: Race Relations in the United States.* New York: W. W. Norton, 1965.

Boyle, Sarah Patton. *The Desegregated Heart: A Virginian's Stand in Time of Transition.* New York: William Morrow, 1962.

Bradford, Daniel, ed. *Black, White, and Gray: Twenty-one Points of View on the Race Question.* New York: Sheed and Ward, 1964.

Brady, Tom. *Black Monday.* Pamphlet, n.d., Samford University Special Collection, Birmingham, Ala.

Branch, Taylor. *Parting the Waters: America in the King Years, 1954–63*. New York: Simon and Schuster, 1988.

Brinkley, David. *11 Presidents, 4 Wars, 22 Political Conventions, 1 Moon Landing, 3 Assassinations, 2,000 Weeks of News and Other Stuff on Television and 18 Years of Growing Up in North Carolina*. New York: Alfred A. Knopf, 1995.

Brown, Ina Corinne. *Understanding Race Relations*. Englewood Cliffs, N.J.: Prentice-Hall, 1973.

Brown, Joe David. "Birmingham, Alabama: A City in Fear." *Saturday Evening Post*, March 2, 1963, pp. 11–19.

Brownell, Blaine A. "Birmingham, Alabama: New South City in the 1920s." *Journal of Southern History* 38 (February 1972): 21–48.

Caldwell, Erskine. *In Search of Bisco*. New York: Farrar, Straus, and Giroux, 1965.

Calloway-Thomas, Carolyn, and John Louis Lucaites, eds. *Martin Luther King, Jr., and the Sermonic Power of Public Discourse*. Tuscaloosa: University of Alabama Press, 1993.

Campbell, Will D. "The Role of Religion in Segregation Crisis." *New South* 15 (January 1960): 3–11.

Campbell, Will D., and James Y. Holloway, eds. *The Failure and the Hope: Essays of Southern Churchmen*. Grand Rapids: William B. Eerdmans, 1972.

Canzoneri, Robert. *"I Do So Politely": A Voice from the South*. Boston: Houghton Mifflin, 1965.

Carter, Hodding. *First Person Rural*. Garden City, N.Y.: Doubleday, 1963.

Cartwright, Colbert S. "The Church, the World, and Race." *New South* 11 (October 1956): 10–12.

Cash, W. J. *The Mind of the South*. New York: Vintage Books, 1941.

Chalmers, David M. *Hooded Americanism: The History of the Ku Klux Klan*. New York: New Viewpoints, 1976.

Chappell, David L. *Inside Agitators: White Southerners in the Civil Rights Movement*. Baltimore and London: Johns Hopkins University Press, 1994.

———. *A Stone of Hope: Prophetic Religion and the Death of Jim Crow*. Chapel Hill: University of North Carolina Press, 2005.

Clark, E. Culpepper. "The American Dilemma in King's 'Letter from Birmingham Jail.' " In *Martin Luther King, Jr., and the Sermonic Power of Public Discourse*, ed. Carolyn Calloway-Thomas and John Louis Lucaites, 33–49. Tuscaloosa: University of Alabama Press, 1993.

Cobb, James C. *The Selling of the South*. Baton Rouge: Louisiana State University Press, 1983.

Colaiaco, James A. "The American Dream Unfulfilled: Martin Luther King, Jr., and the 'Letter from Birmingham Jail.'" *Phylon* 55 (spring 1984): 1–18.

Cook, James Graham. *The Segregationists*. New York: Appleton-Century-Crofts, 1962.

Cort, David. "The Voices of Birmingham." *Nation* (July 27, 1963): 46–48.

Cotman, John Walton. *Birmingham, JFK, and the Civil Rights Act of 1963*. New York: Peter Lang, 1989.

Cowett, Mark. *Birmingham's Rabbi: Morris Newfield and Alabama, 1895–1940*. Tuscaloosa: University of Alabama Press, 1986.

Cox, J. Robert. "The Fulfillment of Time: King's 'I Have a Dream' Speech (August 28, 1963)." In *Text in Context: Critical Dialogues on Significant Episodes in American Political Rhetoric*, ed. Michael C. Leff and Fred J. Kauffeld, 181–204. Davis, Calif.: Hermagoras Press, 1989.

Creger, Ralph. *A Look Down the Lonesome Road*. New York: Doubleday, 1964.

Dabbs, James McBride. *The Southern Heritage*. New York: Alfred A. Knopf, 1959.

———. *Who Speaks for the South?* New York: Funk and Wagnalls, 1964.

Daniels, Jonathan. *The Jon Daniels Story*. New York: Seabury Press, 1967.

Davidson, James E. *South Avondale Baptist Church, Birmingham, Alabama: Its Pastors, People, and Program, 1887–1974*. Birmingham: South Avondale Baptist, 1977.

Davis, Townsend. *Weary Feet, Rested Souls*. New York: W. W. Norton, 1998.

Dees, Jesse Walter, Jr., and James S. Hadley. *Jim Crow*. Westport, Conn.: Negro Universities Press, 1951.

Downing, Frederick L. *To See the Promised Land: The Faith Pilgrimage of Martin Luther King, Jr.* Macon: Mercer University Press, 1986.

Dubois, W. E. Burghardt. "Strivings of the Negro People." *Atlantic Monthly* (August 1897).

Ducas, George, ed. *Great Documents in Black American History*. With Charles Van Doren. New York: Praeger Publishers, 1970.

Eagles, Charles W. *Outside Agitator: Jon Daniels and the Civil Rights Movement in Alabama*. Chapel Hill: University of North Carolina Press, 1993.

Egerton, John. *A Mind to Stay Here: Profiles from the South*. London: Macmillan, 1970.

———. *Speak Now against the Day: The Generation before the Civil Rights Movement in the South*. New York: Alfred A. Knopf, 1994.

Eighmy, John Lee. *Churches in Cultural Captivity: A History of the Social Attitudes of Southern Baptists*. With revised introduction, conclusion, and bibliography by Sam Hill. Knoxville: University of Tennessee Press, 1987.

Elovitz, Mark H. *A Century of Jewish Life in Dixie: The Birmingham Experience*. Tuscaloosa: University of Alabama Press, 1974.

Eskew, Glenn. *But for Birmingham: The Local and National Movements in the Civil Rights Struggle*. Chapel Hill: University of North Carolina Press, 1997.

Fairclough, Adam. *To Redeem the Soul of America: The Southern Christian Leadership Conference and Martin Luther King, Jr.* Athens: University of Georgia Press, 1987.

Fallin, Wilson, Jr. *The African American Church in Birmingham, Alabama, 1815–1963: A Shelter in the Storm*. New York: Garland Press, 1997.

Findlay, James F. "Religion and Politics in the Sixties: The Churches and the Civil Rights Act of 1964." *Journal of American History* 77 (June 1990): 66–92.

———. *Church People in the Struggle: The National Council of Churches and the Black Freedom Movement, 1950–1970.* New York: Oxford University Press, 1993.

Fisher, Paul L., and Ralph L. Lowenstein, eds. *Race and the News Media.* New York: Frederick A. Praeger, 1967.

Flynt, Wayne. "The Ethics of Democratic Persuasion and the Birmingham Crisis." *Southern Speech Journal* 35 (fall 1969): 40–53.

———. "Dissent in Zion: Alabama Baptists and Social Issues, 1900–1914." *Journal of Southern History* 35 (November 1969): 523–42.

———. "Religion in the Urban South: The Divided Religious Mind of Birmingham, 1900–1930." *Alabama Review* 30 (April 1977): 108–34.

———. *Alabama Baptists: Southern Baptists in the Heart of Dixie.* Tuscaloosa: University of Alabama Press, 1998.

Forman, James. *The Making of Black Revolutionaries: A Personal Account.* New York: Macmillan, 1972.

Frady, Marshall. *Southerners: A Journalist's Odyssey.* New York: New American Library, 1980.

Franklin, John Hope, and Isidore Starr. *The Negro in Twentieth Century America: A Reader on the Struggle for Civil Rights.* New York: Vintage Books, 1967.

Fulkerson, Robert P. "The Public Letter as a Rhetorical Form: Structure, Logic, and Style in King's 'Letter from Birmingham Jail.'" *Quarterly Journal of Speech* 65 (April 1979): 121–36.

Garrow, David. *Protest at Selma: Martin Luther King, Jr., and the Voting Rights Act of 1965.* New Haven: Yale University Press, 1978.

———, ed. *We Shall Overcome: The Civil Rights Movement in the United States in the 1950s and 1960s.* New York: Carlson, 1981.

———. *Bearing the Cross: Martin Luther King, Jr., and the Southern Christian Leadership Conference.* New York: William Morrow, 1986.

———, ed. *Birmingham, Alabama, 1956–1963.* New York: Carlson, 1989.

———, ed. *Martin Luther King, Jr.: Civil Rights Leader, Theologian, Orator.* New York: Carlson, 1989.

Gilbreath, Edward. *Birmingham Revolution: Martin Luther King Jr.'s Epic Challenge to the Church.* Downers Grove, Ill.: InterVarsity Press, 2013.

Gilmore, J. Herbert, Jr. *They Chose to Live: The Racial Agony of an American Church.* Grand Rapids: William B. Eerdmans, 1972.

Goldfield, David R. *Black, White, and Southern: Race Relations and Southern Culture, 1940 to the Present.* Baton Rouge: Louisiana State University Press, 1990.

Goldwin, Robert A., ed. *Civil Disobedience: Five Essays by Martin Luther King, Jr., Herbert J. Storing, Paul Goodman, James Farmer, and Henry V. Jaffa.* Kenyon College: Public Affairs Conference Center, 1968.

Graham, Hugh Davis. *The Civil Rights Era: Origins and Development of National Policy, 1960–1972*. New York, Oxford: Oxford University Press, 1990.

Graves, John Temple. The Fighting South. New York: G. P. Putnam's Sons, 1943.

Gray, Daniel Savage. *Alabama: A Place, a People, a Point of View*. Dubuque, Iowa: Kendall/Hunt, 1977.

Halberstam, David. *The Fifties*. New York: Villard Books, 1993.

Hampton, Henry, Steve Fayer, and Sarah Flynn. *Voices of Freedom: An Oral History of the Civil Rights Movement from the 1950s through the 1980s*. New York: Bantam Books, 1992.

Handy, Robert T., ed., *The Social Gospel in America, 1870–1920*. New York: Oxford University Press, 1966.

———. *A Christian America: Protestant Hopes and Historical Realities*. New York: Oxford University Press, 1971.

Hariman, Robert. "Time and the Reconstitution of Gradualism in King's Address: A Response to Cox." In *Text in Context: Critical Dialogues on Significant Episodes in American Political Rhetoric*, ed. Michael C. Leff and Fred J. Kauffeld, 205–217. Davis, Calif.: Hermagoras Press, 1989.

Harmon, Nolan B. *Encyclopedia of World Methodism*. Nashville: United Methodist Publishing House, 1974.

———. *Ninety Years and Counting: Autobiography of Nolan B. Harmon*. Nashville: Upper Room, 1983.

Harrell, David Edwin, Jr. *White Sects and Black Men in the Recent South*. Nashville: Vanderbilt University Press, 1971.

———. *The Varieties of Southern Evangelicalism*. Macon: Mercer University Press, 1981.

———. "Pluralism, Catholics, Jews, and Sectarians." In *Religion in the South*, ed. Charles Reagan Wilson, 59–72. Jackson: University Press of Mississippi, 1981.

Harris, Carl V. "Reforms in Government Control of Negroes in Birmingham, Alabama, 1890–1920." *Journal of Southern History* 28 (November 1972): 567–600.

———. "Annexation Struggles and Political Power in Birmingham, Alabama, 1890–1910." *Alabama Review* 27 (July 1974): 163–84.

———. *Political Power in Birmingham, 1871–1921*. Knoxville: University of Tennessee Press, 1977.

Haselden, Kyle. *Mandate for White Christians*. Richmond: John Knox Press, 1966.

Hays, Brooks. *A Southern Moderate Speaks*. Chapel Hill: University of North Carolina Press, 1959.

Hemphill, Paul. *Leaving Birmingham: Notes of a Native Son*. New York: Viking Press, 1993.

Hill, Samuel S. "Southern Protestantism and Racial Integration." *Religion in Life: A Christian Quarterly of Opinion and Discussion* 33 (summer 1964): 421–29.

———. *Southern Churches in Crisis*. New York: Holt, Rinehart, and Winston, 1966.

———, ed. *Religion and the Solid South*. Nashville: Abingdon Press, 1972.

———. *The South and the North in American Religion.* Athens: University of Georgia Press, 1980.

———, ed. *Religion in the Southern States: A Historical Study.* Macon: Mercer University Press, 1983.

———, ed. *Encyclopedia of Religion in the South.* Macon: Mercer University Press, 1984.

Hobson, Fred. *But Now I See: The White Southern Racial Conversion Narrative.* Baton Rouge: Louisiana State University Press, 1999.

Hoover, Judith D. "Reconstruction of the Rhetorical Situation in 'Letter from Birmingham Jail.'" In *Martin Luther King, Jr., and the Sermonic Power of Public Discourse,* ed. Carolyn Calloway-Thomas and John Louis Lucaites, 50–65. Tuscaloosa: University of Alabama Press, 1993.

Horowitz, David Alan. "White Southerners' Alienation and Civil Rights: The Response to Corporate Liberalism, 1956–1965." *Journal of Southern History* 54 (May 1988): 173–200.

Ingalls, Robert P. "Antiradical Violence in Birmingham during the 1930s." *Journal of Southern History* 47 (November 1981): 521–44.

Johnson, Charles S. *Patterns of Negro Segregation.* Lexington, Mass.: D. C. Heath, 1968.

Kelley, Robin D.G. *Hammer and Hoe: Alabama's Communists during the Great Depression.* Chapel Hill: University of North Carolina Press, 1990.

Kent, Edward, ed. *Revolution and the Rule of Law.* Englewood Cliffs, N.J.: Prentice-Hall, 1971.

Kilian, Clarence M., ed. *"The Old First" of Birmingham, Alabama: From the Founding in 1873 to the Year of Our Lord 1952.* Birmingham: Birmingham Publishing, 1952.

Killian, Lewis M. "Hypocrisy of 'Delay.'" *New South* 11 (June 1956): 1–3, 12.

———. *White Southerners.* New York: Random House, 1970.

———. *Black and White: Reflections of a White Southern Sociologist.* Dix Hills, N.Y.: General Hall, 1994.

King, Coretta Scott. *My Life with Martin Luther King, Jr.* New York: Holt, Rinehart, and Winston, 1969.

King, Martin Luther, Jr. *Stride toward Freedom: The Montgomery Story.* New York: Harper, 1958.

———. "The Church on the Frontier of Racial Tension." Address given at Southern Baptist Theological Seminary, Louisville, Ky., April 19, 1961. https://digital.library.sbts.edu/bitstream/handle/10392/2751/King-ChurchOnFrontier.pdf?sequence=1&isAllowed=y.

———. *Strength to Love.* New York: Harper and Row, 1963.

———. *The Letter from Birmingham Jail.* Philadelphia: American Friends Service Committee, May 1963.

———. *Letter from a Birmingham Jail.* Music by Paul Reif. New York: Seesaw Music, 1963.

———. *Why We Can't Wait.* New York: Harper and Row, 1964.

———. "The Un-Christian Christian." In *The White Problem in America,* ed. Editors of *Ebony,* 57–63. Chicago: Johnson, 1966.

———. *Where Do We Go from Here: Chaos or Community?* Boston: Beacon Press, 1967.

———. "America's Chief Moral Dilemma." Speech given at the Hungry Club Forum, Atlanta, Ga., May 10, 1967. https://www.theatlantic.com/magazine /archive/2018/02/martin-luther-king-hungry-club-forum/552533/.

———. "Eulogy for the Martyred Children." In *A Testament of Hope: The Essential Writings and Speeches of Martin Luther King, Jr.,* ed. James Melvin Washington, 221–23. San Francisco: HarperSanFrancisco, 1986.

The King-Levison File, part 2 of *The Martin Luther King, Jr., FBI File.* Frederick, Md.: University Publications of America, 1987.

Kirby, Jack Temple. *Darkness at the Dawning: Race and Reform in the Progressive South:* Philadelphia: J. B. Lippincott, 1972.

Klein, Mia. "The *Other* Beauty of Martin Luther King, Jr.'s 'Letter from Birmingham Jail.'" *College Composition and Communication* 32 (February 1981): 30–37.

Kunstler, William. *Deep in My Heart.* New York: William Morrow, 1966.

LaMonte, Edward. *Politics and Welfare in Birmingham, 1900–1975.* Tuscaloosa: University of Alabama Press, 1995.

Lawson, Richard L. *Rhetorical Guide to the Borzoi College Reader.* New York: Alfred A. Knopf, 1967.

Lazenby, Marion Elias. *History of Methodism in Alabama and West Florida.* Birmingham: North Alabama Conference and West Alabama Conference of the Methodist Church, 1968.

Lentz, Richard. *Symbols, the News Magazines, and Martin Luther King.* Baton Rouge: Louisiana State University Press, 1990.

Lewis, John. *Walking the Wind: A Memoir of the Movement.* New York: Simon and Schuster, 1998.

Lincoln, C. Eric. *Race, Religion, and the Continuing American Dilemma.* New York: Hill and Wang, 1984.

Lippy, Charles H. "Towards an Inclusive Church: South Carolina Methodism and Race, 1972–1982." In *Rethinking Methodist History: A Bicentennial Historical Consultation,* ed. Russell E. Richey and Kenneth E. Rowe, 220–27. Nashville: Kingswood Books, 1985.

Lokos, Lionel. *House Divided: The Life and Legacy of Martin Luther King.* New York: Arlington House, 1968.

Lowi, Theodore J., ed. *Private Life and Public Order: The Context of Modern Public Policy.* New York: W. W. Norton, 1968.

Luker, Ralph E. *The Social Gospel in Black and White: American Racial Reform 1885–1912.* Chapel Hill: University of North Carolina Press, 1991.

Lyle, Jack. *The Black American and the Press.* Los Angeles: Ward Ritchie Press, 1968.

Lynd, Staughton, ed. *Nonviolence in America: A Documentary History.* American Heritage Series. Indianapolis: Bobbs-Merrill, 1966.

Lyon, Carter Dalton. *Sanctuaries of Segregation: The Story of the Jackson Church Visit Campaign.* Oxford: University Press of Mississippi, 2017.

Lyons, Thomas T. *Black Leadership in American History.* Menlo Park, Calif.: Addison-Wesley, 1971.

Manis, Andrew Michael. "Religious Experience, Religious Authority, and Civil Rights Leadership: The Case of Birmingham's Reverend Fred Shuttlesworth." In *Cultural Perspectives on the American South,* ed. Charles Reagan Wilson, 5:143–54. New York: Gordon and Breach, 1991.

———. *A Fire You Can't Put Out: The Civil Rights Life of Birmingham's Reverend Fred Shuttlesworth.* Tuscaloosa: University of Alabama Press, 1999.

Marion, John. "An Overview of the Desegregation Controversy." In *Southern Churches and Race Relations: Report of the Second Interracial Consultation Held at the College of the Bible, July 18–22, 1960,* ed. Lewis S. C. Smythe. Lexington, Ky.: College of the Bible, 1960.

Marshall, Catherine. *A Man Called Peter: The Story of Peter Marshall.* New York: McGraw-Hill, 1951.

Marshall, James Williams. *The Presbyterian Church in Alabama.* Montgomery: Presbyterian Historical Society of Alabama, 1977.

Martin, William. *A Prophet with Honor: The Billy Graham Story.* New York: William Morrow, 1991.

Maston, T. B. *Of One: A Study of Christian Principles and Race Relations.* Atlanta: Home Mission Board, Southern Baptist Convention, 1946.

———. *Segregation and Desegregation: A Christian Approach.* New York: Macmillan, 1959.

Matthews, Donald R., and James W. Protho. *Negroes and the New Southern Politics.* New York: Harcourt, Brace, and World, 1966.

Mays, Benjamin E., and Joseph W. Nicholson. "The Genius of the Negro Church." In *The Black Church in America,* ed. Hart M. Nelsen, Raytha L. Yokley, and Anne K. Nelson, 287–91. New York: Basic Books, 1971.

McBeth, Leon. "Southern Baptists and Race since 1947." *Baptist History and Heritage* 7 (July 1972): 155–69.

McGill, Ralph. *A Church, A School.* New York: Abingdon Press, 1959.

———. *The South and the Southerner.* New York: Little, Brown, 1963.

———. "The Southern Moderates Are Still There." In *No Place to Hide: The South and Human Rights.* 2 vols. Macon: Mercer University Press, 1984.

McMillan, George. "Silent White Ministers of the South." *New York Times Magazine,* April 5, 1964, pp. 22, 114.

McNeill, Robert B. *God Wills Us Free: The Ordeal of a Southern Minister.* New York: Hill and Wang, 1965.

Miller, Keith D. *Voices of Deliverance: The Language of Martin Luther King, Jr. and Its Sources.* New York: Free Press, 1992.

Morgan, Charles, Jr. *A Time to Speak.* New York: Harper and Row, 1964. Morris, Willie, ed. *The South Today: 100 Years after Appomattox.* New York: Harper and Row, 1965.

Mott, Wesley T. "The Rhetoric of Martin Luther King, Jr.: 'Letter from Birmingham Jail.'" *Phylon* 36 (December 1975): 411–21.

Murray, Andrew E. *Presbyterians and the Negro: A History.* Philadelphia: Presbyterian Historical Society, 1966.

Murray, Peter C. "The Racial Crisis in the Methodist Church." *Methodist History* 26 (October 1987): 3–14.

Muscatine, Charles, and Marlene Griffith, eds. *The Borzoi College Reader.* 3rd ed. New York: Alfred A. Knopf, 1976.

Muse, Benjamin. *Ten Years of Prelude: The Story of Integration since the Supreme Court's 1954 Decision.* New York: Viking Press, 1964.

Myers, Robert Manson. *Children of Pride: A True Story of Georgia and the Civil War.* New Haven: Yale University Press, 1972.

Myrdal, Gunnar. *An American Dilemma: The Negro Problem and Modern Democracy.* New York: Harper and Brothers, 1944.

Newston, Wesley Phillips. "Lindbergh Comes to Birmingham." *Alabama Review* 26, no. 2 (April 1973).

Niebuhr, H. Richard. *Christ and Culture.* New York: Harper and Row, 1951.

Noll, Mark, et al. *Eerdmans' Handbook to Christianity in America.* Grand Rapids: William B. Eerdmans, 1983.

Norris, Hoke, ed. *We Dissent.* New York: St. Martin's Press, 1962.

Nunnelley, William A. *Bull Connor.* Tuscaloosa: University of Alabama Press, 1991.

Oates, Stephen B. *Let the Trumpet Sound: The Life of Martin Luther King, Jr.* New York: Mentor Press, 1982.

Odum, Howard W. *The Way of the South: Toward the Regional Balance of America.* New York: Macmillan, 1947.

Osborne, George R. "Boycott in Birmingham." *Nation,* May 5, 1962, pp. 397–401.

Peirce, Neal R. "The Southern City Today." In *Dixie Dateline: A Journalistic Portrait of the Contemporary South,* ed. John B. Boles. Houston: Rice University Studies, 1983.

Peters, William. *The Southern Temper.* Garden City, N.Y.: Doubleday, 1959.

Princeton University. *Class of 1921 Thirty-Year Book.* Princeton: Princeton University Press, 1951.

Pulpit Digest. "Southern Ministers Speak Their Minds." *Pulpit Digest* 39 (December 1958): 13–17.

Pyatt, Sherman E., comp. *Martin Luther King, Jr.: An Annotated Bibliography.* Westport, Conn.: Greenwood Press, 1986.

Raines, Howell. *My Soul Is Rested: The Story of the Civil Rights Movement in the Deep South.* New York: Penguin Books, 1977.

Rathbun, John W. "Martin Luther King: The Theology of Social Action." In *Martin Luther King, Jr.: Civil Rights Leader, Theologian, Orator,* ed. David J. Garrow, 743–58. New York: Carlson, 1989.

Ray, Susan Ingram Hunt. *The Major: Harwell G. Davis, Alabama Statesman and Baptist Leader.* Birmingham: Samford University Press, 1991.

Reed, John Shelton. *One South: An Ethnic Approach to Regional Culture.* Baton Rouge: Louisiana State University Press, 1982.

Rogers, William Warren, et al. *Alabama: The History of a Deep South State.* Tuscaloosa: University of Alabama Press, 1994.

Romero, Patricia W. "Martin Luther King and His Challenge to White America." *Negro History Bulletin* 31 (May 1968): 6–8.

Salisbury, Harrison. *Without Fear or Favor: "The New York Times" and Its Times.* New York: Times Books, 1980.

Schlesinger, Arthur M. *Robert Kennedy and His Times.* Boston: Houghton Mifflin, 1978.

Schultke, Flip, and Penelope McPhee. *King Remembered.* New York: Pocket Books, 1986.

Selby, Earl, and Miriam Selby. *Odyssey: Journey through Black America.* New York: G. P. Putnam's Sons, 1971.

Sellers, James. *The South and Christian Ethics.* New York: Associated Press, 1962.

Sessions, Robert Paul. "Are Southern Ministers Failing the South?" *Saturday Evening Post,* May 13, 1961, pp. 37, 82–85, 88.

Shuttlesworth, Fred. "Birmingham Shall Be Free Some Day." *Freedomways,* winter 1964, pp. 16–19.

Silver, James W. *Mississippi: The Closed Society.* New York: Harcourt, Brace and World, 1964.

Sitton, Claude. "Racial Coverage: Planning and Logistics." In *Race and the News Media,* ed. Paul L. Fisher and Ralph L. Lowenstein. New York: Frederick A. Praeger, 1967.

Smith, Donald H. "An Exegesis of Martin Luther King, Jr.'s Social Philosophy." In *Martin Luther King, Jr.: Civil Rights Leader, Theologian, Orator,* ed. David J. Garrow, 829–37. New York: Carlson, 1989.

Smith, Frank E. *Look Away from Dixie.* Baton Rouge: Louisiana State University Press, 1965.

Smith, Kenneth L., and Ira G. Zepp, Jr. *Search for the Beloved Community: The Thinking of Martin Luther King, Jr.* Valley Forge: Judson Press, 1974.

Smith, Petric J. *Long Time Coming: An Insider's Story of the Birmingham Church Bombing That Rocked the World.* Birmingham: Crane Hill, 1994.

Smith, Theophus H. *Conjuring Culture: Biblical Formations of Black America.* New York: Oxford University Press, 1994.

Smythe, Lewis S. C., ed. *Southern Churches and Race Relations: Report of the Second Interracial Consultation Held at the College of the Bible, July 18–22, 1960.* Lexington, Ky.: College of the Bible, 1960.

Snow, Malinda. "Martin Luther King's 'Letter from Birmingham Jail' as Pauline Epistle." *Quarterly Journal of Speech* 71 (August 1985): 318–34.

Sobel, Lester A., ed. *Civil Rights, 1960–66.* New York: Facts on File, 1967.

Sokal, Jason. *There Goes My Everything: White Southerners in the Age of Civil Rights, 1945–1975.* New York: Vintage Press, 2007.

Sosna, Morton. *In Search of the Silent South: Southern Liberals and the Race Issue.* New York: Columbia University Press, 1977.

Southard, Samuel. "Are Southern Churches Silent?" *Christian Century* 80 (November 20, 1963): 1429–32.

Southern, David W. *Gunnar Myrdal and Black-White Relations.* Baton Rouge: Louisiana State University Press, 1987.

Southern Regional Council. "The Churches Speak." *New South* 11 (October 1956): 3–9.

Spillers, Hortense J. "Martin Luther King and the Style of the Black Sermon." *Black Scholar* 3 (September 1971): 14–27.

Stagg, Frank. "Henlee Hulix Barnette: Activist." In *Perspectives in Religious Studies: Essays in Honor of Henlee Hulix Barnette,* ed. Rollin S. Armour. Macon: Mercer University Press, 1991.

Storing, Herbert J., ed. *What Country Have I? Political Writings by Black Americans.* New York: St. Martin's Press, 1970.

Stritch, Thomas. *The Catholic Church in Tennessee: The Sesquicentennial Story.* Nashville: Catholic Center, 1987.

Strong, James. *The New Strong's Exhaustive Concordance of the Bible.* Nashville: Thomas Nelson, 1984.

Sturm, Douglas. "Crisis in the American Republic: The Legal and Political Significance of Martin Luther King's 'Letter from a Birmingham Jail.'" In *Martin Luther King, Jr.: Civil Rights Leader, Theologian, Orator,* ed. David J. Garrow, 931–46. New York: Carlson, 1989.

Taylor, Halsey P., and Victor N. Okada, eds. *The Craft of the Essay.* New York: Harcourt, Brace, Jovanovich, 1977.

Taylor, O. W. *Early Tennessee Baptists, 1769–1872.* Nashville: Executive Board of the Tennessee Baptist Association, 1957.

Thompson, Paul. *The Voice of the Past: Oral History.* New York: Oxford University Press, 1986.

Thornton, J. Mills. *Dividing Lines: Municipal Politics and the Struggle for Civil Rights in Montgomery, Birmingham, and Selma.* Tuscaloosa: University of Alabama Press, 2002.

Tindall, George. *Emergence of the New South, 1913–1945.* Baton Rouge: Louisiana State University Press, 1967.

Valentine, Foy D. *A Historical Study of Southern Baptists and Race Relations, 1917–1947.* New York: Arno Press, 1980.

Vander Zanden, James Wilfrid. *Race Relations in Transition: The Segregation Crisis in the South.* New York: Random House, 1965.

Viorst, Milton. *Fire in the Streets: America in the 1960s.* New York: Simon and Schuster, 1979.

Walker, Alice. *In Search of Our Mother's Gardens: Womanist Prose.* New York: Harcourt, Brace, Jovanovich, 1983.

Wallace, George C. "Inaugural Address." In *Black, White and Gray: Twenty-one Points of View on the Race Question,* ed. Bradford Daniel, 177–89. New York: Sheed and Ward, 1964.

Warren, Robert Penn. *Segregation: The Inner Conflict in the South.* Vintage Books: New York, 1956.

———. *Who Speaks for the Negro?* New York: Random House, 1965.

Washington, James Melvin, ed. *A Testament of Hope: The Essential Writings and Speeches of Martin Luther King, Jr.* San Francisco: HarperSanFrancisco, 1986.

Watters, Pat. *Down to Now: Reflections on the Southern Civil Rights Movement.* New York: Pantheon Books, 1971.

Wechman, Robert J. *Readings and Interpretations of Critical Issues in Modern American Life.* New York: Selected Academic Readings, 1968.

Weisbrot, Robert. *Freedom Bound: A History of America's Civil Rights Movement.* New York: W. W. Norton, 1990.

Westin, Alan F., ed. *Freedom Now: The Civil Rights Struggle in America.* New York: Basic Books, 1964.

Westin, Alan F., and Barry Mahoney. *The Trial of Martin Luther King.* New York: Thomas Y. Crowell, 1974.

Wharton, Vernon Lane. *The Negro in Mississippi, 1865–1890.* Chapel Hill: University of North Carolina Press, 1947.

White, John. *Black Leadership in America: From Booker T. Washington to Jesse Jackson.* New York: Longman Group, 1985.

White, Lewis. "A Current Lament." *New South* 18 (May 1963): 12–13, 15.

White, Ronald C., Jr., and C. Howard Hopkins. *The Social Gospel: Religion and Reform in Changing America.* Philadelphia: Temple University Press, 1976.

Williams, Juan. *Eyes on the Prize: America's Civil Rights Years, 1959–65.* New York: Viking Penguin, 1987.

Williamson, Joel, ed. *The Origins of Segregation.* Lexington, Mass.: D. C. Heath, 1968.

———. *The Crucible of Race: Black-White Relations in the American South since Emancipation.* New York: Oxford University Press, 1984.

Wilson, Charles Reagan. *Baptized in Blood: The Religion of the Lost Cause, 1865–1920.* Athens: University of Georgia Press, 1980.

———. *Religion in the South.* Jackson: University Press of Mississippi, 1981.

Woodward, C. Vann. *The Burden of Southern History.* Baton Rouge: Louisiana State University Press, 1968.

———. *The Strange Career of Jim Crow.* New York: Oxford University Press, 1974.

———. *Thinking Back: The Perils of Writing History.* Baton Rouge: Louisiana State University Press, 1986.

Woofter, Thomas J. *Southern Race Progress: The Wavering Color Line.* Washington, D.C.: Public Affairs Press, 1957.

Workman, William D., Jr. *The Case for the South.* New York: Devin-Adair, 1960.

Worton, Stanley N., ed. *Freedom of Assembly and Petition.* Rochelle Park, N.J.: Hayden, 1978.

Young, Andrew. *An Easy Burden: The Civil Rights Movement and the Transformation of America.* New York: Harper Collins, 1996.

Zepp, Ira J., Jr., and Kenneth L. Smith. *Search for the Beloved Community: The Thinking of Martin Luther King, Jr.* Valley Forge, Pa.: Judson Press, 1974.

Zinn, Howard. *The Southern Mystique.* New York: Alfred A. Knopf, 1964.

Newspapers and Agencies

Alabama Baptist (Birmingham), 1952–1965, 1980, 1993, 2015.

Alabama Churchman (Episcopal; Birmingham), 1938–1969.

Apostle (Episcopal; Birmingham), 1993.

Associated Baptist Press, 2006.

Baltimore Afro-American, 1963.

BaptistPress.com, 2004.

Birmingham News, 1911, 1913, 1938–1976, 1983–1999.

Birmingham Post, 1937.

Birmingham Post-Herald, 1938–1972, 1979.

Birmingham World, 1963.

Catholic Week (Birmingham), 1945–1955, 1963, 1975.

Chicago Defender, 1963.

Chicago Tribune, 1963.

Christian Index, 1963, 1966, 1970.

Cleveland Call and Post, 1963.

Courier-Journal (Ky.), 1957.

Fort Worth (Tex.) Star-Telegram, 1975.

Greensboro (N.C.) Daily News, 1963–1964.
Jackson (Miss.) Clarion-Ledger, 1963.
Los Angeles Times, 1963, 2006.
Louisville Times, 1963.
Memphis Commercial-Appeal, 1964–1972.
Memphis Press Scimitar, 1969.
Methodist Christian Advocate (Birmingham), 1952–1964.
Mobile Press Register, 1960–1961.
Nashville Banner, 1964.
Nashville Tennessean, 1964–1975.
National Register (Catholic), 1969.
New York Herald-Tribune, 1963.
New York Post, 1963.
New York Times, 1921, 1939–1995, 2006.
One Voice (Catholic; Birmingham), 1975.
Southern Shofar, 1995.
Tennessee Register (Catholic; Nashville), 1964–1994.
Wall Street Journal, 1963.
Washington Post, 1963, 1993.

General-Interest Magazines and Journals

Atlantic Monthly, 1897, 1944, 1963.
Business Week, 1962, 1969.
Christian Century, 1962–1963, 1970.
Commonweal, 1963.
Ebony, 1963, 1971, 1988.
Esquire, 1958.
Economist, 1963.
Encore: American and Worldwide News, 1963.
Liberation, 1963.
Nation, 1962–1963.
National Review, 1963.
New Leader, 1963.
New South, 1963.
Newsweek, 1963, 1969, 1979.
New Yorker, 1977.
Phylon, 1963.
Pulpit Digest, 1958.
Saturday Evening Post, 1961, 1963.
Seasons (Samford University), Summer 2001.
Theology Today, 1963.

Time, 1956, 1963, 1967, 1969.

U.S. News and World Report, 1963.

Witness (Birmingham Baptist Association), 1944–1954.

Unpublished Written Works

Corley, Robert Gaines. "The Quest for Racial Harmony: Race Relations in Birmingham, Alabama, 1947–63." Ph.D. diss., University of Virginia, 1979.

Eskew, Glenn Thomas. "But for Birmingham: The Local and National Movements in the Civil Rights Struggle." Ph.D. diss., University of Georgia, 1993.

Grace, D. B. "Official Life of George B. Ward." Unpublished manuscript. Birmingham Public Library Tutwiler Collection of Southern History and Literature, Birmingham, Ala.

Harris, J. Tyra. "Alabama Reaction to the *Brown* Decision, 1954–1956: A Case Study in Early Massive Resistance." Ph.D. diss., Middle Tennessee State University, 1978.

Jones, Terry Lawrence. "Attitudes of Alabama Baptists toward Negroes, 1890–1914." Master's thesis, Samford University, 1968.

LaMonte, Edward Shannon. "Politics and Welfare in Birmingham, Alabama, 1900–1975." Ph.D. diss., University of Chicago, 1976.

Lanier, Martha Louise. "Alabama Methodists and Social Issues, 1900–1914." Master's thesis, Samford University, 1969.

Lawson, T. R. "Swede," and Mrs. Ernest S. Story. "First Baptist Church Centennial, 1872–1972." Samford University Special Collection.

Lilley, Stephen James. "Kind Letters and Support for Dr. Martin Luther King, Jr." Ph.D. diss., University of Massachusetts, 1989.

McGinnis, Timothy Scott. "The Controversy and Division of First Baptist Church, Birmingham, Alabama, 1968–1970." Senior honors thesis, Samford University, May 1990.

Moore, Edward L. "Billy Graham and Martin Luther King, Jr.: An Inquiry into White and Black Revivalistic Traditions." Ph.D. diss., Vanderbilt University, 1979.

Nichols, Michael Cooper. "'Cities Are What Men Make Them': Birmingham, Alabama, Faces the Civil Rights Movement, 1963." Senior honors thesis, Brown University, 1974.

Rahming, Philip A. "The Church and the Civil Rights Movement in the Thought of Martin Luther King, Jr." Th.M.thesis, Southwest Baptist University, 1971.

Rigsby, Enrique DuBois. "A Rhetorical Clash with the Established Order: An Analysis of Protest Strategies and Perceptions of Media Responses, Birmingham, 1963." Ph.D. diss., University of Oregon, 1990.

Sperry, Benjamin O. "Caught 'between Our Moral and Material Selves': Mississippi's Elite White 'Moderates' and Their Role in Changing Race Relations, 1945–1956." Ph.D. diss., Case Western Reserve University, 2010.

Stewart, George R. "Birmingham's Reaction to the 1954 Desegregation Decision." Master's thesis, Samford University, 1967.

Vick, Mary-Helen. "A Survey of the Governing Body of Birmingham, Alabama, 1910–1964." Master's thesis, Alabama College, 1965.

Walker, Eugene P. "A History of the Southern Christian Leadership Conference, 1955–1965: The Evolution of a Southern Strategy for Social Change." Ph.D. diss., Duke University, 1978.

Interviews, Tape Recordings, Video Recordings, Television Shows

Allen, Billy. Telephone interview by author. Transcript. Oklahoma City, Okla., August 9, 1998.

Allen, Joseph. Interview by Sister Rose Sevenich. Transcript. Catholic Diocese of Birmingham (Ala.) Archives, October 2, 1992.

Amaker, Norman. Telephone interview by author. Tape recording. Chicago, Illinois, July 22, 1998.

Carpenter, Doug. Interview by author. Tape recording. Birmingham, Ala., January 27, 1991.

Carter, Charles T. Interview by Evan Musgraves. Digital recording and transcript. Birmingham, Ala., September 13, 2013. Samford University Oral History Collection, Birmingham.

———. Interview by Timothy George. Birmingham, Ala., June 4, 2019. Beeson Podcast (Episode 447), https://www.beesondivinity.com/podcast/2019/transcripts/beeson-podcast-episode-447-carter.txt.

CBS Reports. "Who Speaks for Birmingham?" Transcript of CBS broadcast of May 18, 1961. Hosted by Howard K. Smith. Birmingham Public Library Tutwiler Collection of Southern History and Literature, Birmingham, Ala.

Durick, Joseph A. Interview by author. Tape recording. Bessemer, Ala., February 21, 1992, May 8, 1992, January 28, 1993.

———. Interview by Sister Rose Sevenich. Transcript at Catholic Diocese of Birmingham (Ala.) Archives, October 2, 1992, October 23, 1992.

Grafman, Milton L. Interview by Birmingham Public Library. Tape recording at Birmingham Public Library Department of Archives and Manuscripts. Birmingham, Ala., July 19, 1977, July 27, 1977, August 3, 1977.

———. Telephone interview by author. Tape recording. Birmingham, Ala., March 1, 1991.

———. Interview by author. Tape recording. Birmingham, Ala., March 22, 1995.

Hardin, Paul. Interview by Elliott Wright. Tape recording and transcript. Indianapolis, Ind., April 18, 1980. World Methodist Archives, Lake Junaluska, N.C.

———. Telephone interview by author. Tape recording. Asheville, N.C., October 27, 1992.

Harmon, Nolan. Interview by author. Tape recording. Atlanta, Ga., July 30, 1992.

King: A Film Record from Montgomery to Memphis. Martin Luther King Film Project, 1970. Videocassette.

Love, Katherine Ramage. Telephone interview by author. Tape recording. Pine Bluff, Ark., February 28, 1992.

————. Interview by author. Tape recording. Pine Bluff, Ark., February 2, 1995.

Mackey (King), Willie Pearl. Telephone interview by author. Transcript. Silver Springs, Md., October 25, 1998.

Marshall, Burke. Interview by Anthony Lewis. Transcript. Washington, D.C., June 20, 1964. John F. Kennedy Library, Boston, Mass.

Murray, George M. Telephone interview by author. Tape recording. Fairhope, Ala., October 20, 1992.

————. Interview by author. Tape recording. Fairhope, Ala., March 21, 1995.

Oni, Sam. Interview by Melody An, Sean Kennedy, Alden Moore, Megan Rutherford, and Diandra Walker. Transcript. Macon, Ga., April 22, 2009. http://faculty.mercer.edu/davis_da/fys102/Sam_Oni.pdf.

Porter, John. Interview by author. Tape recording. Birmingham, Ala., May 7, 1992.

Rupp, Peggy. Interview by author. Tape recording. Birmingham, Ala., February 1, 1991.

Shuttlesworth, Fred L. Telephone interview by author. Transcript. Cincinnati, Ohio, April 23, 1992.

————. Interview by author. Tape recording. Birmingham, Ala., March 20, 2003.

Simmons, William. Telephone interview by author. Transcript. Lexington, Ky., August 6, 1998.

Stallings, Earl. "Where Shall I Begin: Reminiscences of Earl Stallings." Tape Recording. Sun City West, Ariz., 1998.

————. Interview by author. Tape recording. Birmingham, Ala., May 26, 2001.

Walker, Wyatt T. Interview by author. Tape recording. New York, N.Y., January 7, 1997.

Walter, Francis X. Interview by author. Tape recording. Birmingham, Ala., March 1, 1991.

Index

68–69; reaction to "Letter from Birmingham Jail," 163, 205–206, 207; integration in South Carolina, 206–207; mentioned, 2, 5, 6, 7, 9, 47, 117, 144, 165–66, 176. *See also* Eight white ministers; Methodists

Hardin, Paul, Sr., 67–68

Harmon, John Wesley, 39–41

Harmon, Nolan Bailey, Jr.: sermons of, 25, 41–42; racial views of, 28–29, 41, 43–45, 46, 163; and Alabama Methodists, 38–39; background of, 39–40; early career of, 40–41; prohibitionist rhetoric of, 41; and law and order concept, 41, 43–44; Central Jurisdiction and, 42–43; critical of Martin Luther King Jr., 43–44; gradualism of 44, 165; name misspelled, 144; reaction to "Letter from Birmingham Jail," 163, 164–66; later career of, 166–67; White House visit of, 185–87 *passim*; mentioned, 2, 5, 6, 7, 9, 47, 67, 68, 69, 117, 174, 207. *See also* Eight white ministers; Methodists

Harmon, Nolan Bailey, Sr., 39–40, 41

Harmon, Rebecca Lamar, 166

Harper's Magazine, 89

Hartsfield, William, 91

Haynes, Henry, 111

Hebrew Union College, 64

Heflin, Tom ("Cotton Tom"), 55

Hill, Samuel S., Jr., 42

Hines, John E., 171–72

Hitler, Adolf, 62, 124, 175, 245

Hodge, Bachman, 38

Holland, E. L., 20–21

Holocaust, 64, 175, 177

Holy Trinity-Holy Cross Greek Orthodox Church (Birmingham), 18, 234

Hoover, Herbert, 55

Hudson, William, 132

Huntley-Brinkley Report, 133

Huntsville Ministers Association, 18

Independent Presbyterian Church (Birmingham), 14

Institute on Judaism for Christian Clergy, 65

Interracial Committee of the Jefferson County Coordinating Council, 32–33

J. J. Newberry's, 102, 276n. 51

Jackson, Emory O., 105

Jefferson, Thomas, 127, 129, 140, 147, 249, 254

Jefferson County, 55, 89, 91, 99, 107

Jefferson County Coordinating Council. *See* Interracial Committee of the Jefferson County Coordinating Council

Jenkins, William A., 107, 108, 131, 230

Jews, 6, 14, 19, 61–62, 124–25, 213. *See also* Anti-Semitism; Grafman, Milton

Jim Crow, 12, 21, 22, 29, 86, 87–88, 90, 105, 174, 208

Joffrion, A. Emile, 18

John Birch Society, 169

John XXIII, Pope, 188

Johnson, Lyndon, 107

Jones, Charles Colcock, Jr., 31

Jones, Charles Colcock, Sr., 31–32, 173

Jones, Clarence, 115, 118–19

Jones, Samuel R., Jr., 223

Jones, Vernon, 172

Jordan, Mortimer, 94

Kean, Charles, 185

Kelly Ingram Park, 113, 114

Kelsey, George, 140

Kennedy, John F., 5, 107, 114–15, 133–34, 147, 180, 185–87 *passim*, 226,

Kennedy, Robert, 104

Kenyatta, Muhammed, 148

Kershaw, Alvin, 62–63

King, A. D., 179

King, Martin Luther, Jr.: criticism of eight white ministers, 2–4, 149; use of press by, 3, 95–96, 97–98, 101, 104, 131–35 *passim*, 137, 227–28; criticisms of, 4, 104–106, 164–65, 178, 184–85, 198–99, 206, 212–13; criticism of moderates, 9, 23–24, 181; comparison to eight white ministers, 24; Birmingham dem-